COMMUNICATION

PRINCIPLES OF TRADITION AND CHANGE

Samuel P. **Wallace**
University of Dayton

Kimberly N. **Rosenfeld**
Cerritos College

David L. **Bodary**
Sinclair Community College

Beth M. **Waggenspack**
Virginia Tech

KENDALL/HUNT PUBLISHING COMPANY
4050 Westmark Drive   Dubuque, Iowa 52002

Book Team

Chairman and Chief Executive Officer   Mark C. Falb
President and Chief Operating Officer   Chad M. Chandlee
Vice President, Higher Education   David L. Tart
Director of National Book Program   Paul B. Carty
Editorial Development Manager   Georgia Botsford
Senior Developmental Editor   Angela Willenbring
Vice President, Operations   Timothy J. Beitzel
Assistant Vice President, Production Services   Christine E. O'Brien
Senior Production Editor   Mary Melloy
Permissions Editor   Renae Horstman
Cover Designer   Janell Edwards
Web Project Manager   Billee Jo Hefel

Brief Contents

Contents

Preface

Colleges and universities across the country approach the basic communication course from a variety of perspectives. The traditional form of the basic course usually teaches public speaking and argumentation. Other approaches include interpersonal communication, small group communication, or a mixture of communication topics. This book is designed for use in the "mixed" course, commonly known in the field as the hybrid, or blend, course. This includes traditional public speaking topics, but it also incorporates small-group decision making, interviewing, and interpersonal communication, all of which are essential for achieving communication goals in social and professional settings.

There are many justifications for the hybrid course, but only two will be cited here. The first justification relates to the structure of the field of communication. Although the study of communication has roots in rhetorical practice, theory, and criticism, spanning over 2000 years, contemporary study of communication is composed of rhetorical scholars and those trained in the social sciences. A hybrid course emphasizing all the areas of study and research will more fully represent the field as it exists in the twenty-first century.

The second justification for the hybrid course is the trend in higher education requiring graduates to meet a defined level of competence in basic skills necessary to effectively function in today's social, professional, and political environments. Among those basic outcomes assessment skills are written and spoken communication, technology/information literacy, critical thinking, and quantitative and scientific reasoning. In addition, most institutions require "oral competencies" for graduation. However, successful functioning in a complex society requires abilities in addition to public-speaking skills. Most major decisions of consequence are made in groups, where business and personal relationships must be established and maintained, and information must be gathered and disseminated for a multiplicity of purposes through the interview. The hybrid course exposes students to a broad range of skills and strategies necessary to function effectively in our communication-saturated world.

The field of communication has many components, and its graduates have to be competent in communication skills in several different contexts to function effectively in society. Therefore, this text and its accompanying web features are designed for courses that embrace the *hybrid* perspective. Included are several dimensions needed by a strategic, successful communicator:

- A limited exposure to basic communication theory is provided. While the focus of the hybrid course is to train students to formulate communication strategies and to execute those strategies with practical skills, any applied application must have a sound base in theory. Students who understand *why* the strategies and skills are essential will be more able to successfully *apply* them. In addition to a chapter devoted to theory, theoretical insight is a running theme throughout the text.

- Fundamental principles of communication that cross all contexts are explored in chapters examining critical thinking, source credibility, and verbal and nonverbal communication.

- Examples and illustrations that provide a current perspective on communication in action are employed throughout the text. Students will reflect on the impact that communication has on daily activities as the text supplies supporting materials ranging from popular culture to political discourse, historical reflection to civic engagement, and multicultural perspectives to family and professional applications.

- The development of a probing mind is reflected through internal chapter questions. Rather than simply being told what the concepts are, students are encouraged to ask questions that will assist in the development of strategic communication plans.

- The interpersonal communication context is analyzed. This unit includes a chapter that explores establishing, building, and maintaining interpersonal relationships, and two chapters concerned with planning and executing information gathering and employment interviews.

- The task-oriented, small group context is investigated. The three chapters in this unit speak to the structure and development of groups; the use of influence and control in managing and directing groups; and a chapter on decision-making strategies that provide a practical guide to making decisions of consequence.

- Public presentations are discussed, with a dual focus on informative and persuasive public speaking. Included are sections on the practical planning, research, organization, and delivery of contemporary public presentations.

The overall goal of the text is to get students "on the road" to developing their communication skills. Nobody expects the students to become expert communicators by the end of the term. Skills will evolve over time with experience and exposure to life situations. However, we hope to accomplish our course goals and establish a strong foundation by exposing students to communication theory and challenging them with problems that must be solved across a variety of communication contexts. We are confident that by encouraging students to apply theory to better understand human communication, they will be able to create and execute strategies that lead to achieving their goals.

As students progress through the units, they are challenged to consider their roles as communicators in each of the contexts. To be successful in these contexts, students have to be able to ask questions that sharpen their understanding of the complexity of communication and adapt to changing audiences and contexts. They must be aware of relevant aspects of the situation (analysis of audience, self, and context), formulate a strategy (planning), and exhibit the appropriate behaviors (skills) to accomplish the goals.

Chapter 1—Introduction: Why Study Communication?

Communication is a complex, multidisciplinary process in which participants create meaning by using symbols and behavior to send and receive messages with a social and cultural context. This book will help the reader formulate strategies and learn the skills necessary to accomplish communication goals.

Chapter 2—What Is Communication?

This chapter focuses on the theories used to guide communicators in the formulation of strategies to achieve communication goals. The many definitions of communication all share common characteristics.

Chapter 3—What Is the Impact of Critical Thinking in Communication?

Critical thinking is the ability to analyze and evaluate information on the basis of evidence, with the ultimate goal of sharing it with others. This chapter discusses the development of perceptual skills, knowledge-gathering skills, and researching skills needed for critical thinking.

Chapter 4—What Is the Power of Verbal and Nonverbal Communication?

This chapter explains language as a shared system of symbols and structures in organized patterns to express thoughts and feelings and offers strategies for using language effectively. It illustrates the six functions nonverbal messages perform to create meaning and defines the types of nonverbal communication.

Chapter 5—How Can I Become a Credible Source?

Credibility is dynamic, and its qualities include character, intelligence, goodwill, and charisma. This chapter also discusses speech anxiety and offers techniques for managing it.

Chapter 6—How Do Interpersonal Relationships Affect Communication?

The concept of relationships as contextual is explained, as well as the stages of relationships. Conflicts and relationship termination are explored, as well as the parameters of virtual relationships.

Chapter 7—What Should I Know about Interviewing?

This chapter explains the parts of an interview and how to prepare for an interview. It also discusses the kinds of questions that are most useful in an interview situation.

Chapter 8—How Do I Participate in an Interview?

Information-gathering interviews and employment interviews are the focus of this chapter. Preparation and planning, including a discussion of resumes, cover letters, and thank-you letters is included.

Chapter 9—Why Do We Use Groups to Solve Problems and Make Decisions?

Small groups are defined as a collection of people who work together either voluntarily or involuntarily to achieve a goal or solve a problem. The advantages and the drawbacks of group work, including group roles and tips for handling disruptive members is discussed.

Chapter 10—What Are the Roles of Leadership and Power in Group Dynamics?

Leadership is the ability to influence people; power is the ability to control them. Leadership styles and power bases are analyzed, as well as conflict within small groups.

Chapter 11—How Can My Group Make Decisions?

The circumstances of decisions of consequence are defined here, and the seven-step strategy for making quality decisions is outlined. Groupthink is analyzed as a detriment to good decision-making.

Chapter 12—Audience: Who Are You Communicating With?

Assessing your audience and the context is crucial for effective communication. This chapter provides strategies for analyzing and adapting to the audience.

Chapter 13—How Should I Construct My Message?

Selection is a decision strategy of determining your topic and purpose, meeting the audience's needs, and choosing the proper supporting evidence. This chapter focuses on the introduction, body, and conclusion of the speech as well as connectives that tie the speech together.

Chapter 14—How Do I Deliver a Message?

Effective delivery involves both verbal and nonverbal message management, tailored for the intended audience and content. Different speech styles, effective verbal and physical delivery and presentation aids are explored in this chapter.

Chapter 15—What Should You Know about an Informative Message?

This chapter explains delivery strategies that are important for presenting an informative message. It defines descriptive speeches, briefings, expository speeches, narratives, and explains the role of credibility in an informative speech.

Chapter 16—What Is Persuasive Communication?

Persuasion is a process of social influence, involving the preparation and presentation of messages that affect others' beliefs, values, attitudes and actions. This chapter focuses on the three types of persuasive propositions, lists essential elements of effective persuasion, and explains flaws of a persuasive argument.

INTENDED AUDIENCE

Students

The intended audience for this book includes beginning as well as advanced college students, and we acknowledge that many of them take the course because it is required. Even so, we assume the course is mostly populated with students who want to learn communication strategies and skills necessary for accomplishing goals in their professional, social, and personal lives.

Instructors

This book is designed for courses taught by a variety of instructors, as is typical for many basic courses in communication. Both new and veteran graduate students, adjunct faculty, and seasoned, experienced full-time faculty should all be able to effectively use this material. The companion web site and instructor resources are available to provide guidance and teaching ideas.

FEATURES

The "book" as we have been describing it actually consists of a print volume and a companion web site. The web portion has been designed to provide a significant collection of resources for the instructor and the student. Additional text material and links to relevant information on the companion web site allow instructors to choose the depth of the content that is appropriate to his or her students. Each chapter contains information and explanations used to prepare students for a considerable series of cognitive and behavioral activities. Students will gain understanding and experience in planning strategies and executing skills in the various communication contexts. We understand that students learn in many different ways, so this product provides multiple means for active learning and application of the course content.

Both students and instructors have access to online content that is integrated chapter by chapter with the text to enrich student learning. The web access code is included on the inside front cover of the textbook.

Look for the web icon in the text margins to direct you to various interactive tools.

Combining the print text with the companion web site will provide the following for each chapter:

- Chapter Pre-Test
- Learning objectives appropriate to the chapter
- Poll questions
- Text content (with additional text material on the companion web site)
- Links to related sites of interest
- Collaborative and interactive assignments
- Feedback form for students to report responses to the material or ask clarification on "muddy" issues
- Chapter Post-Test
- Video explanations of key concepts
- Glossary and flashcards

INSTRUCTOR RESOURCES

The companion web site for this textbook is much more than a typical ancillary included with the adoption of this book. The companion web site and the print volume are integrated and work together to provide a coherent and comprehensive experience. The web site portion of the course package is a complete, fully customizable course management system. It includes:

- Online testing capability and test banks for every chapter
- Interactive grade book (accessible by students)
- Intra-course email/messaging
- Course assessments using our assessment materials, your materials, or both
- Online polling
- Learning objectives
- Interactive assignments

COURSE DESIGN

The resources provided in this package include the print volume and the companion web site.

This material is designed to be taught in at least three different formats:

- A *traditional* face-to-face class taught in a traditional classroom setting.
- A true *hybrid* class in which students meet face-to-face and are engaged in online, interactive activities outside of class. This design has numerous learning benefits related to student engagement and motivation. It can also be used to reduce actual "seat time" in case travel is an issue, or to liberate class time so it can be better used for meaningful interaction between instructors and students.
- Completely *online* as a distance learning class.

Acknowledgments

We would like to thank our families for tolerating our absence and preoccupation with writing this book. We promise to make it up to you! We'll go camping and biking, play cards and games, and maybe even fix the leaky faucet in the kitchen or finish painting the basement. We'll come out of the computer space to hear your stories and fully enjoy family life once again.

We would like to thank the reviewers who took us to task on earlier drafts of this book. Your comments were on target and significantly improved the final product. The reviewers include:

Stephanie Ahlfeldt
Concordia College

Robert Arend
Miramar College

Don Asay
Treasure Valley Community College

Richard Barnes
Concordia University of Wisconsin

Melissa Beall
University of Northern Iowa

Kathy Berggren
Cornell University

Kathryn Black Lance
Pine Technical College

Nathan Brackeen
Central Alabama Community College

Kathy Brady
University of Wisconsin–Whitewater

Sandra Burris
Bowling Green State University–Firelands College

David Byland
Oklahoma Baptist University

Cristina Cardenas
Galveston College

Linda Combs
Daytona Beach Community College

Ed Coursey
Tompkins Cortland Community College

Peter Croisant
Geneva College

Thao Dang-Williams
St. Louis Community College at Forest Park

Kathryn Dederichs
Minneapolis Community and Technical College

Jean Dewitt
University of Houston–Downtown

Anie Dubosse
Norwalk Community College

Heather Erickson
Emerson College

Penny Eubank
Oklahoma Christian University

Dawn Fitzpatrick
Anne Arundel Community College

John Fritch
University of Northern Iowa

Richard Groetzinger
Heidelberg College

Karen A. Hamburg
Camden County College

Lisa Harris
Lenoir-Rhyne College

Mark Henderson
Jackson State University

Don Henschel
Midwestern State University

Daniel Higgins
Heidelberg College

Janet Sue Hinton
East Mississippi Community College

Rick Hogrefe
Crafton Hills College

Angela Hoppe-Nagao
Cerritos College

Peggy Huey
University of Tampa

Susan Kilgard
Anne Arundel Community College

Michele King
The College of William and Mary

Kara Laskowski
Shippensburg University

Terence Lynberg
Mesa and Mira Costa

Danny Marshall
Pierce College

Jill McCall
Moorpark College

Yolanda Monroe
Gadsden State Community College

Thomas Morra
Northern Virginia Community College

Lori Norin
University of Arkansas–Fort Smith

Kekeli Nuviadenu
Bethune-Cookman College

Fellina Nwadike
Coppin State University

Kathryn O'Sullivan
Northern Virginia Community College

Ruth Parent
Keene State College

Maria Parnell
Brevard Community College

Kelly Petkus
Austin Community College

Kim Alyse Popkave
Montgomery County Community College

Diana Rehling
St. Cloud State University

William Richter
Lenoir-Rhyne College

Mary Rupert
Gonzaga University

Carol Sams
Columbia Basin College

Karen Schlag
University of Houston–Downtown

Christopher Shar
Towson University

Rosie Soy
Hudson County Community College-Jersey City

Bill Stone
Northeast Mississippi Community College

Scott Swanson
Scott Community College

Henry Tkachuk
Concordia College

Matt Walker
Northwest Missouri State University

Sheryl-Anne Welch
University of Wisconsin–Whitewater

Janet Winslow
Clinton Community College

A very special thanks goes to Great River Technologies for helping us to integrate our materials into a powerful and user-friendly web presence. We appreciate your commitment and look forward to an ongoing partnership. Thanks to Hank Roubicek for his creative contributions that brought the video portions of the web material to life.

Finally, we would very much like to thank Paul Carty and Angela Willenbring of Kendall/Hunt Publishing. You put up with a lot from us, yet you were always friendly and kept us on task. We sincerely appreciate your patience, diplomacy, professionalism, and your sense of humor!

About the Authors

Sam Wallace, Ph.D. is an associate professor in the Department of Communication at the University of Dayton. A former basic course director with many years of experience, Sam is a past chair of the Basic Course Division of the National Communication Association and he was the first chair of the Basic Course Interest Group for the Central States Communication Association. He was president of the Ohio Communication Association and a past editor of the *Ohio Speech Journal*. In addition, Sam has directed or co-directed the Basic Course Conference in Dayton, Columbus, Las Vegas, and Phoenix.

Sam has authored, co-authored, and co-edited several books, articles in national and state journals, and convention papers. He has served on the editorial boards of *The Ohio Speech Journal*, *The Basic Communication Course Annual*, and *Communication Teacher*. His research interests include communication pedagogy, innovation in the classroom and in organizations, and the role of space and environment in the learning process.

Kimberly Rosenfeld, M.A. is a professor of Speech Communication at Cerritos College in Los Angeles, California where she teaches courses in interpersonal communication, fundamentals of oral communication, argumentation and persuasion, intercultural communication, organizational communication, and public speaking.

Over the past fifteen years, she has participated in multiple technology-related grants and served as chair of the Speech Department. As a member of the Carnegie Foundation Grant writing team, she mentored faculty in designing studies to improve teaching and learning and to communicate research results to the public on the web. While a faculty researcher and campus mentor on the Visual Knowledge Project (VKP) lead by Georgetown University, Kimberly researched the use of handheld computers in the classroom. While participating in Teacher TRAC's preparing Tomorrow's Teachers to Use Technology (PT3) grant awarded by the U.S. Department of Education, she integrated new media ranging from handheld computers to the internet within the communication curriculum.

Kimberly has presented her work at numerous conferences including those of the National Communication Association and the Western States Communication Association.

David L. Bodary, Ph.D. is a professor in the Communication Arts Department at Sinclair Community College in Ohio. He has a Bachelor of Science degree in Communication from Eastern Michigan University and a Master of Arts and Doctorate in Communication Studies from Wayne State University in Detroit, Michigan. As a full-time faculty member David teaches a variety of communication courses including interpersonal communication, effective public speaking, principles of interviewing, small group communication, and business and professional communication.

David has been recognized for meritorious teaching many times since joining Sinclair Community College in 1994. He is a member of the National Communication Association, the Central States Communication Association and the Ohio Communication Association where he has served in a variety of leadership and governance roles. David was honored with a National Institute for Staff and Organizational Development (NISOD) teaching excellence award in May of 2008. David has authored numerous articles and workbooks. He was lead developer of the *Blueprint for Success—Ten Truths of Leadership* training materials for L.M. Berry and Associates and is a certified facilitator of *High Involvement Teamwork* training by Richard Chang and Associates.

Beth M. Waggenspack, Ph.D. is an associate professor in the Department of Communication at Virginia Tech in Blacksburg, Virginia, where she teaches undergraduate and graduate courses in rhetorical history, theory, and criticism, along with the introductory "survey of the discipline's theory" course. Beth has won three college-level awards for teaching and one for advising while at Virginia Tech. As a result, she attained one of the university's highest academic honors, the Alumni Teaching Award and induction into the Academy of Teaching Excellence, representing the scholarship of teaching and learning.

In addition to teaching, Beth carries on an active scholarly research program in two areas. The first focuses on political communication, especially women's roles in that arena. A first ladies' scholar, she has written extensively about Helen Herron Taft and Eleanor Roosevelt. Her scholarship also includes book chapters, journal articles, and conference presentations on Marian Wright Edelman, Elizabeth Cady Stanton, Dorothy Fuldheim, and Lucy Stone. She wrote several chapters on women's contributions to rhetorical theory and practice for *The Rhetoric of Western Thought*. Beth's second research program revolves around adoption issues and communication. She was the author of a groundbreaking study of the media's images of adoption and is currently working with the Evan B. Donaldson Adoption Institute on a white paper extending that research.

1

INTRODUCTION: WHY STUDY COMMUNICATION?

LEARNING OBJECTIVES

After reading this chapter, you should understand the following concepts:

- Communication is a complex, multidisciplinary process in which participants create meaning by using symbols and behavior to send and receive messages with a social and cultural context.
- The freedoms of speech, of the press, of association, of assembly, and of petition constitute the freedom of expression represent—the right to communicate.
- The rapid growth of technology enhances our abilities to communicate, but also complicates the issues of communication.
- Several themes are woven into this text, each involving values that are represented in your rights and responsibilities to communicate.
- This book is designed to help the reader formulate strategies and learn the skills necessary to accomplish communication goals, with the understanding that expertise is not acquired over a semester but is honed with time and practice.

KEYWORDS

communication
freedom of expression
culture

INTRODUCTION

Have you ever experienced a communication gap? Try this. Which of the following statements can you interpret or translate?

Hey, don't bogart the brewski. Everythingi copasetic. It's gnarly.[1]

What It Is, What It Is? The Man came around today, can you dig it? Yeah, that's sick.[2]

The dinks next door just barf me out. They are such hosers.[3]

The straight edge is a buzz kill. Let's dip. Don't go there! Back in the day we were tight![4]

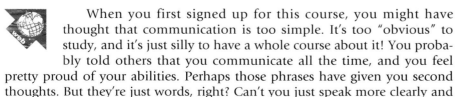 When you first signed up for this course, you might have thought that communication is too simple. It's too "obvious" to study, and it's just silly to have a whole course about it! You probably told others that you communicate all the time, and you feel pretty proud of your abilities. Perhaps those phrases have given you second thoughts. But they're just words, right? Can't you just speak more clearly and

Why would you have to study communication when you do it every day?
© digitalskillet, 2008, Shutterstock.

resolve any confusion those phrases might have created? Do you really need a whole course just about word choice? Is that what this course is?

You might think that studying communication is a waste of time because it's nothing more than common sense. Because you have been communicating all your life and seem to be reasonably good at it, you figure there *can't* be much to it, right? You should be spending your academic time more profitably, considering topics that *should* be studied. We should be studying how to fly an airplane or how to practice medicine, because those things are complex and people don't just intuitively learn how to navigate through heavy clouds or how to successfully remove a spleen. However, there is no need to study communication—we do that every day!

Because communicating is so familiar to everyone, it is often taken for granted and, as a result, it is ignored. The only time we really ever pay attention to or notice the communication process is when something goes wrong or if some rule is violated. Instead of waiting around for a communication disaster to strike, the purpose of this course is to challenge you to call your participation in the communication process into question and raise it to the level of conscious awareness. At this level you can examine it, take it apart, put it back together, and use that new awareness to improve your own abilities as a communicator.

Think for a minute *how* and *how often* you communicate. Not only do you carry on conversations with others, work successfully in groups with them, participate in interviews, make presentations, and tell entertaining stories, but you also have to have a pretty good facility with various electronic communication tools that provide you with efficient means of reaching out to others. In their book *Connecting to the Net.Generation: What Higher Education Professionals Need to Know about Today's College Students*, Reynol Junco and Jeanna Mastrodicasa revealed the following information gathered in a survey of 7,705 college students in the United States:[5]

- 97 percent own a computer.
- 94 percent own a cell phone.
- 76 percent use instant messaging.
- 15 percent of IM users are logged on 24 hours a day/7 days a week.
- 34 percent use Web sites as their primary source of news.
- 28 percent own a blog, and 44 percent read blogs.
- 49 percent download music using peer-to-peer file sharing.
- 75 percent of students have a Facebook account.
- 60 percent own some type of expensive portable music and/or video device such as an iPod.

Do these figures surprise you? Do you think these media have an effect on how you communicate and what you expect from others? Add in the work groups, commuting partners, friends and family members that you talk with daily. All of these influence how you develop relationships with others, your awareness of things going on near and far, the ways that you view time, what you think is important, and a thousand other perceptions. Your beliefs, attitudes, and values are all affected by the amount, type, and success of your communication efforts. For example, if you use many of those media, you probably expect responses more quickly than someone from a previous generation. You might think that finding information is better done on a computer than by personal interviews or even reading a book or a print newspaper. Your means of telling others about yourself have expanded, leaving both privacy and personal safety at risk. You can create images of yourself that reflect what you'd like to be, rather than what you are. Your language evolves with blinding speed, with new words being coined daily and shared immediately. You live in a communication-saturated world, where symbols evolve, media change, and people adapt.

How does the media you use affect your communication with others?
© Konstantin Sutyagin, 2008, Shutterstock.

Are you starting to believe that communication is much more complex than you first realized? Theorists and researchers have studied it for hundreds of years, attempting to discover what constitutes effective communication, involving different sources, messages, audiences, contexts, and purposes. Other studies have investigated the use of technology ranging from Sumerian writing and its impact on later Egyptian hieroglyphics, through the impact of print and photography, to electronic means ranging from the telegraph to the computer, PDAs, cell phones, and emerging new technologies. These studies have been undertaken by researchers in diverse fields such as art, anthropology, history, philosophy, computer science, linguistics, sociology, psychology, English, and a relatively new field called **communication.**

Today, the study of communication spans multidisciplinary interests and has developed interlocking and independent theoretical approaches. This text will introduce you to the basics of the theories and practice of some of those approaches to communication in different contexts. Ranging from the situational contexts of intrapersonal, interpersonal, and small group communication, to interviewing and finally public speaking, you'll traverse the discipline. Although you will find that these different contexts allow you to examine the communication process more clearly, the categorization is not perfect, because you'll find overlap among the strategies suggested in different contexts. For instance, you'll learn about being seen as credible,

Depending on the situation, different communication strategies are most effective.
© Dmitriy Shironosov, 2008, Shutterstock.

understanding an audience, and how to engage in verbal and nonverbal communication. There are some basic assumptions and ideas about each of these topics, but the contexts in which you use the strategies will differ. You'll see that when you prepare a speech, you'll want to engage in critical thinking, research, organization, and consider delivery strategies. You might also have to conduct an interview or participate in a small group discussion. In a small group, you still will have to think critically, analyze your audience, and organize and present your ideas. But delivery concerns are different in public speaking than they are in interviewing. Participating in an interview requires a different mind-set (roles and norms) than does leading a small group. Good communication depends on developing a set of strategies designed to help you to understand one another and cooperate to create meaning with others. As a result of taking this class, you'll discover that you have a broad view of strategic choices to consider in a number of different communication contexts.

Maybe you're starting to be convinced that this text might teach you some necessary skills, but you'll be exposed to more than skill competency. Communication involves considering cultural values and issues, along with developing shared meaning with others.

WHAT IS THE IMPACT OF COMMUNICATION STUDY BEYOND SKILLS?

Why is competent communication important to almost anything we do?
© Laurence Gough, 2008, Shutterstock.

Communication is important and central to nearly all that we do. Think about it. We make our laws through a process of debate and voting in legislatures. Our legal system depends on people to make a good case; to present and interpret evidence in a compelling way to allow important decisions to be made. Our political system requires citizens to make decisions concerning candidates for office, laws to adopt, and where to spend tax money. Religion, culture, science, and education all involve a series of beliefs passed along to each new generation by the people who hold those beliefs. It's all done through communication. Fundamental to our American culture is the right to use our ability to communicate. Let's consider the freedoms and responsibilities inherent in that right in an attempt to discover the complexity of communication.

The freedoms of speech, of the press, of association, of assembly, and of petition: this set of guarantees, protected by the First Amendment, constitutes the concept of **freedom of expression.** They represent the right to communicate. Without this freedom, other fundamental rights, like the right to vote and to participate in our own governance, would lack force. Members of a democratic society have both the right and responsibility to participate in governance. At the very least, you should be an informed voter. But being an informed voter requires doing research and interpreting and critically analyzing information and values related to candidates and issues. This activity often means that you have to sift through and weigh heaps of campaign slogans, sound bytes, and promises to get to the "meat" of the matter.

The essence of being a citizen in a democratic society goes beyond the privilege of voting, however. From childhood, you may have been taught the core values of being an individual, of tolerating the differences and diversity of others, or of having the right to speak and think as you want. You learn to express your mind, to speak out against decisions you disagree with, to praise people who do a good job, to associate with whomever you want, and to criticize both individuals and government. This freedom of expression is the essence of a democracy. Let's consider a few examples that demonstrate the nation's commitment to freedom of expression and how it has been tested.

When the country music group the Dixie Chicks' lead singer Natalie Maines said at a London concert on March 10, 2003, that she was "ashamed the president of the United States is from Texas," the backlash started. Country music stations across the country pulled Dixie Chicks' songs from their playlists, others called for boycotts of their concerts, and some organizations sponsored bonfires in which the group's CDs were destroyed.[6] In response, on his Web site, Bruce Springsteen defended the group's right to say what they believe. He asserted that they are American artists who were using their right to free speech, and that anyone who thought it was right to punish them for speaking out is un-American.[7]

Is burning the American flag an issue of the freedom of expression? In 1989, the Supreme Court ruled in the case of *Texas v. Johnson* that the First Amendment rights of citizens to engage in free speech, even if that speech is "offensive," outweigh the government's interest in protecting the American flag as a symbol of American unity. The action of flag burning, as repugnant as it may be to many citizens, was defined by the Supreme Court and Texas Court of Criminal Appeals as an example of "symbolic speech."[8] For the majority opinion, Justice Brennan wrote: "If there is a bedrock principle underlying the First Amendment, it is that the Government may not prohibit the expression of an idea simply because society finds the idea itself offensive or disagreeable. Punishing desecration of the flag dilutes the very freedom that makes this emblem so revered, and worth revering."[9]

What about protest marches and sit-ins? What about protesting the actions of the courts? Are these activities representative of freedom of expression? In 1963, the Southern Christian Leadership Coalition mounted a campaign that focused on direct action, committed to ending segregation in Birmingham, Alabama. The campaign began with a series of mass meetings, including one featuring civil rights leader Martin Luther King Jr., who spoke about the philosophy of nonviolence and appealed to the volunteers to practice its methods. The actions included lunch counter sit-ins, marches on City Hall, a boycott of downtown merchants, sit-ins at the library, and a voter registration march. When the city government obtained a court injunction directing an end to all protests, King and the SCLC disobeyed the court order, and on April 12, King was arrested in Birmingham. He was kept in solitary confinement and was allowed only minimal contact. It was at this time that King penned his famous Letter from the Birmingham Jail.[10]

The rapid growth of technology enhances our abilities to communicate and adds additional cautions to what we say and how we say it. It has multiplied the channels by which we can create relationships, gather information, conduct business, and make decisions. The 2005 Pew Foundation's Major Moments Survey showed increases in the number of Americans who report that the Internet played a crucial or important role in various aspects of their lives.[11] Consider the growth of blogs, "web logs," which allow anyone with a computer to post thoughts, opinions, histories, anecdotes, and political ideas to a worldwide platform, unhindered by time and distance. Blogger and public relations writer Jeneane Sessum of Atlanta is the founder of Blog Sisters, a group blog with more than 100 female members from around

How has technology changed the way we communicate with others?
© Kurhan, 2008, Shutterstock.

the world. The group discusses everything from gender and international politics to family life and career quandaries, without fear of being censored. Sessum says, "Blogs make it really easy to express yourself. It's an amazing tool to help you figure out who you are, what you care about and to connect with other human beings. Plus, it's a place for me to exercise my voice. I've been so busy writing for clients that I've never kept up with my personal writing. Blogging has really helped me refine my voice."[13]

Martin Luther King Jr.'s Letter from Birmingham Jail

Sometimes a law is just on its face and unjust in its application. For instance, I have been arrested on a charge of parading without a permit. Now, there is nothing wrong in having an ordinance which requires a permit for a parade. But such an ordinance becomes unjust when it is used to maintain segregation and to deny citizens the First Amendment privilege of peaceful assembly and protest.

I hope you are able to embrace the distinction I am trying to point out. In no sense do I advocate evading or defying the law, as would the rabid segregationist. That would lead to anarchy. One who breaks an unjust law must do so openly, lovingly, and with a willingness to accept the penalty. I submit that an individual who breaks a law that conscience tells him is unjust and who willingly accepts the penalty of imprisonment in order to arouse the conscience of the community over its injustice, is in reality expressing the highest respect for law.[12]

Does the existence of blogs raise questions about freedom of expression? Some critics assert that bloggers have transformed the Internet into a virtual soapbox, resulting in an impact on the public dialogue with questions about social responsibility and the law. Bradley Smith, chairman of the Federal Elections Commission (FEC), has suggested that there is a need to regulate political speech in blogs, saying that bloggers could soon invite federal punishment if they improperly link to a campaign's Web site.[14]

Broadcast media have a responsibility to check sources when providing news coverage. On September 20, 2004, CBS news anchor Dan Rather apologized for a "mistake in judgment" in relying on apparently bogus documents for a *60 Minutes* report about President George W. Bush's time in the Texas Air National Guard. In his on-air statement, Rather said,

> Now, after extensive additional interviews, I no longer have the confidence in these documents that would allow us to continue vouching for them journalistically. I find we have been misled on the key question of how our source for the documents came into possession of these papers. That, combined with some of the questions that have been raised in public and in the press, leads me to a point where—if I knew then what I know now—I would not have gone ahead with the story as it was aired, and I certainly would not have used the documents in question. But we did use the documents. We made a mistake in judgment, and for that I am sorry.

Rather's admission of a mistake resulted in great damage to the CBS news division's credibility. Boston *Phoenix* media writer Dan Kennedy said, "They were way too late in acknowledging there may be problems with this. The short-term damage is just horrendous. You have a large percentage of the public believing—falsely, I would argue—that the media are suffused with liberal bias, and this just plays right into that."[15]

There are many examples of the impact of communication rights and responsibilities that span the entire history of the United States. Freedom of expression is codified in law, and it is part of who we are as Americans. The core values represented in the right to express your thoughts and to communicate freely with others are central to our society. These values are vital to the attainment and advancement of knowledge and the search for the truth. These are only a few examples of instances where the privilege and attendant responsibility of freedom of expression have impacted your life. In this text, we will "bring it home" by your participation in discussions about the freedom of expression in your daily life in personal and public arenas.

Now it's time to ask: How does this concept of communication responsibilities impact what you'll learn in this course?

WHAT ARE THE THEMES OF THIS TEXT?

Several themes are woven into the fabric of the course material in the print volume and the companion Web site. These illustrate the key assumptions and topics that you'll discover. Each also involves values that are represented in your rights and responsibilities to communicate.

- *Transactional perspective:* The assumption that participants cooperate to create meaning is clearly described and explained in the theory chapter and is reflected in the explanations for all communication contexts treated in the book. Public speaking, group decision making, interviewing, and interpersonal communication are all transactional processes. Messages are sent and received by all participants simultaneously in a cooperative effort to create and share meaning.
- *Critical thinking:* Participants in communication should be able to formulate and argue their own opinions and propositions and not merely accept as true what is taken from the media or heard from other people.
- *Participants:* Understanding communication assumes an understanding of the people who participate in communication. We assume that the meaning participants give to messages is influenced by a myriad of factors: the self-concept of the participant, the intentions or goals of the participant, the totality of experience of the participant, and the other participants.
- *Context:* Communication is influenced by the various physical, symbolic, and social contexts in which it occurs.
- *Culture:* Communication is influenced by the culture in which it occurs and by the cultural perspectives of the participants. Think of **culture** as a *community of meaning;* we all belong to multiple cultures and we come into contact with other cultures on a professional and social basis every day.
- *Technology:* We live in a world in which communication between and among people is more and more often mediated by some form of technology. From the responsibilities of sound research and investigation, to the use of instantaneous communication technology used to facilitate regional and global collaboration, to the effective use of presentational materials, you will be asked to consider the development and use of technology to enhance your message.

SUMMARY

You're now ready to begin your study of unique features of the communication discipline, along with its attendant values and responsibilities. You will bring your established abilities into the mix, but you will also begin to take into account aspects of communicating that you never considered before. *Communication is serious, complex, and important!* By the end of this book, we want you to believe this is true. Perhaps more importantly, though, we want to challenge you to become a full and influential participant communicating in personal, business, and civic affairs.

Before you can accept this challenge and begin your exploration of the strategies communication requires, you need to consider the scope of communication via a definition. *Communication is a process in which participants create meaning by using symbols and behavior to send and receive messages within a social and cultural context.* This book is devoted to helping you understand and apply this definition so you will be able to formulate strategies and learn the skills necessary for accomplishing all of your communication goals. You are not likely to become an expert communicator by the time you complete this course, but you should have a good start. You'll be exposed to a series of questions in every chapter that will lead to some beliefs, attitudes, and values, along with skills. Like any expertise that you learn, your competence improves with time, practice, and use. The goal of this text is to assist you in developing strategies and practicing skills in a variety of communication contexts.

ENDNOTES

1. Samples of 1960s slang, defined at 1960s slang, http://www.cougartown.com/slang.html (accessed Sept. 23, 2007).

2. 1970s slang, http://www.inthe70s.com/generated/terms.shtml (accessed Sept. 23, 2007).

3. 1980s slang, http://www.i80s.com/80s_slang/slang1.htm (accessed Sept. 23, 2007).

4. http://www.inthe90s.com/generated/terms.shtml (accessed Sept. 23, 2007).

5. Junco, Reynol and Jeanna Mastrodicasa, *Connecting to the Net.Generation: What Higher Education Professionals Need to Know About Today's College Students.* (Washington, DC: National Association of Student Personnel Administrators, 2007).

6. CNN.Com/Entertainment. Dixie Chicks pulled from air after bashing Bush. March 14, 2003 (accessed June 14, 2007).

7. BBC News (bbc.co.uk) Springsteen backs under-fire Dixies. April 28, 2003 (accessed June 14, 2007).

8. *Texas vs. Johnson*, 491 U.S. 397. (June 21, 1989).

9. PBS.Org PBS Online. United States v. Eichman. Issue: Burning the American Flag. (Undated) (accessed June 18, 2007).

10. Stanford University. King Encyclopedia. "Birmingham Campaign." (accessed June 18, 2007).

11. Horrigan, John and Lee Rainie. "The Internet's Growing Role in Life's Major Moments." (April 19, 2006.) Pew Internet & American Life Project, http://www.pewinternet.org/PPF/r/181/report_display.asp (accessed June 20, 2007).

12. MLK Online. "Letter from Birmingham Jail, April 16, 1963." (accessed March 30, 2008).

13. Trimbath, Karen. "Women Go Blogging and Find Freedom of Speech." Women's eNews. August 2, 2004 http://www.womensenews.org/article.cfm/dyn/aid/1934 (accessed June 22, 2007).

14. "Are Blogs Protected under the First Amendment?" http://www.legalzoom.com/articles/article_content/article14006.html (accessed June 22, 2007).

15. Kurtz, Howard. "Rather Admits 'Mistake in Judgment.'" (September 21, 2004) http://washingtonpost.com/wp-dyn/articles/A35531-2004Sep20_2.html (accessed June 22, 2007).

WHAT IS COMMUNICATION?

LEARNING OBJECTIVES

After reading this chapter, you should understand the following concepts:

- The goal of communication is to build theory used to guide communicators in the formulation of strategies to achieve communication goals.
- There are many definitions of communication, but they share common characteristics: Communication is a process, messages are sent and received, participants interact in social contexts, and meaning is created and shared through symbols and behavior.
- The action model was the necessary first step in the evolution of communication models, but it has a weakness in that it lacks interaction.
- The interaction model includes the important aspect of feedback.
- The transactional model recognizes that communication is a process, it is irreversible, it means shared responsibility, and it occurs in context and culture.

INTRODUCTION

"Oh, that's just a theory. It doesn't mean anything!"

Have you heard this before? There is a common misconception that a **theory** is the same thing as a "guess." A theory is a "shot from the hip," or it's a "Monday morning quarterback's" explanation of why his team won or lost on Sunday. Sometimes you hear people express doubt about "relativity" or "evolution" because they are "only theories," and not fact. Not true! A theory is not idle speculation unsupported by evidence that is spontaneously created or made up.

 Theories are not guesses! Littlejohn states, "Any attempt to explain or represent an experience is a theory; an idea of how something happens."[1] Kerlinger says that a theory is "a set of interrelated constructs (concepts), definitions, and propositions that present a systematic view of phenomena by specifying relations among variables, with the purpose of explaining and predicting the phenomena."[2]

KEYWORDS

theory
empirical
Aristotle
Claude Shannon
Warren Weaver
source
message
code
encoded
transmitted
channel
receiver
decodes
destination
noise
action model
interaction model
Wilbur Schramm
David Berlo
feedback
transactional model
process
participant
carrier
environmental noise
psychological noise
physical context
social context
culture

WHAT IS THE NATURE OF COMMUNICATION THEORY?

Our definition is that a theory is *an attempt to describe, predict, and / or explain an experience or phenomenon.* The purpose of generating a theory is the attempt to *understand* something:

- Theory is a collection of statements or conceptual assumptions.
- It specifies the relationships among concepts or variables and provides a basis for predicting behavior of a phenomenon.
- It explains a phenomenon.

Here's an illustration from the distant past:

Og the cave dweller comes out of his cave in the morning and sees the sun shining in the east. When Og visits the village well later in the day, he and his friends are able to *describe* what happened: "When I came out of my cave, I saw the bright light in the sky!" They can all try to agree on the description, and they will all know what happened.

Og the cave dweller systematically observes the environment.
© 2008, JupiterImages Corporation.

Over the next several months, Og and his pals emerge from their caves every morning, and every morning they see the sun in the eastern sky. They also notice that the sun has moved to the western sky when they return to their caves in the evening. After several conversations at the village well, they discover or recognize that a *pattern* seems to exist in the behavior of the sun. In the morning, the bright light is over there. But in the evening, the bright light is on the other side. They set up an observational plan to see if their pattern holds up. In the mornings, when Og comes from his cave (which faces south), he looks to his left and he *expects* to see the sun. There it is! Eureka! The observations support the hypothesis (or informed assumption) that the sun will rise in the east! Og and his associates can now *predict* the behavior of the sun!

Og is attempting to build a theory. He is able to describe and predict, but he still comes up short because he does not understand *why* the sun behaves as it does. Og still has much uncertainty about the sun's behavior, and that makes him and all the rest of us humans uncomfortable. So we continue to study it. Now, please "fast forward" from this point several thousand years when, after gathering lots and lots of information, we were finally able to *explain* why the sun appears to rise in the east and set in the west.

Og and his buddies made some observations of phenomena and were able to describe it, then they noticed patterns in the phenomena and were able to predict its behavior. They might have even tried to explain the activity they observed, but they did not have enough knowledge to make a good explanation. The explanation came much later and is beyond the scope of this book. But you can go look it up!

What they *did* do was create a partial theory, and that theory was based on empirical observation. Not bad for cave dwellers! **Empirical** means that knowledge claims are based on observations of reality (i.e., the real world) and are not merely subjective speculation based on the observer's perspective. The conclusions are based on *observed* evidence, which helps the observer

Observation ⟶ Pattern Recognition ⟶ Theory ⟶ Hypotheses ⟶ Observation

remain more objective.[3] The cycle of study is repeated over and over: Observation is made, which leads to recognizing a pattern; attempts to predict and explain are made, which become basic theories; the theories help the observer create new hypotheses (predictions) about the behavior of the phenomenon; observation is made and the information analyzed in search of patterns; and those recognized patterns add to the basic theory.[4] As this cycle repeats itself, the body of theory becomes larger and more sophisticated, and the field of study matures.

The goal of any field of study, including communication, is to *build theory*. The body of communication theory is subsequently used to guide communicators in the formulation of strategies for achieving communication goals and to help communicators understand what skills are necessary for carrying out the strategies.

The purpose of this chapter is to help you understand the basic theory supporting human communication behavior. The skills and strategies necessary to accomplish your communication goals are derived from this theory. This chapter includes the following:

- A definition of communication
- An evolution of conceptions of communication
- A transactional model of communication
- A discussion of essential terms

HOW IS COMMUNICATION DEFINED?

Defining communication is not quite as easy as it sounds because almost all people, even scholars, think they know what it is. We all communicate every day, so we all have an opinion. The problem is that nearly nobody agrees! Clevenger says that the term *communication* is one of the most "overworked terms in the English language."[5]

To try to make sense of the literally hundreds of different definitions, we will examine some significant attempts to define communication, and then we will draw out the commonalities in the attempt to build our own point of view. Here are some influential examples:

- An individual transmits stimuli to modify the behavior of other individuals.[6]
- Social interaction occurs through symbols and message systems.[7]
- A source transmits a message to receiver(s) with conscious intent to affect the latter's behavior.[8]
- "Senders and receivers of messages interact in given social contexts."[9]
- "Shared meaning through symbolic processes" is created.[10]
- There is mutual creation of shared meaning through the simultaneous interpretation and response to verbal and nonverbal behaviors in a specific context."[11]
- "Communication occurs when one person sends and receives messages that are distorted by noise, occur within a context, have some effect, and provide some opportunity for feedback."[12]

Take a Closer Look

What do these definitions have in common?

· Communication is a process.
· Messages are sent and received.
· Participants interact in social contexts.
· Meaning is created and shared through the use of symbols and behavior.

The perspective of this book is that *communication is a process in which participants create meaning by using symbols and behavior to send and receive messages within a social and cultural context.* This perspective will be expanded and explained in the remainder of this chapter.

HOW HAVE THE CONCEPTIONS OF COMMUNICATION EVOLVED?

Now that we have a working definition of communication, let's examine where it came from. This section looks at classic models of communication spanning about 2,500 years. The goal of this section is to illustrate the evolution of the communication perspective taken by this book; to show you how we arrived at the point of view that influences every strategy and skill that we teach. We believe that if you understand why we teach it, you will be more motivated to learn and to use this point of view to plan and execute your own communication strategies!

WHAT ARE THE MODELS OF COMMUNICATION?

You have seen and used a map many times. If you are looking for a particular street in your town, you pick up a map to find where the street is and to learn how to get there from where you are. A map is not your town, however, but a *representation* of your town. It's a picture or drawing that helps you understand the way your town is arranged. A *model* is the very same thing. But instead of representing a physical space, like a town, the model represents a process, or the way something happens.

The models discussed here represent three views of communication that have enjoyed popularity over the years. Those three views are action (or linear), interaction, and transaction. These models help illustrate and explain the current view of communication, the transactional perspective. Each will be discussed in the following pages.

As a map represents a place, a model represents a process.
© Stephen VanHorn, 2008, Shutterstock.

The Action Model

Although many perspectives of communication contributed to what we are calling the action model, Aristotle and the Shannon and Weaver models had the most impact.

We'll start with **Aristotle,** a philosopher, scientist, and teacher who lived in ancient Greece. Educated by Plato and the son of a physician, he was trained as a biologist.[13] He was skilled at observing and describing, and at categorizing his observations.[14] Aristotle found himself interested in nearly all things that occupied the attention of the citizens of Athens, including the study of speaking.

Ancient Athens was a democracy, and all citizens had the right and opportunity to influence public affairs and public policy. The more articulate citizens were able to affect events by persuading or influencing other citizens and law makers in public meetings. Because individual citizens had a voice, teachers of public speaking and persuasion were always in demand.

Aristotle's *Rhetoric* is a published collection of his teachings,[15] and it has been suggested that it is the "most important single work on persuasion ever written."[16] The focus of the *Rhetoric* is primarily on the speaker and the message. Some, but little, attention is paid to the audience. The philosophy is that a well-crafted message delivered by a credible speaker will have the desired effect with the audience. If Aristotle had a model of persuasion, the simple version would probably look something like this:

Aristotle used his observation skills to study communication in ancient Greece.
© 2008 JupiterImages Corporation.

> WELL-CRAFTED MESSAGE + CREDIBLE SOURCE = DESIRED EFFECT

Aristotle's contribution to communication would not have been this model. His contributions came in the form of instructions for how to use logic and emotions (*logos* and *pathos*) to craft a message, and how to establish and build credibility as a speaker or source of a message (*ethos*).

For the second time in this chapter, please fast forward in time, but this time only about two thousand years. Stop when you get to the 1940s, and we'll take a look at **Claude Shannon** and **Warren Weaver**. Claude Shannon was a mathematician who worked at Bell Labs, and he was interested in ways to make more efficient use of telephone lines for the transmission of voices. He was not concerned about human communication, but he was very focused on electronic communication. Shannon teamed with Warren Weaver, a scientist and mathematician, to publish the *Mathematical Theory of Communication*. Shannon's focus was on the engineering aspects of the theory, while Weaver was more interested in the human and other implications. Communication scholars found this model to be very useful in helping them to explain *human* communication.[17]

The Shannon–Weaver model is consistent with Aristotle's point of view, and it extends it to include a transmitter, a channel, and a receiver. It also introduces the concept of *noise* to the explanation. The process is illustrated in Figure 2.1. The **source** (a person) initiates a **message** that is turned into a **code** (language), and the **encoded** message is sent **(transmitted)** through a **channel** (sound waves created by the voice, or some mediated signal). The **receiver decodes** the signal (turning it again into a message), which is sent to the **destination** (the other person). **Noise** is anything that can interfere with the signal. See Figure 2.1.

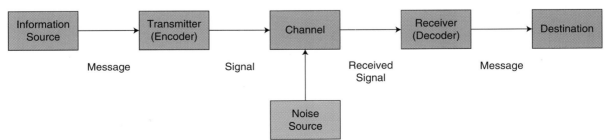

Figure 2.1
The Shannon–Weaver Mathematical Model

A message in a bottle lacks the interaction we have in everyday conversations.
© R. Gino Santa Maria, 2008, Shutterstock.

This model helps to understand human communication, but it has a significant shortcoming: it doesn't adequately capture the reality or the complexity of the process. It assumes that the participants in the process take on discrete speaker or listener roles, and that while one person speaks, the other person quietly listens with no response, until the speaker is finished. Then the roles are reversed. Then the roles are reversed again, and again and again, until the conversation is complete. *Human communication is arguably not that linear!* It is equivalent to placing a message in a bottle, throwing it into the sea, and waiting for it to reach the proper destination. The person (receiver) removes the message from the bottle, reads the message, writes a new message, places it back in the bottle, and throws it back into the sea. The model works, but it doesn't represent the way that we communicate in everyday conversations. It lacks *interaction!*

As you consider the two models just discussed, you can see that they are primarily concerned with the source of the message and the content of the message itself. The focus is on the source and how he or she constructs and delivers the message. So a source that creates well-designed messages has done everything possible to ensure effective communication. Say the right thing and you will be successful! If something goes wrong, or if the source is not clearly understood by the potential receiver, the **action model** states that the fault is with the source. However, when everything goes well and the message is clearly understood, it is because the source crafted and sent a good-quality message. See Figure 2.2 for a depiction of the action model. The action model was the necessary first step in the evolution of the contemporary communication model.

SOURCE ———————— Message ————————→ **RECEIVER**
                       Channel

Figure 2.2
Action Model

The Interaction Model

The **interaction model** remains linear, like the action model, but it begins to view the source and receiver as a team in the communication process.

Wilbur Schramm introduced a model of communication that includes a notion of *interaction*.[18] The Schramm model does not consider the context or environment in which the communication takes place, and it does not explicitly treat codes (language) or noise. Although it is still very linear, it describes the dual roles played by the participants instead of viewing one as a source (speaker) and the other as a receiver (listener), and it makes a strong case for *interaction* among the participants. The flow of information can be seen as more ongoing or continuous, rather than a linear, back-and-forth type of flow. The conception of communication is emerging as a *process*. See Figure 2.3.

David Berlo, in *The Process of Communication*, began to discuss process and the complexity of communication.[19] This model fully includes the receiver, and it places importance on the *relationship* between the source and receiver. It also illustrates that the source and receiver are not just reacting to the environment or each other, but that each possesses individual differences

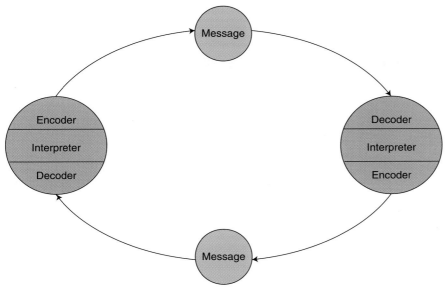

Figure 2.3
Schramm's Model of Communication

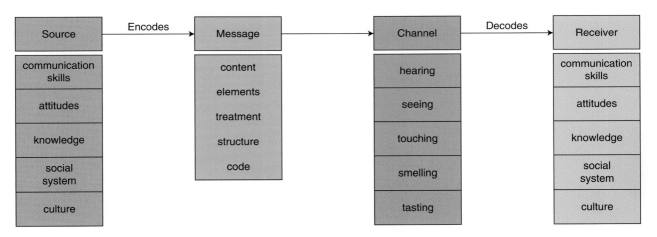

Figure 2.4
Berlo's Model of Communication

based on knowledge and attitudes, and that each operates within a cultural and social system that influences meaning. Because we all have different knowledge and attitudes, we interpret or give meaning to messages in different ways. This makes human communication very complex!

Although it was not explicitly mentioned in the model (see Figure 2.4), Berlo discussed the notion of **feedback** in his book. Feedback is information that is routed to the source, or fed back, from the receiver. Berlo said, "Feedback provides the source with information concerning his success in accomplishing his objective. In doing this, it exerts control over future messages which the source encodes."[20]

Figure 2.5
Interaction Model

Berlo completed the loop left unfinished by the Shannon–Weaver model. The source encodes a message, sent through a channel to a receiver, who decodes it and assigns meaning. The receiver then sends a message back to the source (feedback) indicating, among other things, that the message was understood. Even though this is still a linear model, we are getting closer to a model that begins to capture the nature of human communication. But it's not quite there yet!

These two models, and models like them, can be *summarized* in what we call the *interaction model* (see Figure 2.5). A source sends a message through a noise-filled channel to a receiver. The receiver responds to the source through feedback, which is a message sent by the receiver to the source through a noise-filled channel. The core of the interaction model is that the source is the originator and that the receiver creates feedback to that message. Like the action model, the interaction model implies that the process is linear; that is, communicators take turns being first a source then a receiver, and so on. The interaction model was the second step in the evolution of the contemporary communication model.

The Transactional Model

More contemporary conceptions view communication as an ongoing process in which all participants send and receive messages simultaneously. All participants are both speakers *and* listeners.[21] "A person is giving feedback, talking, responding, acting, and reacting through a communication event."[22] The **transactional model** incorporates this point of view along with the notion that the creation of the meaning of a message is not the sole responsibility of the source or the receiver, but a responsibility that is shared among all participants in a communication situation or event.

Properties of Transactional Communication. To get a clear view of the transactional model of communication, it is necessary to understand the important properties of communication. Properties include process, irreversibility, shared responsibility, context, and culture. These five properties are discussed in this section.

Communication Is a Process. Many conceptualizations of communication describe it as a **process.** The notion of process is not unique to communication; it comes to us from the literature of *theoretical physics*. A little closer to home, the notion of process and its relationship to human behavior can be found in *general systems theory.*[23] Although we use this term all the time, it's important to understand what the term *process* implies.

Process implies that communication is *continuous* and ongoing. It is *dynamic:* It never stops. Barnlund[24] says that a process has no beginning and no end. It constantly changes and evolves, new information and experience is added, and it becomes even more complex.[25] There is ongoing and constant mutual influence of the participants.[26] Participants are *constantly* sending and receiving verbal and nonverbal messages. You can try to take a "snapshot" of a single episode, and you can observe the date and time of its beginning and ending, but you can't say that this is where the communication began and ended. Heisenberg stated that to observe a process requires bringing it to a halt.[27] This gives us a fuzzy look at what is really happening, because stopping a process alters the process. So we have to do the best we can to observe, understand, and participate in communication events.

Consider, for example, a father asking his son to practice his saxophone. The father says, "Pete, please go to your room and practice your saxophone for 20 minutes." Pete (clearly annoyed) responds, "Come on, Dad! I'm right in the middle of this video game. Can't I do it later?" The father immediately gets angry and sends Pete to his room "to think about what he has done," followed by 20 minutes of saxophone practice.

The episode seems to be over, but we wonder why the young man was so annoyed at being asked to practice and why the father got angry so quickly. Could it be that this was only *one* installment in a series of episodes in which the father tries to get Pete to practice? Or could it be that Pete was having some difficulty with the saxophone that made him not want to practice? Or is there something else going on that we can't see in only this one episode? Will this episode affect future episodes?

The answer to the last question is yes! Communication is influenced by events that come before it, and it influences events that follow it.

Communication Is Irreversible. Messages are sent and received, and all participants give meaning to those messages as they happen. Once the behavior has occurred, it becomes part of history and can't be reversed. Have you ever said something that you wish you could take back? It doesn't matter if you meant it or not; once it's out there, you have to deal with it.

As mentioned in a previous section, the prior experience or history of the participants influences the meaning created in the current interaction. Even if you try to take something back or pretend it didn't happen, it still has influence in the current and future interactions. Occasionally, in a court case, an attorney or a witness will say something that the judge decides is inappropriate to the case, and he or she will instruct the jury to "disregard" the statement. Do you think the members of the jury are able to remove the statement from their memories? Have you ever heard that as a member of a jury? What did you do?

A friend of ours was asked the question that no married person wants to hear. While clothes shopping, the spouse asked, "Do these pants make me look fat?" Instead of pretending not to hear the question or saying an emphatic no, our friend said, "The pants are very nice, honey. It's your backside that makes you look fat!" For almost a whole minute, it seemed pretty funny. Multiple attempts to take back the comment failed. That communication episode affected the meaning of nearly every conversation they had for several months. *Communication is irreversible.* And you thought this book would have no practical advice!

> "You are the master of the *unspoken* word. Once the word is spoken, you are its slave."
> —Anonymous

Communication Means Shared Responsibility. Poor communication is not the fault of *one* participant in a conversation. If communication breaks down, you can't blame it on the "other guy." It is the fault of *all* the participants. The transactional perspective implies that it is the responsibility of all participants to cooperate to create a shared meaning. Even if a few of the participants are deficient in some communication skills, it is the responsibility of each person to adapt to the situation and ensure that everyone understands. Even the less capable have responsibilities: If they do not understand, they have the responsibility to ask the other participants to help them understand. *All participants cooperate to create meaning.*

How does your culture affect communication?
© 2008 JupiterImages Corporation.

Communication Occurs in a Context. The participants in the communication event affect or influence each other, and they are also affected and influenced by the context or environment in which the communication event occurs.

Communication Occurs within Cultures. Much like context, the participants are affected or influenced by the culture of which they are members and by the culture in which the communication event takes place.

Specifics of the Transaction Model. The evolution of communication theory through the action and interaction models has brought us to the current perspective, the transaction model. This book is based on the transaction model, and all of the communication strategies we suggest are based on the model and its properties.

Wallace and others view the transactional perspective as *the joint creation of shared meaning through the simultaneous perception of verbal and nonverbal behaviors within a specific context.*[28] Although you are speaking or sending messages, you constantly receive and give meaning to information from the environment and from other participants. Similarly, while you are listening to another participant, you are sending nonverbal messages through eye contact, facial expressions, posture, and body movements. So we don't really take turns being the source and receiver as illustrated by the action and interaction models. Instead, we are constantly sending *and* receiving messages!

How do you prepare for a meeting with a new business associate?
© Kiselev Andrey Valerevich, 2008, Shutterstock.

For example, a husband asks a wife if she minds if he plays golf on a Saturday afternoon. All the time he is asking the question, he is constantly scanning for every nonverbal clue to find out how she really feels. It might be her posture, or the way she looks at (or away from) him, or a particular facial expression, or some combination of everything that provides her response long before she speaks. Lots of information is being exchanged in this situation, which helps this couple create and share meaning.

Think about the first time you met your girlfriend's or boyfriend's parents. Think about your first date with somebody you were really interested in. Or consider meeting a potential client for a business deal. Doing business is important to both participants, so you both are very careful to gather all the available information to reduce uncertainty, become more comfortable, and formulate and confirm strategies for accomplishing communication goals. You use the information to create and share meaning!

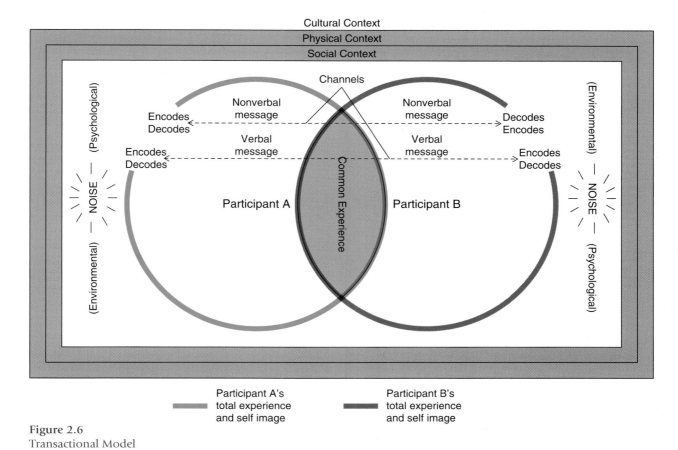

Figure 2.6
Transactional Model

In the transaction model, *participants create shared meaning* by simultaneously sending and receiving verbal and nonverbal messages within a specific context. Please see Figure 2.6 for a depiction of the model. The transaction model is reflected and applied in every chapter of this book.

WHAT DO THE TERMS MEAN?

We know that you're tired of all the theory talk, but we have to define some terms so that we are all on the same page. All of these terms have been used in this chapter, but some have been used in different ways in the various models. This section will establish the way each term will be used throughout the book.

Communicators/Participants

Although the action and interaction models use the terms *source* and *receiver* or *speaker* and *listener*, we will simply use the term **participant.** Because there is no exchange of speaker and listener roles, and because all persons in communication events are simultaneously sending and receiving verbal and nonverbal messages, the terms used in earlier models are no longer descriptive.

The message contains the content of the thought we wish to share with other participants.

Encoding/Decoding

Communication is symbolic. That is, we use symbols to convey our thoughts to each other in the effort to create meaning. When we have a thought or idea that we want to share with others, we must first translate that thought into a set of symbols, or a language, that the other participants will be able to understand. This process of converting our thoughts to symbols is called encoding.

In turn, when we listen to or receive symbols/language, we have to translate that language into thoughts. That is, we give "meaning" to the symbols. This process is called decoding. Symbols are used to represent objects or ideas.

Channel

The means by which a message is conducted or transmitted is the channel. Berlo says that a channel (or medium) is a **carrier** of messages.[29] As such, a channel can be sound waves that travel from a participant's mouth to another participant's ear. It can also be a form of sound amplification to reach a crowd of people in a large room. A channel can also be a radio or television signal, or a book or a newspaper that carries messages to millions of people. More recently, the Internet is a very popular channel for carrying messages to individuals or large groups of people.

Noise

Noise is anything that interferes with or distorts the transmission of the signal. **Environmental noise** is interference with the signal as it moves from the source to the destination. This could take the form of sounds in the room that prevent the receiver from hearing the message; it could be static on a telephone line, or even a dropped call on a cellular phone. **Psychological noise** takes place inside the sender or receiver, such as misunderstanding or failing to remember what was heard.

Context

Context can be viewed as physical or social. The **physical context** is made up of the space surrounding the communication event, or the place in which the communication event occurs. The context could be a classroom, a meeting room at work, a church, a physician's office, your house, your favorite "night spot," or about any other place you can imagine. The place in which the event takes place influences communication behaviors and the meanings attributed to them. How would your behavior change if you moved from your favorite night spot to a classroom? Would you behave the same way?

The **social context** considers the nature of the event taking place in a physical context. The social expectations tied to particular events influence meaning attributed to communication. Even though you were still in a classroom, you would behave differently during an exam than during a group work session. You would behave differently

How does an event's context affect communication?
© 2008 JupiterImages Corporation.

in church during a funeral than celebrating a festive holiday, and you would certainly behave differently while playing bingo in the church basement!

Culture

The **culture** in which the communication occurs and the native cultures of the participants can influence meaning. People belong to a variety of nations, traditions, groups, and organizations, each of which has its own point of view, values, and norms.[30] A culture is made up of the collective beliefs or principles on which a community or part of a community of people is based. These beliefs are often passed from generation to generation and provide a perspective through which the community makes sense of its experiences. The culture, then, provides a very powerful context or backdrop for communication events and has a profound influence on the meaning that participants create and share.

SUMMARY

That's enough of the theory, at least for the moment. Let's get to the application! Keep in mind, however, that a solid understanding of the basics of the transactional model will provide a lot of help to you as you attempt to plan strategies and practice your skills to help you achieve your communication goals.

ENDNOTES

1. S. Littlejohn, *Theories of Human Communication* (Belmont, CA: Wadsworth, 1999), 2.

2. F. Kerlinger, *Foundations of Behavioral Research* (New York: Holt, Rinehart, and Winston, 1973), 9.

3. M. Polanyi, *Personal Knowledge* (Chicago: University of Chicago Press, 1958).

4. W. Wallace, *The Logic of Science in Sociology* (Chicago: Aldine, 1971).

5. T. Clevenger, "Can One Not Communicate? A Conflict of Models," *Communication Studies* 42 (1991), 351.

6. C. Hovland, I. Janis, and H. Kelley, *Communication and Persuasion* (New Haven, CT: Yale University Press, 1953).

7. G. Gerbner, "On Defining Communication: Still Another View," *Journal of Communication* 16 (1966), 99–103.

8. G. Miller, "On Defining Communication: Another Stab," *Journal of Communication* 16 (1966), 92.

9. K. Sereno and C. D. Mortensen, *Foundations of Communication Theory* (New York: Harper & Row, 1970), 5.

10. J. Makay, *Public Speaking: Theory into Practice* (Dubuque, IA: Kendall/Hunt, 2000), 9.

11. L. Hugenberg, S. Wallace, and D. Yoder, *Creating Competent Communication* (Dubuque, IA: Kendall/Hunt, 2003), 4.

12. J. DeVito, *Human Communication: The Basic Course* (Boston, Allyn & Bacon, 2006), 2.

13. J. Golden, G. Berquist, W. Coleman, and J. Sproule, *The Rhetoric of Western Thought, 8th ed.* (Dubuque, IA: Kendall/Hunt, 2003).

14. D. Stanton, and G. Berquist, "Aristotle's Rhetoric: Empiricism or Conjecture?" *Southern Speech Communication Journal* 41 (1975), 69–81.

15. L. Cooper, *The Rhetoric of Aristotle* (New York: Appleton-Century-Crofts, 1932).

16. Golden et al., 65.

17. C. Shannon, and W. Weaver, *The Mathematical Theory of Communication* (Urbana: University of Illinois Press, 1949). Also W. Weaver, "The Mathematics of Communication," in C. D. Mortensen (ed.), *Basic Readings in Communication Theory* (New York: Harper & Row, 1979).

18. W. Schramm, "How Communication Works," in W. Schramm, (ed.), *The Process and Effects of Communication* (Urbana: University of Illinois Press, 1954).

19. D. Berlo, *The Process of Communication* (New York: Holt, Rinehart, and Winston, 1960).

20. Ibid pp. 111–112.

21. Barnlund, D. (1970). "A Transactional Model of Communication," in *Foundations of Communication Theory*, Sereno, K. and Mortensen, C. D. (eds.). New York: Harper & Row, 1970. Also P. Watzlawick, *How Real Is Real? Confusion, Disinformation, Communication: An Anecdotal Introduction to Communications Theory* (New York: Vintage, 1977).

22. M. Burgoon and M. Ruffner, *Human Communication.* (New York: Holt, Rinehart, & Winston, 1978), 9.

23. E. Lazlo, *The Systems View of the World: A Holistic Vision for Our Time* (New York: Hampton Press, 1996). Also L. von Bertalanffy, *General System Theory: Foundations, Development, Applications* (New York: Braziller, 1976).

24. Barnlund.

25. F. Dance, "Toward a Theory of Human Communication," In F. Dance (ed.), *Human Communication Theory: Original Essays* (New York: Holt, 1967).

26. K. Miller, *Communication Theories: Perspectives, Processes, and Contexts* (New York: McGraw-Hill, 2005).

27. W. Heisenberg, *The Physical Principles of Quantum Theory* (Chicago: University of Chicago Press, 1930).

28. S. Wallace, D. Yoder, L. Hugenberg, and C. Horvath, *Creating Competent Communication*, 5th ed. (Dubuque, IA: Kendall/Hunt, 2006).

29. Berlo.

30. Yoder, Hugenberg, and Wallace. *Creating Competent Communication.* (Dubuque, IA: Kendall/Hunt, 1993).

REFERENCES

T. Newcomb, "An Approach to the Study of Communicative Acts," *Psychological review* 60 (1953), 393–404.

P. Watzlawick, J. Beavin, and D. Jackson, *Pragmatics of Human Communication* (New York: Norton, 1967).

3

WHAT IS THE IMPACT OF CRITICAL THINKING IN COMMUNICATION?

LEARNING OBJECTIVES

After reading this chapter, you should understand the following concepts:

- Critical thinking is the ability to analyze and evaluate information on the basis of evidence, with the ultimate goal of sharing it with others.
- Sponge thinkers and panning-for-gold thinkers process critical information differently.
- Critical thinkers must develop perceptual skills, knowledge-gathering skills, and researching skills.
- Perception involves selection, organization, and interpretation. It is based on the principles of subjectivity, stability, and meaningfulness.
- Listening is an important element of critical thinking, so it is important to remove listening barriers.
- Knowledge gathering involves collecting evidence in the form of examples, statistics, testimony, narratives, and analogies to help you achieve your communication goal.
- Researching skills are your ability to find and use sources such as your own knowledge and experiences, interviews, surveys, online searches, and print resources to present ideas in a meaningful way for your listener.

INTRODUCTION

Consider how many times a day you are bombarded with information and opinions. How do you decide what information to keep and what to toss? How do you know what to accept? Think about the amount of information you are exposed to on television alone. According to the A. C. Nielsen Co., the average American watches more than four hours of television each day (twenty-eight hours per week, or two months of nonstop television-watching per year). In a sixty-five-year life, a person will have spent nine years glued to the tube.[1] The number of TV commercials seen by the average person by age sixty-five is 2 million.[2]

Now let's assume that you do not watch television; your preferred medium is the Internet. According to the Pew Internet & American Life project, on an average day, about 94 million American adults use the Internet.

How much TV do you
typically watch each day?
© MalibuBooks, 2008, Shutterstock.

Here are some of the things they do on a typical day:[3]

- 60 percent send or read e-mail
- 41 percent use a search engine to find information
- 37 percent get news
- 80 percent look for health or medical information
- 15 percent watch a video on a video-sharing site like YouTube or Google Video

Let us consider Internet use by children. According to MediaWise:[4]

- Nearly 45 percent of homes with children ages twelve to seventeen have Internet access.
- Children between the ages of five and eighteen will spend an estimated $1.3 billion online by 2002.
- 67 percent of online teens (ages thirteen to eighteen) and 37 percent of online children (ages five to twelve) have researched product items or bought products online.
- Most children and teens use the Internet for e-mailing, search engines, games, music, and homework.

You are living in an information-saturated environment where you must make sense of it all. If you take that one step further, think about sharing what you know with others. Communication allows you to take an active role in the world, lets you participate in civil dialogue, causes you to express views and opinions, and requires you to attempt to make yourself understood. The focus of this chapter is to help you to understand the role of critical thinking in communication as you plan and construct your message. First, we will consider the two thinking styles that are at your disposal. Second, you will learn about the three kinds of knowledge and the skills for their use which must be developed as the basis for critical thinking. Then we will discuss how to strategically prepare for sharing your message with others by learning about the audience through analysis of their demographic, psychographic, and contextual expectations.

Critical thinking is defined as an investigation whose purpose is to explore a situation, phenomenon, question, or problem to arrive at a hypothesis or conclusion that integrates all available information and that can be convincingly justified. Putting it more simply, critical thinking is the ability to analyze and evaluate information on the basis of well-supported reasons and evidence, with the ultimate goal of sharing it with others. Critical thinking is useful in creating an argument, reading or evaluating an essay or Web site, listening to a speech or lecture, participating in group decision making, or even making a purchasing decision. Our examination of critical thinking begins with a perspective of the two thinking styles that people employ.

WHAT ARE CRITICAL THINKING STYLES?

Browne and Keeley suggest that there are two alternative thinking styles that people use.[5] The first, the *sponge* approach, allows you to absorb as much information as you can, just as an absorbent sponge soaks up water. It is a pretty easy way to take in information, because you can remain passive, especially if the material is not too complex. Being a sponge is not necessarily bad: The more information you soak up, the greater your ability to understand how complex issues can be. Knowledge can always be saved and retrieved later; think of this as summary without analysis (like what you might do when you underline in a textbook!). But the problem with sponge thinking is that you end up with gobs of information and no real means for deciding which to keep and which to eliminate. If you cannot select which information to maintain and which to reject, then you might only know what you ran across last. You may end up taking ideas for granted, not considering what to accept or reject, and you may ignore the limits of your perceptual ability. You will find it difficult to create a message based on so much unsorted data.

When you pan for gold, you decide which items to keep and which to discard.
© Robert Gubbins, 2008, Shutterstock.

Most of us prefer to consider ourselves as people who think critically or analytically. That is, we like to keep certain pieces of information and eliminate others, based on some type of criteria. If you want to choose wisely, however, you need to interact with the incoming data. The *panning-for-gold* style of thinking, according to Browne and Keeley, requires active participation as you try to determine the worth of what you hear and read.[6] It requires a questioning attitude that is the heart of critical thinking. It is a challenge to the intellect to utilize this method, because it means that you have to plan how to think, which can be tedious. But in the end, your thinking will probably be stronger and more reliable, and you should be better able to develop a strategic, audience-oriented message, which is essential for successful communication.

To understand the difference between the two thinking styles, put yourself in the shoes of each type of thinker. If you are a sponge thinker, you are focused on getting as much knowledge as you can. You develop skills in memory, note taking, and summarizing. It is not really that important to understand the information or to decide if the information is important or worthy of remembering; you just want to soak it all in. Now consider panning-for-gold thinking. Although you want to gain new information and understanding, you consider the information in light of personal standards for uncovering the truth. You try to comprehend in order to create a stronger base of belief for yourself.

Consider an example of the two styles: You hear from your friend that your school is thinking about changing athletic conferences. If this happens, your friend has heard, the school will need to change its mascot because there already is one of those in the new conference. Your friend tells you that everyone is upset about this change, because it will probably mean that your sports team will not be the best of the conference. He admits, though, that his advisor thinks that this change will probably result in more academic scholarships, greater study-abroad opportunities, and more national recognition for your school. However, your friend reminds you, "Nothing good has ever happened when a school enters a conference. That school loses its identity and becomes something no one recognizes." Your friend then asks you for your opinion on changing conferences.

A sponge thinker would take all this information in, trying to create a judgment, as the friend has requested. If you are using this approach, you probably will rely on your own feelings about your mascot, your sports team, your current conference, members of the new conference, and academic offerings. You will know whether your friend has been trustworthy in the past in what he tells you. But do you know if the information you have just gotten really can form the basis of a judgment on your part? A panning-for-gold thinker would ask questions about the information:

- What does "thinking about changing" really mean? Does this mean that preliminary negotiations have begun? Does it mean that an idea is being floated?
- Who is "everyone" that is upset? What is the source of that statement?
- What are the facts of the potential merge? Are they even known yet?
- Is your friend's advisor in a particular position to be able to offer expert testimony about the outcome of such a merger?
- What are the pros and cons of a merger? What have the mergers of other schools into conferences resulted in for those schools? Can you compare your school to those situations?

Questioning the information you receive allows you to choose what to believe and then to make more critical judgments. When you ask questions, you might discover that the information is incomplete or faulty, that the sources are not credible, or that the assertions being made are unsubstantiated. In every sense, the panning-for-gold thinker will approach thinking as an interactive activity. It is much more difficult than sponge thinking, partly because you have had more experience in sponge thinking, and partly because panning-for-gold means that you have to expend energy. But be honest: most of us *are* lazy, and panning means that you have to work hard at thinking.

HOW DO I BECOME A CRITICAL THINKER?

Let us now assume that you want to be the panning-for-gold type of thinker; you want to question what you hear and to determine what you will believe. This analysis and evaluation is essential for critical thinking. You sense that this type of thinking will not only help you to understand your world more clearly, but it might also result in your creating a more effective message. But in order to know *what* to ask about, you need to know about the kinds of knowledge that are important for critical thinking and the lenses that help to focus us.

The Hallmarks of Critical Thinking

Critical thinking provides us with three kinds of knowledge: organized knowledge, skill knowledge, and understanding.

- *Organized knowledge.* The first, **organized knowledge,** is often called your intellect. It consists of your informed beliefs, what you think is real. For instance, do you know what day it is? Do you have mathematical knowledge of what addition and subtraction rules are? Do you know what is meant by the *Final Four?*

- *Skill knowledge.* **Skill knowledge** consists of your grasp of how to do something. Can you apply those mathematical rules to balancing your financial accounts? Are you able to discuss the method by which teams are chosen for the Final Four?

- *Understanding.* **Understanding,** the third type of knowledge, combines skill with intellect to create insight. In understanding, you grasp the complexity of ideas and evaluate how they impact other concepts. Can you articulate why the Everyday Math program used in public schools employs practical applications of mathematics, rather than asking children to memorize by rote the times tables? Can you discuss the pros and cons of various teams' selections for the March Madness tournament?

The three kinds of knowledge are useful in different situations, and you may be called to use them for different reasons. If you are following instructions, then you need to have skill knowledge. But if you plan to explain how to do something to someone else, transferring that skill knowledge to someone else, you need to be able to go beyond skill into understanding. Organized knowledge is essential for living day to day; you have to have beliefs that serve as the fundamental basis of who you are. If you don't know what a term means, then you can't go past that most basic intellect that constitutes organized knowledge.

Essential Skills for Effective Critical Thinking

To think critically, you apply different skills to gather and focus information. The skills that are essential are perceptual skills, knowledge-gathering skills, and researching skills:

- *Perceptual skills.* **Perceptual skills** engage physical and psychological dimensions, resulting in an interaction between the senses and the external environment. If you wear contact lenses and lose one, your physical ability to see things at a distance might be impaired, possibly causing you to miss something important. If you think that taking a communication class is the sure way to an easy A, you might be disturbed by the reality that the theories and strategies of communicating with others is complex. Your perceptions in both cases will lead your thinking astray.

What skills do you need to apply to think critically?
© Dainis Derics, 2008, Shutterstock.

- *Knowledge-gathering skills.* Here, we are not talking about the physical or mental ability to decode words; it is something much more. **Knowledge-gathering skills** include your ability to read and to listen. Listening involves more than hearing, as you will learn later in this chapter. In the same way, reading is not "just" decoding symbols; it is comprehending meaning, grasping tone and spirit, and evaluating the worth of the material.
- *Researching skills.* **Researching skills** consist of your ability to seek and to gather information. What sources can you access? You have a repertoire of sources such as databases, Internet-based resources, personal interviews, books, journals, and magazines, surveys, and focus groups.

Let us try some simple exercises to discover these skills before we explore them in greater depth.

Copy these nine dots on a sheet of paper. Then connect them using four straight lines. You may cross over lines, but you may not pick your pen or pencil up off the paper, nor may you retrace a line.

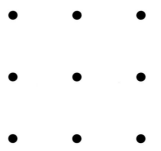

Your ability or inability to do this task is a result of your perceptual skill. Do you expect to be able to connect a box-shaped series of dots when you have four lines to use? Most of us expect to be able to make a box. But the directions disallow that, because you cannot connect all the dots with four lines (that one in the middle becomes problematic with a box shape). You feel constrained by the presumed (and perceived) shape, and you cannot think outside of the box!

Now let us imagine that your instructor has just announced in front of the whole class that she wants to see you at the end of the hour. No other information is given. Your mind begins to race. You wonder about the instructor's tone: Did she sound angry? Was she looking at me? You consider what you have possibly done that would require having to see the instructor. You may even have flashbacks to the last time you were called into the instructor's presence! You are engaging in knowledge-gathering. You record the information and try to establish its worth and meaning in a context beyond "simple" decoding.

Try this problem from Marilyn vos Savant's column in *Parade* magazine to test your knowledge-gathering skills:[7] What can you find in these words: dogma, resin, minor, facet, somber, labor, tirade, dormer. *Hint:* Try whistling while you work out your answer. (*Answer:* The first two letters of each word spells out the tones of the musical scale: do, re, mi, fa, so,la, ti, do.)

Finally, what if you were asked to complete this analogy: George Washington is to one as William Howard Taft is to ———. Now, you might know that Taft was a president of the United States, and you might know that an analogy requires you to do some type of this-is-like-that thinking, so you can employ your knowledge and perceptual lenses. But unless you memorized the presidents sometime back in elementary school and can retrieve the correct rank number, it is likely you would need to go to an outside source to discover the answer. Where exactly would you go? You might do an Internet search, ask your great uncle or political science professor, or even remember to look the answer up in a book. Your researching skills require you to know what kind of information to seek and where likely sources of information might be.

In the remainder of this chapter, let us probe these skills more closely in order to appreciate their importance for critical thinking.

WHAT ROLE DOES PERCEPTION PLAY IN CRITICAL THINKING?

To engage in critical thinking, we have to begin with the most fundamental of our skill abilities: our perceptions. The concept of **perception** can be defined in many ways, but simply put, it is our set of beliefs concerning what is out there. For more detail, let us consider two views. John Chaffee, a professor of humanities specializing in critical thinking, says that perceiving involves actively selecting, organizing, and interpreting what is experienced by your senses.[8] Thus, perception involves what you can see, hear, feel, smell, and taste; you use these sensations to experience and to make sense of the world. Communication Professor Julia T. Wood says that perception is an active process of selecting, organizing, and interpreting people, objects, events, situations, and activities.[9] It is how we attach significance to the world around us.

Process of Perception

If we combine the previous definitions, perception involves our senses, employs a process of interaction, and results in an understanding of some experience in order to make sense of the world. Returning to Wood's definition, perception involves three interactive processes: selection, organization, and interpretation:

Selection. First is **selection.** Because your senses are bombarded by sights, sounds, and smells (at the minimum), you have developed a method of focusing that narrows your attention to selected stimuli. Stop reading right now and focus on the sounds around you. Did you notice them as you were holding this book? Can you close your eyes and picture what page you were on? Are there any pleasant or unpleasant smells around you? Reflect on the stimuli you were actively conscious of and those you eliminated from awareness. This selection of stimuli is necessary and typical of perceptions; you cannot make all stimuli relevant, so you focus on the ones that you have defined as important to whatever task you are currently engaged in.

Perhaps you remember a time when a pot boiled over. Even though dinner was important, your attention had been drawn away by a phone call. One perception (the phone's ring) shifted your perception away from the boiling pot. This perceptual process is important for a communicator, because you can use it to your advantage. We know that some stimuli will draw attention because they are particularly relevant, immediate, or intense. If you talk about something that your listener relates to, it is likely that issue will draw greater interest. If you attempt to catch initial attention by a soft voice, it is unlikely that will work, simply because it is not very intense. If your audience cannot see what you are showing them, their visual limits will likely result in their tuning out.

Organization. The second perceptual process is **organization.** We all try to structure perceptions in order to make sense of them. You will learn later that there are many strategies for structuring public speeches, group meetings, and interviews to accomplish desired goals. For now, we will simply say that each of us applies certain cognitive patterns, or perceptions. Those patterns are developed through experience. If you have never smelled certain spices, then you cannot sort them into the correct meaning of what kind of food is cooking; if you have developed stereotypical patterns that suggest all members of a certain ethnic group have a certain intellectual level, then you might assume that a new colleague from that group has that intellect.

Interpretation. **Interpretation** happens when you assign meaning to your perceptions. Once your brain has selected and organized the stimuli, it has to create meaning. For instance, if you are given a set of numbers, how do you know what they mean?

231 7620

904 38 7231

5468 9960 0075 1234

The first set appears to be a phone number, without the area code. The second set might be structured like a social security number. The third set appears to be similar to a credit card number. How do you know this? Part of your interpretation comes from the way the numbers are structured (organized), but part has to come from your experience. If you have never seen a social security number, you cannot interpret the second set in that way; it might not have any meaning. Similarly, if someone you know suddenly stops talking to you, you recognize the change in a pattern, but you interpret what has "caused" this silence to occur based on your own experiences, beliefs, values, and attitudes. Did Joan stop talking to you because you hurt her feelings? Is she sick and hoarse? Each of those interpretations is different, but they are based on the same initial perception of silence. Depending on your interpretation, your next communication encounter with Joan will be markedly different.

Other strategic perceptual techniques will be developed later in this text, but you need to remember that an audience's perceptions will greatly influence your ability to communicate successfully with them. The process of perception, involving selection, organization, and interpretation, describes the active steps we engage in to develop meaning.

Perception Principles

Three basic principles of perception might offer a deeper understanding of the complexity of the perception process. Subjectivity, stability, and meaningfulness describe the various filters that each of us employs when we attempt to create meaning from stimuli.

Subjectivity. **Subjectivity** refers to perceptions that are unique to your personal experience, views, or mental state. The most obvious source of subjectivity is your **physiology;** you differ from another in your physical sensory ability. Next time you are at the grocery store, look at what people are wearing on their feet. Some will be in sandals, others in boots, some in shoes, and some may try to shop barefoot! Each person's footwear choice indicates a degree of sensitivity to temperature and texture. Similarly, what might be hot chili to you might be mild to another. Music that is "too loud" for some may be "too quiet" for others. Ten million American men—7 percent of the male population—either cannot distinguish red from green, or see red and green differently from

Perception Principles

Subjectivity—Perceptions that are unique to your personal experience, views, or mental state. Sources include:

Physiology: physical sensory ability

Culture and experiences: beliefs, values, norms and ways of interpreting experiences

Psychological: affected by the perceptual choices you make

Selective exposure: you choose consistent information

Selective attention: you choose to pay attention to known stimuli

Selective interpretation: you interpret ambiguous stimuli to be consistent with what you know

Selective retention: you remember more accurately those things that are consistent with what you know

Stability—The predictability that we need in life; managed in two ways:

Assimilation: you interpret the stimuli you receive to fit what you already know or expect

Accommodation: you change what you know to fit the incoming perceptual data

Meaningfulness—Refers to the ways that we project comprehension or understanding onto perceptions; achieved in several ways:

Contrast: you say something is like (or unlike) something you know

Familiar versus the novel: you understand what you've experienced, but something new is much more difficult to understand

Closure: you fill in details of an incomplete picture

Repetition: if it happened before, you expect it to happen again

most people. This is the most common form of color blindness, but it affects only 0.4 percent of women.[10] That knowledge might impact your strategic choice of color on a graph. In the same way, about 10 percent of the population is left-handed; this means that some of us experience an anti-lefty bias that assaults us; scissors are useless, power tools (such as circular saws) are dangerous, and pens smear and make writing illegible. In giving instructions, it might be important to consider handedness. Consider how awkward it might be for a leftie to learn to use a tool meant for the right-handed worker. Many physiological states can influence perception. When you are tired or ill, you may be less able to react to a friend's humor and may take offense at a comment that normally would not make you blink.

A second subjectivity source involves psychological aspects created by our culture and experiences. **Culture** refers to the community of meaning to which we belong (beliefs, values, norms, and ways of interpreting experience that are shared by those around us). As Americans, we tend to subjectively view the world through basic assumptions of various rights: to freedom of speech, to pursue religious beliefs, to be all that we can be. Other cultures do not have those assumptions, yet we do not become aware of that until we are questioned. For instance, in the United States, many adoptive families openly celebrate how their families were created, and they consider the birth parents as part of their extended family. In other countries, adoption is still a shameful state, and if one is forced to make a decision to place the child for adoption, it is shrouded in secrecy and mystery.

To envision this aspect of subjectivity, consider your reactions to the following examples. Past Olympic media coverage highlighted the adoption stories of 2006 American bronze medalist (men's mogul) Toby Dawson, adopted at age three from South Korea, and 1984 gold medalist Scott Hamilton,

It's not easy to be left-handed in a world that's more accommodating to right-handed people.
© Glen Jones, 2008, Shutterstock.

adopted at six weeks from the United States. Run-D.M.C. group member, Darryl "D.M.C." McDaniels, revealed on a 2006 VH1 documentary that he was adopted as an infant but only learned that at age thirty-five.[11] Wendy's founder Dave Thomas started a foundation to celebrate adoption, because he had been adopted from foster care. Your beliefs and experience with adoption, whether you have a member of your family who is adopted or if you are adopted, will impact the way that you view these stories, and, in turn, whether you donate to adoption causes, watch programs about adoption, or even consider adoption yourself.

In the same way, modern Western culture integrates technology and speed into nearly everything about living: we expect things to happen quickly (instant messages, instant photos, instant oatmeal). How does our speed expectation impact our perceptions of other cultures where patience and leisure are the norm, such as Mexico and Nepal?

Psychological subjectivity is affected by the perceptual choices that you make, either intentionally or not.[12] *Selective exposure* suggests that you choose to seek consistent information or to expose yourself to certain contexts where you will feel comfortable with the stimuli. For example, you may attend only one style of play (let's say musicals) rather than going to Greek tragedies, comedies, farces, or melodramas, because psychologically, a musical is pleasant to your eyes and ears. You know what to expect and feel at ease with the context, story line, characters, and addition of music to the overall experience.

Have you ever been surprised to learn what's really in that new food you just tasted?
© Simone van den Berg, 2008, Shutterstock.

Selective attention suggests that people choose to expose themselves or pay attention to certain stimuli already present, to key in on certain phenomenon, because these are more similar to their experiences or beliefs. Perhaps you listen only to one kind of music because that is what you know; the thought of going to a country concert when you are an opera fan may just be too much to ask! If you engage in *selective interpretation*, you interpret ambiguous stimuli so that it becomes consistent with what you know. Imagine that you are given some new food to taste, and it looks pretty much like chicken. You may interpret what you taste as a unique flavor of barbeque chicken, only later to find out that it was alligator! *Selective retention* suggests that you will remember more accurately messages that are consistent with interests, views and beliefs than those that are in contrast with your values and beliefs. Because of the vast amounts of information you are bombarded with, you decide what to keep in the memory, narrowing the informational flow once again. When parents ask children to do household chores, those children seem to have an uncanny ability to remember only the chores that are the easiest or the ones they want to do. Perhaps you are more likely to remember the parts of your professor's lecture that you agree with and to forget the parts that do not correspond to your beliefs.

If you expect that you're eating sausage pizza, the first bite will taste like sausage.
© Mariusz Szachowski, 2008, Shutterstock.

Stability.   A second perception principle, **stability,** refers to the predictability that we need in life. The concept of organization suggests that we pattern what we perceive in order to get stimuli to "fit" into our preconceived ways of thinking. Stability can be managed in two basic ways. *Assimilation* is when you interpret the stimuli you receive to fit what you already know or expect. In simple terms, you "bend" the incoming information so that it fits what you know. If you know that your family always orders sausage pizza, that first bite you take of that pizza will taste like sausage, because you are certain that's what they order. Until you are informed that the topping is really tofu, you expect that the pizza guy has brought you sausage. *Accommodation* occurs when you change what you know to fit the incoming perceptual data. For instance, if you believe that your friend is honest but you see her looking on someone else's test, you might change your perception of what constitutes cheating.

Meaningfulness. Finally, **meaningfulness,** the third perception principle, refers to the ways that we project comprehension or understanding onto perceptions. This is achieved in several ways. You might employ *contrast*, where you say that something is like (or unlike) something that you know. Is the latest reality show anything like *Survivor,* which you cannot stand? You might compare a political candidate to an earlier politician you admired, giving him your vote. Someone you are interviewing with might think that you are too similar to the person she just fired, so she cannot take a chance on you.

A second technique is through the *familiar versus the novel:* You can understand something that you have experienced, but something new is much more difficult to understand. Until you have had your house burn down around you, it is hard to really understand the range of emotions of those who have lived through this. You might never have heard of being a CASA volunteer, so you cannot imagine volunteering for this valuable child advocacy service when you hear a speech about it.

With *closure,* you fill in the details of an incomplete picture. You are given an assignment, but once you try to complete the task, you realize that you do not know exactly what is expected. When you cannot reach your instructor, you make some decisions about what you think she means for you to do. Even *repetition* is a means for creating meaningfulness; if something has happened before, then you expect it to happen again. If you have been snubbed by a colleague several times, you will not be able to attribute friendship meaning when that person suddenly treats you as his best buddy in a meeting; you might assume his behavior is a political move.

Errors in Perception. Perceptions are fundamental to critical thinking, and they are confounded by multiple opportunities to be imperfect. There are many reasons for these perceptual errors, and understanding their source may make for a more perceptive communication event. One reason is that we are influenced by the immediately obvious. You observe two children fighting on a playground, and you immediately assume that the one who is hitting the other must have started the fight. When you intercede, you concentrate your message on the "guilty" one. We also cling to those first impressions, because again, our interpretations are rarely questioned. If a church is the place you first meet someone, you might think that she is a devout member of that church, even though it might be her first time there. Third, we assume that others think like we do, so we do not question our perceptions. Maybe you like junk mail, cyberjokes, and the like, so you pass them on. Others may despise getting bombarded with this same material. Maybe your mother appreciates "constructive criticism," but you do not. As previously noted, we have different sensory abilities, so our facility to see or hear something is likely different from someone else's; where a road sign may be perfectly clear to you, the passenger, your friend the driver may miss it because he cannot see that far.

How do your own experiences affect your perception of other cultures?
© 2008, JupiterImages Corporation.

Each person involved in a car accident has his own perception of what really happened.
© Vuk Vukmirovic, 2008, Shutterstock.

We also have different experiences through our culture, education, character, and activities, so our perceptions are impacted. If you are a football fan, you may watch the game from a technician's point of view, noticing how the linebackers play defense and the variety of coaching plays. A non–football-loving friend who attends the game with you may focus on the cheer squad and the band. In another example, a builder sees the new house construction differently than the first-time homeowner. Finally, different perceptual expectations may be part of the context: Where you are may determine what you expect to see or to hear. A car accident is perceived quite differently by the drivers, witnesses, and attending officer. What each party communicates about that experience will likely be significantly different. If you are at a concert, you probably expect to hear music and not a political pitch, so your perception of the politician who uses the concert as a fundraiser will probably be negative.

What can you gain from this brief foray into perception? The knowledge you gain from your perceptions is vivid, personal, and often accepted uncritically. Your perceptions are experiential, selective, perhaps inaccurate, and likely evaluative. Every dimension of what you know is directly impacted by your perceptions. You cannot engage in critical thinking without considering your perceptions. The same is true of your listener: you cannot communicate with another until you have considered his or her perceptions.

Critical Thinking Skills

This chapter looks at three skill components for effective critical thinking:

1. Listening
2. Knowledge gathering
3. Researching

HOW DOES LISTENING FIT INTO CRITICAL THINKING?

When you need to check your spelling, do you write the word down to see if it feels right? Do you need to see the word to check it? Or do you sound out the word? What about your behavior when you meet someone for a second or third time. Do you remember that person by what you did together, or do you remember where you met? Is it easier for you to remember a name or what you talked about? One last scenario: When reading, do you prefer action stories, descriptive scenes, or narratives where the characters talk? Each one of these situations reveals something about your learning style, or the different approaches that people take to acquire knowledge. In each case, the first example suggests a tactile learner (learn by feeling or touching); the second is a visual learner (learn by seeing); and the third is an auditory learner (learn by listening). Your preferred styles guide the way you learn. They also change the way you internally represent experiences, the way you recall information, and even the words you choose. Everybody has a mix of learning styles; you may have one dominant style, or you may even use different styles in different circumstances. But why is this important to know in a chapter about audience?

When you create and then present a message, you want to adapt it to your audience in order to create shared meaning. You'll consider how you can organize thoughts through vivid words; you'll try to keep your ideas moving by effective structure and transitions. Your ideas may be supported by presentational aids that supplement your words, ones that give your audience something else to look to for understanding. These strategies will help the visual learners who think in pictures and the tactile persons who need action or hands-on information. But you'll also need to consider how your audience perceives ideas through listening, auditory processing. Just as writing clarifies and documents the spoken message, verbally clarifying the spoken message before, during, and after a presentation enhances listening comprehension. You could create a well organized and supported speech about the needs for reducing truck emissions, but if you don't present it in a way designed to enhance our listening, it's likely that your message won't have an impact. Listening is an essential dimension of our critical thinking skills.

Listening

Multiple definitions of listening exist, but we'll use the one from the International Listening Association, which defines **listening** as the active process of receiving, constructing meaning from, and responding to spoken and/or nonverbal messages.[13] It involves the ability to retain information as well as to react empathetically and/or appreciatively to spoken and/or nonverbal messages.[14] This complex definition offers several important considerations.

Listening is *active*. Ralph Nichols, one of the earliest scholars to study listening, said listening is "not involuntary," and that it is a skill that is the "oldest, most used, and the most important element to interpersonal communication."[15] **Hearing** is a passive physiological process where the ear receives sound. Brownell says that the accurate reception of sounds requires you to focus attention on the speaker, discriminate among sounds, and concentrate.[16] That means that the listener has to be physically able to hear; the physiological receptors must be working. But it also puts a burden on the speaker: you have to make sure that your audience is in a position to hear the sounds you're about to make; you have to consider your volume, rate, and pitch, along with the acoustics. Hearing becomes listening when you engage in the active, psychological activity that requires effort and motivation.

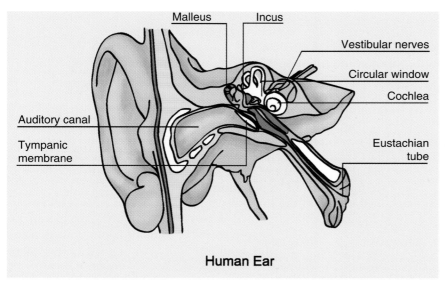

Human Ear

Listening is an active process; hearing is the passive physiological process where the ear receives sound.
© TAOLMOR, 2008, Shutterstock.

Listening is *a process* with implications for speaker and listener. The term *process* implies an activity that is continuous and ongoing. We usually take this process for granted, but there is a major difference between hearing and the complex task of listening. In fact, you could have excellent hearing and still be a terrible listener. This process is also transactional; listening can't occur unless both a sender and a receiver are involved. Have you ever left a lecture feeling cheated because you didn't get much out of the message? Did you then blame the teacher? Don't be lulled into thinking that effective interaction is the sole responsibility of the sender; successful communication is a shared enterprise, a process involving the sending and receiving of messages.

Receiving is a physiological activity in which verbal and nonverbal messages stimulate our senses. If a sound is made, your eardrums vibrate. You can see the nonverbal behavior of people all around you. In addition when receiving, you focus on specific stimuli and reject others.

Constructing meaning occurs as you interpret the stimuli, creating understanding for yourself that you later use as future referents. At the same time you are placing meaning on the stimuli that meets your prior perceptions, you are inferring what the message means to the speaker. You try to fit the message into ideas you already recognize, into what you know about the speaker, into your immediate context, and into your culture. That means that you also have to place that meaning into previously created categories; there simply are too many stimuli for us to keep them all, so we sort and interpret. At the same time, you judge the message for its usefulness and accuracy. That leads to the need for retaining, remembering, or storing the message for later recall.

Reacting is when you respond to the message, providing feedback to the sender. Some examples of responding behaviors are focusing your eye contact on the person you are listening to, using facial expressions to encourage the person to continue, adjusting your posture to lean toward the speaker, or asking questions.

Listening involves our *interpretation of nonverbal cues* that add to meaning. You listen with more than just your physical ability to receive sounds. Listening cues can include perceptions of the speaker's vocal pitch and volume, rate of speaking, use of verbal fillers (such as "uh," "um," "OK," "you know," and "like"), facial expression, eye contact, gestures, and posture. Think of it this way: you listen with more than just your ears! Research tells us that spoken words only account for 30 to 35 percent of the meaning. The rest is transmitted through nonverbal communication that only can be detected through visual and auditory listening.[17]

As you can see by this definition, listening involves those perception skills of selection, organization, and interpretation. You have to be able to perceive sounds, select which ones to keep, and then organize them into meaning that you can reflect back to the sender. Now, armed with a sense of what constitutes listening, let's look at some of the research findings on effective listening.

There are many reasons to put effort into effective listening. Listening has been identified as one of the top skills employers seek in entry-level employees as well as those being promoted.[18] Listening accounts for approximately one-third of the characteristics perceivers use to evaluate communication competence in co-workers.[19] Listening is an important component in how people judge communicative competence in the workplace.[20] Further, individual performance in an organization is found to be directly related to listening ability or perceived listening effectiveness. Consider your life right now as a student. Research tells us that college students spend nearly half of their communication time listening, about one-third of it speaking, and less than one-third of it reading and writing.[21] Effective listening is associated with school success, but not with any major personality dimensions.[22] A number of research studies show that there is a correlation between listening and academic success. A student with high grades also usually has the strongest listening skills; students with the lowest grades usually demonstrate the weakest listening skills.[23] Listening also impacts us in intrapersonal and interpersonal ways. Confident individuals listen to message content better than individuals who lack confidence.[24] Listening is tied to effective leadership.[25] Those with a high people-orientation have a low apprehension for receiving information.[26] In health care contexts, the largest indicators of patient satisfaction with physician's communication skills include empathy and listening. Effective listening has been called a significant predictor for patient satisfaction.[27] As you can tell, the research on listening is broad, but one significant conclusion can be made: Successful listening improves communication.

Earlier in this chapter you learned that critical thinking requires you to analyze and to evaluate information; you gather that information through listening as well as reading. When you listen effectively, you can reflect on what the other person is thinking or feeling by considering her perspective. You place yourself in her shoes, seeing through her eyes and listening through her ears. Even though your viewpoint may be different or you may not agree with the other person, as you listen, you try to understand from her viewpoint. To communicate effectively, you must avoid barriers to listening and practice strategies for effective listening. Although this could be considered as a receiver-only task, in reality, it involves both the receiver and the message sender. In this chapter, we're considering listening as an aspect of critical thinking. In a later chapter, you'll learn what a speaker can do to assist the audience in effective listening.

Barriers to Listening

Listening involves those perception skills of selection, organization, and interpretation that you're already familiar with. You have to select specific stimuli from the wide array that come at you; that selection means that you make decisions about what is important for your needs. You organize perceptions by applying mental structures that represent familiar patterns of understanding. Interpretation happens when you assign meaning to the stimuli that you have selected and organized. But we create listening barriers when we fail to choose, structure, or attach meaning to what we're listening to. There are eight listening stumbling blocks that most of us can relate to. They're not the result of conscious design or irrational bias; they're limited perceptual strategies that we've developed over the years to make listening easier. Unfortunately, "easier" doesn't mean more effective. Because many elements of the communication situation compete for attention, selecting and maintaining a focus on the other person's message requires conscious effort.

Personal Listening Barriers

As a critical thinker, you need to strategically employ the perception principles of subjectivity (your unique perceptions), stability (your unique means of creating predictability), and meaningfulness (developing understanding) every time you listen. Here are some simple guidelines that will work within these principles.

Stumbling Blocks to Listening

- *Noise is anything that distorts message reception.* This could include physical or external noise (cell phone ringtones or work crews); semantic noise (words not understood or with a different meaning than the speaker); physiological noise (biological influences like being tired or hungry); and psychological noise (cognitive influences like biases or prejudices). It takes energy to pay attention, and we are easily distracted by other noises.

- *Daydreaming, an absentminded dreaming state, is caused by a lack of focused concentration.* The average person talks at a rate of about 125 to 175 words per minute, but you can listen at a rate of up to 450 words per minute.[28] Unfortunately, this means that you think faster than you listen, so it's easy for the brain to attempt to multitask while sound waves are perceived. You're familiar with this: It's the same thing as channel surfing. While you mindlessly and randomly move up and down the television channels, you get glimpses of programs, but you really can't grasp the intent or content of any of them. The same thing happens when you daydream: you come in and out of the listening process, lapsing into fantasy states. The problem is extended when you forget to return from these mental side trips often enough to keep up with the other person's message. It takes a great deal of self-discipline to stay focused on a message. This job becomes especially difficult when you are not particularly interested in what the others are saying.

- *A shorter attention span, which is the length of time you'll stick with a message without being distracted, also contributes to ineffective listening.* Our limited attention span means that only part of your memory will be activated at any one time. The most easily activated area is the most familiar one, the one encountered most

What could she do to improve her listening skills?
© Jamie Wilson, 2008, Shutterstock.

often. It's just easier to focus on some stimuli than others. This trend in shortened attention spans has been reflected by advertisements, television shows, sermons, and political messages, all of which have shifted towards shorter, simpler messages.[29] The result of shorter attention spans is that not only do you activate only part of your memory, making retrieval difficult, but you tend to tune out ideas that are long or complex.

- *Information overload can also impede listening.* Noise can be overwhelming, so we find it easy (or necessary) to tune out. Each day we are bombarded with e-mail, faxes, texts, cell phone calls, and other technology that we're supposed to process and answer. According to David Shenk, this creates a "toxic environment

Both physical and psychological subjectivity can be oriented by some simple reminders. When you listen, try to keep your mind focused on your listening goal (you could be looking for pleasure or fun, in order to empathize, to evaluate or judge, or to gather information). Search for areas of interest. Ask yourself, "What is in this message for me?" and look for that, even if it's only one story, one statistic, or the way the speaker uses her voice. Eliminate noise whenever possible; resist those mental and physical distrac-

of continuous overstimulation" that leads to growing stress and an inability to unwind.[30]

- *Jumping to conclusions happens when we think we know what's about to come next.* It's easy to make assumptions in order to predict what follows; once your mind gets moving in a direction, it tends to keep going. Try this test:

  What do you call a funny story? joke

  What are you when you have no money? broke

  What's another word for Coca Cola? Coke

  What's the white of an egg?

  It isn't yolk, it's albumen. Were you tricked? Most people are. The brain likes to race ahead, because it already knows the answer. When you jump to conclusions, it's very possible that you'll miss parts of the speaker's points.

- *Being mentally sluggish is the result of a lack of effort.* It takes energy and practice to listen well. Sometimes, you're just too tired to listen, and you don't have the liveliness needed to stay with the message. More often, though, a lack of effort can be a result of a declaration that you're just not interested in the topic. You declare it dry, boring, or unimportant, so why bother to listen?

- *Focusing on the speaker rather than the message often occurs when you can't get past different physical, cultural, or ethnic characteristics of your speaker.* Have you ever instantaneously judged a storekeeper or teacher by the way she looks or the accent he has? Have you decided that you can't possibly listen or learn from this person? These snap judgments based on appearance or voice will result in a loss of attentiveness on the message. Too many people reject listening to others on the basis of

How can you make the effort to listen when the subject matter doesn't interest you?
© Lisa F. Young, 2008, Shutterstock.

how they look or sound; if all you see or hear is the gender, skin color or hair style, traditional ethnic attire, or accent, your unfavorable reaction stops you from being a good listener.

- *Receiver apprehension, or the fear of misinterpreting or of not being able to adjust psychologically to messages presented by others, can impede effective listening.*[31] You are unsure if you will be able to communicate effectively. For instance, you might worry that you won't understand the topic, or won't know how to respond. Receiver apprehension might also come about when you are so interested in what you have to say that you listen mainly to find an opening to get your two cents in. When your listening apprehension becomes too intense, your mental ability to attend to, understand, and remember information decreases.[32] You become preoccupied with the communication situation, yourself, and the other, and you fail to listen to the other message.

tions. You have to make a conscious effort to keep yourself on track when you're too hot or cold, when the speaker isn't dynamic and speaks much slower than your mind works, when you're concerned about an upcoming test, or if you think the topic is too hard to concentrate on. Work past that short attention span that is so much easier to apply. Check yourself on occasion. Ask yourself, "Am I really paying attention?"

Ask a question to clarify and hold your interest in the speaker's message.
© Lorraine Swanson, 2008, Shutterstock.

Stability patterns get stimuli to fit into our preconceived ways of thinking through assimilation and accommodation. Consider how your bias plays a role when speaking with people different from you. Do you focus more on the person or the ideas? You can overcome a personal bias if you concentrate on the content of the message, not the delivery or how the speaker looks. Suspend your judgment: skip what you perceive as delivery errors or cultural disparities in favor of focusing on the message. Another idea is to be more flexible in your listening; if you are a note taker, cut down the number you take, or don't take any at all. If you're concerned that you might have to respond, listen to the central ideas of what is being said and don't let your mind race ahead trying to devise a response.

Meaningfulness describes how we establish comprehension or understanding by the familiar, contrast, and repetition. If you tend to jump to conclusions, it's probably because you think you know what the speaker is going to say next. To correct that, hold your fire. Remember that the world is structured in many ways and that not everyone sees things as you do. Don't judge what you're listening to until the speaker completes the message. Don't interrupt. Do ask questions for clarification; it's silly to sit there in the dark when one or two clarifications could turn the light on. Those questions could be ones directed to yourself (what have I just been told? How does that relate to something that came earlier? Is it similar to something I already know? Does the evidence meet with my beliefs?), or directed at the speaker when ideas lack clarity.

Remember, you have to work at listening. You've probably become pretty good at faking attention, being easily distracted, resisting difficult ideas, daydreaming, and tolerating noise. But don't worry, you can overcome these bad habits. Effective listening is active and requires diligent practice on your part. You have to engage in behaviors that will support success. You have to be mentally and physically prepared to receive a message and you must participate in the active process along with the sender. But if you make the effort and take the time to improve your listening, you might reap the rewards of getting higher grades or a better job evaluation, be more empathic with others, and feel more self-confident.

As the listener, you're half responsible for effective communication (the sender is the other 50 percent, and you'll see how you can build in message strategies to help your audience to listen in a later chapter). Let's turn our attention now to applying critical thinking skills to knowledge gathering—finding evidence that we can use to support our perceptions and to share with others.

WHAT ARE THE STRATEGIC ELEMENTS OF KNOWLEDGE GATHERING?

Before you can start to create a message, you have to apply your knowledge-gathering skills, which rely on your abilities to read and to listen. This isn't simply the physical or mental ability to decode words into meaning. Knowledge gathering is much more than just hearing and reading. You know that listening is an active process. Listening involves more than hearing, as you have just seen. In the same way, reading is not "just" decoding symbols; it is comprehending meaning, grasping tone and spirit, and evaluating worth of

---

Five Major Evidence Categories

Examples: Single instances that illustrate or explain in an attempt to make a concept meaningful
> **Simple:** brief references lacking detail
> **Extended:** more elaborate, creating a vivid image
> **Hypothetical:** ask the audience to "Imagine the following . . ."
> **Actual:** real life, real cases

Statistics: Numbers that indicate relationships between phenomena

Testimony: The comments of others
> **Expert:** judgment or interpretation made by authorities in the subject area
> **Peer:** testimony from someone who is not a recognized expert

Narratives: Stories that elaborate an idea
> **Anecdote:** a brief, amusing story

Analogies: Show a similarity between features of two ideas, objects, or people in order to create a comparison between the familiar and unfamiliar
> **Figurative:** compare things in two different categories
> **Literal:** compare two things of the same category

---

the materials. The complex process of knowledge gathering requires an understanding of the strategic elements called supporting materials that will form your ideas and your message content, and the means by which you can discover them.

At its heart, **knowledge gathering** means identifying the data or evidence that you will need in order to reach your communication goal of information-giving, persuading, or expressing value. Think of **evidence** as the material that you use to support your ideas, to enhance interest, or even to establish an emotional response. Evidence (also called *supporting material*) is used primarily to develop comprehension within the audience, but it also can help to clarify your own thoughts and make your position compelling and memorable. When you provide evidence, you support your position and build your credibility, but evidence is only as good as the audience perceives it to be. Five major evidence categories (examples, statistics, testimony, narratives, and analogies) will help you to develop those critical thinking questions which are an essential part of the planning process. Understanding how others might perceive your evidence will also help you to strategize as you develop your message.

Examples

Examples are single instances that illustrate or explain in an attempt to make a concept meaningful. *Simple* examples are brief references lacking detail, usually used to make something concrete quickly. These are especially beneficial when the audience is already familiar with something. For instance, if you asked, "Remember the story of Johnny Appleseed? How he planted trees everywhere?" you would not need to provide further detail as you continued your speech about the power of the individual. *Extended* examples are more elaborate, and they are needed when you have to create a vivid image that the audience needs for comprehension. Imagine telling someone about the life of Lindy Boggs, who, at the age of eighty-one, was appointed by President Clinton as U.S. Ambassador to the Holy See (Vatican), the first woman envoy to that posting. You might provide an extended example something like the following.

> At twenty-four, Lindy Boggs came to Washington, D.C. from Louisiana with her newly elected husband, Congressman Hale Boggs. She artfully played the role of political wife, running her husband's congressional campaigns, managing his Capitol Hill office, belonging to the "right" wives' committees, and chairing numerous organizations such as John F. Kennedy's and Lyndon Johnson's inaugural ball committees. At the same time she raised three children who would come into prominence in their own right, including her youngest child, NPR and ABC-TV's Cokie Roberts.

As well as being simple or extended, examples may be hypothetical or actual. *Hypothetical* examples ask the audience to "Imagine the following . . ." You can create a hypothetical example when you do not have an actual example to make your point clearly; you should create a realistic illustration of what you want to portray. "So imagine the typical elementary school child diagnosed with ADHD. She exhibits the qualities of . . ." You can use the hypothetical example to depict something that you cannot represent with a specific person. *Actual* examples come from real life, real cases. They have the benefit of authenticity.

Statistics

Using statistics can enhance your credibility, but you need to explain what they mean.
© Doreen Salcher, 2008, Shutterstock.

Statistics, the second type of evidence, are numbers that indicate relationships between phenomena. They allow you to quickly portray a large amount of information, such as the number of students who receive financial aid, the growth of the national debt, or the numbers of voters who support or deny a particular position. They can explain recurring characteristics, such as how many teens use violent video games, along with their economic and social status. Statistics have the benefit of enhancing a speaker's credibility but they require perceptual assistance from their user. For instance, you may need to decipher a statistic into meaningful information for your audience. If data show that in 2005, it was projected that pet owners in the United States would spend $8.6 billion on veterinary care,[33] you might want to "translate" that finding by explaining that this meant that dog owners spent, on average, $211 on routine veterinary visits and cat owners spent $179. Rather than talking about the hundreds of people who require TTY service on their phones, you might explain that this means one in every eight people knows someone who uses the service. There are fairly simple guidelines to consider when you use statistics: use only ones from reliable sources; double-check statistics; use the most recent statistics available and make sure that you are using comparable statistics. Finally, always articulate the source of your statistics. Consider the following example.

> If you said that since 1798, only 2 percent of members of Congress have been women, according to the Center for American Women and Politics, that would be the case. However, in 2006, eighty-one women served in the U.S. Congress. In 2006, women held eighty-one, or 15.1 percent, of the 535 seats in the 109th U.S. Congress—fourteen, or 14.0 percent, of the 100 seats in the Senate and sixty-

seven, or 15.4 percent, of the 435 seats in the House of Representatives. In addition, three women serve as delegates to the House from Guam, the Virgin Islands and Washington, DC.[34]

How would you compare these statistics?

Testimony

A third type of evidence, **testimony,** consists of the comments of others. These "others" may be authorities or peers. *Expert testimony* is the judgment or interpretation made by authorities in the subject area. The key to expert testimony is that the source must be a recognized authority on the subject. A communication professor may be an expert on the concept of communication apprehension because of her years of study and research, but that does not make her an expert on the importance of Omega-3 supplements on human health. *Peer testimony* comes from someone who is not a recognized expert yet, someone who is recognized by the audience as in a position to know. Jon Stewart of the *Daily Show* is a comedian, not a historian. So, you might quote his political humor when he said, "Critics have noted Schwarzenegger's only previous government experience was serving under President Bush senior as chairman of the Council of Physical Fitness, a largely symbolic office, where Schwarzenegger's only responsibility was doing hundreds of jumping jacks he was going to do anyway."[35] But you should not use this quote in detailing the rise of Arnold Schwarzenegger as a political figure.

Expert testimony is subject evidence that is supplied by someone of authority.
© János Gehring, 2008, Shutterstock.

You often rely on the experiences of your friends and their opinions when deciding what movie to see, what class to take, or what store to visit. You may choose to use direct testimony (a verbatim quotation from the source) or you may summarize the source's position. For example, if talking about the role of Elizabeth Cady Stanton's legacy in nineteenth-century religion, you might say that historian Kathi Kern's first chapter in *Mrs. Stanton's Bible,* titled "'The Sunset of Life': Elizabeth Cady Stanton and the Polemics of Autobiography," describes the autobiography as more than entertainment and more than autobiography. Specifically, Kern said "Stanton remembered selectively, omitted some events completely, and created a new form for her life story."[36]

When using testimony, it is necessary to give credit to that person and source, to select sources that your audience will respect (or furnish them with credentials by which to judge the source), and to accurately represent the source's words.

Narratives

Narratives, the fourth type of evidence, are stories that elaborate an idea. A short narrative, called an **anecdote,** is often a brief, amusing story that can be used to capture audience attention. In explaining how a child is a "quirky" kid, for instance, you might explain that rather than building snowmen, he builds alien space ships, "War of the World" tripods, and destructo-beams. Longer narratives often reflect personal experiences, historical tales, or accounts that reinforce the point you are attempting to make in a humorous, sentimental, or dramatic way.

Example: Using a Narrative

Narratives can help your audience remember your point. If you were discussing the role of the first lady in the United States, for example, you might tell the story of Marian Anderson and Eleanor Roosevelt:

> In 1939, Marian Anderson's manager, Sol Hurok, and Howard University tried to secure a performance for her at Constitution Hall in Washington, D.C. The Daughters of the American Revolution, who owned the hall, refused to accommodate Anderson. The rebuff was widely publicized when Eleanor Roosevelt, herself a member of the D.A.R., publicly resigned from the organization in protest.
>
> In her letter to the D.A.R., she wrote, "I am in complete disagreement with the attitude taken in refusing Constitution Hall to a great artist . . . You had an opportunity to lead in an enlightened way and it seems to me that your organization has failed." Outraged, the "Marian Anderson Committee" formed to petition the D.A.R. and likened the organization's action to those of Hitler's racist regime.
>
> In response, Eleanor and the Committee arranged for Marian to give her concert on the steps of the Lincoln Memorial with the Mall of Washington as her auditorium. Symbolically, the concert took place on Easter Sunday, April 9, 1939.[37]

The key to using narratives is to remember that they are a longer form, that they need to directly relate to the point that you are making, and that the audience will be the judge of their truth.

Analogies

Analogies show a similarity between features of two ideas, objects, or people, in order to create a comparison between the familiar and unfamiliar. Analogies offer comparisons by demonstrating how something known is like something unknown: how one class is like another, how one town is similar to another, how a civilization compares to one that preceded it. For instance, your doctor may explain to you that your heart is like a pump, because both circulate fluid. She might point out that when a pump gets jammed by rust, the water stops flowing; the same is true with plaque clogging your arteries, causing the heart to stop pumping. **Figurative analogies** compare things in two different categories. If you compare clothes shopping to looking for a mate, you might be able to come up with some similarities: when shopping, you're looking for the right fit, for something that makes you comfortable, and that will be long lasting. Figurative analogies are especially useful when your audience is unclear about something you're talking about, because they make things more vivid by that comparison with the known. Literal analogies compare two things of the same category, like two friends, two search engines (Google versus Yahoo!), or two kinds of movies (action versus historical drama). They're useful because they're simple and draw commonalities.

Although analogies are often effective in establishing a line of thinking, they also can break down as the comparisons are drawn out. You want to make sure that your analogy does not break down. We traditionally refer to

How would you compare clothes shopping to looking for a mate?
© Andrew Armyagov, 2008, Shutterstock.

America as a *melting pot*, welcoming people from many different countries, races, and religions, all hoping to find freedom, new opportunities, and a better way of life. But is it really? What if your audience says that a melting pot suggests that ingredients are assimilated into one new thing. If they carry out that analogy, what are the impacts of the Internet, ethnic identity politics, niche advertising, and globalization? What exactly does it mean to be an American? As another example, a literal analogy comparing one type of car to another (an SUV to a Volkswagen) may find the audience unable to see the similarities at all, even as you attempt to point out headroom, wheel base, reliability, and so on. Analogies are often creative and easy to come up with, though, and they can be an effective means of drawing the audience into your message.

Your message must have a variety of evidence in order to support and clarify your ideas. You will have to strategically choose among the five categories (examples, statistics, testimony, narratives, and analogies) based on your audience, your topic, and your goals. Knowledge gathering cannot occur without using researching skills, or locating the evidence that supports your ideas. As we move to the third skill component, remember that your perceptions and your knowledge, as well as the message you are able to create, are influenced by the kinds of inquiry you conduct.

WHAT RESEARCHING SKILLS SHOULD I DEVELOP AND USE?

Researching skills are your abilities to seek and to gather information. You need a variety of sources to access; when one will not provide you the data you need, another might. Although it might be totally appropriate to rely solely on your own organized knowledge in an informal interpersonal situation (explaining to a friend what your job entails), it is more likely that with more complex communication events, you will need to supply other kinds of evidence that require you to go beyond what you know. Do you know how to use Internet-based resources; personal interviews; books, journals, and magazines; surveys and focus groups? How people will perceive your message is impacted by the resources you used in gathering that evidence. Conducting research is a basic critical thinking activity: It requires you to consider what you know (your organized knowledge), what you are able to do (your ability to use different research sources), and your understanding (your ability to develop insight from what you gather). Let us consider some of the research resources that you might utilize as you develop your researching lens, no matter what communication context you will be set in.

Your own understanding (your intellect, your knowledge base) is the most obvious of starting points for inquiry. Do you have a clear definition to share? Have you personal experiences that you might develop? Do you have a position to forward or to defend? Clearly, without a sense of purpose or goal (to inform, persuade, or share emotion or value) you will be without direction for research. Brainstorming at the start of constructing a message is a fair way to create a base. But research does not stop with the self. That is where the research begins.

Perhaps you need to talk with others to gather some initial impressions. The use of the *initial informative interview*, where you begin to gather information or to understand another's perspective, can often give you additional

Take a Closer Look

Where Does Information Come from?

- Your understanding— intellect, knowledge base
- Interviewing
- Surveys
- Online searches
- Print resources

What would you do to prepare for an interview so you get the information you need?
© icyimage, 2008, Shutterstock.

direction. There may be campus or community organizations that have experts who may supply you with information on your topic. If you choose to conduct an interview, you need to plan ahead for the specifics of what you hope to achieve. Prepare a list of questions in advance, carefully record the information you gather, and invite the interviewee to offer any information that he or she might think is relevant.

You may also want to employ *survey research* that asks a number of people about their opinions, views, or beliefs. Initial surveys are useful when you are trying to gauge public opinion in order to learn about the potential audience's range of knowledge about your subject. You probably do this already, such as when you ask several acquaintances their views on a new movie, an upcoming sporting event, or even a class to take. More formally, constructing a survey that will provide you with useful information can be a time-consuming process, but there are some general guidelines you should consider. Make sure you are choosing respondents that reflect the population whose opinions you seek. For instance, do you want to know how students feel about an issue? Work on your questions so to avoid bias and to limit their scope. You would not ask, "Don't you agree that the government is ridiculous on its stand to legalize drugs?" Focus your questions so that the response is limited but can be developed in a series of questions. (Do you favor President Bush's "No Child Left Behind" program? If yes, tell me why.)

It is more likely, however, that when you think of research, you immediately think of going "somewhere else" to locate evidence. These resources are diverse and appropriate in different ways.

Online services allow you to access a wealth of information on just about any topic. A search engine indexes the contents of the Web after you submit keywords in its search box. It then transmits your search simultaneously to several individual search engines and their databases of Web pages. There are many types of search engines at your disposal:

- Crawler-based search engines such as Google scan and index documents that contain the keyword or phrase that you plug in.
- Meta-search engines such as Dogpile and Clusty search a variety of individual search engines at the same time.
- Subject directories or human directories like Yahoo! are searchable databases of Web sites that have been reviewed by human editors.

Depending on the kind of information you need, you would select a different search engine. Very defined information such as a quotation or specific term can be found via a search engine, because it searches for those concepts that might be buried inside of other documents. If you want to find a higher-quality (more reputable) set of sites, use a subject directory such as the Librarian's Index (www.lii.org), Academic Info (www.academicinfo.us), or Google directory (directory.Google.com).

Using a search engine, you can type a keyword or phrase and be presented with Web sites that may (or may not) be relevant to your topic. For instance, a Google search of the term "American Idol" came up with an amazing 32,200,000 sites for that topic. That demonstrates the difficulty with using the Internet as a source of information: How do you know what information is credible or reliable? There is no systematic procedure for checking

---

Example: Internet Databases

- EBSCO Host: Eleven databases including Communication and Mass Media Complete, ERICMEDLINE, PsycINFO, and PsycARTICLES
- InfoTrac: News and periodical articles on a wide range of topics: business, computers, current events, economics, education, environmental issues, health care, hobbies, humanities, law, literature and art, politics, science, social sciences, sports, technology, and many general-interest topics
- JSTOR: Archival collections of journals in electronic format, with some titles dating back into the nineteenth century, primarily from social sciences and humanities fields
- LexisNexis Academic: Access to over 1 billion full-text documents covering a wide variety of subjects, including news, business, legal research, medical, and reference

---

Internet information accuracy. Anybody can create a Web site and put content on it. Bias may be hidden; there may or may not be tests for the claims given. Most university libraries have created guidelines for students to employ when evaluating Internet resources. At Virginia Tech, the site is called "Evaluating Internet Information" *(http://www.lib.vt.edu/help/instruct/evaluate/evaluating .html)*, and it suggests evaluating Internet sources in terms of four tests:

1. *Authority:* Note the author's qualifications, look for contact information.
2. *Coverage:* Assess the depth and relevance of the material on the page.
3. *Currency:* Is the page dated? Are its links current?
4. *Objectivity:* Is the page a presentation of facts and not designed to sway opinion? Is the page free of advertisements or sponsored links?[38]

Not only can you search Web sites from the computer, but you can also locate indexes, databases, and other information retrieval systems. Indexes and databases let you search a topic or a library's holdings; some even summarize publications. Some of these include general-interest databases. These cover a broad range of multiple subjects, which are good places to start.

In addition, there are specialized databases for fields such as agriculture, biology, medical sciences, architecture, business, engineering, physical sciences, human sciences, performing arts, and languages and literature, to name a few. You can also browse databases by types of information, such as directories, historical texts, encyclopedias and dictionaries, biographical resources, statistical data, and specialized reference tools.

To learn how to access any online service, you should check with *a reference librarian* with expertise in their use. Most college libraries offer programs that can help you to quickly develop some level of competence in exploring indexes and databases. Consider learning how to use these online services as a means of improving your organized knowledge; you will discover what sources can supply you with the information or evidence you need in order to achieve your purpose.

In the electronic age, it may seem old-fashioned even to consider *print resources.* Many of them have been converted for electronic use, but there still are books, journals, newspapers, reports, and reference works that might exist

You may still find that you need to visit the library to complete your topic research. © MARKABOND, 2008, Shutterstock.

only in hard copy form. Books offer you detail and perspective, for they examine a subject in depth. Newspapers or other periodicals are regularly published, and usually report on the major issues, events, and people of the time. They might provide information on historical or special topics. Of course, there are Web sites tied to most newspapers and periodicals. The U.S. Government Printing Office publishes all the information collected and produced by the federal government; most state and local agencies also provide information that can be a primary source. Reference works such as encyclopedias, almanacs, atlases, and biographical reference works offer summaries, specific data, historical background, geographical information, and even quotations for your use.

HOW DO I MAINTAIN MY INFORMATION?

No matter what resource you use, you will want to keep a working bibliography of your resources. There is nothing worse than finding "just the right" piece of evidence and then failing to remember where it came from! Beyond the personal frustration, you need to provide that source to your audience for their use, to reinforce your credibility, and to avoid charges of plagiarism by citing the source. If using electronic resources, bookmark the sites you use and keep written records of the bibliographic information (including the URL and date retrieved). For every source you use, develop a system that you use consistently to record all information. Some instructors suggest note cards; other say keep an electronic database. Whatever method you choose, pattern your materials in a way that makes sense for your own retrieval. At a minimum, you should document the following:

- Name of author or editor
- Title of publication
- Volume or edition number, if applicable
- Publisher and place of publication (if only published on line, give URL)
- Date and year of publication
- Page numbers of publication
- Specific evidence (and page numbers for that evidence)

What should you *not* do when utilizing your researching skills? You should not plagiarize, or use another's ideas or words without referring to that source. You should not make up information, falsify data, or make up a source. This would include "changing" a quotation to make it fit your needs, changing or inflating numbers, or claiming that someone else's idea began with you. Conducting ethical research is at the heart of critical thinking.

Now you have some ideas about what constitutes knowledge and how critical thinking is employed in creating that intellectual base. But communication is not solely about what you know; it is also about how you share that information with others. In order to communicate, you have to transform that inner critical thinking into the strategic dimensions of planning communication goals and analyzing and adapting to your audience. This involves goal-setting and analysis of the audience. You'll learn about those aspects of effective communication strategy in the next chapter.

SUMMARY

Do you watch the morning or evening news? It often seems filled with reports of criminal behavior: mass killings with no apparent motive; people wrongly accused of a crime who are convicted, jailed, and released years later when new evidence shows up; and car crashes that happen because of reckless behavior. When you hear these stories, what runs through your mind? Who would do something like this? What could we have done to stop it? How could something like this happen? Why didn't the police find the original criminal before? When will people learn to drive safely? The overall question you're faced with, given all the news reports, is actually this: How do you make sense of what you've heard?

At the beginning of this chapter, you were reminded of the amount of information that you are faced with every day. You employ critical thinking skills as you decide what to do with that data: How do you take it all in? Should you absorb it all as a sponge, or should you employ panning-for-gold techniques that allow you to sort the information into useful arenas? As you sort that information, you ask yourself about its purpose. It may be important for your basic comprehension (knowledge); you may need it to perform some activity (skills); or it may combine with other pieces to provide insight into something more complex that you need to analyze and evaluate (understanding). You have become aware that different skills are at work, helping you to filter and categorize that information: your perceptions gained through reading and listening attempt to attach meaning; your knowledge gathering tells you how different types of evidence work; your researching ability lets you evaluate and search for confirmation.

Now consider the news stories you hear: Do they supply testimony or example? Do they tell you where their statistics were developed? Does the story seem to make sense to you, or do you have some questions about its believability? When you hear those news stories, if you're a critical thinker, you engage in a process that allows you to respond to them. You decide whether to believe what you're hearing and seeing. This chapter showed you how we all try to make sense of what we see and hear. But if you want to be an effective communicator, you have to strategically choose how to organize the information and present those ideas in a meaningful way for your listener. Understanding the audience is essential to successful communication, and that's the next step to consider.

ENDNOTES

1. Norman Herr, "Television & Health: TV-Free America," *The Sourcebook for Teaching Science,* 2001, *http://www.csun.edu/~vceed002/health/docs/tv&health.html#tv_stats* (accessed January 30, 2006).

2. Ibid.

3. Pew Internet & American Life project. http://www.pewinternet.org/trends/Daily_Internet_Activities_2.15.08.htm

4. National Institute on Media and the Family, "Internet Advertising and Children," Minneapolis, *http://www.mediafamily.org/facts/facts_internetads.shtml* (accessed July 14, 2007).

5. M. Neil Browne and Stuart M. Keeley, *Asking the Right Questions,* 7th ed. (Upper Saddle River, NJ: Pearson Education, 2004), 3.

6. Ibid p. 4

7. Marilyn vos Savant, "Ask Marilyn" *Parade*, (Feb. 19, 2006), 18.

8. John Chaffee, *Thinking Critically: A Concise Guide* (Boston: Hougton Mifflin, 2004), 110.

9. Julia T. Wood, *Communication in Our Lives*, 4th ed. (Belmont, CA: Thomson Wadsworth, 2006), 39.

10. Howard Hughes Medical Institute, "Color Blindness: More Prevalent Among Males," *http://www.hhmi.org/senses/b130.html* (accessed February 1, 2006).

11. Darryl McDaniels, *http://www.me-dmc.com/*, Official Web site of Darryl McDaniels (accessed Jan. 3, 2007).

12. These perceptual processes are basic to avoidance of cognitive dissonance. See Leon Festinger, *A Theory of Cognitive Dissonance* (Stanford, CA: Stanford University Press, 1957).

13. E. C. Glenn, "A Content Analysis of Fifty Definitions of Listening," *Journal of the International Listening Association* 3 (1989): 21–31.

14. International Listening Association, "An International Listening Association Definition of Listening," *Listening Post* 53 (1995): 1.

15. R. Nichols, (1957). *Are You Listening?* (New York: McGraw-Hill, 1957): vii.

16. J. Brownell, *Listening Attitudes, Principles, and Skills*, 3d ed. (Rockleigh, NJ: Allyn and Bacon, 2005), 14.

17. R. L. Birdwhistell, *Kinesics and Context* (Philadelphia: University of Pennsylvania Press, 1970).

18. See for example, AICPA, *"Highlighted Responses from the Association for Accounting marketing survey. Creating the Future Agenda for the Profession—Managing Partner Perspective," http://www.aicpa.org/pubs/tpcpa/feb2001/hilight.htm* (accessed September 15, 2007).

19. C. L. Arnold, "An Examination of the Role of Listening in Judgments of Communication Competence in Co-Workers," *Journal of Business Communication* 32 (2) (1995): 123–129.

20. J. W. Haas and C. L. Arnold, "An Examination of the Role of Listening in Judgments of Communication Competence in Co-workers," *Journal of Business Communication* 32 (2) (1995): 123–139.

21. L. Barker, R. Edwards, C. Gaines, et al., "An Investigation of Proportional Time Spent in Various Communicating Activities by College Students," *Journal of Applied Communication Research* 8 (1980): 101–109.

22. R. Bommelje, J. M. Houston, and R. Smither, "Personality Characteristics of Effective Listeners: A Five-factor Perspective," *International Journal of Listening* 17 (2003): 32–46.

23. C. Coakley and A. Wolvin, "Listening in the Educational Environment," in *Listening in Everyday Life: A Personal and Professional Approach*, ed. D. Borisoff and M. Purdy (Lanham, M.D: University Press of America, 1991) 163–164.

24. A. J. Clark, "Communication Confidence and Listening Competence: An Investigation of the Relationships of Willingness to Communicate, Communication Apprehension, and Receiver Apprehension to Comprehension of Content and Emotional Meaning in Spoken Messages," *Communication Education* 38 (3) (1989): 237–249.

25. S. D. Johnson, and C. Bechler, "Examining the Relationship between Listening Effectiveness and Leadership Emergence: Perceptions, Behaviors, and Recall," *Small Group Research* 29 (4) (1998): 452–471.

26. G. D. Bodie and W. A. Villaume, "Aspects of Receiving Information: The Relationship between Listening Preferences, Communication Apprehension, Receiver Apprehension, and Communicator Style," *International Journal of Listening* 17 (2003): 47–67.

27. M. B. Wanzer, M. Booth-Butterfield, and M. K. Gruber, "Perceptions of Health Care Providers' Communication: Relationships between Patient-centered Communication and Satisfaction," *Health Communication* 16 (3) (2004): 363–384.

28. R. P. Carver, R. L. Johnson, and H. L. Friedman, "Factor Analysis of the Ability to Comprehend Time-compressed Speech," Final report for the National Institute for Health, Washington, DC: American Institute for Research, 1970.

29. A new strategy for commercial advertising is to cut down the length of the commercial significantly, to only five seconds. This confronts the issue of shorter audience attention spans. By reducing the time of the commercial, advertisers are also reducing the likelihood that viewers will change channels during the commercial break. *http://news.powerpr.com/public/blog/169913* (accessed Sept. 15, 2007). If you'd like to read a social critique of how television is impacting our attention span, read Neil Postman, *Amusing Ourselves to Death: Public Discourse in the Age of Show Business* (New York: Penguin Books, 1985).

30. D. Shenk, *Data Smog* (NY, NY: Harper One, 1997).

31. M. Fitch-Hauser, D. A. Barker, and A. Hughes, "Receiver Apprehension and Listening Comprehension: A Linear or Curvilinear Relationship?" *Southern Communication Journal* (1988): 62–71.

32. R. Taylor, *Behavioral Decision Making.* (Glenview, IL: Scott, Foresman, 1984).

33. JAVMA news, "Statistics Reveal Strength of Human-animal Bond," July 1, 2005, *http://www.avma.org/onlnews/javma/jul05/050701k.asp* (accessed February 10, 2006).

34. Center for American Women and Politics, *http://www.cawp.rutgers.edu/Facts2.html,* Eagleton Institute of Politics (accessed July 16, 2007).

35. http://www.brainyquote.com/quotes/authors/j/jon_stewart.html Brainy Media "Jon Stewart Quotes," (accessed July 14, 2007).

36. K. Kern, *Mrs. Stanton's Bible.* (Ithaca: Cornell University Press, 2001).

37. The American Experience, "Marian Anderson 1897–1993," *http://www.pbs.org/wgbh/amex/eleanor/peopleevents/pande06.html,* PBS Online (accessed February 9, 2006).

38. Another example of a tutorial on meta-search engines is at *http://www.lib.berkeley.edu/TeachingLib/Guides/Internet/MetaSearch.html* UC Berkeley—Teaching Library Internet Workshops. Here, you can find an analysis of the strengths and weaknesses of some major search engines (accessed Jan. 2, 2007).

REFERENCES

V. P. Goby and J. H. Lewis, "The Key Role of Listening in Business: A Study of the Singapore Insurance Industry," *Business Communication Quarterly* 63 (2) (June 2000): 41–51.

G. E. Hynes and V. Bhatia, "Graduate Business Students' Preferences for the Managerial Communication Course Curriculum," *Business Communication Quarterly* 59 (2) (1996): 45–55.

L. A. Janusik, "Teaching Listening. What Do We Know? What Should We Know?" *International Journal of Listening* 16 (2002): 5–39.

K. K. Waner, "Business Communication Competencies Needed by Employees as Perceived by Business Faculty and Business Professionals," *Business Communication Quarterly* 58 (4), (1995) 51–56.

J. L. Winsor, D. B. Curtis, and R. D. Stephens, "National Preferences in Business and Communication Education: A Survey Update," *JACA* 3 (1997): 170–179.

WHAT IS THE POWER OF VERBAL AND NONVERBAL COMMUNICATION?

LEARNING OBJECTIVES

After reading this chapter, you should understand the following concepts:

- Language is a shared system of symbols and structures in organized patterns to express thoughts and feelings.
- Language is arbitrary, it changes over time, it consists of denotative and connotative meaning, and it is structured by rules.
- The semantic triangle, Sapir–Whorf hypothesis, and muted group theory are three models that help explain how meaning is created.
- Strategies for using language effectively involve using accurate and appropriate language, using unbiased language, and avoiding verbal distractions.
- We constantly send nonverbal messages that present an image of ourselves to others, so it important to be aware of what those messages are saying.
- Nonverbal communication is often ambiguous, continuous, unconscious, sometimes learned and intentional—and usually, more believed than verbal communication.
- Nonverbal messages perform six functions to create meaning: complementing, substituting, repeating, contradicting, regulating, and deceiving.
- Types of nonverbal communication include body movement, use of space, dress and appearance, and eye contact.

INTRODUCTION

Using words to describe magic is like using a screwdriver to cut roast beef.
—Tom Robbins, twentieth century American author

Better wise language than well-combed hair.
—Icelandic Proverb

All credibility, all good conscience, all evidence of truth come only from the senses.
—Friedrich Wilhelm Nietzsche, nineteenth century German philosopher

Eloquence is the power to translate a truth into language perfectly intelligible to the person to whom you speak.
—Ralph Waldo Emerson, nineteenth century U.S. poet, essayist

Get in touch with the way the other person feels. Feelings are 55 percent body language, 38 percent tone and 7 percent words.
—author unknown

The limits of my language means the limits of my world.
—Ludwig Wittgenstein, twentieth century philosopher

The eyes are the windows to the soul.
—Yousuf Karsh, twentieth century Canadian photographer

The difference between the right word and the almost right word is the difference between lightning and a lightning bug.
—Mark Twain, nineteenth century American author

Dialogue should simply be a sound among other sounds, just something that comes out of the mouths of people whose eyes tell the story in visual terms.
—Alfred Hitchcock, twentieth century film director

Through these quotations, you've just been exposed to the *power of verbal and nonverbal communication* to define our beliefs, expose our values, and share our experiences. The words that you use and the nonverbal behaviors that accompany them are critically important as you communicate, because they have the ability to clarify your ideas to others or to confuse them. In this chapter, you'll learn about verbal language and nonverbal communication, to discover how they are used to create shared meaning.

Verbal language and nonverbal communication are used to create shared meaning.
© 2008, JupiterImages.

WHAT IS LANGUAGE?

So what do we know about language? Linguists estimate that there are about 5,000 to 6,000 different languages spoken in the world today; about 200 languages have a million or more native speakers. Mandarin Chinese is the most common, followed by Hindi, English, Spanish, and Bengali.[1] However, as technology continues to shrink the communication world, English is becoming more dominant in mediated communication. According to Internet World Stats, which charts usage and population statistics, the top ten languages used in the Web are English (31% of all Internet users), Chinese (15.7%), Spanish (8.7%), Japanese (7.4%), and French and German (5% each).[2] English is one of the official languages of the United Nation, the International Olympic Committee, in academics and in the sciences.[3] English is also the language spoken by air traffic controllers worldwide. Yet the English that we speak in the United States is really a hybrid, using vocabulary taken from many sources, influenced by media, technology, and globalization. Let's consider what all of this means for you as you try to share meaning with others.

Language is a shared system of symbols structured in organized patterns to express thoughts and feelings. **Symbols** are arbitrary labels that we give to some idea or phenomenon. For example, the word *run* represents an action that we do, while *bottle* signifies a container for a liquid. Words are symbols, but not all symbols are words. Music, photographs, and logos are also symbols that stand for something else, as do nonverbal actions such as "OK," and "I don't know." However, in this section, we're going to focus on words as symbols. Note that the definition of language says that it's structured and shared. Languages have a **grammar** (syntax, a patterned set of rules that aid in meaning). You've learned grammar as you've been taught how to write, and it's become an unconscious part of your daily communication. Take, for example, this sentence:

The glokkish Vriks mounged oupily on the brangest Ildas.

Now, we can answer these questions:

Who did something? The Vriks mounged.

What kind of Vriks are they? Glokkish

How did they mounge? Oupily

On what did they mounge? The Ildas

What kind of Ildas are they? Brangest

English is the language spoken by airline pilots and air traffic controllers all over the world. © 2008, JupiterImages.

You might have difficulty identifying noun, verb, adverb, and adjective, but because you know the grammar of the English language, you're still able to decipher what this sentence is telling you because of the pattern, even if the symbols themselves lack meaning for now. That leads to the next part of the definition: *symbols must be shared in order to be understood.* George Herbert Mead's Symbolic Interaction Theory asserts that meaning is **intersubjective;** that means that **meaning** *can exist only when people share common interpretations of the symbols they exchange.*[4] So if you were given a picture of Vriks and were told that these were ancient hill people of a particular region of the country, you'd have a start at meaning!

In order to get a grasp on language, this section will uncover basic principles about language, introduce to you a few theoretical perspectives, and then will suggest language strategies to enhance your communication.

WHAT ARE THE BASIC PRINCIPLES OF LANGUAGE?

There are some basic principles of language. It is arbitrary, it changes over time, it consists of denotative and connotative meanings, and it is structured by rules. Let's look at these more closely.

Arbitrary

"Language is arbitrary" means that *symbols do not have a one-to-one connection with what they represent.* What is the computer form that you use if you take a test? Is it a bubble sheet? A scantron? An opscan? Each of these names has no natural connection to that piece of paper, and it's likely that at different universities, it's called different names. Because language is arbitrary, people in groups agree on labels to use, creating private codes. That's why your organization might have specialized terms, why the military uses codes, and why your family uses nicknames that only they understand. The language that you create within that group creates group meaning and culture. The arbitrary element of language also adds to its ambiguity; meanings just aren't stable. To me, a test is the same as an exam; to you, a test might be less than an exam. If you say to me, "I'll call you later," how do I define the term *later?* We often fall into the trap of thinking that everyone understands us, but the reality is, it's an amazing thing that we share meaning at all!

Changes over Time

Language *changes over time* in vocabulary, as well as syntax. New vocabulary is required for the latest inventions, for entertainment and leisure pursuits, for political use. In 2007, the top television buzzwords included *surge* and *D'oh,* while in 2006, they were *truthiness* and *wikiality.*[5] How many of those words play a role in your culture today? Words like *cell phones* and *Internet* didn't exist fifty years ago, for example. In addition, no two people use a language in exactly the same way. Teens and young adults often use different words and phrases than their parents. The vocabulary and phrases people use may depend on where they live, their age, education level, social status, and other factors. Through our interactions, we pick up new words and phases, and then we integrate them into our communication.

How is your language different from your parents' and grandparents'?
© 2008, JupiterImages.

Consists of Denotative and Connotative Meanings

Denotative meanings, the literal, dictionary definitions, are precise and objective. **Connotative meanings** reflect your personal, subjective definitions. They add layers of experience and emotions to meaning. Elizabeth J. Natalle examined this dichotomy in a case study of urban music, examining how our language has evolved over the years to include more negative connotation regarding talk about women as compared to talk about men. Think about *chick, sweetie, sugar pie* and *old maid,* versus *stud, hunk, playboy,* and *bachelor.* Do you get a different image? Using a study of rap music, she attempted to clarify how urban music names a particular world, creates male community, and has implications for power and gendered relationships.[6]

A simpler way to consider denotative and connotative meanings is to examine the terms President Bush used to describe the terrorists who crashed the planes on Sept. 11, 2001. Bush's labels on that day in various locations began with "those folks who committed this act" (remarks by the president

© Cartoon Stock,
www.CartoonStock.com.

when he first heard that two planes crashed into World Trade Center)[7] to
"those responsible for these cowardly acts" (remarks by the president upon
arrival at Barksdale Air Force Base)[8] to "those who are behind these evil acts"
and "the terrorists who committed these acts" (statement by the president in
his address to the nation).[9] Consider how the connotative meaning shaped
the image of the perpetrators.

David K. Berlo[10] provided several assumptions about meaning:

- Meanings are in people.
- Communication does not consist of the transmission of meanings, but of
  the transmission of messages.
- Meanings are not in the message; they are in the message users.
- Words do not mean at all; only people mean.
- People can have similar meanings only to the extent that they have had,
  or can anticipate having, similar experiences.
- Meanings are never fixed; as experience changes, so meanings change.
- No two people can have exactly the same meaning for anything.

These ideas echo the idea that when you use words, you need to be aware of
the extent to which meaning is shared. For example, when an adoptive parent
sees those "adopt a highway" locator signs, it's probable that that person sees
something different than others might. "Adopt a" programs might be seen as
confusing and misleading others about the term *adoption*. An adoptive parent
might say that you don't adopt a road, a zoo animal, or a Cabbage Patch doll.
Adoption is a means of family building, and it has a very subjective, emotional meaning.[11] To the town official who erected the sign, it's a representation of the good work being done by some group to keep the highway clean.

What does this sign's language
mean to you?
© Robert J. Beyers II, 2008,
Shutterstock.

Structured by Rules

As we understand and use the rules of language, we begin to share meaning. Think of rules as a shared understanding of what language means, as well as an understanding of what kind of language is appropriate in various contexts. Many of the rules you use weren't consciously learned; you gathered them from interactions with other people. Some, however, were learned aspects of your culture.

Phonological rules *regulate how words sound when you pronounce them.* They help us organize language. For instance, the word *lead* could be used to suggest a behavior that you do (you *lead* the group to show them the way) or a kind of toxic metallic element (*lead* paint in windows is harmful to children). Do you enjoy getting a *present,* or did you *present* one to someone else? Another example of phonological rules is demonstrated by your understanding of how letters sound when they're grouped in a particular way. Take for instance the letters *omb.* Now put a t in front of them, and you have *tomb.* Put a c in front, and it becomes *comb.* Put a b in front, and you have *bomb.* See how the sounds shift?

The way we make singular nouns plural is also phonological. It's not as simple as adding the letter s to the end of a word. The sound changes too: dog/dogs (sounds like a *z* at the end); cook/cooks (sounds like an *ess*); bus/buses (sounds like *ess-ez*). English has many inconsistent phonological rules like these, which makes making errors quite typical, especially for non-native English speakers.

Syntactical rules *present the arrangement of a language, how the symbols are organized.* You saw that earlier in the "glokkish Vriks" example; you're usually unaware of the syntactical rules until they're violated. In English, we put adjectives prior to most nouns: I live in a red house. In French, you live in a house red (the adjective follows the noun).

Semantic rules *govern the meaning of specific symbols.* Because words are abstractions, we need rules to tell us what they mean in particular situations. Take, for example, the headline, "School Needs to Be Aired." What does that mean? Is the school so smelly that it needs to be refreshed? Or are the needs of the school going to be broadcast or spoken in a public forum? Words can be interpreted in more than one way, and we need semantic rules to lead us to shared meaning. Although these three kinds of rules help us to pattern language, there are also rules that help us guide the entire communication event.[12]

Regulative rules *tell us when, how, where, and with whom we can talk about certain things.* You know when it's OK to interrupt someone; you know when turn-taking is expected. You may be enrolled in classes where you are expected to express your opinion; in other classes, you know to hold your tongue. How do you feel about public displays of affection? When is it OK to correct your boss? These regulative rules help us to maintain respect, reveal information about ourselves, and interact with others.

Constitutive rules *tell us how to "count" different kinds of communication.* These rules reveal what you feel is appropriate. You know that when someone waves or blows kisses, that person is showing affection or friendliness. You know what topics you can discuss with your parents, friends, teachers, co-workers, and strangers. You have rules that reveal your expectations for communication with different people; you expect your doctor to be informative and firm with advice, and you anticipate that your friend will compli-

You can count on a close friend for comfort when you have a problem.
© 2008, JupiterImages.

ment you and empathize. As we interact with others, we begin to grasp and use the rules. For instance, when you start a new job, you take in the rules on whom to talk with, how to talk with supervisors and co-workers, and what topics are appropriate, along with the mechanics of how to talk and the meaning of job-specific words. Interestingly enough, you might not even be aware of the rules until they're broken!

HOW DO THEORISTS DESCRIBE LANGUAGE AND MEANING?

Can you picture a book, a pen, a laptop, and a horse? Your ability to conjure up these images means that you've been exposed to the symbols that represent them in the English language. How about the picture shown on the right? What do you see? If you said "keys," then that shows how you have acquired language; you've been taught that these things are associated with the symbol "keys." How are you able to do those connections? There are a great number of perspectives related to language, meaning, and symbols. In this section, you'll be exposed to three models that present varying perspectives on the way that meaning is created.

© Costin Cojocaru, 2008, Shutterstock.

Semantic Triangle

One of the models that demonstrate how words come to have meaning is the **semantic triangle**.[13] Ogden and Richards suggest that a major problem with communication is that we tend to treat *words* as if they were the *thing*. As a result, we confuse the symbol for the thing or object.

At the bottom right hand of the triangle is the **referent,** the thing that we want to communicate about that exists in reality. As we travel up the right side, we find the **reference(s),** which consist of thoughts, experiences, and feelings about the referent. This is a causal connection; seeing the object

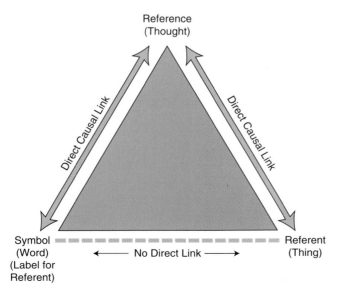

The Semantic Triangle— Ogden & Richards, 1923.

results in those thoughts. Another causal connection exists as you travel down the left side of the triangle, to the *symbol*, or *word*. That's the label we apply to that referent.

The problem is that there is not a direct connection between a symbol and referent; it's an indirect connection, shown by the dotted line. According to this model, it's that indirect link between *referent* and *symbol* that creates the greatest potential for communication misunderstandings. We assume that others share our references, and we think that they must use the same label or symbol because of that shared state of being. A simple example should help.

A mom is teaching her son words by reading simple children's books— books about tools, farms, trucks, zoos, and dinosaurs. Usually, this reading activity happens on the front porch. One day, the mom sees the neighbor's cat sneaking up on her birdfeeders, and under her breath, she mutters something about the "stupid cat." The next day, the toddler goes off to day care, and when mom comes to pick him up, she's met by the teacher. She laughingly tells how she was reading a book about animals that day, and when she got to the page with cute kittens on it, the little boy yelled out, "Stupid cat." The embarrassed mother just learned a lesson about the semantic triangle. For her, the referent (cat) evokes images of bird-murdering, allergy-causing felines (references). She creates the label "stupid cat." (symbol). When the boy sees a picture of one, he naturally thinks that is what those things are called. Unfortunately, that's not the universal name!

You can experience the same thing: If you tell others that you own a dog, what referent do you think they apply the label to? The semantic triangle is a practical tool that helps us to understand the relationship of referent, references, and symbol, or thing, thoughts, and word. It reminds us that one word doesn't necessarily evoke the same meaning in any two people.

Sapir–Whorf Hypothesis

Another theoretical approach to language is the *Sapir–Whorf hypothesis*[14] (also known as the theory of linguistic relativity). According to this approach, your perception of reality is determined by your thought processes, and your thought processes are limited by your language. Therefore, language shapes reality. Your culture determines your language, which, in turn, determines the way that you categorize thoughts about the world and your experiences in it. If you don't have the words to describe or explain something, then you can't really know it or talk about it.

For example, researchers Linda Perry and Deborah Ballard-Reisch suggest that existing language does not represent the reality that biological sex comes in more forms than female and male, gender identities are not neatly ascribed to one's biological sex, and sexual orientation does not fit snugly into, "I like men, I like women, I like both, I like neither," choices. They also assert that evolving new language such as the word *gendex* (representing the dynamic interplay of a person's sexual identity, sex preference, sexual orientation, and gender identity) can work against biases and discrimination.[15] Another example is the concept of *bipolar disorder*. It used to be called *manic depressive*, and it refers to a mood disorder characterized by unusual shifts in a person's mood, energy, and ability to function.[16] But if you don't know what that illness is, you might just agree with a family member who says, "You're just going through a phase." The lack of language restricts our ability to perceive the world. Reality is embedded in your language.

Muted Group Theory

As these perspectives suggest, the *words* that you use are powerful. They have the ability to express attitudes and to represent values. Communication scholar Cheris Kramarae developed the *muted group theory* to suggest that power and status are connected, and because muted groups lack the power of appropriate language, they have no voice and receive little attention.[17] Kramarae noted, "The language of a particular culture does not serve all its speakers, for not all speakers contribute in an equal fashion to its formulation. Women (and members of other subordinate groups) are not as free or as able as men are to say what they wish, when and where they wish, because the words and the norms for their use have been formulated by the dominant group, men."[18] She asserts that language serves men better than women (and perhaps European Americans better than African Americans or other groups) because the European American men's experiences are named clearly in language, and the experiences of other groups (women, people with disabilities, and ethnic minorities) are not. Due to this problem with language, muted groups appear less articulate than men in public settings.

The muted group theory suggests that language serves men better than women.
© 2008, JupiterImages.

The task of muted groups is to conceptualize a thought and then scan the vocabulary that is suited to men's thinking for the best way to encode the idea. The term *sexual harassment* is an example. Although the act of harassment has existed for centuries, it wasn't until sex discrimination was prohibited by Title VII of the 1964 Civil Rights Act. It also took the Clarence Hill–Anita Thomas hearing in 1991 to make the term *gender discrimination* part of the popular dialogue, as the media focused attention on the workplace issue.

Because they are rendered inarticulate, muted groups are silenced in a variety of ways. Ridicule happens when the group's language is trivialized (men talk, women gab). Ritual creates dominance (the woman changes her name at the wedding ceremony but the man doesn't). Control happens as the media present some points of view and ignore others (we don't hear from the elderly or homeless). Harassment results from the control that men exert over public spaces (women get verbal threats couched as compliments when they walk down the streets). This theory affirms that as muted groups create more language to express their experiences and as all people come to have similar experiences, inequalities of language (and the power that comes with it) should change.

Each of these perspectives demonstrates how language impacts meaning. They show how we believe meaning comes into being, how we are limited by the language we possess, and how language wields power. By now, you should be sensitive to the many ways that you can miscommunicate, or at least communicate ineffectively through language choices. How can you become more sensitive to strategic language choices?

HOW CAN I USE LANGUAGE EFFECTIVELY?

Communication scholar Julia T. Wood says that the single most important guideline is to engage in a **dual perspective**, recognizing another person's point of view and taking that into account as you communicate. Wood suggests that you should understand both your own and another's point of view and acknowledge each when you communicate.[19] You'll see that concept played out throughout this text; you need to consider your audience's beliefs, attitudes, and values as you create your message. Here are some strategic tips for effective language use to maintain that dual perspective.

Use Accurate Language

Make sure you are using the term correctly, and if you're unsure if the audience will understand your meaning, define it. You'll learn about defining in the chapter on informative speaking. Remember, what makes perfect sense to you may be gobbledygook to me. When the doctor tells you that you have a rather large contusion, do you know what that is?

Use Appropriate Language

Appropriate means that the language you use is suitable for the context, for the audience, for the topic, and for you. Some occasions call for more formal language (proposals to a client), while others will let slang pass (texting a friend). Some audiences expect technical language, while others need simple terms. Off-color humor might work in certain instances and with specific groups, but you probably shouldn't choose to use it at a church gathering. You need to consider if your audience utilizes **regionalisms** (words or phrases that are specific to one part of the country) or **jargon** (specialized professional language) as you speak with them.

It's important to use appropriate language for the occasion.
© 2008, JupiterImages.

Your topic also can determine suitable language. Some topics call for lots of vivid language and imagery, while others are better suited to simplicity. If you are honoring your boss upon his retirement, then the topic probably calls for words that evoke appreciation and emotion. But if you're telling someone how to put together a computer table, then simple explanatory words are expected. Finally, you need to use words that are appropriate to you. You have developed your own style of language over the years; do you use the same words as your parents? Don't try to use words that just don't flow easily from your mind; it's not going to sound like you.

Use Unbiased Language

Biased language includes any language that defames a subgroup (women; people from specific ethnic, religious, or racial groups; people with disabilities) or eliminates them from consideration. Even if you would never think about using language that defames anyone else, you can fall into using language that more subtly discriminates. Sexist language is replete with this: We use the masculine pronoun (he, him) when we don't have a referent. So if you personify "the judge," "the executive," "the director," as male by using the pronoun *he*, you eliminate one whole subgroup from consideration.

The same holds true when you use the word *man* in occupational terms, when the job holders could be either male or female. Examples are fireman, policeman, garbage man, chairman; they're easily made nonsexist by saying firefighter, police officer, garbage collector, and chair or presiding officer. Finally, while the generic use of *man* (like in mankind) originally was used to denote both men and women, its meaning has become more specific to adult males. It's simple to change the word to be more inclusive: mankind becomes people or human beings; man-made becomes manufactured; the common man becomes the average person.

The *Associated Press Stylebook* has a lengthy entry on "disabled, handicapped, impaired" terminology, including when to use (and not to use) terms such as *blind, deaf, mute, wheelchair-user,* and so on. A separate entry on *retarded* says "mentally retarded" is the preferred term. The World Bank advises using *persons with disabilities* and *disabled people,* not handicapped.

Use appropriate labels when referring to sexual orientation. The terms *lesbians, gay men,* and *bisexuals* or *bisexual women and men* are preferred to the term *homosexuals* (because the emphasis on the latter is on sex, while the former all refer to the whole person, not just the sex partner he or she chooses). In general, try to find out what the people's preferences are, and be specific when applicable. For instance, if all the subjects are either Navajo or Cree, stating this is more accurate than calling them Native Americans.

Avoid Verbal Distractions

If you divert the audience from your intended meaning by using confusing words, your credibility will be lowered and your audience may become lost. The following are distractions:

- **Slang** *consists of words that are short-lived, arbitrarily changed, and often vulgar ideas.* Slang excludes people from a group. Internet slang was usually created to save keystrokes and consists of "u" for *you,* "r" for *are,* and "4" for *for.* Poker slang includes *dead man's hand* (two pair, aces, and eights); to *act* (make a play); and *going all in* (betting all of your chips on the hand). *Daggy* means out of fashion or uncool; *fives* means to reserve a seat.[20]
- **Cliches** or **trite words** *have been overused and lose power or impact.* The Unicorn Hunters of Lake Superior University keeps a list of banished words that is regularly updated. In 2007, it listed words such as combined celebrity names (*Brangelina* and *Tomcat*), *awesome* (because it no longer means majestic), and *undocumented alien* (just use the word *illegal*).[21]
- **Loaded words** *sound like they're describing, but they're actually revealing your attitude.* When speaking of abortion, consider the different image created by the terms *unborn child* or *fetus.* Are you *thrifty* but your friend is *cheap*? How about your brother; is he one of those *health-nuts* who is dedicated to the cult of marathoning? Colorful language is entertaining, but if it distorts the meaning or distracts the audience, then don't use it.
- **Empty words** *are overworked exaggerations.* They lose their strength because their meaning is exaggerated. How many products are advertised as *new and improved* or *supersized*? What exactly does that mean?
- **Derogatory language** *consists of words that are degrading or tasteless.* If you use degrading terms to refer to ethnic groups (*Polack* for a person of Polish descent; *Chink* for someone from China; *Spic* for an Italian) then you are guilty of verbal bigotry.
- **Equivocal words** *have more than one correct denotative meaning.* A famous example is of a nurse telling a patient that he "wouldn't be needing" the books he asked to be brought from home. Although she meant that he was going home that day and could read there, the patient took that to mean that he was near death and wouldn't have time to read. One time while evaluating a debate, an instructor encountered students arguing the issue of the legalization of marijuana. The side arguing for the legalization used the Bible, citing chapter and verse and asserting that God

created the grass and said, "The grass is good." This sent the other side into a tailspin as they tried to refute the biblical passage. This simple equivocal use of the term *grass* lost the debate for the opposition!

WHAT SHOULD YOU TAKE FROM THIS SECTION ON LANGUAGE?

Because our language is arbitrary and evolving, it's easy to be misunderstood. You can attempt to enhance shared meaning by remembering that language is a shared system of symbols; through language, you share ideas, articulate values, transmit information, reveal experiences, and maintain relationships. Language is essential to your ability to think and to operate within the many cultures (community of meaning) that you travel through. You should be sensitive to the words you choose as you attempt to connect with others. Now let's turn our attention to the other means by which you create meaning: your nonverbal communication behaviors.

WHAT IS NONVERBAL COMMUNICATION?

Pretend you are hoarse and the doctor has told you not to speak at all for the next three days. Nor can you IM or text or do any other computer-related communication. How would you do the following?

- Let your friend know that you can't hear her. Or tell her that she's talking too loudly.
- Tell your lab partner that you want him to come where you are.
- Show the teacher that you don't know the answer to the question she just asked you.
- Let a child know that he needs to settle down; his play is getting too rough.
- Tell your significant other that you're not angry, and everything is OK.
- Express disappointment over a loss by your team, which always seems to lose the lead in the last two minutes.
- Signify that you're running late and have to leave.

How hard would it be to make yourself understood? What you've just attempted to do without verbal language is present a message nonverbally. We all constantly send nonverbal messages, giving our receivers all types of cues about ourselves. An awareness of nonverbal communication is important: your nonverbal behaviors present an image of yourself to those around you. They tell others how you want to relate to them, and they may reveal emotions or feelings that you either are trying to hide or simply can't express.

In the remainder of this chapter, you will be introduced to some of the elements of the study of nonverbal communication in the hopes of creating a greater awareness of these elements of the message. You will examine *definitions* of nonverbal communication, its *functions*, and *types* of nonverbal communication. Along the way, we will provide examples and illustrations to help you understand the applications of various nonverbal behaviors and how they can be used to help you interpret the messages of other people. You should also gain some insight into how to use nonverbal behaviors to enhance your own communication.

WHAT IS THE NATURE OF NONVERBAL COMMUNICATION?

Although nonverbal communication is a complex system of behaviors and meanings, its basic definition *can be* fairly straightforward. Here are four definitions for comparison:

1. All types of communication that do not rely on words or other linguistic systems[22]
2. Any message other than written or spoken words that conveys meaning[23]
3. Anything in a message besides the words themselves[24]
4. Messages expressed by nonlinguistic means[25]

Taking these definitions and the body of related research into consideration, we propose a very simple definition: nonverbal communication is *all nonlinguistic aspects of communication.* That definition covers quite a lot of territory. Except for the actual words that we speak, *everything* else is classified as nonverbal communication. The way you move, the tone of your voice, the way you use your eyes, the way you occupy and use space, the way you dress, the shape of your body, your facial expressions, the way you smell, your hand gestures, and the way you pronounce (or mispronounce) words are all considered nonverbal communication. Some of these behaviors have meaning independent of language or other behaviors; others have meaning only when considered with what is said, the context and culture in which a communication event takes place, and the relationship between the communicators.

Maybe you're getting a hint of the richness of nonverbal expression. Without any formal training, you already are able to interpret messages that others send nonverbally. Your skill level, however, may not be as strong as you think, so keep in mind the goal of increasing strategic communication as you continue. Researchers have also been fascinated with the extent to which nonverbal communication impacts meaning, and their findings provide glimpses into the impact of nonverbals on shared meanings and culture. If nothing else, by the end of this section, you will discover that the study of nonverbal communication has come a long way since it was referred to only as *body language!*

What can you say about her nonverbal communication?
© mehmet alci, 2008, Shutterstock.

WHAT ARE THE CHARACTERISTICS OF NONVERBAL COMMUNICATION?

Ambiguous

Most nonverbal behaviors have no generally accepted meaning. Instead, the connection between the behavior and its meaning is vague or *ambiguous,* leaving understanding open to various interpretations. The meaning we apply to words is fairly specific, but the meaning we give to nonverbal communication is nonspecific. The meanings you attribute to nonverbal behaviors are heavily dependent on the relationship between you and the others you're interacting with, the nature of the communication event, the content of the words that accompanies it, and the culture in which the event takes place. For example,

In the United States, a thumbs-up is appropriate for celebrating.
© Jason Stitt, 2008, Shutterstock.

consider the ubiquitous "thumbs up" hand gesture. In the United States it means, "OK" or "very good." In some eastern cultures, however, it is considered an insult and an obscene hand gesture. In Great Britain, Australia, and New Zealand, it could be a signal used by hitchhikers who are thumbing a lift; it could be an OK signal; it also could be an insult signal meaning "up yours" or "sit on this" when the thumb is jerked sharply upward. In Indonesia, the thumb gesture means "good job" in response to someone who has completed an excellent job, or "delicious" when great food is tasted. In another context, if you smile at a joke, that's understood in an entirely different way than if you do it after someone misses a chair and falls to the ground. A smile could also show affection, embarrassment, or even be used to hide pain or anger. As you can see, it is possible to find several meanings for the same nonverbal behavior, and it is possible to find several nonverbal behaviors that mean the same thing.[26]

Continuous

With verbal communication, if you stop speaking, listeners can't attribute any more meaning to your words. Nonverbal communication, by contrast, is so pervasive and complex that others can continue to gather meaning, even if you are doing absolutely nothing! The mere act of doing nothing can send a message; you might blush, stutter, wring your hands, or sweat unintentionally, causing others to react to you. You might not mean to send a message, but your lack of intention to communicate doesn't prevent other people from assigning meaning to your behavior. In addition, your appearance, the expression on your face, your posture, where (or if) you are seated, and how you use the space around you all provide information that is subject to interpretation by others.

Sometimes Unplanned and Unconscious

Nonverbal communication can be either unconscious or intentional, but most of our nonverbal behaviors are exhibited without much or any conscious thought. You rarely plan or think carefully about your nonverbal behaviors. When you are angry, it is naturally expressed on your face as well as elsewhere in your body. The same is true for how your voice changes when you're nervous, how your arms cross when you're feeling defensive, or how you scratch your head when you're unsure of something. These expressions and behaviors are rarely planned or structured; they just happen suddenly and without conscious thought.

Sometimes Learned and Intentional

What can you tell by this woman's expression?
© Steve Luker, 2008, Shutterstock.

Saying that some nonverbal behaviors are natural or occur without conscious thought doesn't mean that people are born with a *complete inventory* of instinctive nonverbal behaviors. Much of your nonverbal behavior is *learned* rather than instinctive or innate. You learn the "proper" way to sit or approach, how close to stand next to someone, how to look at others, how to use touch, all from your experiences and your culture. You have been taught their meaning through your experience in interactions with other people. As a result, you can structure some nonverbal behaviors to send intentional messages, such as disapproval when you shake your head from side to side or give a "high five" to show excitement. However, unlike the formal training you received in reading, writing, and speaking, you learned (and continue to learn) nonverbal communication in a much less formal and unceremonious way, and you use it in a much less precise way than spoken language. But *because* many of these behaviors are learned, you can actively work to improve your nonverbal skills. There is a debate as to whether unintentional nonverbal behaviors really count as communication. Since others incorporate their understanding of our nonverbals as part of shared meaning, we're going to say that intentional and unintentional nonverbals both are worth recognizing here.[27] Our position is that it's nearly impossible not to communicate nonverbally.

More Believable than Verbal

Communication textbooks have been saying for years that, when verbal and nonverbal messages contradict each other, people typically believe the nonverbal message. Because nonverbal is more spontaneous and less conscious, we don't or can't manipulate it as easily as we can control verbal communication. When you were younger and your parents thought that you might be lying to them, they would say, "Look me in the eye and say that again." Your face was more believable to them than what you were saying verbally. Your nonverbal messages would tell them the truth. How could this be so?

Research suggests that between 65 percent and 93 percent of the meaning people attribute to messages comes from the nonverbal channel.[28] There is a small fudge factor in those percentages, however, because the Mehrabian and Ferris study assumed up to 93 percent of meaning came from nonverbal messages in situations *where no other background information* was available.[29] The reality is that many factors affect the meaning given to messages, including how familiar the communicators are with the language being spoken, cultural knowledge, and even individual differences in personality characteristics.[30]

Regardless of the exact percentage of meaning that comes from the verbal or nonverbal channels, we still appear to get more meaning from the nonverbal channel. Unless you are very good at controlling all your nonverbal behaviors, your parents can probably still know when you are not telling the truth.

WHAT ARE THE FUNCTIONS OF NONVERBAL COMMUNICATION?

Types of nonverbal communication will be described a little later in the chapter, but you first need to understand what part nonverbals play in the communication process. Nonverbal communication performs six general functions that add information and insight to nonverbal messages to help us create meaning. Those functions are complementing, substituting, repeating, contradicting, regulating, and deceiving.

Complementing Verbal Messages

If someone shakes your hand while saying "Congratulations" at your college graduation, the handshake gives added meaning to the verbal message. Gestures, tone of voice, facial expressions, and other nonverbal behaviors can clarify, reinforce, accent, or add to the meaning of verbal messages. For instance, if you are angry with a friend and are telling him off, pounding your hand into your fist would add depth to your meaning. These nonverbal behaviors are usually not consciously planned, but they are spontaneous reactions to the context and the verbal message.

Substituting for Verbal Messages

You can use a nonverbal message *in the place of* a verbal message. A substituting behavior can be a clear "stop" hand gesture; it can be nodding the head up and down to say yes; or it can be a shoulder shrug to indicate "I don't know." When you use this kind of gesture, you don't have to supply any verbal message for the meaning to be clear to others. However, keep in mind that your nonverbals may be interpreted differently, given what you have learned from your context and culture. As an example, someone in Japan might act in a controlled fashion, while someone from the Mideast might seem more emotional, even when both are feeling the same intensity of emotion. Your interpretation of those postures, without accompanying verbals, might lead you to the wrong conclusions.

Repeating Verbal Messages

If a stranger on your college campus asks you for directions to the administration building, you might reply, "Carty Hall is two blocks south of here." While you are delivering the verbal message, you also *repeat* the message by pointing to the south. The gesture reinforces the meaning of the verbal message and provides a clear orientation to listeners who are unfamiliar with the campus.

Nonverbal messages can substitute for verbal messages. What specific messages are being sent by the people in these photos?
© 2008, JupiterImages.

Contradicting Verbal Messages

Nonverbal messages sometimes *contradict* the verbal message. It can be done by accident, such as when you say "turn right" but you point to the left. Or it could be done without thinking (unconsciously), such as when you have a sour expression on your face as you tell your former girlfriend how much you "really like" her new boyfriend. Finally, you could use planned nonverbal behaviors, such as a wink of the eye and a sarcastic tone of voice, to contradict the verbal message, "Nice hat!" A famous example of this contradiction happened in September 1960, when 70 million U.S. viewers tuned in to watch Senator John Kennedy of Massachusetts and Vice President Richard Nixon in the first-ever televised presidential debate. The so-called Great Debates were television's first attempt to offer voters a chance to see the presidential candidates "in person" and head to head. Nixon was more well known, since he had been on the political scene as senator and two-term vice president. He had made a career out of fighting communism right in the midst of the Cold War. Kennedy was a relative newcomer, having served only a brief and undistinguished time as senator; he had no foreign affairs experience. Expectations were low for Kennedy; there seemed to be a huge reputation disparity between them.

"The street you are looking for is about one mile to the east." Nonverbal messages repeat verbal messages.
© 2008, JupiterImages.

During the debate, their points were fairly even. But it was the visual contrast between the two men that was astounding. Nixon had seriously injured his knee, had lost weight, and had recently suffered from the flu. When the first debate came, he was underweight and pasty looking, with a murky 5:00 shadow darkening his lower face. He wore a white, poorly fitting shirt and a gray suit that nearly blended into the background set, and he refused to wear make-up, even though he was advised to do so. Kennedy supplemented his tan with make-up, wore a dark suit, and had been coached on how to sit and where to look when he wasn't speaking. Kennedy's smooth delivery made him credible, because he came off as confident, vibrant, and poised. Nixon looked tired, pasty, and uncomfortable (he sweated heavily).

Polls taken after the first debate showed that most people who listened to it on the radio felt that Nixon had won, while most who watched it on television declared Kennedy the victor. Those television viewers focused on what they saw, not what they heard.[31]

Contradictory messages can be difficult for others to interpret, so it's important to monitor your nonverbal behaviors. People have a tendency to prefer the meaning of the nonverbal message when it conflicts with the verbal, so when you say turn right, you should try to point to the right. Or if you don't want your former girlfriend to know how jealous you are of her new boyfriend, try to guard against making that sour face. Most adults, however, will interpret the "Nice hat" comment as sarcasm and clearly understand the message.

Is there sarcasm detected in the "nice hat" comment?
© 2008, JupiterImages.

Regulating the Flow of Communication

Nonverbal behaviors help us to control the verbal messages we're presenting. To prevent chaos when two are more people are engaged in conversation, we use a system of signals to indicate whose turn it is speak. Think about that. How do you know when it is appropriate for you to begin speaking in a group or in a classroom? When you're talking, no one is there saying, "Now, it's your turn." You might use tone of voice to indicate that you want to speak and silence to show that you're ready to yield the floor. If you don't want to be interrupted, you might not make eye contact with the potential interruptor. If you expect an answer, you might directly look at the other person.[32] You probably also use nonverbals to let others know that you're trying to control their talk. Have you ever started to put your computer or lecture materials away before the professor is done speaking? You use nonverbal behavior to indicate that you want to speak, that you are finished speaking, that you want to continue speaking, or that you do not want to speak at all. The nonverbal signals include tone of voice, posture, gestures, eye contact, and other behaviors.

Deceiving Listeners

Sometimes, your nonverbal behaviors are attempts to mislead somebody or hide the truth. This deception doesn't have to be malicious or mean. If you're a poker player, you might wear sunglasses in order to shield your eyes; pupils dilate when you're excited, and you want to keep that excitement close to your vest. Sometimes, you deceive to protect yourself or the other person, like when you pat someone on the back and say, "Everything will be all right," even when you know it won't.

There are many movies based on the premise that you can learn to nonverbally behave like someone you're not in order to deceive others. In *Tootsie* (1982), Dustin Hoffman becomes the female star of a television soap opera. Robin Williams stars as *Mrs. Doubtfire* (1993), dressing as a woman so he can see his children. In *The Birdcage* (1996), Robin Williams attempts to teach Nathan Lane how to do an exaggerated John Wayne walk to disguise his effeminate stroll. *Mulan* (1998) is a young woman wanting to fight the Huns in the place of her father, so she poses as a male to join the army. *Big Momma's House* (2000) stars Martin Lawrence, who plays an FBI agent who goes undercover and dresses as a heavy-set woman. In *White Chicks* (2004) Shawn Wayans and Marlon Wayans are sibling FBI agents who must protect two cruise line heiresses from a kidnapping plot. Finally, in *The Lord of the Rings: The Return of the King* (2004), Éowyn dresses as a soldier to be allowed to fight with the men.

A great deal of research on deception has practical implications. For instance, some occupations, such as lawyers and actors, require you to act differently than you might feel. Research has found that they are more successful at deception than the rest of the general population.[33] People who monitor themselves have been found to be more effective in hiding deception cues than are people who are not as self-aware.[34] Just think about the last time you told someone a "white lie." Were you a little nervous? How did you show that? Did the words come easily? Did you stammer or have to search for words? When you fib, you have to weigh the consequences of being caught versus the need to fib (telling a child that Santa or the Easter Bunny exists). You have to look and act sincere and believable, even though you're churning inside. If you can look composed and natural, then you are more likely to be a successful liar.[35] In fact, research tells us that people with a greater social skills repertoire and more communication competence will generally be more proficient, alert, confident, and expressive, and less fidgety, nervous and rigid, making them more skilled at deception than others.[36]

Now that you see the many roles that nonverbals can play in communication, let's turn from the functions to the categories of nonverbal communication.

WHAT ARE THE TYPES OF NONVERBAL COMMUNICATION?

Although many types of behaviors can communicate, available space and the focus of this book limit our discussion of nonverbal communication to body movement (kinesics), the use of space (proxemics), dress and appearance, and eye contact (occulesics). Vocalics, or paralanguage (the use of the voice), is covered in the chapter on delivery.

Body Movement/Kinesics

(Birdwhistell first identified **kinesics,** or the study of our use of the body to communicate. It includes gestures, posture, facial expressions, and other body movements.[37] Five research themes have emerged in kinesics: the use of emblems, illustrators, regulators, affect displays, and adaptors. A brief look at all five themes will provide a good orientation to the complex ways that we can use our bodies to send messages.

Emblems. An **emblem** is a nonverbal behavior that has a distinct verbal referent or even a denotative definition, and it is often used to send a specific message to others. The verbal referent is typically one or two words of a short phrase. For example, the "thumbs-up" hand gesture is listed in many dictionaries and is defined as a *gesture of approval*. There is a high level of agreement about the meaning of an emblem within cultures, but not usually across cultures.[38]

Most emblems are created with the hands, but we can create them in other ways. For example, a shoulder shrug suggests "I don't know," or a wrinkled nose indicates that "something stinks." But the emblems we are most familiar with are usually hand gestures. Try to make the gesture that goes with each of the following meanings:

- "Sit down beside me."
- "Follow me."
- "I can't hear you."
- "Be quiet!"
- "Shame on you!"

- "OK."
- "I promise."
- "What time is it?"
- "Good bye!"

In addition to everyday conversation, emblems are used by divers while under water, by police officers directing traffic, by construction workers, and by catchers, pitchers, and managers during baseball games. Don't forget the very familiar and more or less universal signal some people use to indicate displeasure with other drivers! Keep in mind, though, that the emblems you know are not always shared. The hand gesture we use for "come here," with the hand palm up with the index finger extending in and out three or four times, has a very different meaning in Latin America. It means that you are romantically interested in the person, and is considered a solicitation. Emblems can replace the verbal or reinforce it.

Police officers use emblems when directing traffic.
© Andrew Barker, 2008, Shutterstock.

Illustrators. An **illustrator** is a gesture that is used *with* language to emphasize, stress, or repeat what is being said. It can be used to give directions, show the size or shape of something, and give clarification. Can you imagine trying to explain to a new parent how to "burp" a baby without using illustrators? Can you give directions to the campus library with your hands in your pockets? Sure you could, but the illustrators add much meaning and clarification to your directions or instructions; they help with that function of clarifying. In a study done several years ago, speakers were found to be more persuasive when they used illustrators than when they did not.[39] More recent research has even extended the importance of illustrators. Robert Krauss found that gestures do more than amplify or accent verbal communication. They also help people retrieve ideas and words, such as when you try to define a term with a spatial meaning such as underneath, next to, and above, which Krauss calls *lexical retrieval.* If not done to excess, "talking with your hands" can be a very good thing!

A common communication regulator is a turn-requesting signal.
© 2008, JupiterImages.

Regulators. A **regulator** is a turn-taking signal that helps control the flow, the pace, and turn-taking in conversations, and you learned about their coordinating role earlier. If a group of people are talking and trying to share meaning, they must take turns speaking, and taking turns requires cooperation among the communicators. To accomplish this cooperation, along with the content of the conversation, participants must also communicate about who will speak next and when that turn will begin. Regulators help us with this task.[40]

Weimann and Knapp and Argyle identified four categories of turn related signals in a typical conversation:[41]

1. *Turn requesting* signals: These are used by a nonspeaker to take the floor. Nonverbal regulators used to request a turn include rapid head nods, forward leaning posture, and increased eye contact with the speaker.
2. *Turn yielding* signals: The speaker uses these to give up the floor. Nonverbal regulators used to yield a turn include increased eye contact with a nonspeaker, leaning back from a forward posture, or a sudden end to gesturing used while speaking.
3. *Turn maintenance* signals: These are used by the speaker to keep the floor (i.e., continue speaking). Nonverbal signals used to keep the turn include speaking louder or faster (increasing volume or rate of speech), continuing to gesture, or avoiding eye contact with the person requesting the turn.
4. *Back channel* signals: Nonspeaker refuses a turn that has been offered by the speaker. Nonverbal signals used to refuse a turn include nodding the head and avoiding eye contact with the person exhibiting a turn-yielding signal.

Affect Displays. An **affect display** is a form of nonverbal behavior that expresses emotions. Although this behavior is most often associated with facial expressions, affect can also be expressed through posture and gestures. These behaviors cannot only express the type of emotion being experienced, but can also express the intensity of the emotion. A smile suggests that you are happy. A slumped-over posture and a scowl on your face can suggest that you are unhappy, while your clinched fists and tense muscles can communicate just *how* unhappy you might be.

Can you make judgments about the nature and intensity of the emotions expressed on these faces?
© 2008, JupiterImages.

The emotions communicated by your face and body can affect the way you are perceived by other people. People who smile spontaneously are often considered by others to be more likable and more approachable than people who do not smile or people who just pretend to smile.[42]

Adaptors.

Adaptors are behaviors that can indicate our internal conditions or feelings to other people. We tend to use these behaviors when we become excited or anxious. Think about the kind of things that you do in communication situations when you feel nervous or excited. Do you scratch your head? Bite your nails? Play with your glasses? Rub your nose? You might not know, because most people are not aware of displaying these behaviors.

Adaptors are generally considered the least desirable type of nonverbal communication. Self-touching in this way could be a distraction to the audience, and it is often perceived as a sign of anxiety. One study found that deceivers bob their heads more often than people who tell the truth.[43] Cultural guidelines may prohibit these behaviors, too. Wriggling your nose or having a disgusted facial look to show that you're repulsed seems to have a universal meaning.[44]

What do these adaptors tell you about the internal feelings of the people in the photos?
© 2008, JupiterImages.

However, in some cultures, people are socialized to mask emotional cues, and in others they're taught to emphasize them. Latin Americans will usually greet friends and relatives more personally than do Americans. Everyone hugs, including the men. Men usually also greet woman with *besitos*, meaning they touch cheeks while making a kissing noise with their lips. Women also greet other women with *besitos*. These little kisses are purely friendly and have no romantic meaning. Maslow and colleagues[45] suggested that the anxiety displayed by adaptors can be interpreted by other communicators as a sign of deception; you are anxious because you are not being honest with the others and you fear being discovered!

Use of Space/Proxemics

The study of proxemics is typically divided into two applications: The use of personal space and how people claim and mark territory as their own. Most of us don't even think about the impact of space on our relationships, but research has shown that your use of space can influence shared meaning and impact your relationship. Knapp and Hall[46] found that our use of space can seriously affect our ability to achieve desired goals. Both applications can be used and managed by people to communicate fairly specific messages, and they can provide evidence to help us make judgments about person using the space.

Personal Space. When you consider the idea of **personal space,** think of a small amount of portable space that you carry around with you all the time. You control who is and who is not permitted inside of that space. Permission to enter that space is granted based on the relationship you have with that person, the context of the encounter, the culture in which you live, and your own personal preferences and tolerances. For example, you would be likely to allow business and professional colleagues to be reasonably close to you; you would allow good friends to be very close to you; and you would allow romantic partners to be closer still, even to the point of touching. In addition, you might allow people that you don't know to be very close to you in the appropriate context, like a crowded elevator or a busy airport.

When someone enters your space without permission, you can interpret it as a lack of courtesy, or even as a threat. You will feel uncomfortable, so you can either wait for the trespasser to move out of your space, or you can move away until you feel comfortable again.

The range of personal space varies across cultures. The box describes spaces typical to the culture in the United States. If you visit the United Kingdom, you will notice that these spaces are slightly expanded; that is, the British prefer just a bit more distance between people. By contrast, many Eastern cultures, including Asia and the Middle East, prefer a smaller distance. When these cultures meet, people from the United States often feel "crowded" by people from Asian cultures, while people from Japan might think that Americans are "cold" or "stand-offish" because of the increased interpersonal distances. As you can see, there is no shortage of opportunities for misunderstanding! Burgoon suggests that we want to stay near others, but we also want to maintain some distance—think about the dilemma this causes![47] Try to be sensitive to cultural norms when you assign meaning to the use of personal space.

Personal Distances

Hall recognized characteristic distances maintained between people in the U.S. culture, depending on their perceived relationships.[48] The distance categories are *intimate, personal, social,* and *public.*

Type	Distance	Who Is Permitted/Context
Intimate Distance  © Andrejs Pidjass, 2008, Shutterstock.	touching to 18 inches	**Who:** Spouses and family members, boyfriends and girlfriends, and very close friends. **Context:** A date with your spouse.
Personal Distance  © 2008, JupiterImages.	18 inches to 4 feet	**Who:** Good friends and people you know well. **Context:** Having lunch with a good friend or co-worker.
Social Distance  © 2008, JupiterImages.	4 feet to 12 feet	**Who:** Business associates, teachers, and people you know but with whom you have a professional but less social relationship. **Context:** A business meeting, small group discussion, or an employment interview.
Public Distance  © 2008, JupiterImages.	12 feet and beyond	**Who:** A person you don't know; a stranger on the street. **Context:** Giving a presentation to a large group; walking downtown on a public sidewalk.

Relationships affect the way we use space. Based on the use of space, describe the relationships in these photos. Be specific about the nonverbal clues that indicate the relationship.
(Photo credits: *left, center,* © 2008, JupiterImages, *right,* © Factoria singular fotografia, 2008, Shutterstock.)

Sometimes we allow our personal space to be violated.
© Racheal Grazias, 2008, Shutterstock.

Territoriality. We also have a tendency to claim space as our own. We have just looked at personal space, which is portable space that you carry around with you. Territory, by contrast, is not mobile; it stays in one place. You can think of territory as a kind of extension of you that is projected on to space or objects. Space that you occupy or control, and objects that belong to you or that you use regularly, are all important to you. If any person not authorized by you occupies that space or touches those objects, you feel violated and threatened. To help describe this kind of attachment to places and things, we turn to Altman, who classified territory into three categories: primary, secondary, and public.[49]

Primary territory is space or those items that you personally control. This includes personal items that only you would use, like your clothes and your toothbrush. It also includes the private spaces in your house like your bathroom and bedroom. Many people treat still other places as primary territory such as their car, their office at work, and even their refrigerator!

People mark their territory in many ways.
© 2008, JupiterImages.

Secondary territory is not your private property. That is, it is not owned by you, but it is typically associated with you. Examples of secondary territory include the desk you always use in class, the seat you always sit in at the office conference table, your favorite fishing spot at the lake, or your usual table at the library.

Public territory is available to anyone, so any space that you try to claim is only temporary. You might define your space on the beach by using markers such as blankets, beach chairs, or umbrellas. Or you might spread out your books and notes at the library to claim space on a work table. Our use of the territory lasts as long as we are using it, or as long as other people respect our markers.[50]

Most of us pay little attention to these claims of space, and we probably don't even realize that we do it. However, these claims come clearly to our attention when they are violated. It seems like there is almost nothing worse than walking into the classroom on the day of the big exam to find someone else in your seat! Sure, any seat will work just as well, but that is *your* seat where you feel most comfortable and confident. We tend to feel violated whenever any unauthorized person uses our space or touches our stuff!

Lyman and Scott identified three levels of **intrusion of territory:** violation, invasion, and contamination.[51] A *violation* happens when your space or your stuff is used without your permission, like when a neighbor borrows one of your tools without asking first. An *invasion* occurs when an unauthorized person enters the territory that you have claimed with markers. They might move your books and notes at the library (while you were looking for a book) and take over your space at the table, or they could cut in front of you in a check-out line at the grocery store. Finally, a *contamination* occurs when space that you claim is used without your authorization, but your evidence of the use is not the presence of the user but objects left behind. For example, you arrive at your office in the morning to find cups and fast food wrappers on your desk. There is nobody in your office, but you know somebody *was* there, and he or she was eating at your desk. Territory that you claim as your own should not be used by anyone without your permission. How you respond to territory depends very much on who invaded the territory and why it was invaded, which you'll see explained in expectancy violations theory, which follows later in this chapter.

Dress/Appearance

Your appearance, along with the way you dress, influences the way other people respond to you. In some situations, your appearance can be the *primary* factor that determines the response of others.[52] *Physical attractiveness*, as well as personal grooming and hygiene, weigh heavily on judgments that are made about you every day. If that's not enough pressure, along with protecting you from the environment and fulfilling cultural requirements for modesty, *clothing* is also a potent source of nonverbal information about you. Morris tells us that clothing sends continuous signals about us and who we think we are.[53] For example, watch the scene in the 1990 movie *Pretty Woman* when the character played by Julia Roberts first enters a "high-class" clothing store and is treated poorly by the staff. What about her appearance led to that treatment?

No one likes to have their territory violated.
© 2008, JupiterImages.

Among other qualities, clothing can suggest social and economic status, education, level of success, or trustworthiness and character. Morris suggests that clothing can be a cultural display and one that communicates something special about the wearer.[54] People have a tendency to express certain values central to their belief systems that indicate the kind of people they perceive themselves to be. Katz tells us that we hold and express particular attitudes to satisfy this need and that those attitudes reflect a positive view of ourselves.[55] Clothing and appearance are consistent with this concept. For example, if you consider yourself to be the "artistic" type, or a successful business person, or a talented athlete, your clothing choices will likely reflect that self image.

Gordon et al., suggests that clothing fulfills a number of symbolic functions:[56]

- Traditional and religious ceremonies often involve specific clothing.
- Self-beautification (real or imagined) is often reflected in clothing.
- Clothing expresses cultural values regarding sexual identity and practice.
- Clothes differentiate roles and levels of authority.
- Clothing is used in the acquisition and display of status.

Think about the way you dress and why you make those clothing choices. What are you trying to say? Are you trying to fit in? Are you trying to identify yourself with a particular group? Are you trying to show respect for an occasion or person?

Clothing is not the only aspect of appearance to consider. Think of the other personal choices people make with tattoos, body art, and personal grooming. What are the impacts of blue hair, black nail colors, Mohawks or dreadlocks, multiple piercing and colorful tattoos? You have the right to communicate about yourself in any way you want, but remember that if you go against cultural norms, you may be creating perceptual barriers that impede communication. Your appearance is a prime source of information that others use to make judgments about you. Try to use some care when making choices about how you should look in particular situations. You can always maintain your individuality, but you should also dress to show respect for the occasion and the people that you will be coming into contact with. If you have to give a presentation for a business group, for example, you can show your respect for the group by dressing in more formal attire. Wearing jeans with ripped out knees may say a lot about who you think you are, but wearing the suit for the business group also communicates who you think you are. You are someone who combines your own needs with a respect for the needs of other people!

How could her tattoos impact others' perceptions?
© Ronald Sumners, 2008, Shutterstock.

Eye Movement/Occulesics

In many Western cultures, including the United States, making **eye contact** with another person is considered a sign of sincerity, caring, honesty, and sometimes power or status.[57] Pearson found that men sometimes use eye contact to challenge others and to assert themselves.[58] Women tend to hold eye contact more than men, regardless of the sex of the person that they're interacting with.[59] Some Eastern cultures view eye contact with others as an impolite invasion of privacy and they especially disapprove of eye contact with a person of higher status. In another study, it was found that inner-city

African-American persuaders look continually at the listener, and African American listeners tend to look away from the persuader most of the time. The opposite is true of middle-class Whites; as persuaders, they look only occasionally at the listener, and White listeners look continuously at the persuader. This could explain why the two groups could have incorrect inferences about the amount of interest the other has when they communicate.[60]

We consider the use of eye contact to be an essential tool for achieving communication goals. In U.S. culture, how does it make you feel when someone will not make eye contact with you? Do you trust this person? Do you suspect his or her motives?

Eye contact helps us communicate in at least four ways: It can open a channel of communication, demonstrate concern, gather feedback, and moderate anxiety.[61]

Open a Communication Channel. You can let others know that you would like to communicate with them by simply looking at them. A brief moment of eye contact can open a channel of communication and make other messages possible.

Demonstrate Concern. Engaging other people in eye contact during conversations shows a concern for them, as well as your commitment that they understand your message. In addition, eye contact can be used to communicate liking and attraction.

Gather Feedback. If you would like information about what other people are thinking, take a look at their eyes. You won't be able to read thoughts, but you can certainly find clues to indicate that they are listening, that they understand the message, and perhaps that they care about what you are saying. The old adage that speakers should look at the back wall of the room when giving a public speech is pretty bad advice; you will miss out on critical information about the frame of mind of audience members, as well as other feedback essential to achieving your goals.

Moderate Anxiety. When speakers get nervous or anxious during a public presentation, they have a tendency to avoid eye contact with the listeners by either looking at the floor, the back wall of the room, or at their notes. As they continue to stare at the floor, anxiety (fear of unknown outcomes) continues to build. Occasionally, but rarely, anxiety can build to the point at which it completely takes over, and the speaker freezes. You can avoid this scenario through *careful preparation* for the event, and by allowing the listeners to provide you with support. By *establishing eye contact* with members of your audience, you will see listeners smiling at you or expressing support with their posture, head nods, or other behaviors. Not looking at the audience or conversational partners removes your opportunity to get or give supportive feedback. When others notice your anxiety, they usually want to help you. Look at the audience, feel the support and try to relax, and then refocus on your communication goals.

By making eye contact with others, you can find clues about their level of understanding and interest.
© Dmitriy Shironosov, 2008, Shutterstock.

HOW DOES THEORY DESCRIBE NONVERBAL BEHAVIOR'S IMPACT ON RELATIONSHIPS?

Have you ever played elevator games with strangers? You know, you enter an empty elevator and take the "power position" by the buttons. At the next floor, someone enters and either asks you to push the button for a floor or reaches in front of you to select a floor and then retreats to the opposite corner away from you. There's no further talk or eye contact. The next person who enters does the same thing, finding a corner. Everyone faces the doors, anticipates its opening, watching the numbers change as if by magic. If others enter, their volume drops to a hush, or they stop talking until they leave. Now, have you ever tried *this*? Get on an elevator and keep walking until you face the back wall. After all, that's how you entered, right? Go stand right next to the power person, real close. Keep talking real loud. Sit down on your backpack or luggage. What do you think will happen? How will others react to you?

One theory that attempts to explain the influence of nonverbal communication on meaning and relationships is **expectancy violations theory.** Judee Burgoon said that "nonverbal cues are an inherent and essential part of message creation (production) and interpretation (processing)."[62] Expectancy violations theory (EVT) suggests that we hold expectations about the nonverbal behavior of others. It asserts that when communicative norms are violated, the violation may be perceived either favorably or unfavorably, depending on the perception that the receiver has of the violator. Burgoon's early writing on EVT integrated Hall's ideas on personal space (which you read about earlier) as a core aspect of the theory.[63] EVT says that our *expectancies* are the thoughts and behaviors anticipated when we interact with another.

We have expectations of how others ought to think and behave. Levine says that these expectancies are a result of social norms, stereotypes, and your own personal idiosyncrasies, and these expectancies cause us to interact with others.[64] We have both preinteractional and interactional expectations. *Preinteractional* expectations are made up of the skills and knowledge you bring to an interaction; *interactional expectations* are your skills and knowledge that let you carry out the interaction.

Another basic idea of EVT is that we learn our expectations from our cultures: You've learned what kind of touching is appropriate with whom, how to greet a stranger, and where to stand in relationship with another, for example.

Finally, EVT says that we make predictions about others based on their nonverbal behavior. So how does this work? Let's say you're standing in line at the grocery store, and the person in front of you looks at what you're about to buy and then makes eye contact with you. At first, you might be uncomfortable, thinking that the person is judging you by the way she is eyeing your groceries. If she then gives you a warm smile and points to her big pile containing the same things, you might feel a bit more comfortable. You've made predictions based on nonverbal behavior: The person is not threatening or judging you negatively.

But EVT is about *violations* of our expectations. Burgoon says that when people deviate from expectations, that deviation is judged based on the other's ability to reward us. A reward could be something as simple as a smile, friendliness, or acknowledgment of competence. This potential to reward is called *communicator reward valence*, which is the interactants' ability to reward or punish and the positive and negative characteristics they have. Someone in power, like your professor for instance, may have more communicator reward valence than a stranger, because the professor has the power of grades and probably has more credibility for you. If someone violates our expectations, these deviations cause *arousal*, an increased attention to the deviation.[65] Cognitive arousal is mental awareness of the deviation; physical arousal involves physiological heightening. For instance, if a person stares at you, you might wonder why he's doing that (cognitive arousal) or you might start to sweat (physical arousal). Once arousal happens, threats occur. Your *threat threshold* is the tolerance you have for deviations; how threatened do you feel? Maybe you don't mind if another person stands too close; maybe you can't put up with someone staring at you. The size of your threat threshold is based on how you view the person who is deviating from your expectations; what is that other's communicator reward valence? Then you add in the *violation valence*, which consists of your positive or negative value placed towards the deviations from your expectations.

When someone violates one of your expectations (for instance, he touches you when you didn't expect it), you interpret the meaning of that violation and decide if you like it or not. If you don't like it, then the violation valence is negative; if the surprise was pleasant (even though you didn't expect it), then the violation valence is positive. The theory predicts that if a violation is ambiguous, then the communicator reward valence will influence how you interpret and evaluate the violation. If the person is someone you like, then you'll positively evaluate his violation; if you don't like him, then you'll negatively evaluate his violation. Take a simple example of how someone is dressed. On an interview, there are certain expectations of how you should look. If you go in wearing jeans and a t-shirt and the company wants its workers to wear suits,

On an interview, you want to be positively evaluated.
© iofoto, 2008, Shutterstock.

then you've violated expectancies. It's pretty likely that you don't have any power here, or any way to reward the company for hiring you. Thus, the interviewer will evaluate you negatively, feeling aroused that you didn't understand such a basic concept like appropriate attire. However, what if you are a highly sought-after, uniquely imaginative individual that the company has been pursuing? Your violation of the dress code might be seen positively; you're bold and creative, just like they thought. EVT is an interesting theory that focuses on what we expect nonverbally in conversations, as well as suggesting what happens when our expectations aren't met. It's very practical in applications across many contexts.

WHAT ARE THE KEY POINTS TO REMEMBER ABOUT NONVERBAL COMMUNICATION?

Nonverbal communication is a complex combination of behaviors that form a source of information used by other people to make sense of messages that you send. Even though much of your nonverbal behavior is spontaneous and unconscious, you should realize that it contributes a significant percentage of the meaning that people attribute to your messages. As such, you should try as hard as you can to be a good self-monitor and pay close attention to your nonverbal behaviors. However, nonverbal behavior is also a source of information for you. It can help you to more accurately interpret the communication of others, so pay attention!

Be careful to not overgeneralize the meanings of particular nonverbal cues. The specific meaning of any nonverbal behavior is typically dependent on multiple factors, including (but not limited to) culture, the relationship between the people communicating, the specific communication context, and individual characteristics of the participants. You wouldn't want others to make stereotypical assumptions about your behavior, so make sure that you don't make those same assumptions about the behavior of others. Gather as much information as possible before reaching conclusions. Sometimes a touch is just a touch!

SUMMARY

Verbal and nonverbal communication are powerful, critically important elements in the creation of shared meaning, because they have the ability to clarify your ideas to others or to confuse them. It's not always easy to use language or nonverbal behavior correctly, because both are arbitrary and ambiguous. The relationship that words or movements have with ideas is not based on a concrete characteristic; instead, you are relying on the ability of the audience to associate your symbols with their cognitions (beliefs, attitudes, and values). You've been exposed to some theoretical explanations of how these attempts to create meaning work in our lives. We interpret language and nonverbal communication because of our particular culture, which provides a frame of reference on how to assign meaning. In order to be a competent communicator, you need to remain aware that your words aren't always understood as you mean them to be and that your nonverbal behavior can supplement or contradict those words. The next chapters will let you put those meanings into action!

ENDNOTES

1. Language and Culture, Introduction, http://anthro.palomar.edu/language/language_1.htm.

2. "Internet World Users by Language," Internet World Stats, http://www.internetworldstats.com/stats7.htm (accessed Sept. 22, 2007).

3. In 1997, the Science Citation Index reported that 95 percent of its articles were written in English, even though only half of them came from authors in English-speaking countries. David Graddol, "The Future of English?" (digital edition), http://www.britishcouncil.org/de/learning-elt-future.pdf (accessed Sep. 22, 2007).

4. G. H. Mead, *Mind, Self and Society; From the Standpoint of a Social Behaviorist* (Chicago: University of Chicago Press, 1934).

5. "Top Television Buzzwords of 2007," The Global Language Monitor. http://www.languagemonitor.com/wst_pagell.html (accessed Sept. 22, 2007).

6. E. Natalle, with J. L. Flippen, "Urban Music: Gendered Language in Rapping," in Philip Backlund and M. R. Williams (ed.) *Readings in Gender Communication* (Belmont, CA: Wadsworth-Thompson, 2004), 140–149.

7. "Remarks by the President after Two Planes Crashed into World Trade Center," http://www.whitehouse.gov/news/releases/2001/09/20010911.html (accessed Sept. 22, 2007).

8. "Remarks by the President Upon Arrival at Barksdale Air Force Base," http://www.whitehouse.gov/news/releases/2001/09/20010911-1.html (accessed Sept. 22, 2007).

9. "Statement by the President in His Address to the Nation," http://www.whitehouse.gov/news/releases/2001/09/20010911-16.html (accessed Sept. 22, 2007).

10. D. Berlo, *The Process of Communication* (New York, Holt, Rinehart and Winston Inc., 1960).

11. "Adopt-a Confusion" Perspectives Press, http://www.perspectivespress.com/pjadopta.html (accessed Sept. 22, 2007).

12. Cronen, Pearce, and Snavely 1979. Vernon E. Cronen, W. Barnett Pearce, and Lonna Snavely (1979). "A Theory of Rule Structure and Forms of Episodes, and a Study of Unwanted Repetitive Patterns (URPs)," pp.225–240 in Dan Nimmo, ed. Communication Yearbook III. Edison, NJ: Transaction Books.

13. C. K. Ogden and I. A. Richards, *The Meaning of Meaning,* 8th ed. (New York, Harcourt, Brace & World, 1923), 9–12.

14. S. Trenholm, *Thinking through Communication* (Boston: Allyn and Bacon, 2000), 87.

15. L. A. M. Perry and D. Ballard-Reisch, "There's a Rainbow in the Closet," in Philip Backlund and M. R. Williams (ed.), *Readings in Gender Communication* (Belmont, CA: Wadsworth-Thompson, 2004), 17–34.

16. Bipolar.com http://www.bipolar.com/ (accessed May 1, 2008).

17. C. Kramarae, *Women and Men Speaking: Frameworks for Analysis* (Rowley, MA: Newbury House, 1981), 1.

18. Ibid.

19. J. T. Wood. *Communication in Our Lives,* 4th ed. (Belmont, CA: Thompson Wadsworth, 2006), 137.

20. Urban dictionary http://www.urbandictionary.com/ (accessed Sept. 12, 2007).

21. Lake Superior State University, "List of Banished Words," http://stuft.vox.com/library/post/lakesuperior-state-university-2007-list-of-banished-words.html (accessed Sept. 12, 2007).

22. M. Orbe and C. Bruess, *Contemporary Issues in Interpersonal Communication* (Los Angeles: Roxbury, 2005).

23. D. O'Hair, G. Friedrich, and L. Dixon, *Strategic Communication in Business and the Professions* (Boston: Houghton Mifflin, 2005).

24. K. Adams and G. Galanes, *Communicating in Groups: Applications and Skills* (Boston: McGraw-Hill, 2006).

25. R. Adler, L. Rosenfeld, and R. Proctor, *Interplay: The Process of Interpersonal Communication* (New York: Oxford University Press, 2004).

26. J. Burgoon and A. Bacue, "Nonverbal Communication Skills," in J. Greene and B. Burleson (eds.), *Handbook of Communication and Social Interaction Skills* (Mahwah, NJ: Lawrence Erlbaum, 2003).

27. F. Manusov, "Perceiving Nonverbal Messages: Effects of Immidiacy and Encoded Intent on Receiver Judgements," *Western Journal of Speech Communication* 55 (Summer 1991), 235–253. Also M. Knapp and Hall, *Nonverbal Communication in Human Interaction,* 6th ed. (2005).

28. R. L. Birdwhistell, "Background to Kinesics." *Etc.* 13, (1955), 10–18.

29. A. Mehrabian and S. Ferris, "Inference of Attitudes from Nonverbal Communication in Two Channels," *Journal of Consulting Psychology* 31 (1967), 248–252.

30. J. Shapiro, "Responsivity to Facial and Linguistic Cues," *Journal of Communication,* 18 (1968), 11–17. Also L. Vande Creek and J. Watkins, "Responses to incongruent verbal and nonverbal emotional cues," *Journal of Communication,* 22 (1972), 311–316; and D. Solomon and F. Ali, "Influence of Verbal Content and Intonation on Meaning Attributions of First-and-Second-Language Speakers," *Journal of Social Psychology,* 95 (1975), 3–8.

31. "The Kennedy-Nixon Presidential Debates, 1960," The Museum of Broadcast Communications, http://www.museum.tv/archives/etv/k/htmlk/kennedy-nixon/kennedy-nixon.htm (accessed May 1, 2008).

32. K. Drummond and R. Hopper, "Acknowledgment Tokens in Series," *Communication Reports* 6, (1993), 47–53.

33. R. Riggio and H. Freeman,"Individual Differences and Cues to Deception," *Journal of Personality and Social Psyhchology* 45 (1983), 899–915.

34. J. Burgoon, D. Buller, L. Guerrero, and C. Feldman, "Interpersonal Deception: VI, Effects on Preinteractinal and International Factors on Deceiver and Observer Perceptions of Deception Success," *Communication Studies,* 45 (1994), 263–280.

35. A. Vrij, K. Edward, K. Roberts, and R. Bull, (2002). Detecting deceit via analysis of verbal and nonverbal behavior. *Journal of Nonverbal Behavior* 24, 239–263.

36. Burgoon et al.

37. R. Birdwhistell, *Kinesics and Context* (Philadelphia: University of Pennsylvania Press, 1970).

38. P. Ekman, "Movements with Precise Meanings," *Journal of Communication* 26 (1976), 14–26.

39. A. Mehrabian and M. Williams, "Nonverbal Concomitants of Perceived and Intended Persuasiveness," *Journal of Personality and Social Psychology* 13 (1969), 37–58.

40. G. Savage (1978). Endings and beginnings: Turn taking and the small group in Wall, V. (ed.), Small Group Communication: Selected Readings (Columbus, OH: Collegiate).

41. J. Weimann and M. Knapp, "Turn Taking and Conversations," *Journal of Communication* 25 (1975), 75–92. Also M. Argyle, *Bodily Communication* (New York: International Universities Press, 1975).

42. G. Gladstone and G. Parker, "When You're Smiling, Does the Whole World Smile for You?" *Australasian Psychiatry* 10 (2002), 144–146.

43. W. Donaghy and B. F. Dooley, "Head Movement, Gender, and Deceptive Communication," *Communication Reports* 7 (1994), 67–75.

44. J. Martin and T. Nakayama, *Intercultural Communication in Contexts* (New York: McGraw Hill, 2000).

45. C. Maslow, K. Yoselson, and H. London, "Persuasiveness of Confidence Expressed via Language and Body Language," *British Journal of Social and Clinical Psychology,* 10 (1971), 234–240.

46. Knapp and Hall, 2005.

47. J. Burgoon, "A Communication Model of Personal Space Violations: Explication and an Initial Test," *Human Communication Research,* 4 (1978), 129–142. Also J. Burgoon, "Nonverbal Signals," in M. Knapp and G. Miller (eds.), *Handbook of Interpersonal Communication* (Thousand Oaks, CA: Sage, 1994); and J. Burgoon, "Spatial Relationships in Small Groups," in R. Cathcart, L. Samovar, and L. Heaman, *Small Group Communication: Theory and Practice* (Madison, WI: Brown, 1996).

48. E. T. Hall, *The Silent Language* (Garden City, NY: Doubleday, 1959); and E. T. Hall, "A System for the Notation of Proxemic Behavior," *American Anthropologist,* 65 (1963), 1003–1026.

49. I. Altman, *The Environment and Social Behavior* (Monterey, CA: Brooks Cole, 1975).

50. L. Malandro, L. Barker, and D. Barker, *Nonverbal Communication* (New York: Random House, 1989).

51. S. Lyman and M. Scott, "Territoriality: A Neglected Sociological Dimension," *Social Problems* 15 (1967), 236–249.

52. M. Knapp, *Essentials of Nonverbal Communication* (New York: Holt, Rinehart & Winston, 1992).

53. D. Morris, *Manwatching: A Field Guide to Human Behavior* (New York: Harry N. Abrams, 1977).

54. Ibid.

55. D. Katz, "The Functional Approach to the Study of Attitudes," *Public Opinion Quarterly* 24 (1960), 163–204.

56. W. Gordon, C. Teagler, and D. Infante, "Women's Clothing as Predictors of Dress at Work, Job Satisfaction, and Career Advancement," *Southern States Speech Communication Journal* 47 (1982), 422–434.

57. P. Andersen, *Nonverbal Communication: Forms and Functions* (Mountain View, CA: Mayfield, 1999). Also D. Leathers, *Successful Nonverbal Communication: Principles and Applications*, 3rd ed. (Boston: Allyn and Bacon, 1997).

58. J. Pearson, *Gender and Communication* (Dubuque, IA: William C. Brown, 1985).

59. J. Wood, *Gendered Lives: Communication, Gender, and Culture*, 5th ed. (Belmont, CA: Wadsworth, 2002), 141.

60. S. Rosenberg, S. Kahn, and T. Tran, "Creating a Political Image: Shaping Appearance and Manipulating the Vote," *Political Behavior* 13 (1991), 347.

61. S. Wallace, D. Yoder, L. Hugenberg, and C. Horvath, *Creating Competent Communication: Interviewing.* (Dubuque, IA: Kendall/Hunt Publishing, 2006).

62. Burgoon, 1994.

63. Burgoon, 1978.

64. T. R. Levine, L. Anders, J. Banas, K. Baum, K. Endo, A. Hu, and C. Wong, "Norms, Expectations, and Deception: A Norm Violation Model of Veracity Judgments," *Communication Monographs* 67 (2000), 123–137.

65. Burgoon, 1978. P. 133

REFERENCES

D. Berlo (1960). *The Process of Communication.* New York, Holt, Rinehart and Winston Inc.

S. Campo, K. A. Cameron, D. Brossard, and M. Frazer (2004) "Social norms and expectancy violations theories: Assessing the effectiveness of health communication campaigns." Communication Monographs 71, 448–470

P. Ekman and W. Friesen (1975). *Unmasking the face.* Englewood Cliffs, NJ: Prentice-Hall.

P. Ekman and W. Friesen (1969). The repertoire of nonverbal behavior: Categories, origins, usage, and coding. *Semiotica, 1,* 49–98.

R. Gass and J. Seiter (2003). *Persuasion, social influence, and compliance gaining.* Boston: Allyn & Bacon.

D. Graddol (2000). The Future of English? (digital edition). http://www.britishcouncil.org/de/learning-elt-future.pdf

J. Hornick (1992). Tactile stimulation and consumer response. *Journal of consumer research, 19,* 449–458.

L. Howells and S. Becker (1962). Seating arrangement as leadership emergence. *Journal of abnormal and social psychology, 64,* 148–150.

D. Kaufman and J. Mahoney (1999). The effect of waitress touch on alcohol consumption in dyads. *Journal of social psychology, 139,* 261–267.

C. Kramarae (1981), Women and men speaking: Frameworks for analysis. Rowley, MA: Newbury house.

R. M. Krauss and U. Hadar (1999). The role of speech-related arm/hand gestures in word retrieval. In, R. Campbell & L. Messing (Eds.), Gesture, speech, and sign (pp. 93–116). Oxford: Oxford University Press.

E. Morsella and R. M. Krauss (in press). The role of gestures in spatial working memory and speech. American Journal of Psychology. http://www.columbia.edu/cu/psychology/commlab/publications.html (retrieved Sept. 28, 2007)

G. H. Mead (1934). *Mind, self and society; From the standpoint of a social behaviorist.* Chicago: University of Chicago press.

E. Natalle and J. Flippen (2004). Urban Music: Gendered language in Rapping. In Backlund, P., and Williams, M. (ed) *Readings in Gender Communication.* Belmont, CA: Wadsworth-Thompson. 140–149.

C. K. Ogden and I. A. Richards (1923). *The Meaning of Meaning.* New York, Harcourt, Brace & World, Inc., 9–12.

L. Perry and D. Ballard-Reisch (2004). There's a Rainbow in the closet. In Backlund, P., & Williams, M. (ed.). *Readings in Gender Communication*, Belmont, CA: Wadsworth-Thompson, 2004, 17–34.

S. Rosenberg, S. Kahn, and T. Tran (1991). "Creating a political image: Shaping appearance and manipulating the vote." Political Behavior 13, 345–367 P. 347

G. Savage (1978). Endings and beginnings: Turn taking and the small group. In Wall, V. (ed). *Small group communication: Selected readings*. Columbus: Collegiate.

F. Strodtbeck and L. Hook (1961). The social dimensions of a twelve man jury table. *Sociometry, 24,* 297–415.

G. Trager (1958). Paralanguage: A first approximation. *Studies in linguistics, 13,* 1–12.

S. Trenholm (2000). *Thinking through Communication*. Boston: Allyn and Bacon.

J. Wood (2006). *Communication in Our Lives, Fourth Ed.* Belmont, CA: Thompson Wadsworth, 2006.

How Can I Become a Credible Source?

LEARNING OBJECTIVES

After reading this chapter, you should understand the following concepts:

- The qualities of credibility include character, intelligence, goodwill, and charisma.
- Credibility is dynamic, and creating a credible persona is not without risk.
- Speech anxiety has physiological, cognitive, and behavioral dimensions to it. Its causes can be situational or traitlike.
- Speech anxiety can be managed using techniques such as visualization, systematic desensitization, and cognitive restructuring.

INTRODUCTION

Imagine that you are going to sit in for a late-night talk-show host, and you get to choose your guests. One will be an important politician or social leader, one will be an actor or director, and one will be a musician or writer. These people can be living or dead. Who would you choose, and why? The *why* reveals what is important to you when you consider the draw of these guests. Are you interested in people who have made a difference? Perhaps it is power that lures you. Maybe it is someone's sex appeal or the characters that person has played. There might be something about a singer that compels you. (Think of the voting in shows like *American Idol*. Does the best singer win, or is there something else at work there?) We know that audiences are deeply affected by their perceptions of the person who is delivering the message. They may accept or reject the message based on how well the other dresses, vocally or physically presents ideas, or even some unknown quality involving "likeability." These audience perceptions of believability are known as the speaker's *ethos* or *credibility*.

Credibility is constructed; it is developed, maintained, and changed through communication activity. Keep in mind that credibility is the *impression* of others that are placed on a source, but rather than repeating *perception of credibility*, this chapter will use the simple term. Credibility might be applied to a person, to an organization, or even to a Web site or other media form. In examining credibility, we will consider the qualities that affect credibility, the stages that credibility may progress through, and strategies that you can make use of when attempting to enhance others' perceptions.[1] In addition, we will explore communication apprehension, which limits your ability to be an effective, credible communicator.

KEYWORDS

credibility
character
intelligence
goodwill
charisma
initial credibility
derived credibility
terminal credibility
mystification
speech anxiety
communication
  apprehension
physiological dimensions
cognitive dimensions
behavioral dimensions
situational anxiety
traitlike anxiety
visualization
systematic desensitization
cognitive restructuring

WHAT ARE THE QUALITIES OF CREDIBILITY?

In Book Two of his *Rhetoric,* Aristotle investigated the qualities that make up the audience's perception of the speaker's ethos. The first quality, *character,* involves the perceived integrity, sincerity, honesty, or trustworthiness of the communicator. The second, *intelligence,* is based on a perception of the speaker's apparent expertise, competence, or knowledge. The third, *goodwill,* consists of the audience's perception that the speaker has its best interest at heart; the speaker is not communicating just for self-betterment.[2] In contemporary studies, a fourth quality, *charisma,* has been added. Charisma is a sense of power, energy, or attractiveness that draws an audience in.[3]

While a communicator may have strategies that impact these four qualities, it is essential to remember that your believability exists in the audience's minds. We know that these qualities are perceived differently by receivers. Think about someone that you find very attractive; a friend might wonder aloud at your taste. You might think that someone who has many degrees is very smart; your friend might say that this person's foul language shows he is not. Preteens might idolize Paris, Britney, Lindsay, and Nicole (their last names aren't even important); their parents probably wonder why bad behavior is a draw.

In addition, the perception of credibility elements might clash. President Bill Clinton was a Rhodes Scholar; that suggests intelligence. Yet his extramarital affair cast doubt on his character. You might pine for a beautiful member of the opposite sex and find her very charismatic, but you are dismayed as you watch her cut down everyone around her, showing a lack of goodwill. In another vein, who do you believe when selecting what course to take, what restaurant to eat at, where to get your news? How do you make those decisions? Perhaps you follow the media polls that proclaim whose approval ratings are rising or falling, who is the most beautiful, who is the most powerful.[4] Credibility is essential to communicating, and you cannot accurately predict how the audience will perceive you. However, there are some simple techniques that you can consider to enhance audience impressions. Hopefully, you believe in what you are communicating; sincerity shows in the words you choose and the manner in which you speak or write.

Character

Character includes perception of integrity, honor, trust, altruism, and ethics. President Dwight D. Eisenhower said this:

> In order to be a leader a man must have followers. And to have followers, a man must have their confidence. Hence, the supreme quality for a leader is unquestionably integrity. Without it, no real success is possible, no matter whether it is on a section gang, a football field, in an army, or in an office. If a man's associates find him guilty of being phony, if they find that he lacks forthright integrity, he will fail. His teachings and actions must square with each other. The first great need, therefore, is integrity and high purpose.[5]

One strategy to enhance character is to maintain eye contact with your listeners. Think about someone who will not look at you as he speaks; how do you judge his character? Most likely, you feel that he is less than honest or is trying to hide something. Eye contact is an essential feature of delivery, and it can add a dimension to your audience's perception of your honesty. As an example, here's what Synchronics Group, a pre-trial consulting firm recommends:

> Losing eye contact is particularly devastating in the courtroom. A good opposing counsel will pick up on the hesitation and attack the witness with it.
>
> Maintaining a steady eye contact under assault makes your witness look steadfast and invincible in the eyes of the jurors. Jurors often do not understand the questions that are being asked, or the answers that are being offered, during cross-examination. They might miss the substance of the power play, but they are aware of the struggle. And any witness who meets the verbal assaults of opposing counsel without batting an eye communicates self-confidence and authority.[6]

Maintaining steady eye contact makes you look steadfast in the eyes of jurors.
© Tim Pannell/Corbis

You could also use personal examples that show you have experienced what you are talking about; self-narratives have the power to create credibility. For instance, if your speech is about immigration reform, your credibility will be given added weight if you can relate to the struggles that immigrants go through, either because you came to the United States via immigration, or because you have association with those who have those experiences. Members of the audience may think, "Well, if that's happened to him, I can see how it impacts me." In this way, you will be seen as "practicing what you preach." In one class, a female student revealed that she was a breast cancer survivor. She explained how she had gone through chemo at twenty-one. The young audience's perception of her ethos was much stronger than if she had just said, "You should check for breast cancer," because in this case, it was someone their age who shared her actual experience.

Intelligence

Intelligence is a perception of competence, expertise, and knowledge. Intelligence can be projected by careful preparation, supporting details, and clear language. Your messages (whether they are speeches, group presentations, interviews, or other communication activities) should be supported by research, should provide a variety of believable supporting materials, and should use appropriate language. Other chapters deal with gathering evidence and developing delivery strategies, and later in this chapter you'll think about language, but think of it this way for now. How much do you believe someone when you ask, "Where were you?" and the answer is, "Around." What about someone who argues that you should really see this new movie, "Because it is good."

You need to provide supporting materials that let the audience know that you have a grasp of the facts. Cite the research that you've conducted; if you can include sources that are respected by your listeners, your credibility will be enhanced. Explain your competence or expertise; why should your listeners believe you? Did you experience this topic? Did you investigate it through research? What qualifies you to speak on this subject?

You also need to speak in terms that the audience will immediately grasp, or you need to define your terms so you are speaking at their level. You'll learn some definition techniques when you read about informative speaking, but for now, just remember that your audience will be lost if they're not using a term in the same way as you are. If you think that *criticism* means judging or analyzing, and your audience perceives it to be negative statements, a simple concept can become very confusing.

You can also help the audience's perceptions of your intelligence by skillful delivery, which is covered in its own chapter. We tend to attribute expertise to someone who exudes confidence and competence in speaking or writing. A hesitant vocal or physical delivery may create an impression of someone who is unsure of the facts. Someone who uses instant messaging (IM) to send an important response to a job offer may be seen as not qualified; the IM language and acronyms, designed for the simplistic context, are not appropriate for "more important" communication. Think of delivery as all of the ways you send that message. Is the impact of the message, "I want to break up with you," different if it is sent via text message, e-mail, phone message, through a third party, or in person? Yes, the message is important, but it is safe to assume that the *way* it is delivered will also receive much attention in terms of perceiving your ethos.

Goodwill

Goodwill suggests to the audience that you care for them more than yourself. Goodwill is an aspect that your message should naturally create, because communication centers on strategies that make speaking other-directed. If you have done an adequate context analysis of the audience and occasion, you know what is needed to let the audience know their needs come first.

One specific technique of enhancing the impression of goodwill is to adapt your supporting materials to the audience whenever possible. This means, for example, that statistics should be translated into specific audience terms so they are understandable. If you were trying to convince people to spay or neuter their pets, you need to drive that home. The U.S. Humane Society says that the average number of litters a fertile dog can produce in one year is two. That results in an average number six to ten puppies. In six years, one female dog and her offspring can theoretically produce 67,000 dogs.[7] Imagine translating that number into the members of your audience. How many dogs would they have to adopt to manage that number? How would those numbers look when visually displayed without numerals? You might also use examples to which the audience can relate; find out how many are pet owners, how many have visited a shelter, how many know someone who has gotten a pet but has acted irresponsibly toward that pet because veterinary care costs too much? In addition to adapting your supports, your use of language that reflects the culture and level of the group is essential.

Finally, your use of clear organization, including summaries for listening guidance and specific structure, will also give the audience a sense that you care about their understanding. If you want to see the "anti-goodwill" strategies in action, think about poorly planned meetings, jokes told that have made you uncomfortable, stores where salespeople hover over you (making you think that they are waiting for you to shoplift), or classes where the language is so far over your head that the instructor might as well be speaking in a foreign tongue. Goodwill places an expectation on you: When you communicate, you need to show the audience that you have put them ahead of yourself.

Charisma

But what about **charisma?** Is it something you are born with? We cannot all be Brad Pitt, Nelson Mandella, Jennifer Lopez, Billy Graham, or Saddam Hussein (and perhaps when you read some of those names, your reaction was, "Those people do not have charisma, as far as I'm concerned.") This element is probably the most difficult to conceptualize and to promote, because it is the most personal, individualized, and fleeting. Max Weber defined someone possessing charisma as "an individual personality set apart from ordinary people and endowed with supernatural, superhuman powers, and heroic qualities. In short part Hero, and part Superman/Superwoman."[8]

Do you know someone who has that special "something?"
© Aurelio, 2008, Shutterstock.

If you think about people who have that "something," people you would like to be around because of the energy, life, and personality they possess, your list would probably be very different from someone else's.[9] Your list might include former president Ronald Reagan, country singer Tim McGraw, Quincy Jones, your best friend, your favorite elementary teacher, and the late Reverend Jerry Falwell. Someone else might scoff at all of these choices. Certainly, all of these people are very different from each other, but each has a fascination for you. Although you might not appreciate the positions they took, you might admire something about them. It is difficult to identify exactly what makes a person charismatic, but there appear to be a few strategies that you can try to give your message a feeling of energy, which is an element of charisma. In speaking, you can truly be enthusiastic about your topic. If you are disinterested or bored, it will show in your manner, and your speech will be flat. You can appear dynamic and alive in front of your audience; a person whose delivery is low-keyed, riveted to a manuscript, and hidden behind a lectern will not inspire much personal confidence on your part.

Enthusiasm can be contagious; if you can connect with the audience by showing that you are enthusiastic about your message, it's likely that the audience will take on some of that passion.

Projecting Charisma with Fonts

If you are presenting materials visually, consider color composition, font type and size, and amount of information presented—each might suggest some aspect of personality. If you do not believe that, reflect on how you perceive the following statement, each presented in a different font type:

Secretary of State Condoleezza Rice told off her critics with a stern look and said, "We do not comment on terrorist investigations."

Secretary of State Condoleezza Rice told off her critics with a stern look and said, "We do not comment on terrorist investigations."

Secretary of State Condoleezza Rice told off her critics with a stern look and said, "We do not comment on terrorist investigations."

Secretary of State Condoleezza Rice told off her critics with a stern look and said, "We do not comment on terrorist investigations."

Do the fonts chosen impact how you read this statement? Do they suggest a different "personality" behind the statement?

Let's sum up the suggestions for a communicator to have input on the audience's impression for credibility. Be prepared. Have a well organized, well-supported message, and be flexible enough to alter it if needed. Be ready to answer questions competently. Use language that is adapted to the audience; you do not want to insult them by talking down, but if you have any doubts about their ability to comprehend what you're saying, then define, describe, and illustrate with examples. If you share group affiliation (because of your age, location, educational or work experiences, cultural background, or organizational membership), be sure to incorporate those affiliations into your message if appropriate by referring to them or using supporting materials which will reinforce them. Persuading another by talking his or her language by "speech, gesture, tonality, order, image, attitude, and idea," is called *identification* by rhetorical theorist Kenneth Burke.[10] In simpler terms, this is called establishing common ground, or *homophily.* If a listener feels that you both share similar backgrounds, attributes, concerns, beliefs, and values, you are more likely to be believed. Infomercials make millions of dollars a year on that premise, despite questionable product claims and late-night direct response marketing.[11]

HOW DOES CREDIBILITY CHANGE?

Because credibility is dynamic, ideas about what constitutes it vary because of era, context, and culture. Martha Stewart's image was the personification of gracious living as portrayed in her magazines and two popular television programs, as the author of several books and hundreds of articles on homemaking, and commercial spokeswoman for K-Mart. In 2001, she was named one of the thirty most powerful women in America, and third most powerful woman in America by *Ladies Home Journal.* However, in 2004, her personal stock trading brought charges of insider trading by the Justice Department and the Securities Exchange Commission. Although she maintained her innocence, in 2004 a jury found Stewart guilty of misleading federal investigators and obstructing an investigation; she eventually served a five-month prison sentence. Since then, Stewart has worked to rebuild her reputation and her "brand."[12] *Time* magazine in 2005 called her a person who shapes our lives, naming Stewart as one of the nation's top 100 "Builders and Titans."[13] In 2007, *Forbes* magazine listed her as one of the twenty richest women in entertainment, despite the fact that she had been forced to step down as CEO from her namesake company, Martha Stewart Living Omnimedia. Stewart's rise and fall is a good example of credibility's dynamic nature.

Our understanding of ethos has evolved over the years. Although the classical Greeks believed that a person's credibility existed only during the communication act, today we recognize that ethos is a complex web of past and present impressions. What you have done before impacts the way an audience accepts your current ideas, and that blend, in turn, affects the impression that they take away from you. As an example, think about your feeling toward a past historical figure such as Franklin D. Roosevelt, Martin Luther King Jr., Betty Ford, Neil Armstrong, or Cesar Chavez. Our knowledge of them is based on what we have gleaned from texts, classes, and perhaps television or movies. Perhaps you have no clear image of them at all. But ask your parents or grandparents about those people and their reactions will probably be quite different. They will probably have strong images of speeches or actions these figures took, stands they made, or ways they looked. Your family members' characterizations of those historical figures' ethos are, therefore, dissimilar to yours.

The stages of credibility demonstrate both how credibility is a personal perception and how it progresses or evolves.[14] **Initial credibility** is the perception of the source prior to exposure to a message. Simply put, it is your reputation, the images that establish your credibility before the listener encounters you. As a result, initial credibility is built on known accomplishments, positions or roles, and titles. Sometimes, your initial credibility is established by something as simple as an introduction or statement in a program. However, with the growth of social networking sites, initial credibility has been discovered in other ways. Employers have begun to use search engines such as Google or Yahoo! when they conduct background checks. But as reported in the *New York Times*, some recruiters are looking up applicants on social networking sites such as Facebook, MySpace, Xanga, Orkut, and Friendster, where college students often post risqué or teasing photographs and provocative comments about drinking, recreational drug use, and sexual exploits in what some mistakenly believe is relative privacy. When viewed by corporate recruiters or admissions officials at graduate and professional schools, such pages can make students look immature and unprofessional, at best.[15] Warren Buffett, U.S. business executive and CEO of Berkshire Hathaway, noted the importance of reputation when he said, "It takes 20 years to build a reputation and five minutes to ruin it."[16] What the audience knows about you or your organization, or what is revealed to them about you prior to your message, influences their expectations of the communication event and message to come. **Derived credibility** is the believability you produce in your audience's mind as you present the message. It consists of your organization, supporting materials, delivery, and connection that the audience receives as they process the message. You'll focus on elements of derived credibility throughout this text as you learn strategies for creating and adapting all sorts of messages for different contexts. Finally, **terminal credibility** is the cumulative result of initial and derived credibility. It's the image that the audience carries of you at the end of the message, and it usually forms the next round of initial credibility.

All three of these stages are dynamic. You could begin with low initial credibility (the audience doesn't know anything about you, for instance, except that you hold a low title or come from a rival school). As you present your ideas, your well-developed points, sound supporting materials and dynamic delivery combine to give the audience a more positive perspective of you; your derived credibility rises. By the end of your message, the audience is ready to agree to your proposal; terminal credibility is high.

When the final book in the *Harry Potter* series was imminent, people worldwide were buzzing with guesses about its content. *Harry Potter and the Deathly Hallows* enjoyed widespread popularity (initial credibility). That can be demonstrated by some astounding figures: Barnes & Noble expected to presell 1 million copies of the book; Amazon.com received 600,000 orders; and Scholastic Books ordered an initial printing of 12 million books in preparation for the worldwide launch. Prior to the July 21, 2007, installment, the entire Harry Potter series had sold roughly 325 million copies around the world in 64 different languages.[17] When the book was released, most fans and critics gave it positive reviews. Michiko Kakutani, a book critic of the *New York Times*, said that the book gave "good old-fashioned closure: a big-screen,

Are the photos you've posted on the Web ones you'd want a potential employer to see?
© Carsten Reisinger, 2008, Shutterstock.

heart-racing, bone-chilling confrontation and an epilogue that clearly lays out people's fates. Getting to the finish line is not seamless—the last part of *Harry Potter and the Deathly Hallows*, the seventh and final book in the series, has some lumpy passages of exposition and a couple of clunky detours—but the overall conclusion and its determination of the main characters' story lines possess a convincing inevitability that make some of the prepublication speculation seem curiously blinkered in retrospect."[18] Thousands of fans reported staying up all night to read their copies. Derived credibility was nearly uniformly high; the book kept readers on edge, right to the end. And how do you evaluate terminal credibility? Marty Dodge of Blogcritics online magazine summed it up this way:

> *Harry Potter and the Deathly Hallows* is probably not Rowling's best book in the series, and adults might find it to be a bit thin at times. It reads a bit rushed, and there are some spelling errors and plot glitches. But taken as a whole series, Rowling has done something only few other authors like Tolkien have done. She has created a series of books that can be read by child and adult alike and enjoyed in similar but slightly different ways. One just has to wonder if Rowling will be allowed to finish with Potter and what she has planned for her next novel.[19]

As you can see, the high positive anticipation led to continued positive derived credibility, with the final feeling seeming to be satisfaction, relief, and wonder about what's next. You could predict that if author J. K. Rowling chose to write a sequel (or prequel, or spin off), that the book would begin with high initial credibility.

Credibility is a changing factor, based on a number of elements. The only constant is that ethos exists within the mind of the audience, and your listeners or readers attribute character, intelligence, goodwill, and charisma based on their own unique perceptions. Those perceptions can change because of time, context, and message content, and you have a limited means of impacting those perceptions.

The creation of a credible persona is not easy; in fact, it carries some peril with it. When you open yourself up to others by sharing your ideas or values, you are taking a risk. What if others do not agree? What if they find your ideas to be ridiculous or wrong? When you attempt to establish yourself as an authority (in order to persuade), others might think you lack expertise or are trying to come off as a know-it-all. But because credibility is an essential factor in communication, it is worth the risk. There are some pretty simple strategies that you can use to enhance your audience's perception of your credibility. You can use **mystification,** which is the use of special jargon to imply that you have special authority or expertise (but remember, if your audience does not know the meaning of the jargon, you might confuse them). The use of humor can be employed positively: self-deprecating humor (making fun of yourself) is especially successful if you already enjoy high credibility. However, the negative side of humor is that the audience might evaluate your message as a joke rather than an important issue. Showing dispositional similarity (demonstrating similar views) lets the audience identify with your ideas. Citing sources of evidence and using sources that the audience already accepts can add to your credibility. All-in-all, though, the needs of the audience will often override extensive considerations of a persuader's credibility. For example, let's say that you like an instructor because she's entertaining, but your friend might find humor less important because the friend needs to have a clear explanation of technical material. When your friend asks for your opinion (or you do a search on Rate My Professors.com)[20] the impressions given may not meet you friend's needs.

Now you have an idea about the complex perception of credibility and how it impacts an audience. Later chapters in this text pose questions and offer strategies for influencing some of those perceptions: you'll learn about verbal and nonverbal communication, about different communication contexts and roles, and about a host of other ideas. But one issue potentially has a direct impact on your ability to enhance credibility, no matter the topic, audience, or context. That's **speech anxiety,** commonly called *stage fright.*

WHAT IS SPEECH ANXIETY?

Comedian Jerry Seinfeld said, "According to most studies, people's number one fear is public speaking. Number two is death. Death is number two. Does that sound right? This means to the average person, if you go to a funeral, you're better off in the casket than doing the eulogy."[21] Seinfield's comedic take on communication apprehension probably rings true with a good number of people who are reading this text. Virginia Richmond and James McCroskey reported that almost 95 percent of people surveyed said that they had some degree of anxiety about communicating in some situations.[22] The concepts of communication apprehension and speech anxiety are among the most researched areas in communication.[23] Let's consider how those ideas are described, and then we'll consider causes and strategies for managing yourself in the face of this common feeling.

Communication apprehension (CA) has been defined as an "individual level of fear or anxiety associated with either real or anticipated communication with another person or persons."[24] Furthermore, we know that your tendency to feel anxious when you're communicating can be "specific to a few settings (public speaking) or may exist in most everyday communication situations, or may even be part of a general anxiety trait that arises in many facets of an individual's life."[25] People who suffer from extreme communication apprehension often remain silent rather than speaking out; they fear speaking out in any context, even interpersonal and group discussions. Among the fears that a person with communication apprehension may have is that of speech anxiety, the level of fear you experience when you anticipate or actually speak to an audience. We'll assume that you don't have the deep fear that communication apprehensives do, but rather you've experienced speech anxiety. The symptoms will sound familiar.

Let's consider anxiety first: that feeling of apprehension and fear characterized by physical symptoms such as palpitations, sweating, and feelings of stress.[26] When faced with speaking with others, you may feel your knees knock or your hands tremble, hear your voice quiver, get a dry mouth or feel like you're spitting everywhere, sweat, blush, or be unable to think or find the words that you're wanting to say. That's because your speech anxiety has physiological, cognitive, and behavioral dimensions to it.

Physiological dimensions are caused because your body puts out hormones and adrenaline that overloads your system. Your heart beats faster, and your blood pressure rises. Blood vessels that deliver blood to your face dilate and they open up or relax a little. More blood than usual flows to the

How anxious do you feel at the prospect of having to speak in front of an audience?
© 2008, JupiterImages Corporation.

skin of your face, and you blush. You sweat because you are hot, and that's how you regulate your body temperature. As more adrenalin courses through your system, you tremble or shake. You feel like you're operating in high speed, so you start breathing more heavily (or not at all) and there's little that you can do about it. Guess what? There's little you can do to control these natural reactions, and for the most part, they really don't interfere with your ability to communicate. If you focus on these reactions, you become more self-conscious, so the simple solution is to remain other-conscious. There will be other strategies given at the end of this section, but keep in mind that what your body does, it does.[27]

Cognitive dimensions of speech anxiety are our mental images and often are the result of prior negative experiences. If you got negative feedback on a prior speech or if you froze up on that last interview, it's natural to think of the next occasion with a sense of dread. If you're told that talking to someone is a horrible trial or that public speaking is horrible, you'll expect something bad to happen. No one likes to make a mistake in front of others, and if you fear that you're going to be inadequate or want to avoid criticism, then you may find yourself at a loss for words. The problem is that you're exhibiting irrational thinking. You think to yourself, "No one will listen to me," or "I'll never remember all this stuff." That idea of *catastrophic failure* is prompted by the idea that if you assume that something bad can happen, then it will. You're anticipating something bad happening, making the situation worse.

You might suffer from the *pursuit of approval*, where you expect yourself to perform perfectly. No one expects that flawlessness; why should you? If you seek approval and feel that audience endorsement is vital, then you've set yourself a hard task. How can you please everyone in the audience? You can't please all the people all of the time, so you should set reachable goals. Finally, if you *exaggerate*, you overgeneralize by making one error or negative experience seem like it defines you. Have you ever said, "I was blushing so much that people couldn't help but notice," or "I can't believe I forgot that part of my message. How dumb can I be?" You should probably see that all of these negative self-conversations should be "curable." If you engage in negative self-talk, you will encourage yourself to look for the worst. Remember that old children's story called *The Little Engine That Could?* His statement was, "I think I can." As simple as that sounds, it's sound advice for you.

Behavioral dimensions are the result of a lack of control over your delivery. You speak too softly or rapidly; you sway or pace; you fail to make eye contact with anyone. Your notes don't help you like you thought they would, or you don't know what to do with your hands while talking. Your message is replete with stuttering and vocalized pauses, such as "like" and "um." These behaviors usually are caused by a lack of experience, a repertoire of communication strategies, and deficient practice. In other words, the behavioral dimensions of speech anxiety are easy to fix, and you'll be given a host of strategies in the chapter covering delivery.

Causes of Speech Anxiety

Much of the early research that dealt with communication apprehension couched it as a personality trait, but now most researchers consider communication apprehension (and speech anxiety) to include both trait and situation views.[28] The causes of speech anxiety are fairly obvious. **Situational anx-**

iety is the result of being placed in a particular context, and the real or imagined aspects of that situation cause anxiety. Research has articulated five situational factors can contribute to this kind of anxiety. We tend to be more anxious in these situations:[29]

1. We are communicating with people who we don't know or who seem different from us.
2. We are put in new or unusual situations.
3. We feel that we're in the spotlight or conspicuous and everyone is attending to us.
4. We think we're being evaluated (formal situations).
5. We've had a past failure in a particular speaking situation.[30]

Situational anxiety, as you can see, often results from a lack of experience in a certain context or from trying to meet cultural expectations. **Traitlike anxiety,** by contrast, is more chronic and is a result of your temperament and personality. *Traitlike* refers to a relatively stable and enduring predisposition of an individual towards experiencing fear and/or anxiety across a wide range of communication contexts.[31] People with traitlike anxiety interfere with communication across all contexts: public speaking, talking on the phone, meeting strangers, singing, and so on. The Personal Report of Communication Apprehension can help identify those with severe traitlike anxiety, who can benefit from more in-depth work with professionals to reduce anxiety, because this aspect isn't bound by a context.

Do you feel particularly anxious when you're starting school in unfamiliar surroundings?
© Jason Stitt, 2008, Shutterstock.

Managing Speech Anxiety

It might seem highly desirable if you could just not have any anxiety at all, but in truth, a bit of nervousness isn't a bad thing. Motley suggests that it helps to be a bit nervous when you want to do your best. If you are lackadaisical about making a speech, you probably won't do a good job on it.[32] There are several different techniques that can help; some work on situational anxiety, and others can assist those with traitlike anxiety.

Visualization involves the reduction of anxiety by imagining positive speaking experiences. Visualization has also been called guided imagery, mental rehearsal, and mediation; the basic techniques and concepts are the same. When you engage in visualization, you create a mental image of what you want to happen or feel. Athletes use this technique all the time as they imagine themselves jumping a hurdle or catching a ball; you probably do, too, when you "pump yourself up" prior to doing something important.

Research tells us that positive visualization can be especially effective if you have chronic apprehension.[33] When you visualize, you begin by imagining the context, including images of a time when you did well or thinking of your best performance to come. You try to step into the feeling, imagining the context in detail and thinking about how good you'll feel performing your task. You can involve many of your senses: visual images (how the audience will look), kinesthetic (how your body will feel), auditory (how confident your voice will sound). As you repeat visualization, you keep rehearsing the mental image, just as you will the actual communication event. The idea is that your mental rehearsal will train you to be able to do what you've been imagining.

Systematic desensitization focuses on reducing tensions that surround a feared event.[34] This method has been used for treating all sorts of fears, from snakes and spiders to fear of flying or heights. In systematic desensitization,

Positive visualization can help you imagine a good performance and make that happen.
© 2008, JupiterImages Corporation.

you learn how to relax; this lessens the physiological dimension of speech anxiety. Usually, you learn deep muscle relaxation (tensing and relaxing different muscle groups until you are aware of the different sensations). Then, as you're relaxed, you start to picture yourself in that anxiety-producing state (for instance, packing for a trip—you're not even thinking about being on an airplane yet). As you go through the technique, you put yourself in greater anxiety-producing contexts (ending with flying over the ocean). The goal is to learn to use those calm and relaxed sensations with being in the situation that scares you.

Cognitive restructuring assists you in changing how you think about speaking situations.[35] This technique suggests that the problem you're encountering is the result of irrational beliefs, not the speaking situation. Earlier, you read about the cognitive dimension of speech anxiety: fear of failure, exaggeration, and the pursuit of approval. Each of these creates personal expectations that are impossible to attain. That's what makes you feel anxious. In cognitive restructuring, you learn to stop negative self-talk. One of the ways that complements this is to receive training in the task that you set yourself for failure. Skills training like you're getting in this class (learning to create effective speeches, conduct successful interviews, participate in effective group work) should help you to reduce anxiety.[36]

These techniques for reducing speech anxiety are all useful, and researchers are still working on identifying which ones work best for different people. Most likely, the best technique is a combination of several of them, used in the order of the kind of anxiety you feel.[37] For instance, if thinking about doing a speech makes you feel inadequate about your ability, you might take this approach:

1. Begin with cognitive restructuring. Tell yourself that you're learning great skills and you can do this! You don't need to be brilliant to succeed!
2. Go on the systematic desensitization. Focus on deep muscle relaxation. Let go of the tension.
3. End with visualization (Imagine yourself in the speech, or even practice it with a friend beforehand).

If you're worried about talking with your doctor about some physical problem, it might help to begin with visualization, imagining yourself in her office, and then move to cognitive restructuring, thinking about the questions you'll pose. The key is to work on the anxiety and not let it control you.

SUMMARY

Credibility is co-constructed between you and your audience. When we interact, our credibility is created, maintained, and changed as it evolves through stages. Remember, credibility is the impression that others have of you, and they assess you on the basis of four qualities (character, intelligence, goodwill, and charisma). You have strategies to use as you try to influence the other's perceptions of you. Speech anxiety is common and natural to all of us; in fact, it's a necessary part of interaction because it keeps us alert and involved. At the same time, it can limit your ability to be perceived as an effective, credible communicator. By understanding the causes of speech anxiety and learning some techniques for managing it, you can become more effective in all communication transactions.

Five Tips for Overcoming Speech Anxiety

1. *Be aware.* Remember, anxiety often comes from a sense that you don't know what you're facing and you won't succeed. If you can reduce the unknown (analyze your audience and occasion, visit the location, talk with others who have had similar experiences), you can visualize what is about to come.

2. *Be confident in your message and purpose.* You know that an audience perceives your credibility based on their view of your intelligence and competence. That means that you should (whenever possible) talk about things you know about, organize your ideas, and conduct appropriate research for the audience and the occasion. A lack of confidence comes when you talk yourself into disbelief: you tell yourself that you really don't know what you're doing and that no one could be interested in what you have to say. Know your message and present it appropriately to the audience and occasion.

3. *Be strategic in handling anxiety.* There are many tips throughout this text for different situations, but here are some pretty general strategies you can use.
   - Keep things out of your hands, because you'll tend to play with those items unconsciously. That means empty your pocket, take off bracelets and watches, and try not to hold notes.
   - Make sure your hair is pulled out of the way and your glasses aren't slipping; you don't want to be fiddling with your face while talking.
   - Do some stretches before you speak, like rolling your head around to loosen up your neck, or shrugging your shoulders to release tension. Simple isometric exercises will work and don't have to be obvious. Isometrics is a form of resistance training where you use your muscles to exert a force either against an immovable object or to hold the muscle in a fixed position for a specific length of time. You can press your palms together, extend your fingers out to lengthen them, or press your feet down while sitting to isolate your leg muscles.
   - Get a drink of water before you speak, and if you tend to get a "cotton mouth," keep some water handy but out of the way of swinging arms.
   - Practice what you're going to say and time it; then remember where you should be in the message at what time point.
   - Look for a friendly face in the audience and talk to that person.

4. *Be reasonable about your anxiety.* Remember, it's natural to have anxiety, but it's not rational to expect the worst. You're not going to fail, the audience isn't going to laugh at you (unless that's your goal), and whatever you do won't lead to the end of the world.

5. *Be positive about yourself.* Credibility also rests in character and charisma. If you tell yourself that you're not smart, it will show in your demeanor. Believe in yourself, and we will, too.

We continuously send and receive messages in our efforts to create shared meaning. Those messages impact our credibility. Luckily for us, communication is a process, and making a mistake when interacting with another does not necessarily mean failure in the communication attempt. You have the ability to enhance the audience's perceptions of you, and the next chapters will let you see how credibility works in different contexts and with different transactions.

ENDNOTES

1. For some examples of how the communication field has studied the credibility concept, consider the following recent articles: David K. Berlo, James B. Lemert, and Robert J. Mertz, "Dimensions for Evaluating the Acceptability of Message Sources," *Public Opinion Quarterly* 33 (1969): 563–576. Also Lanette Pogue and Kimo Ahyun, "The Effect of Teacher Nonverbal Immediacy and Credibility on Student Motivation and Affective Learning," *Communication Education* 55 (3) (July 2006): 331–344; "Can Corporate Blogs Ever Really Be Credible?" *Business Communicator* 7 (2) (June 2006): 1–2; Spiro Kiousis and Daniela V. Dimitrova, "Differential Impact of Web Site Content: Exploring the Influence of Source (Public Relations versus News), Modality, and Participation on College Students' Perceptions," *Public Relations Review* 32 (2) (June 2006): 177–179 and J. Glascock and T. Ruggiero, "The Relationship of Ethnicity and Sex to Professor Credibility at a Culturally Diverse University," *Communication Education* 55 (2) (April 2006): 197–207.

2. Richard C. Jebb, (trans.). *The Rhetoric of Aristotle* (Cambridge: University Press, 1909): 69.

3. Max Weber defined charisma as a certain quality of an individual personality, by virtue of which s/he is set apart from ordinary people and treated as endowed with supernatural, superhuman, or at least specifically exceptional powers or qualities. These are such as are not accessible to the ordinary person, but are regarded as of divine origin or as exemplary, and on the basis of them the individual concerned is treated as a leader. "Max Weber," http://business.nmsu.edu/~dboje/teaching/503/weber_links.html (accessed Feb. 21, 2006). For some examples of communication research on the concept, see, for example, William L. Gardner, "Perceptions of Leader Charisma, Effectiveness, and Integrity," *Management Communication Quarterly*, 16 (4) (May 2003): 502; Mark Anderson, "Pancho Villa and the Marlboro Man: American-Style Charisma in the Marketplace of Ideas," *Media History* 7 (2) (Dec. 2001): 171–181.

4. For examples of different polls, see the Gallup organization at http://www.gallup.com/or the *Entertainment Weekly* polls at http://www.ew.com/ew/critmass/index.html. Also, two articles speak to media and charisma: T. Sheafer, "Charismatic Skill and Media Legitimacy: An Actor-Centered Approach to Understanding the Political Communication Competition," *Communication Research*, 28 (6) (Dec. 2001): 711; and B. Briller, "Heroes and Other Villains: Politics, TV and Charisma," *Television Quarterly* 30 (2) (Fall 1999): 31.

5. Peggy Anderson, (ed.) *Dwight D. Eisenhower, Great Quotes from Great Leaders*, (Lombard: Great Quotations, 1989).

6. "Importance of Eye Contact," http://www.synchronicsgroup.com/tips/eye_contact.html, The Synchronics Group San Francisco, CA (accessed Sept. 11, 2007). Copyright © 2007. Reprinted with permission.

7. Humane Society of the United States, "HSUS Pet Overpopulation Estimates," http://www.hsus.org/pets/ issues_affecting_our_pets/pet_overpopulation_and_ownership_statistics/hsus_pet_overpopulation_estimates.html (accessed July 16, 2007).

8. Max Weber, *Max Weber: The Theory of Social and Economic Organization*, translated by A. M. Henderson and Talcott Parsons (New York: The Free Press, 1947). For examples of research on charisma, see R. J. House, and B. Shamir, "Toward the Integration of Transformational, Charismatic, and Visionary Theories," in M. Chemers and R. Ayman (eds.), *Leadership Theory and Research: Perspectives and Directions* (New York: Academic Press, 1993): 81–107 and J. M. Howell, "Two Faces of Charisma: Socialized and Personalized Leadership in Organizations," in J. A. Conger and R. N. Kanungo (eds.), *Charismatic Leadership: The Elusive Factor in Organizational Effectiveness* (San Francisco: Jossey-Bass, 1988), 213–236.

9. K. J. Klein and R. J. House, "On Fire: Charismatic Leadership and Levels of Analysis," *Leadership Quarterly* 6 (2) (1995): 183–198. Also Jane A. Halpert, "The Dimensionality of Charisma," *Journal of Business and Psychology*, 4, no. 4 (June 1990): 399–410 and Jeffrey D. Kudisch, Mark L. Poteet, Gregory H. Dobbins, Michael C. Rush and Joyce E. A. Russell, "Expert Power, Referent Power, and Charisma: Toward the Resolution of a Theoretical Debate," *Journal of Business and Psychology* 10 (2) (1995): 177–195.

10. Kenneth Burke, *A Rhetoric of Motives* (Berkeley: University of California Press, 1950), 3–46.

11. See a video example of the creation of an infomercial by NBC's *Dateline* at http://www.msnbc.msn.com/id/ 14856571/"From the inside out" John Larson (Sept. 15, 2006). For a simple history of Infomercials, see http://www.answers.com/topic/infomercial?cat=biz-fin.

12. MarthaStewart.com, http://www.marthastewart.com/ (accessed Sept. 14, 2007).

13. Donald Trump, "Martha Stewart, the Domestic Diva is Back." http://www.time.com/time/subscriber/2005/time100/builders/100stewart.html (accessed Sept. 14, 2007).

14. James C. McCroskey, *An Introduction to Rhetorical Communication*, 7th ed. (Boston: Allyn and Bacon, 1997), 91–101.

15. Alan Finder, "For Some, Online Persona Undermines a Résumé" (June 11, 2006), http://www.nytimes.com/2006/06/11/us/11recruit.html (accessed Sept. 13, 2007).

16. Warren Buffet quotation, http://thinkexist.com/quotation/it_takes-years_to_build_a_reputation_and_five/151205.html (accessed Sept. 13, 2007).

17. "Fan Frenzy over Harry Potter Book 7: Harry Potter and the Deathly Hallows—MuggleNet.com Book Tour," (May 17, 2007), http://www.randomsandiego.com/blog/2007/05/17/mugglenetcom-book-tour-fan-frenzy-over-harry-potter-book-7-harry-potter-and-the-deathly-hallows/ (accessed Sept. 11, 2007).

18. Michiko Kakutani, "An Epic Showdown as Harry Potter Is Initiated into Adulthood," http://www.nytimes.com/2007/07/19/books/19potter.html (accessed July 19, 2007).

19. Marty Dodge Book Review, "Harry Potter and the Deathly Hallows by J. K. Rowling," http://blogcritics.org/archives/2007/07/21/154457.php (accessed July 21, 2007).

20. http://www.ratemyprofessors.com/index.jsp

21. Jerry Seinfeld. Thinkexist.com. http://thinkexist.com/quotes/Jerry_Seinfeld/ (accessed July 17, 2007).

22. V. Richmond and J. McCroskey, *Communication: Apprehension, Avoidance, and Effectiveness* (Scottsdale, AZ: Gorsuch Scarisbrick, 2005).

23. Much of the research on the concepts have been done by James C. McCroskey and his colleagues, who have made significant contributions to our understanding of the concept and how to measure it. The primary measure of communication apprehension, the Personal Report of Communication Apprehension (PRCA), was first developed in 1970. A new edition is available on the Web site that accompanies this text. Dr. McCroskey's Web site at http://www.jamescmccroskey.com/provides links to all of his published articles, many of which can be downloaded.

24. J. C. McCroskey, "Oral Communication Apprehension: A Summary of Recent Theory and Research," *Human Communication Research* 4 (1977), 78–96.

25. P. G. Friedman, *Shyness and Reticence in Students* (Washington, D.C.: National Education Association, 1980), 181 520.

26. MedicineNet.com, "Anxiety Definition. Mental Health Disorders," http://www.medterms.com/script/main/art.asp?articlekey=9947 (accessed Sept. 30, 2007).

27. A good source on the facets of behavior associated with speech anxiety is A. Mulac and A. Sherman, "Behavior Assessment of Speech Anxiety," *Quarterly Journal of Speech* 60, no. 2 (1974), p. 138.

28. McCroskey, 1977.

29. Ibid.

30. M. Motley and J. Molloy, "An Efficacy Test of a New Therapy for Public Speaking Anxiety," *Journal of Applied Communication Research* 22 (1994), 48–58. Also J. C. McCroskey, "The Communication Apprehension Perspective," in J. C. McCroskey and J. A. Daly (eds.), *Avoiding Communication: Shyness, Reticence, and Communication Apprehension* (London: Sage Publications Inc., 1994), 13–38.

31. Most researchers agree that there may be a hereditary component to apprehension. (McCroskey 1982; McCroskey 1984) Children are born with certain personality predispositions or tendencies that affects how they will react to environmental stimuli. However, although heredity may have an impact on traitlike CA, most researchers propose that the patterns of reinforcement that an individual experiences in the environment are the dominant components.

32. M. Motley, COM Therapy. In J. A. Daly, J. C. McCroskey, J. Ayres, T. Hopf, and D. Ayers (eds.)

33. J. Ayres, and T. Hopf, "The Long-term Effect of Visualization in the Classroom: A Brief Research Report," *Communication Education*, 39, 75–78. Also J. Ayres, T. Hopf, and D. Ayres, "An Examination of Whether Imaging Ability Enhances the Effectiveness of an Intervention Designed to Reduce Speech Anxiety," *Communication Education* 443 (1990), 252–258.

34. Richmond and McCroskey, *Communication: Apprehension, Avoidance, and Effectiveness,* 5th ed. (Scottsdale, AZ: Gorsuch Scarisbrick, 2000).

35. Motley and Molloy, 1994.

36. L. Kelly, G. Phillips, and J. Keaen, *Teaching People to Speak Well: Training and Remediation of Communication Reticence* (Cresskill, NJ: Hampton, 1995).

37. M. Allen, J. Hunter, and W. Donahue, "Meta-analysis of Self-report Data on the Effectiveness of Public Speaking Anxiety Treatment Techniques," *Communication Education* 38, (1989): 54–76; K. Dwyer, "The Multidimensional Model: Teaching Students to Self-manage High Communication Apprehension by Self-selecting Treatments," *Communication Education* 49, (2000).

How Do Interpersonal Relationships Affect Communication?

LEARNING OBJECTIVES

After reading this chapter, you should understand the following concepts:

- Relationships are contextual: They depend on where we meet people, who they are in relation to us, and in what environment we interact.
- Relationships proceed through the stages of initiation, maintenance, and termination.
- Self-disclosure often helps initiate communication as relationships develop.
- Maintaining relationships takes time and effort. Good communication skills enhance relationships.
- Conflicts are inevitable in relationships, but appropriate communication skills can lead to a successful resolution, resulting in improved relationships.
- Relationships terminate for many reasons: social exchange theory helps explain relationship dissolution.
- Virtual relationships are relatively new, offering much more freedom to interact without concern for appearances, but requiring many of the same rules that govern face-to-face relationships.

KEYWORDS

culture
occulesics
self-disclosure
norm of reciprocity
Johari Window
six degrees of separation
dialectics
autonomy/connection
openness/closedness
novelty/predictability
compromise
collaboration
social exchange theory

INTRODUCTION

Communication skills are not limited to public speaking. They expand to our daily lives through the relationships we form. Relationships have been written about and referenced dating back to ancient times, evidencing just how critical they are to our lives. Aristotle philosophized about their use, Shakespeare wrote amazing plays depicting their duality and necessity, and many religious books provide believers with guidance in how to interact within them. The vital nature of relationships is supported by the numerous studies linking close relationships to life satisfaction and overall health. A 2004 report from the National Center for Health Statistics found that married people are less likely to smoke, drink heavily, or to be physically inactive than people who are not married.[1] Additionally, they are less likely to suffer from headaches or

Close relationships are an essential element for a satisfying, healthy life.
© 2008, JupiterImages Corporation.

serious psychological stress.[2] The benefits of relationships are not only for those who have found life partners; they are also for those who are recovering from illness, and for general life satisfaction, especially as we age.[3]

Although we need relationships for our survival, the relationships we form can cause us both happiness and grief. Through our communication we not only create, maintain, and terminate relationships, but we also affect their quality. Our relationships affect multiple aspects of our existence, whether they are friendships we have at work or school, romantic involvements that evolve into long-term commitments, or relationships with our family members. Each relationship comes with its unique challenges, and each takes time and effort if it is to be maintained.

Before we get started, take a moment to note some information about three relationships most important to you at this moment.

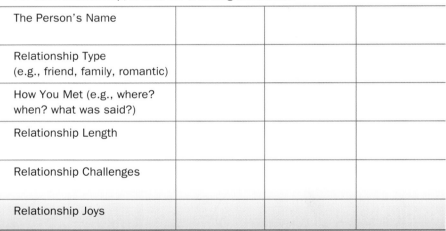

Take a Closer Look

Your Most Important Relationships
For each relationship, record the following information

The Person's Name			
Relationship Type (e.g., friend, family, romantic)			
How You Met (e.g., where? when? what was said?)			
Relationship Length			
Relationship Challenges			
Relationship Joys			

Using this list, you can reflect on these relationships as you learn about various communication concepts throughout the chapter. It can help you focus on your own approach to and uses of communication within these relationships.

WHAT ARE THE RELATIONSHIP GENRES?

As you reflect on your list of relationships, you will probably notice that they vary in type. Many of our relationships are contextual; they depend on where we met the person, who they are in relation to us (family versus nonfamily), and in what environment we interact. For example, many students develop lasting friendships at school or at campus jobs. These friendships are different from those relationships you have with your family members, business colleagues, and romantic partners. Each is a type of relationship with very different expectations for communication and its outcomes.

Relationships take time and effort to be maintained, whether they are friendships, romances, or family.
© 2008, JupiterImages Corporation.

We will begin with a brief discussion of the various relationship genres. Here you will be introduced to friendships, family relationships, romantic relationships, professional/collegial relationships, and virtual relationships. We will explore their definitions and the variation in expectations, and discuss factors influencing each relationship type, such as age, gender, culture, and technology. Let us begin with relationships that impact us at a very early age: friendships.

How are your friendships different from other relationships you have?
© 2008, JupiterImages Corporation.

Friendships

The friendships you develop and foster are one of your strongest forms of support. This is not a new idea. Great thinkers of the past, such as Aristotle, have written about the importance of friendships. In his book *Nicomachean Ethics*, Aristotle argues that

> without friends no one would choose to live, though he had all other goods; even rich men and those in possession of office and of dominating power are thought to need friends most of all; for what is the use of such prosperity without the opportunity of beneficence.[4]

What is meant by the term *friendship?* Aristotle stated that friendship is one of the greatest virtues, and in order for people to be friends, they need to be well-disposed toward one another and "wish each other's good." Given this definition, we can see that friendship relates to all other types of relationships, for friendships are formed for primarily three reasons: usefulness, pleasure, or goodness.[5] *Usefulness* is characterized by a friend who gets you that job you wanted or a membership to an exclusive club. *Pleasure* comes in the form of a friend who makes you laugh or staves off loneliness. *Virtue* involves valuing a relationship for and of itself.[6]

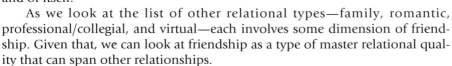

Why do you choose to become friends with someone?
© 2008, JupiterImages Corporation.

As we look at the list of other relational types—family, romantic, professional/collegial, and virtual—each involves some dimension of friendship. Given that, we can look at friendship as a type of master relational quality that can span other relationships.

Family Relationships

We do not choose the families into which we are born or adopted. Yet, family ties are some of the strongest, most emotional, and longest-lasting of all the relationships formed throughout a lifetime. For many, the family can be relied upon to provide the usefulness, pleasure, and goodness of which Aristotle spoke. The connection we have with our families, however, is a special type of relationship where there are strong influences of age, gender, and culture that affect communication expectations and types. Whatever the case in our own families, the manner in which we maintain relationships is bound by status differences linked to culture, age, and gender, and further impacted by the communication strategies we use with family members.

Culture strongly impacts relationships within a family. © 2008, JupiterImages Corporation.

Culture strongly impacts family relationships. Although there are many definitions and applications of culture, for the purpose of this chapter we define **culture** as learned ways of behaving that conform to a particular geographic region or ethnic group. With all of its values, expectations, and approaches to living, culture is taught through modeling. You receive rewards for acceptable behavior, and punishments for unacceptable behavior. It is learned not by explicit instruction, but through our interactions with others. For example, in most cultures there are expectations for how children communicate in the family, by the manner in which they address various family members, by the displays of respect, and by subjects that are talked about or avoided. You can probably think of a time when you were scolded for talking to a parent in a way that was judged disrespectful, either by the tone of your voice or by the words that you used. As an adult, however, using the same tone and words is no longer interpreted as disrespectful. To illustrate this notion further, we can look at our use of eye contact, which is a form of nonverbal communication called **occulesics.** Most people raised in the United States are taught to look an adult in the eye as a sign of respect, whereas, in other cultures (e.g., Far Eastern, Latin American, some African American) the same act is an act of disrespect or defiance.[7]

Family relationships are also influenced by our age and gender. They, too, have a strong link to our culture. In many cultures, there are different behavioral expectations in the family associated with gender such as dress standards, expectations regarding conversational patterns and language use, the chores that should be completed, and the hobbies that family members are expected and allowed to pursue.

This was illustrated in the film *Bend it like Beckman* (2003), which showed a young Indian girl living with her parents in London. Her choice to play soccer disappoints and outrages her parents, as they expect her to conform to the traditional customs where young adult girls do not play soccer but instead marry, cook, clean, and raise children.

Cultural expectations also extend to age. For example, the Egyptian culture has been studied for its formulation of hierarchies according to age, gender, and experience. They rely heavily on ancient traditions for guidance in outlining the proper place and behavior of each person in society.[8]

Family relationships have significant impacts on our lives from the beginning. At some point, committed, romantic relationships also maintain a strong presence for most people.

Romantic Relationships

Romantic relationships usually start as friendships and often evolve into romantic love. As relationships move toward romantic, the communication becomes more personal and affectionate. Romantic relationships can be the most challenging for us because they involve strong emotions that can often work in opposition to rational thought. The complexity of these types of relationships is illustrated by a seventeenth-century French novelist, Mlle de Scudéry, in the novel *La Princess de Clèves*. An ancient map (*Carte du Tendre*) is used to describe the range of emotions that people feel on their quest to love.

The map represents an unknown country called Tendre (Tenderness). It is a topographic and allegorical representation of the country of love, where the lover must find his way to his lady's heart. He begins in the town of New Friendship, enduring many dangers and tests. In doing so, he risks being lost in the dangerous Seas of Enmity or falling into the Lake of Indifference. He must cross three large rivers of Regard, Recognition, and Inclination, and travel through many cities and villages with names like Generosity, Love Letter, Sensibility, Neglect, Pride, and Jealousy. This map is an allegory to describe the challenges and emotional experiences we have as we develop these types of relationships.[9]

Romantic relationships often display very personal and affectionate communication.
© 2008, JupiterImages Corporation.

Professional Relationships

Professional/collegial relationships are formed during the course of professional careers and volunteer commitments. These relationships perform a very important function in our lives. They serve to help us network and can work as a form of support and motivation. The networking literature notes its importance to gain opportunities for jobs, admission to clubs and/or associations, and valuable advice.[10]

Virtual Relationships

With the explosion of the World Wide Web, the virtual environment has established itself as a legitimate context in which to form relationships. Virtual environments include, but are not limited to, teleconferencing, e-mailing, interactive Web sites, chat rooms, bulletin boards, and blogs. Before proceeding, take a moment to familiarize yourself with some common terms related to this type of relationship genre.

Work-related relationships offer support and motivation.
© 2008, JupiterImages Corporation.

Virtual communities span every relationship genre and context. They cross borders, age, physical ability or disability, race, interest, sex, profession, and religion. These communities can be developed around professional and recreational subjects, political parties, medical communities, gaming enthusiasts, technical expertise, sexual orientation, and online dating.

If we look at one of the older formats for communicating in a virtual community, bulletin boards (where individuals posted and responded to messages asynchronously), we see that they evolved into chat rooms where people meet in real time (e.g., instant message) to discuss topics of interest. The format has now evolved further into blogs.

The **blog** (from *Web logs*) invasion has permeated popular culture. As noted in *Time*, "Historians may well date the golden age of the blog from 2004." The history of blogs goes back to about 1999, but it was in 2004 that they gained the most attention, largely because of political debates. Through blogs, people feel as if they are part of a community and, in some cases, an elite group. Blogs have been described to be like "stumbling on a sympathetic haven in the lonely, trackless wilderness of the Internet." They not only feed the need to belong, but it has been argued that blogs provide a platform that

How are relationships different in a virtual community?
© 2008, JupiterImages Corporation.

Defining Virtual Contexts

Avatar: A representation of yourself in the virtual world, whether in the form of a three-dimensional model used in computer games or a two-dimensional icon used on Internet forums and other communities (http://www.techweb.com/encyclopedia).

Blog (WeB LOG): A blog is a digital journal that is available on the Web. The activity of updating a blog is *blogging,* and someone who keeps a blog is a *blogger.* Blogs are typically updated daily using software that allows people with little or no technical background to update and maintain the blog (http://www.matisse.net).

Bulletin board: A congregation of users gathered electronically by modem, where each person can post messages. They began as informal communities but now include political, commercial, adult, and many other kinds of categories (www.netlingo.com).

Chat room: This is a Web site for live, online conversation in which any number of computer users can type messages to each other and communicate in real time. These messages usually appear on an area of the screen next to the user's nickname. Most chat rooms have a particular topic (which you are expected to discuss), but some chat rooms are specifically for meeting other people. Other chat rooms are designed as elaborate 3-D environments, where you select an avatar that represents you in this virtual meeting place (www.netlingo.com).

Cyberspace: This term originated by author William Gibson in his novel *Neuromancer.* Cyberspace is the digital world constructed by computer networks, and in particular, the Internet. Whenever you hear the term *cyberspace,* it generally refers to the online world, which is a place that actually exists as a communications medium, a virtual world (http://www.netlingo.com).

IM (instant messaging): A technology that gives users the ability of exchanging messages in real time with little or no time delay (www.netlingo.com). There are several IM services available that make this possible, such as i-chat and AOL.

Online community, a.k.a. virtual community: These are areas on the Internet that cater to people's common interests. They are virtual in the sense that they exist in cyberspace and do not take up physical space. Communities are formed on Web sites, discussion groups, newsgroups and even in chat rooms, and there are several popular gaming communities online. In general, communities communicate by using a discussion board or forum (www.netlingo.com).

allows for an exchange of ideas free from the biases inherent in many corporate-funded media, allowing people to communicate directly to one another.[11] The blog explosion is another example of the variety of virtual contexts in which we can form relationships.

Virtual relationships enable us to make contact and interact with people from our neighborhoods and around the globe. There has been much talk about the nature of these relationships and their impact on face-to-face relationships, which will be discussed later in this chapter.

HOW DO WE DEVELOP RELATIONSHIPS?

Now that we know about the genres of relationships and the factors influencing them, we will examine the communication strategies typically employed in the stages of relationship development. Relationship development can be looked at in a series of three interrelated stages: initiation, maintenance, and termination:

Relationship Stages

- *Initiation:* How and why do we form relationships?
- *Maintenance:* How do we keep them strong?
- *Termination:* What do we do when they end? Is it possible to end them effectively?

As these stages are discussed, keep in mind they are not fixed; rather, they are more like frameworks for understanding a complex, nonlinear process. Take a moment to think about one of the relationships you listed at the beginning of this chapter. With that relationship in mind, answer the questions in the "Take a Closer Look" box.

Think about the formation of this relationship as we discuss relationship initiation and maintenance.

INITIATION: HOW DO RELATIONSHIPS BEGIN?

Whether we are forming friendships, romantic relationships, or professional contacts, relationships start at the initiation stage. This stage is characterized by several factors. The first is related to the opportunity to interact. Seldom do we form relationships with people whom we come into contact with just once. Most relationships develop as a result of proximity and from extended exposure to each other. That exposure can be in the form of seeing each other at work every day, interacting in an online community on a regular basis, seeing the other person at the gym several days a week, in the general area in which we live (e.g., next door neighbor), at monthly volunteer activities, in classes, or in any other context in which we have repeated contact.

Why are you likely to become friends with your classmates?
© 2008, JupiterImages Corporation.

It is through this repeated contact that you discover a little about the person's identity through nonverbal and verbal communication cues. For example, nonverbally, we come to understand people by their clothing choices (jock, professional, Grateful Dead fan, sophisticate, outdoors type, dancer, etc.) and even the ways in which they move (confidently, shyly, etc.). If it is in an online environment, we may see a picture, interact via Web cam, discern the tone of a typed message, or study the nonverbal make-up of an *avatar* (a representation or icon of the communicator in two or three dimensions).

Once we interact verbally with an individual, we can gain personality insights from his or her approach to conversation. For example, a person who does not engage in conversational exchange (dialogue), but instead monopolizes the conversations (monologue) and ignores all turn-taking signals may be viewed as either egocentric, aggressive, dominant, or nervous. It is from these types of initial cues that we begin to form opinions about whether the person's personality and character is a match with our personality and character.

Mastering the Art of Conversation: The British Pub

An interesting aspect of the British culture illustrates an ease in initiating a conversation: pub culture. It is manifested in the regular practice of visiting the local pub on one's way home from a day's work. Each day individuals in the pub drink, yes, but, more importantly, they talk. It is through this daily informal pub talk, with anyone—strangers, acquaintances, or close friends—that the British are able to master the art of conversation and, subsequently, relationship building.

An American woman reported her experience as she traveled in Great Britain. The British individuals with whom she was talking realized she was not involved in their industry and was not able to contribute to the technical and specialized conversation topic. The individuals in the group immediately changed the subject and they all continued to talk about politics, culture, religion, and many other topics late into the evening.

This idea of taking time to talk is also seen in cafés throughout Europe, where individuals are often seen chatting over a coffee or tea. With the popularity of coffee houses like Starbucks, The Coffee Bean and Tea Leaf, and Boba Tea Houses in the United States these days, there is bound to be a shift in our approach to the art of conversation, as such places are conducive to getting out of our cars, sitting down a bit, and taking time to relax. It will be interesting to see what impact they have on the American approach to conversation. What do you think?

Take a Closer Look

Conversations with One of Your Most Important Relationship Partners

First conversation

- What was the conversation topic?
- What was the conversation duration?

Second conversation

- What was the conversation topic?
- What was the conversation duration?

Self-Disclosure: After Conversation Has Begun

Once we have an initial interaction with someone and choose to talk, we begin to reveal aspects of ourselves the other person would not know unless we told him. This communication act has been called **self-disclosure**. Self-disclosure is what we use to get closer to others, and it often helps us to initiate conversations. Whether we discuss our opinion about a movie or talk about what type of work we do or hobbies we pursue, the act of self disclosing in a relationship typically takes place slowly over time. As our relationships become more intimate, our self-disclosure increases in both the number of topics we talk about and the depth at which we talk about them.

If you were to graph the conversational topics, you would most likely notice two things occurring: (1) the number of topics, or *breadth*, increases, and (2) the extent to which you talk about this topic, or *depth*, increases.

The Norm of Reciprocity. Not only does self-disclosure increase the number of topics and breadth of topics, it is also reciprocated in the process of relationship initiation and development. This phenomenon is referred to as the **norm of reciprocity**.[12] The norm of reciprocity asserts that in order for us to continue to move forward with a relationship, we must feel the person with whom we are communicating is self-disclosing equally, both in depth and breadth. If we are the only ones sharing such information, then we are left feeling vulnerable and untrusting. The message we send in the course of a verbal transaction includes both a content and relational message. The relational message sent when someone does not reciprocate can be perceived as distrust.

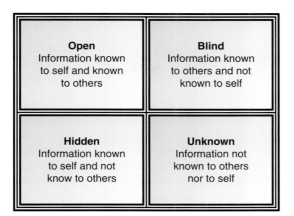

Figure 6.1
Johari Window

The Johari Window. Self-disclosure helps us to learn about others and also about ourselves. It is through the act of revealing information about ourselves that we learn a little more about who we are. This is best illustrated by the **Johari Window.**[13] The creators of the Johari Window, Joe Luft and Harry Ingham (from whom the name *Johari* is formed) say there are four aspects of ourselves that are affected by self-disclosure. Each is a result of what is known or not known to self and to others. The four "windows" consist of (1) open aspects of ourselves, (2) hidden aspects of ourselves, (3) blind aspects of ourselves, and (4) unknown aspects of ourselves. Figure 6.1 illustrates each window.

Close friends feel comfortable sharing private information about themselves with each other.
© 2008, JupiterImages Corporation.

The Open Self. This includes information that is known both to others and to oneself. The information that is revealed here is consistent with the relationship's intimacy level. During the initiation of a relationship, the information in the open window is rather safe, and involves little risk to us. The topics discussed are very general and often nonspecific, but the breadth and depth of information increase as relationships become more intimate. As we share information about ourselves, that information becomes part of our open selves in that particular relationship.

Our open selves vary, depending on the type of relationship. With our close friends, we may discuss information about school in terms of our grades, relationships, and extracurricular activities. When communicating with our families we may also reveal information about school, but the types of topics we discuss and the depth at which we discuss them may differ. For instance, we may discuss information about school projects we have due, and instructors and subjects we are taking, but may not reveal much about our extracurricular activities. All of this depends on the nature of the relationship. Thus, the size of our open self varies in each and every one of our relationships.

The Hidden Self. This aspect of the self includes information that is known by us but not known by others. In a relationship's initial stages, for example, it would seem both awkward and risky (it could put us in a vulnerable position) to reveal too much, too fast. Do you really need to tell your new romantic interest about all the details of your last break-up? Should you reveal your medical problems to a work colleague? Perhaps as the relationship develops it might become appropriate for these topics to be disclosed. However, during the initiation phases of a relationship, there are simply some aspects of who we are that should remain private or hidden.

Our hidden selves may never be fully revealed to any one individual. It is important to understand that fully revealing parts of our hidden selves is not the goal of disclosure. Clearly, there are some aspects of ourselves that should remain private.

The Blind Self. This is the one area of the Johari Window out of our direct control. In essence, it is information about ourselves known to others but not known to us. This would include information about our habits, tendencies, abilities, and/or skill levels. Such aspects of ourselves are typically revealed to us by others who have license to do so, such as close friends, teachers, and parents. This is illustrated when a teacher, for example, reveals to you that you are a natural at speaking, a talented photographer, or a skilled computer programmer, or when a close friend comments on your agility at playing golf or your tendency to use your hands a lot when you talk. It is also a source of information that you can use as corrective feedback.

With each person with whom we build relationships, information about our blind self moves to our open self. As we learn more about who we are, we can work to better realize our full potential.

Your talent for working with children may be unknown until you have the opportunity to try it and do well.
© 2008, JupiterImages Corporation.

The Unknown Self. This aspect of our self includes information that is not known to us or to others. For example, once you undertake a new challenge in your life, sometimes you do not know how you will perform, or if you will like it, or if you have the stamina to handle it. For instance, some people may not know that they are really patient people when working with children until they start volunteering at the local elementary school, YMCA, or Boys and Girls club.

Each pane in the window is interdependent with the others. A change in your *hidden* window will affect the size of your *open* window, and so on. The Johari Window is useful for not only understanding self disclosure but for also understanding ourselves. One of the best ways for us to evolve and to improve in our personal relationships is to be aware of the influence that information from others about ourselves has on who we are and who we are becoming. It is important that we remain open to such information about ourselves.

Now that we have examined self-disclosure in terms of its role in relationship development, we will discuss some self-disclosure guidelines to better understand the ways in which self-disclosure can be either helpful or harmful.

Self-Disclosure Guidelines

Self-disclosure is necessary in nearly all relationships, especially those we would like to become more intimate. Not all of our relationships are of an intimate nature nor do we desire them to be. In such situations, self disclosure is not as important, which explains the fact that we may know some people for a very long time and still reveal very little personal information about ourselves, keeping the relationship at a certain distance. Self-disclosure has its challenges. Knowledge of a few self-disclosure guidelines should help in the effective use of this skill.

Guideline One: Self-Disclosure Should Happen over Time.

Self-disclosing too much too soon can result in inaccurate perceptions, hurt feelings, and negative reactions. Just think of the problems you might encounter if you were to disclose to a co-worker your negative feelings about your boss and this co-worker reported the information to the boss. We should be cognizant of the fact that once something is disclosed, it cannot be taken back; it can leave you vulnerable and it can leave you at the mercy of unethical communicators.

Guideline Two: Be Aware of Strategic Self-Disclosure.

This involves the use of disclosure by others about themselves in order to learn information about you. Using the norm of reciprocity, such individuals disclose information about themselves that they want to know about you. A person might tell you he is divorced or single in hopes that you will reveal in return. A co-worker might disclose the amount of her bonus to find out the amount of yours.

Sometimes others will reveal things about themselves in the hopes that you will respond with your own information. © 2008, JupiterImages Corporation.

Guideline Three: Avoid Over Disclosing.

Individuals have been known to engage in over disclosure in many contexts. Getting something off your mind is cathartic. The classic example of this is the person sitting next to you on a long plane ride who tells you his life story, whether you would like to know it or not. Why do you think this happens? It is safe! For many, the act of self-disclosing to a perfect stranger not only fulfills cathartic purposes but is also safe from the threat that the information may be used against them. If we operate under the assumption that the two of you will never see one another again, then, yes, the self-disclosure certainly is both cathartic and safe. However, it is not always pleasant for the receiver, and may backfire if you cross paths with the individual in another context. Stanly Milgram's notion that came to be called **six degrees of separation** supports this likelihood and illustrates that crossing paths with a stranger again is more likely than you may think.[14]

Guideline Four: Be Aware of Self-Disclosure's Burden.

There are times in life when it is best not to know certain things. Our disclosure can be an unnecessary burden on those to whom we disclose. Examples of this are enacted in numerous movies and TV shows about gangsters. Typically, the "boss" does not disclose information to his family to keep them from being forced to tell if captured by their opponents. This is also a dilemma when families need to choose whether to tell a child he or she is adopted, or to inform a spouse that you think his or her best friend is attractive. The decision is based on the moral and ethical viewpoints of the communicator.

This is important to keep in mind when you are on the receiving end of the disclosure. A high school teacher ran into a problem when a student disclosed her drug use. The student asked the teacher not to tell anyone, especially her parents. The teacher, who wanted to be supportive and keep the confidence of her student, felt torn by the disclosure, but was ethically and professionally obligated to report the use to the proper individuals. This disclosure from the teacher's perspective was important in order to intervene on an illegal and harmful act; however, it was difficult for both the student and the teacher, as his report was seen as a breach of trust.

Disclosure and the Web

The element of anonymity in an online exchange provides a sense of freedom not experienced by those in face-to-face interactions: Freedom from shyness, freedom from self-consciousness, and in most cases, freedom from identity. Such freedom provides individuals with a sense of false confidence which often results in individuals practicing accelerated forms of self-disclosure. This is not necessarily a negative thing, as there are studies indicating the use of disclosure to be easier and more comfortable in online discussions, often resulting in the formation of long-term, real life relationships.[15]

Although disclosure may be accelerated and result in long-term relationship formation, it may not always be helpful and ethical, as researchers Coffey and Woolworth found as they examined virtual forums about strongly emotional local issues.[16] Those who communicated about the situation in this online community forum were found to be aggressive, hostile, and even threatening.

Case in point, communicating on the Web is public communication regardless of one's screen name, and/or avatar, and the guidelines for self-disclosure and ethical communication apply to this context as much as any other. Although we would like to think we are anonymous when communicating in cyber relationships, we really are not.[17] This was true in the infamous Scott Peterson trial where his Internet activity was retrieved by authorities and used as evidence against him.

RELATIONSHIP MAINTENANCE: WHY DON'T MY RELATIONSHIPS LAST?

Relationship maintenance is not always easy. It takes time, effort, and skill. Important relationships, however, are worth such efforts. Often our intentions are good, but we find that our communication with others is not always effective. This is illustrated when you find yourself thinking something along these lines: "The more I talk the worse this seems to get," "That's not what I meant," "You are taking this the wrong way," or "You just do not understand me/the situation/ this relationship." Such thoughts can be attributed to many factors: emotions, habits, lack of understanding, undeveloped communication skills, or lack of knowledge.

Emotion

Emotionally charged situations often result in ineffective communication.
© 2008, JupiterImages Corporation.

Emotion is a powerful part of our human identities. Its power has been illustrated by the numerous studies linking emotional stress to a variety of health problems.[18] Emotion is not only linked to our personal health, but also to our behavior. Daniel Goleman illustrates this point in his books, *Emotional Intelligence: Why it can matter more than IQ* (1997) and *Working with Emotional Intelligence* (1998).[19] Goleman argues that people who are able to succeed at communicating in highly emotional situations are successful at recognizing and controlling their impulsive and emotional responses. Goleman's points are best illustrated by reflecting on your own behavior.

Take a Closer Look

Emotional Communication

Take a moment to think about the following:

- When was the last time you had an argument with someone?
- Who was it?
- What type of relationship was (is) it?
- What was it about?
- How did you behave? (shout, say things you regretted, avoid the person, passively agree to avoid an argument, stay calm)
- Was your communication behavior in this particular conflict typical of you? If not, how do you typically behave?
- If so, what way?
- If not, how does it differ?
- Why do you think it is different?

Many of our communication responses, especially in highly emotional situations, are based on communication habits. These habits are typically consistent with the communication behavior of influential adults who we observed and interacted with throughout our formative years.

Goleman asserts that people who are able to refrain from interacting based purely on emotions are successful in many aspects of their lives, including relationships. Those who can recognize an emotion being experienced and maintain control over it rather than becoming emotionally highjacked are the people who perform best, regardless of IQ.

This is explained further by brain studies indicating when we experience intense emotions like stress, anxiety, or anger, our brains often do not use our working memory (i.e., paying attention, remembering important information), but rather the brain falls back on simple, highly familiar routines. *Routines* refer to habits we learned from the time we were very young. Once we are operating in a routine state, complex thought is put aside.[20] Your brain is not operating at full capacity.[21]

In addition to the emotional habits we form, the knowledge we seek and the skills we work to develop influence our success. Much of our communication is based on habits that have been formed as a result of our life experiences via modeling, trial and error (induction), and our individual learning. These habits are useful in many situations; however, they explain why we do not improve our communication skills. Many of us are not aware of our habits. Once you become aware of ineffective communication habits, you have two choices: you can change or you can remain the same. Many people remain doing the same things because they simply have not developed a better way to communicate, or they do not believe they are capable of change. Many of these beliefs are grounded in the fact that we receive very little communication training in our lives and simply lack the knowledge, have not developed the skill, or have not thought about how our communication affects our relationships with others.

The Marshmallow Experiment and Emotional Intelligence

The ability to resist impulses is the root of all emotional self-control, since all emotions, by their very nature, lead to impulses to act.

A study illustrating the impact that control of our emotional impulses has on our life outcomes was conducted by psychologist Walter Michel during the 1960s. In the study four-year-olds were given the following proposal:

If you will wait until after I run an errand, you can have two marshmallows when I return. If you cannot wait until I return, then you can have a marsh-mallow now, but only one.

The researcher then left a marshmallow on the table and left the room.

The behavior of these children was found to be twice as powerful a predictor of what their SAT scores would be as was IQ at age four. The children who resisted had earned average SAT test scores 210 points (out of 1,600 possible points) higher than those who could not resist temptation. It was found that when these same children were followed and revisited in adulthood, those who were able to resist taking the marshmallow were *still* more intellectually attentive, better able to concentrate, better able to develop close relationships, and showed better self control when frustrated. Goleman concluded that the self-imposed delay of gratification is the essence of emotional self-regulation. Such self-regulation results in one's ability to avoid impulse when doing things such as building a business, solving an algebraic equation, or pursuing the Stanley Cup and results in one's ability to think and work more effectively.

In our reactions to and communication with those with whom we have relationships, it is critical that we be mindful of the power to avoid reacting on impulse, as doing so may result in communicating in ways that permanently damage our relationships.[22]

Relational Clash: An Explanation

Each of our relationships is in a state of change. As we change, so does our interaction with others. This is inevitable, as human beings are not static. We grow more mature and accumulate life experiences. Many relationships experience changes based on a series of tensions that Baxter and Montgomery call dialectics.[23] **Dialectics** are polar opposites. If we examine a conventional definition provided by the Merriam-Webster dictionary, we find that dialectical tension is an "opposition between two interacting forces or elements." Baxter and Montgomery's dialectical theory is consistent with this definition. There are three dialectics, or opposites, at work for each individual in a relationship: autonomy/connection, openness/closedness, and novelty/predictability.

Autonomy/connection has to do with our need to be connected to significant others at times, and at other times, to exert our independence. Relationships typically undergo the greatest connection as they are initiating and developing. It is through communication acts such as self-disclosure and shared experiences that we feel connected with others. However, our feeling of connection can become overwhelming, leaving us feeling as if we need some space in the relationship. That need for space can manifest itself in either a simple fashion (e.g., going out for a walk alone once a day, the gym, the bookstore, shopping, to a sports game or movie) or in a more complex way (e.g., pursuing hobbies independent of the other, taking physical time away from the relationship). It is when these needs are not in harmony with our partner's needs that the relationship may experience strain.

Openness/closedness has to do with our need to share information with others versus our need for privacy, or closedness. Sometimes the needs for privacy may not be observed when partners are seeking closeness, resulting in relational tension.

Novelty/predictability has to do with the excitement and uncertainty level present in a relationship. When relationships are a bit unpredictable, or novel, we feel increased interest in finding out the unknown. This is best explained by reflecting on the first few weeks of a new romantic relationship. Every experience and conversation is new and exciting. Each interaction during this time works to reduce uncertainty, thereby creating predictability. When the relationship is too predictable, individuals may become bored and are not motivated to maintain the relationship. If it is too novel, they may become anxious to the point where they may choose to end the relationship.

These dialectics can be experienced in degrees. Seldom is someone's need for novelty so complete that it does not require some predictable elements. Like children on a seesaw, rocking back and forth, each of these dialectical sets are shifting within our relationships. The problem arises when they are in opposition, such as when one person feels a need for novelty while the other person needs more predictability.

How does a sense of novelty keep you interested in a relationship?
© 2008, JupiterImages Corporation.

CONFLICT MANAGEMENT: BUT, AREN'T WE GOING TO DISAGREE?

The presence of conflict in our relationships is both inevitable and helpful in relational growth, as well as our own self-improvement. Conflict, however, is an occurrence that is often viewed as something undesirable and something to avoid. Many individuals do indeed avoid conflict because they lack the communication skills necessary for a successful outcome. When the appropriate communication skills are employed, conflict can be effectively managed, resulting in improved relationships.

Conflict Styles

Blake and Mouton have identified five communication styles people use when engaged in conflict.[24] In their model, they plot each style on a grid, examining the extent to which the communicator is concerned with getting his or her needs met and/or meeting the needs of others (see Figure 6.2).

Avoidance.   Avoidance is a lose/lose approach to conflict and is characterized by withdrawing from the situation. We may physically leave or we may leave psychologically by not acknowledging that a conflict exists. Withdrawing is problematic because to avoid the conflict is to simply put off the

Take a Closer Look

How Do You Handle Conflict?

Before you continue reading, take a moment to reflect on your communication behavior during your last conflict with someone:

- What was the conflict about?
- How was the conflict resolved?
- What did you say or do to get it resolved?
- If you were able to relive the conflict situation, would you communicate differently?
- Did your communication behavior during this conflict match the behavior of one of your parents?

Many of our communication choices during a conflict are based on the communication patterns we learn as we grow up. The modeling we witness results in the formation of subconscious communication habits typically consistent with the communication behavior of influential adults who we observed and interacted with throughout our formative years.

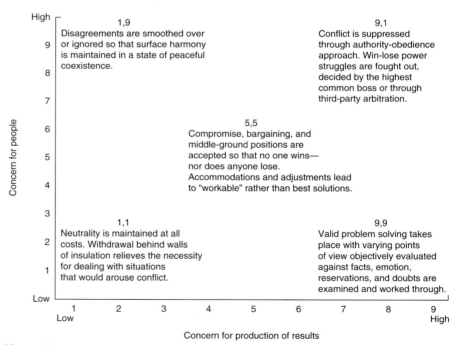

Figure 6.2
Blake and Mouton grid

inevitable, allowing the relationship to reach termination without making any effort to salvage it. Avoidance is not, however, always a negative conflict strategy. It can be positive if we are either too emotional to discuss the reasons we are upset or we simply do not have the time to devote to the discussion. Whenever we use avoidance to cool off before discussing the reasons for our anger, we are using avoidance constructively.

Competition. Competing is a win/lose approach to conflict as the parties are striving to be on top, and not to understand each other. Although there are times when there is no alternative but to compete (a job, love interest), this is not the norm. Most conflict situations allow for mutual negotiations; there is not a winner or a loser.

Accommodation. This is a lose/win approach to conflict and it is characterized by allowing others to have their way. Like those who avoid conflict, accommodation allows us to avoid confrontation and the discomfort often associated with it. This is not an inherently negative approach to conflict, as sometimes it is important that we accommodate (e.g., the issue simply is not that important or not worth the clash). If this is a pattern in communication, however, the person doing the accommodating is left with unmet relational needs. This cannot persist if the relationship is to continue.

Compromise. The two most effective approaches to conflict are compromise and collaboration. **Compromise** is considered a lose/lose approach to conflict in that each party is required to give up something to solve the situation. This is not necessarily a bad thing, but it falls short of collaboration, in that both parties are left somewhat unsatisfied with the outcome. The better of the two is to collaborate.

Collaboration. **Collaboration** is a win/win approach to conflict with each person in the conflict situation leaving the conflict completely satisfied with the outcome. This is a time-consuming approach that takes mutual motivation, time, and effort.

Resolving Conflict through Collaboration

Define the Conflict. The collaborative process involves several steps. Sometimes conflict manifests itself in covert ways. Arguments about the unfinished household chores may really be someone's lack of consideration for another's feelings. Very often this kind of conflict is not easily seen. Thus, accurately defining the conflict is critical to collaboration. Fisher and Ury suggest focusing on mutual interests, not positions; defending a position directs less attention to meeting the underlying concerns of the parties.[25] When defining the nature of the disagreement, individuals should focus on the problem and not attack, blame, or criticize. If you are committed to managing a conflict productively, you need to be mindful of the language used to define the conflict.

It's not always easy to focus on the problem and not attack, blame, or criticize.
© 2008, JupiterImages Corporation.

Poor example: "You made me angry when you didn't do the dishes."

Better example: "When you don't do the dishes, I feel as if my wishes are not important to you."

Poor example: "You are rude."

Better example: "I feel hurt when you talk to me using that harsh tone of voice."

Poor example: "It is all your fault that we are in this financial situation."

Better example: "Let's work together to understand how we got into financial trouble in the first place.

Generate Solution Criteria. We must openly discuss what we hope to get from a resolution. This involves creating mutually agreed upon criteria that the resolution must meet. When approaching the development of such criteria, it is important to engage in perspective taking. That is, to view the conflict from your opponent's position. This is one of the most powerful negotiating tools we can use.[26] It is through perspective taking that we may come to realize the emotion and power of the other party's point of view, and to provide ourselves with other explanations for another's actions.[27] We should also approach this as a cooperative activity to be worked on by all who are involved. Those who are actively involved in the decision-making process are more likely to commit to the solution than those who are not.

Brainstorm Solutions. Once the criteria have been developed, the solutions to the problem should be brainstormed together without judgment. It is a good idea to approach the brainstorming session with clarification that it is not part of the active negotiation. This will enable parties to feel free to express all ideas in creative ways without the fear of premature judgment or premature decision making.[28]

Evaluate and Implement Solutions. The brainstormed solutions that best meet the criteria are the ones to use (three is a manageable number). Temporary implementation is essential, given that we do not know if a solution is going to work until we try it out. Once the solution is temporarily revisited, those involved in the conflict should meet again to discuss its effectiveness. If it is not working, the next best solution is implemented. If none of the solutions work, we move to the next best strategy: compromise.

There is nothing inherently wrong with conflict in our relationships. It is an inevitable part of interacting with others and can work to strengthen our relationships. Successful conflict management is dependent on the communication strategies we use to express our dissatisfaction. When the appropriate strategy is used, the results can be beneficial to the relationship.

Mediation Training and Compromise

Licensed mediators often use compromise to help individuals reach agreements. One commonly used strategy is to have individuals think through their Best Alternative to a Negotiated Agreement (BATNA).[29] This is a starting point to help motivate individuals to work toward mutual resolution. Many individuals who choose to mediate are often in the midst of legal battles that may result in harsh results for the losing party. Those who agree to mediate often realize the best alternative to a negotiated agreement is worse than a compromise (e.g., expensive fines, jail time, loss of job, loss of license to work). Thus, they proceed with an attempt to collaborate or to compromise in the hope that the discussion with the other party and mediator will result in a mutually beneficial decision.

This was illustrated by the example of a woman working as a volunteer mediator in small claims court. She was mediating a case in which a young high school student was working at a car wash drying cars. He was suing his former employer for lost wages and penalties for not giving him his last check within the legally mandated thirty days after his termination. The employer maintained the position that the student quit his job. The student stated that he was fired from his job. Upon the student's leaving, the employer had cut the check and was waiting for the student to pick it up. The student had expected it to be mailed.

Through mediation, the employer decided it would be better to work to solve the problem and avoid further court dates and general hassle. Subsequently, he decided to pay the student well over the amount legally mandated but less than the student was asking. The student refused the payment, abandoned the mediation process, and brought the case in front of the judge. He was given half of the amount of money he would have gotten had he agreed to the compromise. In this situation, the compromise would have prevented unnecessary hassle on the part of the employer and would have provided more money for the student.

RELATIONSHIP TERMINATION: NOW WHAT DO I DO?

Relationships terminate for many reasons: lack of time or motivation, growing apart, or unresolved conflicts. One theory that helps us understand relationship dissolution is **social exchange theory**.[30]

Social exchange theory relates to perceived relational costs and rewards. When we perceive the costs of a relationship to outweigh the rewards, we are likely to terminate the relationship. The costs and rewards of a relationship can manifest themselves in many ways, as they are linked to our unique perceptions. Relationship rewards may be companionship, inspiration, financial stability, or security. A relational cost may be time spent working on the relationship, money spent, psychological energy, or physical energy. When we weigh the costs against the rewards, we expect them to be equal or to be rewarding. If they are not, we either look for alternatives or leave the relationship. See Figure 6.3.

This theory explains why some people stay in relationships that are stressful, difficult, and even abusive. If the person in the relationship perceives the rewards to be acceptable given the costs, he or she will stay in the relationship.

Relational termination may occur for a myriad of reasons: abandonment, mutual decision or circumstance. Depending on the circumstances of the relational dissolution, individuals may react with relief, joy, or profound sadness. When profound sadness is the case, a person may physically leave the relationship, but psychologically move through a grief process. One of the

Sometimes the costs of a relationship are too great and it's time to leave.
© 2008, JupiterImages Corporation.

Rewards	Points	Costs	Points	Total	Balance +/−/=
Companionship	+10	Emotionally draining	−8	= +2	It is well worth the emotional drain.
Fun	+5	Verbally abusive	−15	= −10	It is not worth the fun.
Supportive	+5	Time consuming	−5	= 0	It is a balanced situation

FIGURE 6.3   Social Exchange Theory: A Mathematical Representation

most significant contributors to grief research, Elisabeth Kübler-Ross, out-lined five stages of grief, which are often presented with varying modifica-tions to help us understand this process.[31] From a communication stand-point, these stages are helpful in understanding the communication taking place as relationships terminate. The stages of grieving can be found on the WebCom companion site to this book.

WHY ARE VIRTUAL RELATIONSHIPS SO ATTRACTIVE?

Virtual relationships are definitely here to stay and are manifesting them-selves by way of online dating services, chat rooms, bulletin boards, and blogs. With the success rate of service like Match.com and Love@aol.com, the political influence of blogs, and the general impact virtual communities have on our lives, it is clear that this is a popular context in which people meet and develop relationships.[32]

Life in a virtual world is much different than face-to-face world, as we are given the freedom to interact with others without the need to consider the impact that our dress, looks, or nonverbal communication may have on the relationship. Let us look at some of the findings regarding this special rela-tionship genre.

Virtual Initiation

The nature of online, or cyber, relationships is changing the way we interact with others. As one author so aptly stated, "On-line chat rooms are like bars without knowing what anyone else looks like."[33] Whether the relationship initiates through mutual interests (chat rooms about dogs, scrapbooking, *Star Trek*), in a search for companionship (Match.com) or by curiosity (regular visits to blog spaces or bulletin boards), relationship initiation in this context is different from face-to-face initiation.

In online environments, we do not have the advantage of the same types of nonverbal cues used in face-to-face relationships which help us to under-stand the relational level of a message, the evaluation of someone's immedi-ate response to a comment, or to form a realistic perception.[34] It has been reported that many individuals approach cyber relationships with an unreal-istic outlook. Without physical cues to provide a reality check, it is easy for us to project hopes and dreams onto the person on the other end of the computer terminal.[35] This is not only deceptive, but can also lead to premature intimacy, impulsive actions, and even dangerous decisions. The anonymity of a computer screen makes people bolder, leading them to try on more daring personalities that may result in deception and disappointment.[36]

Do you think that people tend to have unrealistic expectations in virtual relationships?
© 2008, JupiterImages Corporation.

This is not to suggest that all Internet relationships are dangerous, as there are plenty of statistics suggesting that meeting people on the Internet is no more dangerous than meeting someone in various face-to-face environments.[37] Virtual relationships have a positive impact on many people. Senior citizens are one of the fastest-growing groups using the Internet to build new, supportive friendships, and to find romantic love after the loss of a husband or wife. It has enabled self-conscious teenagers to interact more freely,[38] and helped couples to develop stronger relationships than those who date the old-fashioned way.[39] The positive contributions of online relationships are further corroborated by the number of people who do successfully meet and marry after meeting online. Perhaps you know a couple that met on the Internet?

Virtual Maintenance

For those who have been labeled geographically challenged, technology now enables people to maintain friendships, family relationships, and courtships regardless of distance, revolutionizing the ability to continue relational growth even when physically apart. Virtual relationship maintenance also expands our use of technology to maintain relationships at home. Survey results among those who have been deemed Generation Xers revealed that 20 percent of them use their wireless phones to keep track of someone they are dating and 25 percent of wireless users said they perceive having closer relationships now that they own wireless phones.[40] The use of the cell phone continues to impact this maintenance with our ability to text message and to send and receive e-mails and photos.

How have cell phones impacted how you maintain your relationships?
© 2008, JupiterImages Corporation.

Virtual Termination

Relationship termination in the cyber world can be abrupt and difficult. It can be as easy as turning off our computers, changing our e-mail address, and simply not responding to others.

Virtual relationship termination makes the difficult and unpleasant task easier for the one ending the relationship, but much harder for those on the receiving end. As reported in several newspaper articles, a growing number of individuals are using the Internet to break up romantic relationships, end friendships, and even to fire employees.[41] Modern couples can validate and announce to the world the termination of their relationship by updating their profile on My Space.com from "taken" to "single."

Although many communication scholars would agree that there are certain messages that should, without question, be delivered in person, many individuals who lack the confidence, courage, and communication skills are able to avoid such a task by using their computers.

Virtual relationships also affect the termination of many nonvirtual relationships. For example, Brophy found that virtual relationships have been the impetus for the termination of live relationships as cyber romances have been accused of straining marriages to the breaking point.[42] Examining some of the factors influencing virtual relationship development is helpful in understanding communication in this ever-changing context.

SUMMARY

This chapter began with Aristotle and ended with a discussion of virtual relationships. We have discussed various types of relationship genres and influences on those relationships, followed by discussion of relationship initiation, maintenance, and termination and the impact of the virtual world on these stages.

Throughout this chapter, we have seen that, regardless of the century in which we are living or the context in which we form relationships, one fact remains the same: meaningful contact with others is an integral part of our lives affecting our health and life satisfaction.

Our communication skills have a profound impact on the way we initiate, maintain, and terminate relationships. Relationships are not limited in the twenty-first century to the traditional forms of conversation. There are rapidly changing contexts in which we are forming contacts with people around the globe, crossing cultural, gender, age, physical ability or disability, sexual orientation, professional, political, and religious lines.

As communication contexts continue to evolve, so do the communication skills and tools we use to function within them. For example, in virtual relationships, we rely on different types of nonverbal nuances such as the look of a person's avatar, the wording of our messages, and the way a person behaves in an online forum.

As technology evolves, the digital world has offered us an evolution in communication tools. It began with a digital letter, the e-mail, which we can review and refine before sending. Then we moved to exchanging a rapid fire of one-line messages in the form of instant messaging. Now, we are using a virtual face-to-face communication via the combination of a Web cam and a phone. We are in the midst of real-time interpersonal interactions in a virtual world.

A communicator can now pick the method of computer mediated communication that is most comfortable and conducive to the communication goal. In a time when relationships are built, maintained, and terminated in a virtual world, are we going to see the development of new communication techniques and communication tools to transfer the emotional cues of one-on-one contact? How are we going to maintain the complex nonverbal interactions that are part of interpersonal relationships?

ENDNOTES

1. The National Center for Health Statistics. (2004). Accessed January 2, 2005 "http://www.cdc.gov/nchs/" http://www.cdc.gov/nchs/

2. M. Fox, "Marriage Keeps You Healthy, Study Shows," *Facts of File World News Digest: U.S. and World News: 1940–Present* (December 16, 2004).

3. I. Wolcott. The Influence of Family Relationships on Later Life. *Family Matters,* 48, Spring. (1997). Also L. Marcel, I. Connelly, S. Grzybowski, A. Michalos, J. Berkowitz, and H. Thommasen, "Determinants of Rural Physicians' Life and Job Satisfaction," *Social Indicators Research* 69 (1) (October 30, 2004).

4. D. Ross, *Aristotle: The Nicomachean Ethics.* 1998. (Trans.). London: Oxford University Press, 1998 (original work published 350 B.C.E.).

5. Ibid.

6. R. Reeves, "Friendship Is the Invisible Thread Running Through Society," *NS Essay* (April 19, 2004): 29–31.

7. C. H. Dodd, *Dynamics of Intercultural Communication* (5th ed.). Boston: McGraw Hill, 1998. Also R. Axtell, *Dos and Taboos around the World* (2nd ed.) (New York: Wiley, 1990a), R. Axtell, *Dos and Taboos of Hosting International Visitors* (New York: Wiley, 1990b), and M. H. DeFleur, P. Kearney, T. G. Plax, and M. L. DeFleur, *Fundamentals of Human Communication: Social Science in Everyday Life* (3rd ed.). Boston: McGraw Hill, 2005.

8. P. A. Begley. "Communication with Egyptians," in L. Samovar & R. Porter, *Intercultural Communication: A Reader* (Belmont, CA: Thomson Wadsworth, 2003).

9. M. Scudéry, *La princesse de Cleves.* Paris: Gallimard, collection Folio, n 778, 1653.

10. "Networking as Professional Development," *Public Relations Tactics* 12 (1) (2005). Retrieved January 7, 2005, from EBSCO Host Database. Also E. Zimmerman, Before Applying, Check Out the Blogs. *New York Times.* (October 3, 2004).

11. Taylor, C. 10 Things We Learned about Blogs. *Time Magazine.* January 4, 2004.

12. Alvin W. Gouldner, "The Norm of Reciprocity: A Preliminary Statement," *American Sociological Review 25* (1960): 161–178.

13. J. Luft, *Of Human Interaction.* Palo Alto: National Press, 1969.

14. D. Saxbe, "Six Degrees of Separation: Two New Studies Test the 'Six Degrees of Separation' Hypothesis," *Psychology Today.com* (accessed January 2, 2005).

15. H. E. Marano, 2004, December 10. "Cyberspace: Love Online," *Psyched for Success,* http://cms.psychologytoday.com (accessed January 2, 2005).

16. B. Coffey and S. Woolworth, "Destroy the Scum, and Then Neuter Their Families: The Web Forum as a Vehicle for Community Discourse," *Social Science Journal,* 41 (1) (2004).

17. D. Pekoff, "Public Flames and Private Fantasies: When Is Computer-mediated Communication Private?" Paper presented at the Western States Communication Association Conference in San Jose, CA, 1994.

18. R. Glaser, B. Rabin, M. Chesney, S. Gohen, and B. Natelson, "Stress-Induced Immunomodulation," *The Journal of the American Medical Association* 281 (24) (1999). Also C. H. Schenck, M. Mahowald, and R. Sack, "Assessment and Management of Insomnia," *The Journal of the American Medical Association,* 289 (19) (2003) and K. Orth-Gomér, S. Wamala, M. Horsten, K. Schenck-Gustafsson, N. Schneiderman, and M. Mittleman, "Marital Stress Worsens Prognosis in Women with Coronary Heart Disease," *The Journal of the American Medical Association,* (23) (2000): 284.

19. D. Goleman, *Emotional Intelligence: Why It Can Matter More than IQ* (New York: Bantam Books, 1997). Also D. Goleman, *Working with Emotional Intelligence,* New York: Bantam Books, 1998.

20. Goleman, 1998.

21. Warr, P. and Bunce, D. (1995). Trainee Characteristics and the Outcomes of Open Learning. *Personnel Psychology,* 48, 347–375. Also M. Belenky, B. Clinchy, N. Goldberger, and J. Tarule, *Women's Ways of Knowing: The Development of Self, Voice and Mind* (New York: Basic Books, 1982).

22. Goleman 1997.

23. L. A. Baxter, and B. Montgomery, *Relating: Dialogues and Dialectics* (New York: Guilford Press, 1996).

24. R. Blake and J. Mouton. "The Fifth Achievement." *Journal of Applied Behavioral Science* 6 (4) (1970).

25. R. Fisher and W. Ury, *Getting to Yes: Negotiating Agreement Without Giving In* (New York: Penguin Books, 1991).

26. Ibid.

27. D. M. Kolb and J. Williams, (2003). *Everyday Negotiations.* San Francisco: Jossey-Bass, 2003.

28. Fisher and Ury.

29. Society of St.Vincent de Paul Institute for Conflict Management. *Basic Mediation Training Manual: Victim-Offender Reconciliation Program.* 2003.

30. Thibault, J. W. and Kelley, H. (1952). *The Social Psychology of Groups.* New York: John Wiley & Sons. 1952.

31. E. Kübler-Ross, *On Death and Dying.* New York: Touchstone, 1969.

32. Williams, J. Love.com: Virtual Dating Game. *Psychology Today.* (February 14, 2003). Also S. Carpenter, "For Your Type, Keep Typing," *Los Angeles Times,* February 9, 2006, http://www.calendarlive.com/dating/cl-wk-cover9feb09,0,5279441.story (accessed May 21, 2007).

33. S. Roane, *How to Work a Room: The Ultimate Guide to Savvy Socializing In-person and On-line.* New York: Harper Collins, 2000.

34. J. S. McQuillen, "The Influence of Technology on the Initiation of Interpersonal Relationships," *Education* 123 (3) (2003).

35. B. Brophy, "Saturday Night and You're All Alone?" *U.S. News & World Report* 122 (6) (1997). Retrieved January 3, 2005 from from EBSCO Host Database.

36. Ibid.

37. S. Miller and S. Turkle, "Net Worth," *People, 45* (13) (1996). Retrieved January 3, 2005 from EBSCO Host Database. Also K. Springen, "Matchmaker, Matchmaker, Find Me a Web Site," *Newsweek* (August 3, 1998).

38. S. Globus, "The Good the Bad and the Internet," *Current Health 2,* 28 (6) (2002).

39. "Romances that start on the Internet may last longer, researcher says," (2002, April 26) *Chronicle of Higher Education* (48), 33, pA35. Retrieved May 21, 2007 from EBSCO Host Database.

40. T. Ford, "Funny Facts," *RCR Wireless News* 18 (33) (August 16, 1999), EBSCO Host Database (accessed May 21, 2007).

41. D. Aucoin, "To end a romance, just press 'end'." *Boston Globe,* accessed www.boston.com, May 21, 2007. Also Zaslow, J. "High-Tech Breakups are Quick but Inflict a Special Pain: Getting Even with Her.com. (February 14, 2007).*The Wall Street Journal.* Personal Journal, D1, D10.

42. Brophy

REFERENCES

R. B. Adler, L. B. Rosenfeld, N. Towne, and R. F. Proctor II, *Interplay: The Process of Interpersonal Communication* (7th ed.) (New York: Harcourt Brace, 1997).

I. Altman and D. Taylor. *Social Penetration: The Development of Interpersonal Relationships* (New York: Holt, Rinehart & Winston, 1973).

S. Brehm and J. Brehm, *Psychological Reactance: A Theory of Freedom and Control* (New York: Academic Press, 1981).

O. Burkeman, "Keep Your Distance," *The Guardian* (UK), September 14, 1999, http://members.aol.com/nonverbals3/news.htm. (accessed January 7, 2005).

J. R. Gibb, "Defensive Communication," *Journal of Communication* 11 (1961): 141–148.

D. Kersey, *Please Understand Me II: Temperament, Character, Intelligence* (California: Prometheus Nemesis Book Company, 1998).

K. McKenna, A. Green, and M. Gleason, "Relationship Formation on the Internet: What's the Big Attraction?" *Journal of Social Issues* 58 (1) (2002).

Merriam-Webster On-Line Dictionary, http://www.m-w.com/cgi-bin/dictionary/(accessed December 28, 2004).

NetLingo Internet Dictionary 2004. www.netlingo.com (accessed January 14, 2005).

Technology Encyclopedia. www.techweb.com/encyclopedia (accessed May 21, 2007).

WHAT SHOULD I KNOW ABOUT INTERVIEWING?

LEARNING OBJECTIVES

After reading this chapter, you should understand the following concepts:

- Interviewing differs from general conversation in that there is an interviewer and an interviewee, specifically asking and answering questions to further specific goals.
- Open questions are useful for exploring topics in depth, while closed questions limit the answers to allow the interviewer to gather more specific information.
- Biased questions, double-barreled questions, open-to-closed questions, and unreliable questions are all potential hazards when conducting an interview.
- To prepare for an interview, you should have a clear goal and an interview plan for achieving that goal.
- Interviews have an opening, a body, and a closing, which are designed to set the foundation for the interview, accomplish the goals of the interview, and end the interview on a good note.

INTRODUCTION

It's about 3 A.M. on a Wednesday morning and you decide that you should probably try to do a little homework before going to bed. It seems especially important to you, because your calendar says that you have a physics exam at 11 A.M. So you open up your physics notebook and you are faced with "fractals." What the heck is a fractal?

Feeling relaxed, you immediately begin to scan the bold print in the chapter you thought you were covering this week. No fractals. There are plenty of bold-print items talking about "photons," "electromagnetic radiation," and something called "Plank's constant." But there is not a fractal to be found!

Not quite in a panic, and instead of looking in the book's table of contents or subject index, you make up your mind that the only reasonable response to this emergency is to "Google it" and see what you can find. You stumble on "Fractal's World," but you are pretty sure that a fractal is not a cartoon character. Upon further examination, you discover plenty of pictures and illustrations of fractals, including a "fractal of the day," but you don't find an explanation of fractals that you can understand.

KEYWORDS

interviewing
screening interview
counseling or helping interview
primary question
secondary question
open question
closed question
multiple-choice questions
dichotomous questions
biased questions
leading question
loaded question
double-barreled question
open-to-closed question
reliability
interview plan
opening
body
closing

Now nearing panic, but before dropping physics and giving up your child-hood dream of being the first scientist to master cold fusion, you come up with a sound strategy for solving the problem: You sleep on it! At 10:00 A.M. you wake up, put on a hat, and trek off to visit your physics professor. After all, the test is not until 11:00 A.M. There is still plenty of time!

You arrive at your professor's office, knock on the door, and request a few minutes because you have a *quick* question. You say that you couldn't find the term *fractal* in your textbook, and you wonder if you could get a brief definition. After the laughter dies down, the professor gives you the fast answer you asked for, and you go on your way, confident in your ability to "ace" the physics test.

When you return home after the test, you get on the phone and complain to your parents that college is hard and that you just pulled an "all-nighter" to prepare for your physics test. While the parents are feeling sorry for you, you ask if they could send a few dollars to cover some expenses. Recognizing that you are working so hard, they agree to send you as much money as you want.

What do fractals, photons, and cold fusion have to do with interviewing? Probably not much. But during that visit to your professor's office, whether you know it or not, *you conducted an information gathering interview!* When you asked your parents for cash, *you conducted a persuasive interview.* In both cases, you had a specific goal to accomplish. To help achieve those goals, in both cases, you asked questions, and you received answers. A goal orientation and the asking and answering of questions are essential components of an interview.

You probably take part in many interviews every day without really thinking about it. Because interviewing is such a common activity, and because it is central to accomplishing a wide range of goals in our lives, it is important to approach it in a systematic and organized way. Understanding and organizing interviews is the focus of this unit.

WHAT IS INTERVIEWING?

We begin the discussion of **interviewing** with a definition or description of the concept. There will be plenty of information to put on tests, so there is no reason to include a definition just for that purpose. In this case, however, articulating a definition should make the subsequent discussion of the inter-view much more clear if we all begin at the same place.

The examples in the previous section give a reasonable idea of what an interview looks like. In addition, most of us have participated in interviews in either a casual or formal setting, so you probably have a decent idea of what is and what is not an interview. You probably know already that an interview is a *form of interpersonal communication* or conversation, so let's begin there.

Although it is true that all interviews are conversations, you should recognize that *all conversations are not interviews!* The ways in which conversations and interviews differ will help us get a handle on exactly how we should view an interview.

Two Parties

All interviews have two parties: interview*er* and an interview*ee*. More than two people could be participating in the event, but there will still be those two parties. For example, a group of reporters could be questioning the producers of the latest reality show, *Excessive and Unnecessary Ear Alteration,* about the rumor that the program could be turned into a full-length feature film. The group of curious reporters makes up one of the parties: the interviewer. The group of *EUEA* producers is the second party: the interviewee. Keep your fingers crossed that *this* movie never makes it to the theaters!

Questions and Answers

The primary structure of this kind of conversation centers on asking and answering questions. The kind of questions and sequence of questions that are asked are largely determined by the type of interview and goals for that interview. Types of questions and organization of questions will be discussed shortly.

Goals

Both parties in an interview have deliberate and specific goals they wish to accomplish with this event. Typical interview goals include gathering information, giving information, seeking employment, seeking employees, making a sale or creating an impression, helping self or others, evaluating employee performance, and assessment of self or another. The more precise or detailed you can be in determining your goals for an interview, the more clearly you can plan and organize your role in the process. Interview goals provide the purpose of the interview, determine the kinds of questions that will be asked, and, to some extent, affect the structure of the interaction.[1] If the goals of the interview are ambiguous or not well thought out, one or both of the parties will leave the interview unsatisfied.[2]

Awareness

All the people involved should know that they are participating in an interview. They should understand that this is not a casual conversation and that they are guided by their own goals for the interview.

Exchange of Roles

While roles of the parties remain constant, each participant engages in a brisk exchange of speaking and listening roles. Both parties in an interview ask as well as answer questions. There is no formula for determining who talks more in a particular context, but it depends on the type of interview (see following section), the goals of the individual parties for the interview, and the conversational styles of the participants.

A common view of an employment interview, for example, is that the employer (interviewer) asks all or most of the questions and the applicant (interviewee) provides all or most of the answers. This might be true in a **screening interview,** in which the employer is attempting to determine the qualifications of the applicant for the specific job being offered. However, in later interviews, the interviewee could be asking more questions to better

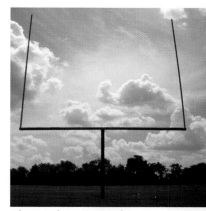

When you think of an interview, does a group of pushy reporters automatically come to mind?
© Milos Jokic, 2008, Shutterstock.

Clear and precise goals are as important for a successful interview as they are in other situations.
© David Lee, 2008, Shutterstock.

In a screening interview, the employer attempts to determine the applicant's qualifications.
© 2008, JupiterImages Corporation.

understand the nature of the specific position and the nature of the company. The applicant wants to know if he or she would like to work for this particular company. In this situation, the interviewer (employer) will likely do more talking to provide the necessary information to the applicant.

In a **counseling** or **helping interview,** a psychologist (interviewer) might ask some questions of the interviewee to determine the kind of problem he or she is experiencing, but then the counselor might do more of the talking to give advice to the interviewee about how to try to solve the problem. In other kinds of counseling interviews, the psychologist could determine that the best way to provide help is to ask questions for the purpose of gently guiding the interviewee to talk about his or her problems. In this case, the interviewer would ask a few questions while the interviewee does all or most of the talking.

WHAT TYPES OF QUESTIONS ARE USED IN INTERVIEWS?

As you already know, all interviews are structured around the asking and answering of questions. Although questions and answers might be viewed as a limitation on the interaction in an interview, there is a wide variety of question types that allow considerable flexibility in the kinds of conversations that you can hold. This section will explore a variety of types of questions and their uses.

Primary and Secondary Questions

A **primary question** is used to introduce topics or new areas of discussion. A primary question is easy to identify because it can stand alone, out of any kind of context, and yet it can still make perfect sense. Here are some examples of primary questions:

- Where did you attend high school?
- What is your opinion of the "designated hitter" rule in baseball?
- For what company have you been working the past two years?

A **secondary question** (or probing question) usually does not make much sense if asked outside of a particular context. This question is used to encourage an interviewee to keep talking, to provide additional or more focused information, or to clarify an answer. If an interviewee doesn't answer a question to the satisfaction of the interviewer, the interviewer can follow up the primary question with a secondary question. Secondary questions can be preplanned and written into your interview plan, or they can just spontaneously emerge during the course of the interview. Some examples of secondary questions that might be used to expand or probe responses to primary questions include the following:

- What classes did you think were the most interesting? (preplanned follow-up)
- Why? What was interesting to you about biology? (spontaneous follow-up)

- Do you think every player should play both offense and defense? (preplanned)
- What's so special about pitchers? (spontaneous)

- Which of those jobs did you like best? (preplanned)
- What was so unusual about that job? (spontaneous)

- Is there anything else that you would like to say?

Why are open questions useful for exploring a topic in depth?
© 2008, JupiterImages Corporation.

To avoid possibly influencing the interviewee's response, make an effort to keep your probing questions as nondirective or neutral as possible. Try not to say (with a shocked or surprised look on your face), "*Why* would you do *that?*" Instead, Willis suggests "Tell me more about that."[3]

In addition to asking an actual question as a secondary or probing question, the interviewer could also simply pause and wait for further response. The pause, combined with a posture and/or facial expression that indicates listening or curiosity can "nudge" an interviewee to provide additional information. It's probably a good idea to list possible probing questions on your interview guide, especially if you anticipate that a question will require some probing to accomplish the information-gathering goals of the interview.

Finally, be careful not to lead the interviewee with your probing questions or suggest an answer. Be as neutral as possible. See the section about biased questions that follows shortly.

Open and Closed Questions

Open Questions.   When using an **open question**, the interviewee has a great deal of freedom in how to respond to the question. An open question can request very general or nonspecific information, and there is usually very little direction provided by the interviewer as to the direction of the desired response. Here are some examples of open questions:

- Tell me what happened.
- How do you feel about smart videogames?
- What do you know about internet telephones?

Open questions can be very useful for exploring a topic in depth because the interviewee can talk about nearly any related topic for as long as he or she wants. Open questions also allow the interviewer to discover facts concerning a topic about which he or she knows very little. So this kind of question is good for exploring and investigation of new areas of interest. They can also be used to learn more about an interviewee's perspectives, priorities, and depth of knowledge of a particular topic.

The use of open questions requires that the interviewer be very skilled. The questions can take time to answer and therefore demand excellent listening skills. In addition, because the interviewer provides little direction for the desired response, the interviewee is free to go off in any direction with the answer. Consider this question asked by the interviewer: "What are your feelings about cable TV?" The purpose of the interview might be to discover the opinions of a community about programming on the local cable TV system. But because the question is so broad, the interviewee might seize that opportunity to complain about how the cable installer scared his dog or dug up his yard when laying the cable. It takes a good deal of interviewer skill to acknowledge that undesirable response and then to gently direct the interviewee to discuss programming. Consequently, in addition to discovering information consistent with the goals of the interview, the interview must also *manage* the interaction to keep the conversation on topic.

Finally, open questions are rarely useful for covering a wide range of topics because of the amount of time necessary for the interviewee to respond to each question. If the goal of the interview is not coverage of a small number of topics in depth, but a larger number of topics, a more closed type of question should be used.

Closed Questions.   In sharp contrast to an open question, a **closed question** attempts to limit or restrict the response and focus the interviewee on providing only the desired information. Closed questions allow the interviewer to better control the topics covered by the interviewee by requiring more precise and specific answers. Examples of closed questions include the following:

- What is your favorite summertime sport?
- What mode of transportation do you use to commute to work every day?
- In what city would you like to live?

Interviewers can use different types of closed questions to accomplish specific interview goals. In addition to the less restrictive questions, you can also use multiple-choice and dichotomous questions.

Multiple-choice questions restrict the interviewee's response options. Public opinion polls and other types of surveys often use this kind of question. Multiple choice is an example of extremely closed questions. They are more common in survey kinds of interviews, but they are occasionally used in more mainstream types of interviews, especially if several people are being interviewed.

Using multiple-choice questions, interviewers are able to collect very specific pieces of information in a relatively short time. The information collected is fairly uncomplicated and easy to summarize, and the responses from many interviewees can be compared because all the collected data are in the same form. In addition, because the responses are restricted and predetermined, the level of interviewer skill and training does not have to be nearly as high as when using open questions. Interviewees are forced to choose the option provided by the interviewer that best describes their responses to the questions.

Even though the interviewers do not need the highest level of skill to use closed questions, the questions themselves must be written with great care. The questions themselves must be clearly worded, and the response lists should be exhaustive and mutually exclusive.

To be *exhaustive*, a list of responses must include all possible answers that could be given by interviewees. For example, in an interview conducted by an automobile manufacturer to gather customer reactions to a new model, the interviewer asked how long the interviewee had owned the car. The possible answers were 3 months, 6 months, 9 months, or 1 year. What if

Multiple Choice Questions

Which one of the following U.S. presidents took office immediately after John F. Kennedy?

a. Dwight D. Eisenhower
b. William J. Clinton
c. Gerald R. Ford
d. Lyndon B. Johnson
e. Harry S. Truman

How many vacation days do you get every year?

a. None
b. Five or less
c. Six to ten
d. Eleven to twenty
e. Twenty one or more

Would you rather live in Dayton, Ohio; Blacksburg, Virginia; or Norwalk, California?

the interviewee had owned the car for only 5 weeks? What is that person to answer? To make this list exhaustive, the responses could be changed to 3 months or less, 4 to 6 months, 7 to 9 months, 10 to 12 months, and more than 12 months. With this change, all interviewees could find a response appropriate to themselves.

Another strategy for achieving exhaustiveness is to include an "other" response. For example, the question you asked is, "With what political party do you affiliate yourself?" Given the variety of existing political parties, the list of responses could be quite long. And even with a long list, you might not cover all the possibilities. However, to make your list exhaustive, you could include several of the more popular parties, and then include an "other" to provide all interviewees with a response.

The responses for multiple choice questions must also be *mutually exclusive*. That is, an interviewee should be able to find only one applicable choice. When constructing this kind of question, you should examine the list and ask if an individual might realistically choose more than one response. Responding to the political party question, it seems unreasonable to expect that anybody would select more than one of those response categories.

Dichotomous questions restrict responses to one of two possible choices. The responses can be a yes/no answer or various two-option answers.

Although this kind of question is easy to ask, easy to answer, and provides results that are easy to summarize, they provide little depth of understanding or insight because they reveal little information beyond what is specifically asked by the interviewer.

As you have likely concluded, closed questions have strengths and weaknesses. On the strength side, they are easy to write, easy to administer, and easy to analyze and compare. Also, they require a lesser level of skill and training to conduct an interview. They also provide the opportunity to precisely direct the flow of an interview and to gather information about a variety of topics in a fairly short time. On the weakness side, closed questions limit the depth of potential responses because of the restrictive format of the question and possible answers.

The kinds of questions that you use really depend on the goals you have for the interview and how you intend to use the information collected in the interview. If you would like to understand the "soul" of the interviewee and find out what makes him or her tick, then more open questions will allow freedom to follow unexpected directions and to explore in depth. However, if you want to collect a variety of information from a large and diverse group of people, perhaps the more closed questions would work better for you. Of course, it's always possible to mix the kinds of questions to achieve your specific interview goals.

> With what political party do you affiliate yourself?
>
> a. Democrat
> b. Republican
> c. Green
> d. Independent
> e. Other _____
>   (please specify)
> f. No party affiliation

> ### Dichotomous Questions
>
> - Are you satisfied or dissatisfied with the course you are taking?
> - Did you complete the assignment for today's class?
> - Do you agree or disagree with the designated hitter rule in baseball?

The kinds of questions you use depend on the goals you have for the interview.
© 2008, JupiterImages Corporation.

Question Hazards and Other Dangers

Biased Questions. Questions phrased in such a way that they would be likely to influence the interviewees' responses are called **biased questions.** You should make every attempt to avoid biased questions, because the responses given do not necessarily represent the true thoughts of the interviewee. Biased questions come in at least two forms: leading questions and loaded questions.

A **leading question** guides the interviewee in the direction of the response preferred by the interviewer or otherwise requires the interviewee to give the socially correct or acceptable response. Leading questions are often used by sales people to persuade customers to buy a product or service.

Leading Questions

- Isn't this a great car?
- Everyone knows that fuels burned by cars and trucks harm the environment and contribute to global warming. Are you in favor of restricting vehicle emissions?
- Aren't golden retrievers fabulous dogs?
- You *actually* listen to talk radio *every day*?
- Most people agree that the governor of the state is doing a great job and should be re-elected. Using the following scale, how would you rate the governor's work in education?

| Great Job | Good Job | Neutral | Poor Job | Very Poor Job |

Similar to a leading question, a **loaded question** can incite emotional responses, give equally disagreeable response alternatives, or place the interviewee in a paradox where any answer is inappropriate. Loaded questions almost always create a defensive reaction from the interviewee and seldom yield usable information. Fortunately, these questions are rarely used, so be careful that you avoid them.

Loaded Questions

- Have you stopped beating your cat?
- Did you get caught cheating on your girlfriend again?

To fix leading or loaded questions, make sure that your questions are *neutral*. That is, the wording of your questions should suggest no particular response. Remember that you are trying to *discover* information by asking questions. You are not merely trying to get interviewees to say something you want them to say. If you can't decide by proofreading them yourself if your questions are neutral, then you can ask others to read them for you. You can also pretest your questions on a very small number of interviewees. In either case, you can ask the readers if they spotted any biased questions. Here's a rewrite of one of the examples:

Fix: Unbiased Question

Which one of the following best represents your opinion of the governor's work in education?

| Great Job | Good Job | Neutral | Poor Job | Very Poor Job |

Double-Barreled Questions. It's pretty easy to place two questions into one question, so you have to be careful to proofread your questions before you include them in your interview plan. With a **double-barreled question,** you would be asking for a single answer to what might be several questions.

For example, a question might ask: "Are you in favor of increases in cable TV and electricity rates for this community?" The question asks for a yes or no response. However, if you say yes, what exactly is it that you are in favor of? Are you in favor of a rate increase for electricity? Are you in favor of a rate increase for cable TV? Or are you in favor of a rate increase for both electricity and cable TV? If you say no, what do you oppose? What if you support the increase in cable rates but oppose the increase in electricity rates? How can this attitude be expressed with a single yes or no answer? Here are other examples:

Double-Barreled Questions

The United States should get out of the post office business and spend the money on preparing for natural disasters or other emergencies.   YES   NO

Do you support the president's position on the hurricane clean-up and tax relief?   YES   NO

To fix double-barreled questions, carefully proofread your questions with a sharp eye out for two-pronged questions. If you spot one, the best fix is to break it down into separate questions, assuming that your interview goals include all the concepts covered in the original question. Keep the issues separate and clear. Looking at the previous example, you could rewrite the question as two new questions:

Fix: Individual Questions

Do you support the president's position on the hurricane clean-up?   YES   NO

Do you support the president's position on tax reform?   YES   NO

Open-to-Closed Questions. With this question hazard, the interviewer begins with a question, but then follows up very quickly with a much more narrow, closed question. Although the question is originally designed to allow the interviewee some depth and flexibility in the response, the follow-up question severely limits the response, and often reduces it to a simple yes or no. Here's an example of an **open-to-closed question.**

Open-to-Closed Questions

Tell me what it's like to be married. *(then immediately follow with)* Do you guys fight a lot? (or) Do you guys go out a lot? (or) Do you enjoy being married?

Can you please describe the position that you have available? Would I get a vacation? (or) Are there educational benefits? (or) Would I get my own office?

In each case, attempting to take advantage of the benefits of open questions, the interviewer begins by looking for some depth in the response. The goal is to allow the interviewee to provide some personal insight. But before the response can be expressed, the interviewer changes the question and limits the interviewee to a very simple answer.

The cure in this case is less a matter of careful proofreading (that is *still* very important!) but more a matter of careful timing and listening to the interviewee's response. Make sure you give the interviewee enough time to fully answer your original open question. Then, if you still would like more information, use your follow-up or probing questions. Be patient!

Question Reliability. Somebody bright and famous *should* have said, "Whatever *can* be misinterpreted *will* be misinterpreted!" Can an interviewee find a meaning for your question other than the one that you intended? Can a group of interviewees find *multiple* meanings for your questions or statements? The answer to these questions should always be, "No!"

Being concerned with **reliability** means that you are concerned with the *consistency* with which other people interpret or give meaning to your questions or statements. You want to make sure that all (or most) of the people who read or hear your questions give the same meaning to them. If you ask, "What color was the mouse?" you would like the interviewees to assume that "mouse" means the furry little creature that somehow got into your house and is living under your bed. You do not want interviewees to assume other meanings for the term, like, for instance, the peripheral accessory that allows you to operate your computer.

If interviewees give different or inconsistent meanings to questions in an interview, the interviewer doesn't really know for certain what question is being answered. Is it the question that I meant to ask? Or is it the question that the interviewee heard? What question am I hearing the response to?

Here's an example. This question was part of a Web-based interview that was trying to measure "vanity" in the interviewees.

Unreliable Question

"If you could significantly improve your body, but that improvement would take ten years off your life, would you do it?"

The question was asking if people would trade ten years of life to significantly improve their looks. As it turns out, people taking the survey gave meaning to the term *improve* in several ways:

- *Improve* means to look better.
- *Improve* means to be more healthy or fit.
- *Improve* means to cure some ailment or deformity.
- *Improve* means to develop big muscles.
- *Improve* means to develop superior athletic abilities.
- *Improve* means to gain or lose weight, or to become shorter or taller.
- *Improve* also meant the enhancement of a variety of body parts!

You can see the problem! Look back at the original question. When you read it, what question did you think was being asked? Did you think *improve* meant to "look better?" Many people did not! What meaning did *you* give to the question?

If you are the interviewer, and you asked that same question to 150 interviewees, how can you possibly summarize the responses to that question? You don't even know what question the people are responding to!

The original question was intended to measure vanity. A simple pretest of the question on a small group of interviewees probably would have identified the reliability problem and allowed the interviewer to make the question more clear. That is, the interviewer can rewrite the question to make it less likely to be interpreted in unintended ways. The rewrite might look like this:

Fix: Reliable Question

"If you could significantly improve your looks, but the improvement would take ten years off your life, would you do it?"

Remember that meanings exist in people, and not in the terms that you use. As a result, any term you use can be interpreted in ways that you did not intend. To prevent this from happening, word your questions very carefully. Proofread every question. For some extra peace of mind, try out or pretest your questions on a small group of people and ask them what meaning they give to the questions.

In addition, try to be as specific as possible when choosing words. Choose words for their clarity and their lack of ambiguity. Try to avoid jargon or specialized words unless your preinterview analysis suggests that the interviewees will clearly understand them.

Open questions often have inherent reliability problems. Because an interview using open questions can follow many different paths with many interviewees, it's nearly impossible to determine if every interviewee is responding to exactly the same question. However, if you carefully plan, word, and test your questions, you can avoid many problems with reliability.

HOW DO I PREPARE FOR AN INTERVIEW?

To prepare for an interview, you should have firmly determined what you want to gain from the interview. In addition, you should have a strategy for reaching your objective.

Goals

As you saw in the definition of an interview, at least one of the parties comes into the situation with a specific goal in mind. So before you begin any kind of interview, you need to pause and reflect on your **goals** for the interaction. Just what do you want to get form this interview? Are you looking for advice, information, employment, attitude change, directions, instructions, motivation, or solutions to a problem?

What do you want to accomplish in the interview? Determine what you want to gain before you participate.
© 2008, JupiterImages Corporation.

When you have made a general determination of your goals, try to narrow the focus and decide what you want to take with you from this specific conversation. Do you want advice on a career choice? Do you need help with a particular problem in your life or career? Do you want to make the "short list" for an employment position? Are you trying to select a major? The more specific your goals, the better you can plan for the interview.

Interview Plan

When you have arrived at a decision about what goals you would like to accomplish in your interview, you should develop an interview plan. The **interview plan** outlines your strategy for goal achievement and it includes the topics that should be discussed as well as the sequence and wording of specific questions. The exact format of the plan is directly tied to your interview goals. The format of your plan can range on a continuum from directed to nondirected.

In a *directed* interview, the interviewer controls the areas of discussion and the pace and flow of the conversation. Questions used in this plan are usually more closed, restricting the focus of the interviewee. If you use a *nondirected* plan, you would include more open questions that allow the interviewee some flexibility of response. As a result, in this type of interview, the interviewee tends to exert more control over the flow of the conversation and, to some extent, the topic areas covered.

As mentioned earlier, the specific plan that you choose depends on your goals for the interview. If you don't know a great deal about the topic, and if you would like to explore that topic in depth with a relatively small number of interviewees, then you should select a more nondirected interview plan. With this plan, the interviewer begins by asking open questions to start the conversation and establish a focus. Because the questions and potential subject areas are broad, the interviewee must be prepared to probe responses and to more completely investigate different content areas. The interviewer therefore has to be very skilled to not only *follow* the flow of the conversation but to *adapt* to the different directions the conversation might take. Here are some examples of questions appropriate to this type of interview plan:

- Tell me about yourself.
- What happened?
- How do you feel about life as a college student?

If a completely nondirected question is not necessary, that is, if you would like to guide the interviewee more toward a specific topic area, you can use a more restrictive question. The question supplies a little more direction about the desired response. Take a look at these examples:

- What is the biggest challenge you see to attending college part time while raising a family?
- What is your biggest concern about life after college?

If this form of the question doesn't bring the amount of focus that you want, you can follow up your open question with probing questions to move the interviewee to the topics you wish to discuss:

What is your biggest concern about life after college?

- Probe: getting a job? (getting a better job?)
- Probe: raising a family?
- Probe: finding a satisfying career?
- Probe: making a meaningful contribution to society?

Using a more directed question form allows the interviewer not only to keep the interviewee focused on appropriate topics, but also to restrict the duration of the responses. Pace is important! You do not want to run out of time or energy before you accomplish your interview goals!

The directed interview plan allows the interviewer to exercise more control over responses and the topics covered. If you are interested in gathering a broad range of information about a topic from a fairly large number of interviewees, then the directed interview is the plan you should choose. Common applications for the directed plan include market surveys and opinion polls which typically interview large numbers of people. In addition, employers who conduct screening interviews of large groups of applicants often use a more directed approach. Each interviewee responds to questions that are usually more closed, worded the same way to improve reliability, and asked in the same order. Here are some examples of questions that might be used in a directed interview plan:

What specific questions could you ask a student about her concerns about life after college?
© aceshot1, 2008, Shutterstock.

Directed Interview Questions

- Which member of the City Council do you think should be the next mayor of the city?
- If you could only make one improvement to this proposal, what would it be?

If you want to completely control the range of possible responses, you can use a multiple choice or standardized response question:

- The County should construct four new recreation centers in the next 3 to 5 years.

  Strongly Agree   Agree   Neutral   Disagree   Strongly Disagree

- Which one of the following is your favorite Simpson's character?
  a. Marge
  b. Homer
  c. Bart
  d. Lisa
  e. Maggie
  f. Other

HOW ARE INTERVIEWS STRUCTURED?

An interview has a recognizable structure much like the structure of a public speech or other messages. There are three main parts to an interview: the opening, the body, and the closing.

Opening

The **opening** or introduction is a critical part of the interview, yet it is often neglected during the planning stages. The opening serves at least three functions critical to the success of the interview. The opening should *set the foundation* of the relationship between the parties that will be further developed during the course of the interview. Some interviewing professionals suggest some small talk or even some self disclosure at this point, but that should be decided case-by-case based on the specific individuals involved and the goals of the interview.[4]

The opening should *motivate* the other party to participate fully in the interaction. You can offer a reward, stress the importance of the interview goals, show respect for the other, or use some other motivational strategy. The important idea is to let the other party know that you hope for and would appreciate full participation.

Finally, the opening should *provide an orientation* to the interviewee about what will take place in the interview. The interviewer should talk about the goals of the interview, what procedures will be followed as the interview progresses, approximately how long the interaction might take, and provide details about what is expected of the interviewee. If appropriate to the type of interview, the interviewer should let the interviewee know how the information collected will be used after the interview.

When the opening is complete, you should try to move smoothly into the body of the interview. This transition might be best achieved by asking an open question.[5] This first question should be nonthreatening and fairly easy to answer. The open question should get the interviewee talking and allow an easy movement into the body.

Body

The **body** is the central part of the interview. It is in this section that much of the information is exchanged and all or most of the interview goals are accomplished. Regardless of the type of interview you are conducting, you will have to arrange the topics covered in the body in a logical and coherent way. This coherent arrangement allows the most efficient use of your time, prevents both parties from being confused or distracted, and dramatically improves the likelihood that the goals of the interview will be realized.

Planning the body of the interview requires choosing the organizational structure or pattern that will best help you realize your goals. Take a look at the following examples and try to decide which one will best suit the goals of your next interview.

Common Organizational Patterns

Spatial. In this organizational pattern, question topics move in a sequence related to physical location. For example, if you are a reporter gathering information about the National Museum of the United States Air Force, you could begin by asking about the Early Flight gallery, then ask about the Modern Flight gallery, and conclude with questions about the gallery containing presidential aircraft.

Topical. Questions in a topical sequence are arranged according to the interests and priorities of the interviewer. A journalist might follow a sequence of who, what, when, where, and why to cover a story. Or the coverage of the Air Force Museum would follow this sequence:

- Propeller-driven aircraft
- Jet-powered aircraft
- Experimental aircraft
- Rockets and missiles

Chronological. Questions are ordered in a time sequence. If you are questioning someone about a work history, you would begin at the first job, and then move through each job until you reach the present. Let's go back to the Air Force Museum for another example:

- Military aircraft from WWI and WWII
- Military aircraft from the Korean War
- Military aircraft from the Vietnam War
- Military aircraft from the Gulf conflicts

Cause-Effect. This sequence is arranged according to the causes of a situation and their effects. For example, if you are interviewing a school board member about the degree of absenteeism in the high schools, you could ask about its causes such as economic conditions, motivation to attend class, or family issues. Then you could ask about some possible effects, such as poor test scores, a rising crime rate, or high unemployment. Some other examples:

- A parent might discuss a student's poor test grades (effect) and then explore the possible causes of those grades.
- A physician could discuss a child's exercise habits (cause) and then discuss the possible effects of a sedentary lifestyle.

Problem-Solution. This sequence moves from the *examination* of a problem to the *solution* of the problem. For example, an appraisal or counseling interview might first focus on the interviewee's problem and then turn to a discussion of solutions. Other examples include the following:

- A school counselor and a student might talk about the student's poor attendance in class and then discuss how the attendance might be improved.
- A professor could discuss problems that students have been experiencing in a particular class at mid-semester, and then have an exchange concerning what could be done to improve the class for the rest of the term.
- A job counselor could discuss why a person seeking employment has had many interviews but has not yet been offered a job. The counselor might discuss with the interviewee how to improve his or her interviewing skills.

Structure and Function. This progression of ideas begins with how something is structured and then turns to a discussion of its function. If you're asking questions about an organization, you might begin with questions about how a particular department or unit is organized or structured. Then you ask questions about what exactly the department does.

What questions could you ask to better understand how the three branches of government work?
© Gary Blakeley, 2008, Shutterstock.

Understanding the Structure and Function of the U.S. Government

Legislative Branch: Consists of the House of Representatives and the Senate. Members of these two bodies are elected by the residents of individual states. The Senate has two members from each state, while membership in the House of Representatives is determined by the populations of each state (structure). The Legislative branch writes the laws of the United States (function).

Q: What makes up the Legislative Branch? (S)
Q: How is membership determined in the House and the Senate? (S)
Q: How many members are in each house? (S)
Q: What does the Senate do? (F)
Q: What does the House of Representatives do? (F)

Executive Branch: Consists of the office of the president of the United States. The president is elected by a vote of all the people of the country (structure). The president is the commander of the armed forces and is charged with enforcing laws (function).

Q: Who can be the president? (S)
Q: How is the president elected? (S)
Q: How does the president enforce the laws? (F)

Judicial Branch: Consists of the Supreme Court of the United States. Judges serving on the Supreme Court are appointed by the president and confirmed by the legislative branch. Judges are appointed for life to the court (structure). The Supreme Court is charged with interpreting the Constitution and applying the laws of the United States (function).

Q: Who can be a member of the Supreme Court? (S)
Q: How many judges are members of the Court? (S)
Q: What does the Supreme Court do? (F)
Q: Why does the Constitution need to be interpreted? (F)

If you're trying to understand the structure and function of the U.S. government, you could ask about the three branches of the government and how they are organized, and then you could ask about what each branch does.

Build the Relationship. Relationships between people in interviewing situations develop in much the same way as relationships between people in other contexts. In cases where the parties do not know each other, the communication that occurs initially is fundamentally superficial because it is based on broad generalizations and assumptions made by each party about the other. Miller assumes that all initial interactions are impersonal or noninterpersonal, and that relationships become more interpersonal as they develop.[6]

Miller and Steinberg explain that individuals relate to each other on three levels: cultural, sociological, and psychological.[7] The relationship begins on the cultural level, and progresses through the sociological toward the psychological level. A brief look at these levels should help you understand how relationships can grow and be maintained during an interview.

On the *cultural* level, individuals do not relate to each other as persons, but only as role occupants or generalized members of a culture. The communicators only know as much about each other as they know about any other member of the culture, so uncertainty is high. Communication takes place on a superficial and somewhat formal level and is often made up of small talk. There is little or no disclosure of personal information. When the relationship gets to the *sociological* level, individuals relate to each other as stereotyped members of groups. One person interprets the behavior of the other based on what is known about the group to which that other is believed to belong. Finally, on the *psychological* level, individuals begin to relate to each other not only as members of a culture or group, but also as unique individuals. This level of relationship can be reached after the communicators have experienced one another's behaviors and have exchanged more personal types of information. They get to know each other!

Why is individual uncertainty high on the cultural level?
© 2008, JupiterImages Corporation.

In an interview, the initial relationship is likely to exist at the cultural level, or at best, if you have done a reasonable amount of research on the other party or organization, at the sociological level. Regardless, uncertainty at either level is high, and each party is trying to feel out the other to find out if he or she can be trusted with more personal information. As the parties interact, and if they begin to build trust, then more and more personal disclosure will take place and the relationship can move toward the psychological level. As a relationship moves through these levels toward the psychological, the relationship becomes more interpersonal.

The more interpersonal the relationship between the parties, the more freely information will be exchanged. If you can move the relationship toward the interpersonal end of the relationship continuum, you will more likely be able to achieve your goals for the interview. The bad news is that it will not always be possible to move into a trusting interpersonal relationship within the course of just one interview. Even so, you should make the effort to make the relationship as interpersonal as the situation permits!

While there are many ways to build relationships in an interview, here are three suggestions:

1. *Take a little risk!* Volunteer some personal information. Allow the other party to get to know you more on a more interpersonal level. You would prefer the interviewer remember you as "Sam from Dayton who has applied for the drafting position," rather than "applicant 356-C." If the employment interviewer gets to know something about you as a person, he or she will be more able to remember you and differentiate you from the rest of the candidates.
2. *Try to create a supportive climate!* A supportive climate is one in which neither party feels threatened by the other. A perception of threat creates an atmosphere of defensiveness in which both parties begin to question each others' intentions and suspect manipulation by the other. The result of this is inaccurate interpretation of meanings and intentions, and information will not be freely exchanged in this atmosphere. You will probably never make it to the psychological level!

Tips for Creating a Supportive Climate

To avoid the formation of a defensive climate, follow Gibb's advice:[8]

- Try to use descriptive statements.
- Try *not* to use evaluative statements.
- Try to remain focused on solving the problem.
- Try *not* to give the impression that you want to exert control over the situation.
- Try to maintain a natural, spontaneous, and engaged point of view.
- Try *not* to give others the impression that you are using a strategy to control the situation or to get whatever you want.
- Try to show a sincere concern and interest in the other.
- Try *not* to appear detached and neutral.
- Try to establish and maintain an atmosphere of equality.
- Try *not* to make the other feel inferior.
- Try to keep an open mind!

3. *Be engaged!* It could be that the most significant thing you do to build and maintain a relationship with an interview (or conversational) partner is to be involved in the interaction. Involvement means full participation in the "here and now" of the interaction without being distracted by factors not connected to the communication. This involvement will not only help you achieve your goals for the interview, but it also communicates an interest in the other participants in the conversation. As the other participants discover that you are genuinely interested and involved in what is happening, they will become more motivated and involved as well. So the outcome of your engagement is the increased commitment to the free exchange of information and to the success of the interview! It's all good!

Transition. When you complete the body of the interview, you should make this very clear to the interviewee. You can do this in a straightforward way by simply saying that the time for the interview is over or that you have no more questions. Be sure that interviewee understands that the questioning is completed.

Closing

Much like the opening, the **closing** of an interview is often overlooked while planning, and it often results in the interviewer attempting to simply "wing it." Because they think that there is nothing left to accomplish when the questioning is over, interviewers have a tendency to rush this phase. If the interviewer's only goal is to collect information, once that information is received, he or she might think that the interview is over. Many times the interviewer will just say "thanks!" and leave, giving no consideration to the interviewee or properly closing the interaction. This kind of "nonclosing" leaves interviewees with a poor impression and would not motivate them to cooperate again should the interviewer require more information.

The closing needs to be carefully considered because it also plays a critical role in the interview process: It provides closure, helps to maintain the relationship that was developed during the interview, and can help motivate the interviewee if further cooperation is needed.

As mentioned before, the interviewee should not have to wonder if the interview is over. The interviewer should *provide closure* by being very clear that the conversation is completed. This can be done by summarizing the content of the interview, letting the interviewee know if there is a next step in the interviewing process (such as multiple employment interviews), reminding the interviewee what will be done with the information collected from the conversation, or even through exhibiting some simple verbal or nonverbal leave-taking behavior.

How can you tell that this interview is finished?
© Phil Date, 2008, Shutterstock.

The interviewer should make a strong effort to *maintain the relationship* that has been created and developed during the interview. Try to keep the relationship upbeat and positive, especially if you will be working together with the interviewee after the interview or if you will need further cooperation at a later time. The effort you make to treat the interviewee with respect and maintain that relationship will motivate him or her to cooperate further if needed. The motivation that you provide will also give the interviewee a sense of satisfaction by knowing that the effort and time in the interview was well spent.

SUMMARY

The next chapter will apply the concepts discussed in this chapter to specific interview contexts. The focus of the chapter is employment/internship interviewing and interviewing to gather information.

ENDNOTES

1. L. Hugenberg, S. Wallace, D. Yoder, and C. Horvath, *Creating Competent Communication*, 4th ed. (Dubuque, IA: Kendall/Hunt, 2005).

2. K. Kacmar, and W. Hochwater, "The Interview as a Communication Event: A Field Examination of Demographic Effects on Interview Outcomes," *Journal of Business Communication* 32 (1995); 207–232; and S. Ralston and R. Brady, "The Relative Influence of Interview Communication Satisfaction on Applicants' Recruitment Interview Decisions," *Journal of Business Communication* 31 (1994); 61–77.

3. G. B. Willis, *Cognitive Interviewing: A Tool for Improving Questionnaire Design* (Thousand Oaks, CA: Sage, 2005).

4. R. Anderson and G. Killenberg, *Interviewing: Speaking, Listening, and Learning for Professional Life* (Mountain View, CA: Mayfield, 1999). Also C. Stewart and W. Cash, *Interviewing: Principles and Practices* (New York: McGraw-Hill, 2003).

5. Stewart and Cash.

6. G. R. Miller, "The Current Status of Theory and Research in Interpersonal Communication," *Human Communication Research*, 4 (1978); 164–178.

7. G. R. Miller and M. Steinberg, "Between People," Palo Alto, CA: SRA (1975).

8. J. Gibb, "Defensive Communication," *Journal of Communication*, 1 (1961), 141–148.

Links of Interest

http://www.abastaff.com/career/interview/interviewtypes_quickguide.htm
Exit Interview
http://jobsearchtech.about.com/cs/interviewtips/a/exit_interview.htm

Audition
http://technicaljobsearch.com/interviews/interviews-1.htm
http://virtual.clemson.edu/SDS/DISORIEN/JOBSKILL/inttypes.htm
http://www.interview-resource.com/types.html
http://careers.usc.edu/docs/handouts/Interview_Different_Types.pdf

Follow up Interview
http://www.jobstor.com/467.0.html
http://www.bc.edu/schools/cas/premed/interview/types/
http://careers.udayton.edu/

HOW DO I PARTICIPATE IN AN INTERVIEW?

LEARNING OBJECTIVES

After reading this chapter, you should understand the following concepts:

- In an information-gathering interview, it is important to prepare and plan questions, listen to the responses, and record the information.
- Employment interviews can take place in different ways, but the goal will be to determine through responses to questions and behavior during the interview whether the person being interviewed is right for the job.
- The best preparation for an employment interview is to make a commitment to listening, get to know yourself, learn to anticipate questions, and plan your responses.
- The questions allowed in employment interviews are much more restricted than other information-gathering interviews, and may not relate to issues of age, sex, race, national origin, marital status, pregnancy, or religious beliefs.
- A resume is an essential tool for communicating contact information, objectives, education, employment history, and related skills.
- A cover letter is the first impression you will make with a company, so it should be free of errors and should highlight the parts of your resume you consider to be most important.
- Thank-you letters keep your name and credentials in front of the decision makers.
- Appearance can be a deciding factor in getting a job.

INTRODUCTION

The previous chapter describes the nature of interviewing, the structure of interviews, and typical types of questions. You are now ready to test your wings and move on to some specific applications of interviewing! Congratulations!

   This chapter will help you prepare for two kinds of actual interviewing experiences: the information-gathering interview and the employment interview. In the information gathering interview, our focus will be on organizing the interview, asking questions, listening to responses, and recording information. You will be the interviewer.

What would you do to prepare yourself for an employment interview?
© iofoto, 2008, Shutterstock.

For the employment interview, our focus will be on your preparation and participation as an interviewee. You will be asked to complete a self inventory, to get to know yourself better, and prepare to answer common questions asked in a screening interview. You will also be asked to construct a resume, write a cover letter to accompany your resume, and write letters of appreciation for interviews.

HOW DO I CONDUCT AN INFORMATION-GATHERING INTERVIEW?

This section will discuss the steps you should take when preparing an **information-gathering interview.** In this type of interview, the focus will be on planning and asking questions, listening to the responses, and recording the information.

Preparation and Planning

To make sure that you have a successful and productive interview, make a plan. A good plan makes it possible that you will get what you want from the interview situation.

Make a plan for your interview that includes specific goals.
© Kenneth William Caleno, 2008, Shutterstock.

The first step in the planning process is to establish your goals for the interview. The more specific your goals, the easier the planning process becomes and the more likely you will have a productive interview. As with any trip you might take, the knowledge of where you are going is enhanced by a detailed plan of how you intend to get there!

The goal in this kind of interview is information. Determine exactly what information you want to gain from the interaction. Are you interested in facts, opinions, descriptions of events or processes, explanations, biographical information, something else? Once you decide on a *general* goal, focus on your *specific* goals. What specific facts or exactly what kind of facts are you looking for?

With this well-articulated goal in mind, next consider *who* should be the subject of your interview. Choose the interviewee according to your goal statement. Who will best help you accomplish this goal?

A clearly thought out and precisely articulated goal will make your questions easier to plan. When your goal is clear, you will know better what to ask. You will also be better able to remain focused on the direction of the interview and keep the interaction on track. In addition, when you communicate your goals to the other party in the interview, he or she will be better able to interpret your questions and help you move toward your goal. Interviewees are willing to help you, or they would not be participating in the first place. Knowledge of what information you are looking for will allow them to help you even more. Also, in the event that your attention span begins to waver or you pull yourself off track by pursuing a false lead, the interviewee can help you find your direction and continue toward your interview goal.

Next, select the type of interview structure and the kind of questions that you will use. The interview structure will, again, depend on your specific goals for the interview. If you are interested in obtaining a description of a small rural town, for example, you could consider using the *spatial* structure. You could begin your questioning by asking about the town's business district, then move to the town square, the neighborhoods, the school, and finally, the parks and recreation facilities. If you are interested in finding out about a process, like how corn is grown, a *chronological* sequence might work best. You could begin by asking about preparation of the fields, then turn to planting procedures, then ask about crop maintenance and irrigation, then harvesting the corn, and finally ask about how corn is used by people. Examine your goal, and then choose your structure.

We suggest that you use questions that are more open that allow the interviewee some measure of flexibility in responding. Because you have goals to accomplish, you want to retain some degree of control over the conversation, so asking completely open questions is not always the best idea. Place a bit of a restriction on your questions so that a specific direction is indicated. Instead of opening your interview with the request to "tell me about corn," try asking, "What is the first step in producing a corn crop?" Or you could be even more specific and directive by asking, "How do you prepare a field for planting corn?"

You should also prepare a series of probing or follow-up questions that you can use (if necessary) to guide your interviewee in the direction that you want to go. If you asked about field preparation, you probably didn't want an explanation about where to find a field for planting corn or what the real estate market prices are for corn fields these days. If you have probing questions at the ready, you can gently refocus the interviewee to the topic you want to discuss.

Finally, prepare a good opening and closing. See Chapter 7 for guidance on the functions of interview openings and closings. It's kind of like the introduction and conclusion of a speech. In this case, however, you should tailor them to the specific person in the interviewee chair and your specific purpose for the interview.

The opening should accomplish the following:

- Begin to build the relationship that should last throughout and beyond the actual interview session.
- State your specific goals for the interview.
- Provide orientation by telling the interviewee how long the session will last, what topics will be covered, and perhaps why he or she was chosen by you to help you accomplish your interview goals.

The closing should do the following:

- Attempt to maintain or continue the relationship that was built during the conversation. It gives the interviewee some satisfaction for participation and it is especially important if you have to ask for further information or clarification after the interview has been completed.
- Thank the interviewee, provide a summary, and bring closure to the conversation.
- Use the opportunity to ask permission to contact interviewee in the future for more information.

How can you stay focused on the interview conversation?
© Stephen Coburn, 2008, Shutterstock.

Listening and Involvement

Paying close attention and carefully listening for the duration of an extended conversation is challenging to all of us, regardless of how intelligent we are or how important the conversation is to us. There are lots of things going on around us and inside our heads that work together to steal our attention away from the here and now of a conversation. The purpose of this section is to give you a basic understanding of listening and the role of distraction, and to examine a few strategies to help you remain focused on the immediate interview conversation.

Listening is the active process of receiving, constructing meaning from, and responding to spoken and/or nonverbal messages. It involves the ability to retain information as well as to react empathetically and/or appreciatively to spoken and/or nonverbal messages.[1]

Listening is an *active*, psychological activity. Active means that it is voluntary and that it requires effort and motivation on our part.[2] The bad news is that most of us are generally poor listeners who only use about 25 percent of our capacity to listen.[3] In addition, we tend to remember only about 50 percent of what we hear immediately after listening to a message and that number drops to 25 percent after two days.[4] In some conversational contexts, we listen even less effectively and remember as little as 10 percent of the content.[5]

So listening is voluntary and active, and many people are passive listeners. When we do listen, we do so with poor efficiency and tend to remember only fairly small percentages of what we hear. If these research findings are true, it appears that we don't have a very high probability of success in information-gathering interviews! If your communication goal in an interview is to gain information, it is important to recognize the general tendency to be inefficient listeners and resolve to become a better listener.

It takes a great deal of energy and self-discipline to keep yourself focused on the here-and-now of your communication, but that is the *goal of good listening.* Berko and others have reported that most of us are able to think much faster than we can talk.[6] As a result, our brains have extra processing capability that does not have to be engaged when we listen to others, and this extra processing capacity can interrupt our concentration on the immediate communication situation. As you listen to others speak, you have the capacity to take what we call **mental road trips** to places beyond the "here and now." You could be thinking about your job, or your house, or your dog, how your favorite baseball team is doing. "Did you turn the iron off this morning?" You are thinking about a *zillion* topics other than what the other person is saying. *The difference between thinking speed and listening speed can be an obstacle to effective listening* when the extra mental capacity causes us to lose focus on the message.[7]

The challenge is to focus attention on the here and now and to ignore any elements irrelevant to the immediate communication situation. Here are some simple strategies that you can use to keep your head in the game.

Do you tend to take a mental road trip when you should be paying attention to someone?
© 2008, JupiterImages Corporation.

Focus on the Content. Focusing on the **content** of the conversation means that you become involved in the communication transaction rather than letting your emotions, environmental factors, or extraneous behaviors interfere with your understanding of what the other person is saying.

Review the Content. Reviewing includes mentally going over the central ideas and summarizing the important information. Focus your attention on the bigger picture because trying to memorize all the small details will distract your attention from the conversation as a whole. Sellnow tells us that it is possible to "listen too hard."[8] It doesn't take much time to get lost in the details. If you are going to remember some elements of a conversation and forget others, you should at least remember the major ideas the other person talked about.[9]

Repeat the Content. Repeat the content to the other person to find out if you truly understood it. The goal of restatement is to check the extent to which both people share meaning. You are essentially asking the question, "This is the meaning I've given to what you have said. Am I correct?"

- If you think you might not have heard the actual words correctly, you could *repeat the words* to check for accurate hearing.
- If you do not understand the meaning of something that was said, you should *paraphrase the content* in your own words, then check with the other party for accuracy.
- If you think you understand the meaning of the content but you do not understand why the person said it, you can *paraphrase the motivation* of the content. "This is why I think you said that. Is that correct?" This is the most difficult kind of paraphrasing, but it is a very useful skill that can dramatically improve your understanding of a message.[10]

These strategies not only allow interview parties to determine the level of comprehension, but they are indicators of the interest in the other's point of view. The strategies provide feedback that tells the other if you are giving the right meaning to the message. If your repetition or paraphrase is inaccurate, the other person can state the message in a different way to help you better understand the intended meaning.

Another challenge to good listening comes when we focus on ourselves and what we are doing instead of the ideas being presented by the other person. It's very easy to be more involved with what you are saying (or are planning to say), rather than attending to the whole conversation. One flustered participant returned from an interview and reported that he was very worried that his tie was crooked and that he wouldn't be able to ask the right questions. He didn't follow the conversation very well and could barely remember what the interviewee said. He was so self-focused that he did not attend to all the elements of the interview situation and was unable to understand the other person.

A common mistake that hampers productive listening is preparing or rehearsing your next statement instead of listening to the response of the other person.[11] It's very important to pay attention to your own behavior (i.e., to be a good self-monitor); your best effort should be made to focus on the message and not so much on yourself.

Recording Information

If you are conducting the interview with the goal of gathering information, you will have to find some method of recording what you learn from the interviewee. The most common methods are to just listen, listen and record the notes after the interview, listen and take notes during the interview, or make an audio or video recording of the interview.

Just Listen. Simply listening and participating in the interview is probably the best way to discover the information that you are looking for in the interview. Abel conducted a study in which two groups of people participated in interviews to gather information.[12] One group took notes during the interview, and the second group took no notes, but just listened. When the reports were compared, the reports from the group that did not take notes were more accurate than those from the group that did take notes. Those people not taking notes were not distracted by the act of taking the notes during the conversation.

Listen Now, Write Notes Later. To take advantage of the increased involvement with the conversation that you have while simply listening, you should write your notes as soon as possible after the actual interview. The longer you wait, the less likely that you will clearly remember what was said.

Taking notes during an interview may work well if you just jot down main ideas.
© 2008, JupiterImages Corporation.

Listen and Take Notes. As if you weren't going to be busy enough during this interview, now we are telling you to take notes! Taking notes *during* an interview is a significant challenge: you have to listen, manage the direction and pace of the interview, and you have to take notes. You have to do this all at the same time!

You have certainly tried to take notes during class, so you know how difficult it can be. If you try to write absolutely everything down, you will likely miss important things that were said while you were focused on writing. This is especially true in this kind of interview.

In addition, such a focus on writing everything down withdraws you from the "here and now" of the communication situation. If you manage to divide your time and attention well enough between listening and note taking, you should have little trouble. If, however, you begin to spend more time and attention on note taking, the situation could quickly deteriorate. Not only will you miss important details, but after a while, the interviewee picks up on your note taking and begins to speak at the speed at which you are taking notes. Not only is this distracting for the interviewee, but any real conversation that you were having will come to a halt and the interview turns into a dictation session. Not good!

The solution to this problem can be found if you revisit your goals for the interview. If your goal is obtaining meticulous detail, then see the section on audio and video recording. If a high level of detail is not exactly what you are looking for, the best solution might be to take notes on a "big picture" or "conceptual" level. Quickly write down main ideas in just enough detail to jog your memory at a later time. In this case, it's a good idea to revisit your notes as soon as you can after the interview and try to fill in as many gaps as you can. It's also another good reason to build and maintain a good relationship with the interviewee: you might need to call to get assistance to fill in the required details. The interview isn't necessarily over when the conversation ends!

Audio or Video Recording. If your goals for the interview require attention to lots of detail, then you should consider an electronic recording of the conversation. If you use an electronic device, make sure you get the permission of the interviewee, and get it in advance of the interview. In addition, when using an electronic device for recording, make sure you have a "Plan B." Electronic gadgets are cool and do some amazing things, but they still break! If you count on Murphy's law, "Whatever can go wrong will go wrong," you will always have a back-up plan if something doesn't work. Don't let a broken gizmo ruin your interview; carefully consider a practical alternative.

Many people using audio recording devices make transcripts of the conversation after the interview. This is a very labor-intensive undertaking, but it captures everything that was said down to the smallest detail. If detail isn't your goal, then you could skip the transcript step and listen to the recording several times for needed quotes or for the level of detail that your goals require.

If your interview goals require even more detail, you could make a video recording. Video captures not only what was said, but facial expressions and gestures that can help you interpret more clearly the meaning of the words. It's especially important that you get permission from the interviewee before making a video recording. But before hauling all that equipment around, go back to the goals for this interview to help you decide if a video record is actually needed. If it doesn't help you achieve your goals, then extra equipment is more likely to become a distraction for you as well as your interviewee.

HOW SHOULD I APPROACH EMPLOYMENT INTERVIEWS?

It is very likely that you have already experienced several employment interviews. Even though they are very common and "everybody has to go through it," skill in this type of interview is essential for career success. Our focus with the **employment interview** will be on interviewee responsibilities: preparation and answering questions. After you get some experience in your chosen career, you will be in more of a position to focus on asking the questions and managing the interview.

Employment interviews come in a variety of different shapes and sizes. The kind of situation that we typically expect is one interviewer to one interviewee, but don't count on that always being the case. You could find yourself sitting at a table with a search committee with *everybody* asking questions. This is becoming more common, so consider it to be a real possibility. You could also be interviewed during a meal, or on the telephone (which *could* be a conference call with a committee), or even over a

You might find yourself in an interview situation where an entire committee asks you questions.
© 2008, JupiterImages Corporation.

video link (which *could* include that same committee). Just be aware that you might not be walking into the exact situation that you expect. If you have some flexibility in your expectations, you will be much less distracted by different interview situations.

The remainder of this chapter is dedicated to helping you prepare for the employment interview and will examine questions that are likely to hear, how to prepare answers for those questions, resume writing, cover letters, and thank-you letters.

Questions and Answers for Employment Interviews

The type of employment interview that is our focus in this chapter is generally called a **screening interview.** A screening interview is usually the first contact you will have with most organizations and is often is conducted by a professional in the human resources department. The purpose of the interview is to determine if the interviewee meets the necessary requirements for the available position. If the interviewee appears to meet the company's criteria for the position, he or she will be invited back for more interviews. These subsequent interviews, often called **selection interviews,** are conducted by supervisors or other members of the department that is hiring the position.

The purpose of the information-gathering interview section was for you to expand your skills in planning an interview, asking questions, maintaining involvement with the interviewee and the flow of a conversation, and accurately recording information. However, the purpose of this section is for you to acquire skills at responding to questions asked in the selection interview. The best preparation for this kind of interview is to make a commitment to listening, get to know yourself very well, anticipate (in a general way) the questions you are likely to encounter, and plan some of your responses.

Make a Commitment to Listening. With any conversation, each participant has to make a commitment to listening and focusing on the communication event. This focus is even more central in an interview because both parties come to the situation with serious and specific goals they wish to accomplish.

In the first part of this chapter, in the discussion of information-gathering interviews, we talked about listening to the other person and carefully attending to the conversation as more and more information is revealed to you. In the employment interview, listening to the other *should* be a little easier than in the information gathering interview. After all, you are the interviewee and you are the person who will do much of the talking. However, there are still significant challenges in this kind of interview that require a great deal of effort and energy from the interviewee.

You will be asked a series of questions. It is important that you understand the question being asked. You need to be sure of the actual words spoken by the interviewer and you need to be sure about what the interviewer means. Make sure that you accurately interpret the questions. If you didn't hear what the interviewer said or you are not clear on what he or she means, ask questions! Let the interviewer *help you* to understand what is being asked. Don't try to pretend that you understand and stumble through the response!

Listen to *your own* responses! What? Listen to what *you* say! Keep track of what you are saying and be sure it is responsive to the question that was asked. Pay attention so that you don't repeat yourself unnecessarily and that you say what you actually mean to say. Also pay attention to *how* you give your responses. Are you communicating an appropriate tone for this kind of conversation?

Finally, try to stay focused on this conversation and do not allow yourself to be distracted. You came to this interview prepared, so you should not become preoccupied with planning your answer to he next question while you are still in the middle of this one! Commit yourself to expend the effort necessary to remain in the "here and now" of this conversation, and maintain that commitment throughout the conversation.

During the interview, make sure you accurately interpret the questions.
© 2008, JupiterImages Corporation.

Get to Know Yourself.   Of course, you already know yourself. You should know yourself better than anybody else knows you. But how good are you at describing and explaining what you know about yourself to others? Most of us aren't very good at it, yet we still try and try, even at the expense of confusing others and boring their socks off! Remember the last time you tried to introduce yourself to a group of people who didn't know you? Does this scenario sound familiar? "Now we will go around the table, and everybody should state their names, what department they work in, and say a few words about themselves so we can all get to know each other better." This hardly ever goes well! But why? Who knows more about you than you?

The reason that self-introductions often have unfortunate results is not a lack of information, but the lack of a plan! We stumble over these introductions because we are organizing and editing a lifetime of information that will somehow be reported to a group of strangers in three or four sentences. If only we knew this question was coming, we could have planned something to say!

Guess what? Questions asking you to describe yourself, your education, your talents, your interests, your goals, your skills, and even your hobbies *are coming in this interview!* Because you know this, you can begin now to plan what to say about yourself.

Anticipate the Questions.   The questions you are likely to be asked in a screening interview are probably not very different from those in the list we have provided. The questions might be worded differently, but the content areas will be similar. You can bet that there will be some surprises, and you'll have to handle those as they come. Our goal in this course is to help minimize surprises and prepare you to tackle the questions we know are coming.

Probably the most common question in a screening interview sounds very much like, "Tell me about yourself!" Many professional interviewers do not like this question and do not recommend asking it. The reason is that nobody knows how to answer it. Even though many of the specialists don't use it, the reality is that you are very likely to hear this question at your screening interview. So you would be wise to prepare a good-quality answer!

You can do a quick *Google* search for employment interview questions and see quite a variety. Here's a short list of questions that you are likely to encounter.

Can you anticipate the questions you're likely to hear in a screening interview?
© 2008, JupiterImages Corporation.

- Tell me about yourself.
- What is your greatest strength? What are your three greatest strengths?

Self-Inventory

Following is a list of questions that you should answer about yourself. Write the answers down. Included on the Web site for this course is an electronic form that you can complete that is designed to help you conduct your inventory. Take a look at these questions:

- What are five characteristics that you believe define who you are?
- What are your work-related strengths and weaknesses?
- What are the strengths and weaknesses of your personality?
- What would your say are your greatest achievements? What did you learn from them?
- What would you say are your greatest failures? What did you learn from them?
- Why did you choose the college or university that you are attending?
- Why did you choose your major? Describe the path you took to choosing this major: include any experiences, courses, teachers, mentors,

role models or significant insights that helped place you on this path.

- What three college courses have you liked the most? Why?
- What three college courses have you liked the least? Why?
- Why are you interested in a career in _____? Describe your path to this career: Include any experiences, courses, teachers, mentors, role models, significant insights, or anything else that helped place you on this path.
- What contribution do you think you can make to the field of _____?
- What do you believe is the most significant challenge currently facing the field of _____?
- What do you think will be the next "growth area" or major development in the field of _____?
- What would you like to be doing five years from now?
- What are your long-range career goals?

- What is your greatest personal strength?
- What is your greatest professional strength?
- What is your greatest weakness?
- What is your greatest personal weakness?
- What is your greatest professional weakness?
- What are your three greatest weaknesses?
- Name one weakness and talk about the steps you have taken to overcome it.
- What is your favorite class (or favorite three classes) in college? Why?
- What is your least favorite class (or three least favorite classes) in college? Why?
- Why did you choose _____ for a major? What got you interested in _____? Describe the path you took to selecting this major.
- What is the last book that you read? (The interviewer might ask you to talk about it. Do *not* say you read a book that you haven't read!)
- Why did you choose _____ as a career? Describe the path you took to choose this career.
- Why did you quit working at _____? (Assumes past employment history)
- What do you like best about your position at _____?
- What do you like least about your position at _____?

This is only a partial list and should not be viewed as exhaustive. However, based on your authors' collective experience, this list contains questions that are frequently used and likely to appear in your screening interview. There will be other questions that you did not anticipate. If you have done your homework, however, you should know yourself well enough to be able to construct a respectable answer for unanticipated topics.

Plan Your Responses. Obviously, you can't anticipate every question, and you will not be able to carefully plan every answer. Perhaps you shouldn't try to plan out *every* response even if you could. You want to sound relaxed and not over practiced or insincere. You can remain spontaneous and still have general responses prepared to questions that you can anticipate.

"Tell Me about Yourself." For example, you can probably count on some form of the "tell me about yourself" question to be asked. How will you answer it?

Our suggestion for preparing your response begins with *research:* Examine your self-inventory. Select three or four significant items or characteristics that you believe describe you. Then select, perhaps, the reason(s) you picked your specific career. Make a list; write it down.

Step two in crafting this response is *organization.* Think of this response as a two-minute speech. As such, your response should have a very brief introduction, three or four main points, and a very brief summation or conclusion. The main points should correspond with the significant characteristics that you believe describe you the best. Mention each characteristic and provide a brief explanation. The first two or three main points should be descriptive of you. The final main point should provide a connection between your characteristics and the company you are interviewing with. You can use this opportunity to describe what a perfect fit can be made with you and this company or with you and this career opportunity.

Strengths and Weaknesses. Another typical question asks about strengths and weaknesses. Go back to your self-inventory and look at it with a very critical eye. Make a list of three or four characteristics that you consider to be strengths, and make sure that you honestly believe them to be strengths. Look at strengths of character and strengths related to your profession.

Now make a list of three or four characteristics that you believe to be weaknesses. This is not always a pleasant task, but a personal weakness is something that you will eventually have to face and make an effort to improve, so look at it as a personal growth exercise. Besides, the question will very likely come up in the interview.

Strengths are much easier to talk about than weaknesses. Don't be shy about discussing your strengths, but don't brag about them either. If you have ways that you live your life or do your work that you are proud of, mention those and maybe talk a little about how you came to be that way. Don't forget to include any strong skills you have learned that might be useful in your professional life.

How can you best respond to a question about what your weaknesses are?
© 2008, JupiterImages Corporation.

When you consider your weaknesses, think about real weaknesses that you have and also think about what you have done or what you could do to overcome them. Even if you don't have it beaten yet, at least you have recognized the weakness and are taking steps to eliminate it. Interviewers are very used to hearing about minor weaknesses that have easy solutions. Even people who believe they are perfect come up with small weaknesses because they know it will come up in an interview. We call these *false weaknesses.* Many of those sound phony to the interviewers (who typically interview a lot of people, so you know they have heard nearly everything!). For example, a typical false weakness is "I'm a perfectionist." This is said to be a weakness because it "takes me longer to do things since I have to do them just right." How many times do you think interviewers hear that one?

A response to the weakness question that we hear a lot is, "I'm a procrastinator." This is a fine response, if you follow up with sincere efforts you have made to overcome it. However, this is often followed up with, "But being a procrastinator is fine because I have found that I work really well under pressure." That kind of response, as well as the attitude toward work that it communicates, should provide some entertainment for the interviewer, but it will *not* land you a job.

A good example of an answer to the weakness question is, "I have been working on my listening skills. I have found myself distracted occasionally when other people talk, and I don't always hear everything they say." Having poor listening skills is certainly a weakness, but you have acknowledged that you have recognized the weakness and that you are trying to improve your skills. You can follow the recognition statement with some specific things you are doing to help you improve. "I now understand that listening is not a passive activity and that it takes a lot of effort to listen well. Now when I talk to other people, I focus much more energy on being involved in the whole conversation and listening carefully. I'm not perfect, but I am certainly improving!" Another possibility is to talk about some specific training in listening that you are taking to help you improve.

Career Choice. Discuss not only the future and where you see your career taking you, but also what effect you could have on the career. How do you think your innovative thinking or skills can influence the field you are entering?

You should also, if appropriate in the interview, talk about the path that brought you to this career. What life experiences or classes or individuals influenced you to be interested in this particular career? What sparked your interest? The answers to these questions can be compelling, and they can be an indication of your dedication and commitment to the career.

Past Employment. Present and past employment is very often discussed in screening interviews. Be able to describe the positions that you have held and what duties you performed. What did you learn from each position? Did you learn any skills, or did you learn something about a work ethic?

You might be asked why you left a particular position. *Never* talk in a negative way about a former employer or position. Maybe the job was temporary, or you didn't plan to be there for the long term. Maybe the position was not challenging enough for you or the company didn't offer the opportunities that you were looking for. There is no reason to "trash" a former employer: Doing so can communicate a characteristic in you that is undesirable to a new employer. So even if you wanted to push your former boss out of a window, take the professional high road and let go of the anger!

These are just a few examples of typical questions and answers. Go through the list of questions in this chapter and critically consider how you would answer each one. Check with friends, teachers, and mentors about other questions that might be asked in this kind of interview. Think about how you can answer the question honestly and in a way that truly describes you and what you think you can contribute to an employer.

EEOC Considerations

The United States has federal and state laws designed to prevent discrimination in the workplace and in hiring practices. A worker or recruit cannot be discriminated against on the basis of age, sex, race, national origin, marital status, pregnancy, or religious beliefs. These laws apply to procedures used by companies for interviewing and hiring new employees.

This means that, when considering a potential new employee, a company can't consider these characteristics when making hiring decisions. As a result, they are not permitted to ask questions during the interview process about any of those topics. These are regarded as "inappropriate" or even "illegal" questions. If you are asked such a question, you do not have to respond to it. Topics covered and questions asked in employment interviews should be focused only on *job-related* issues. Please see Appendix 5 for a brief description of each characteristic and a link to the EEOC Web site for your further research.

Most companies have strict policies related to asking only appropriate questions during interviews, and the interviewers in those companies are normally well trained. It is unlikely that they will ask you an inappropriate question. These companies usually have guidelines on what to do if you think you have been asked an inappropriate question. So if you think such a question was asked in an interview, a good first step is to contact the company's human resources department. If that contact is not satisfying, you should contact the Equal Employment Opportunity Commission (EEOC).

The simple fact that an interviewer asks you an illegal question like those in the box is not a clear indicator that the company is trying to discriminate against you or that it has some hidden agenda in the interview. Very often, when we get engaged and "taken up" in a conversation, we just follow the topics and we let our interest and curiosity dictate the direction. The bad news is that sometimes this curiosity or interest can take the conversation into illegal or inappropriate territory. The inappropriate question *could* be just an honest mistake. However, the interviewer could be trying to obtain information that would violate the Equal Employment Opportunity Commission guidelines against discrimination.

Regardless of the intention of the interviewer, *you* have to be attentive to the kinds of questions you are being asked. Listen carefully to each question you are asked. If you suspect that a question is not appropriate, don't get excited. Plan your response. Your reply to the question does not have to be hostile, and you do not have to "hit the interviewer on the head" with the law. However, you *do* have to call it to the interviewer's attention. You could casually ask, "Why do you want to know that?" Or you could ask how the information requested applies to the requirements of the position you are seeking. There might be a good explanation! If you are satisfied with the explanation, then answer the question. If you are not satisfied with the explanation, politely let the interviewer know, and tell him or her that you are not comfortable with responding to a question that you believe is inappropriate. Let us repeat: It's important to be polite and professional at all times!

It's important to be professional because you (as the interviewee) are walking a thin line in this situation. You certainly have the right, under the law, to refuse to answer a question that is inappropriate. However, what if it does happen to be an honest mistake made by the interviewer, or is a case of your misinterpreting the question? If you immediately get excited, become

Inappropriate Questions in Employment Interviews

Take a look at these examples of questions that are inappropriate for an employment interview. Please note that this is *not* a complete list of all possible forms of discrimination. Some appropriate alternatives are provided.

Issue: Age
Inappropriate question: How old are you?
Inappropriate question: What is your date of birth?
Inappropriate question: What year did you graduate from high school?
Appropriate question: Are you over the age of 18?

Issue: Marital Status
Inappropriate question: Do you have children to care for?
Inappropriate question: Do you have children?
Inappropriate question: Will you need child care services while you work?
Inappropriate question: Does your husband/wife approve of your travel for business?
Appropriate question: Will you be able to travel for business?

Issue: National Origin
Inappropriate question: Where were you born?
Inappropriate question: Where were your parents born?
Inappropriate question: Do you speak English with your family at home?
Inappropriate question: Is your last name Korean?

Issue: Disabilities
Inappropriate question: Do you have any disabilities?
Inappropriate question: Please respond to the following medical questions.
Appropriate question: Are you able to perform all the functions required of this position?

Issue: Religion
Inappropriate question: Are you Catholic?
Inappropriate question: Do you go to church?

openly hostile, and threaten legal action, you have only made a bad situation much worse. If you did misinterpret something that was, in fact, an appropriate question, your chances of actually getting the job are pretty small. Few companies will hire somebody that they know has a short fuse. No matter what happens, be determined to remain professional at all times.

Many companies are so concerned about this issue that the company interviewers operate from a script. The script isn't just a list of topics to be covered in an interview, but many contain the exact wording of each question. The questions are carefully scripted to obtain the necessary information for making a hiring decision without violating the spirit or letter of the anti-discrimination laws. The resulting interviews are frequently lacking in spontaneity, but it helps all involved avoid making costly errors. It also helps prevent placing the interviewee in an awkward situation.

 You and the interviewer should keep in mind at all times that the main goal of any selection interview is to determine your capability to perform the responsibilities of the position. You share in the responsibility to uphold this goal, so be prepared, be attentive, and be professional.

WHAT SHOULD MY RESUME LOOK LIKE?

Even before you schedule an interview, you will probably need to send a resume. You should keep a current resume as an electronic file. But first, you must create one. You should begin this process by collecting all the data that you will need for your **resume.** An easy way to accomplish this is to complete Appendix 1 at the end of this chapter. Once all the data are collected, then you will have little trouble placing the information into your resume.

Your Contact Information

Make sure that the prospective employer has all the information necessary to contact you for an interview. This information must be complete and correct!

Telephone. Include a home and/or cell phone number.
Consider the following advice:

- Provide the area code and the telephone number. If you live outside the United States, be sure to include a country code.
- Make sure the numbers you provide are *correct!*
- If there are other people at your house who might answer the telephone, you should warn them that a prospective employer might call. Ask the others to be courteous and respectful, to offer to take a message for you if you are not there, and to record that message accurately.
- If you have a goofy or silly message on your answering machine or voice mail, now would be a great time to change the message to something more professional. It doesn't have to be cold and stuffy, but make sure it is understandable (speak clearly, don't mumble), friendly (save the sarcasm for your friends and family), and polite. When you record your outgoing greeting on your telephone, listen to it to make sure it says what you want it to say in the way you would like to say it. If you aren't satisfied with the message, record it again and again until you are satisfied with it.

Bad Greeting	Good Greeting
· Whaaaaasssssup! This is BJ. Leave a message. **DO IT!!**	· Hello! This is Brian Jay. I am unable to take your call. Please leave a detailed message and I will return your call as soon as possible.
· I could talk to you now, but I just don't want to. Sigh . . . If you *really, really* want to, I suppose you can leave a message. Sigh . . .	

E-mail. If you plan to give an e-mail address for the prospective employer to respond to, make sure it is professional. If you have an e-mail address at your campus or through your employer, you probably do not have much control. If, however, you use a service that allows you to create your own e-mail name, use some discretion, and keep it clean and professional. It might be a good idea to make the address some version of your name so the prospective employer knows that it's *you* being contacted. Here are a couple of examples:

Bad Addresses	Good Addresses
beerhunter@myprovider.com	Bjay@myprovider.com
born_to_race@myprovider.com	Brian_jay@myprovider.com

 If you participate in an online social site such as FaceBook.com, MySpace.com, or any other site to which the general public has access, review the information you have placed there about yourself. Many prospective employers have begun to search the Web as part of their research into your qualifications and character. *Google* yourself and see what you find (annaivey.com). This is what prospective employers will find also, so don't place anything on a public site that you would be embarrassed for them to know or see.

Address. If you are a full-time student and live on campus, give your *complete* and correct campus address.

357 Smith	357 Smith Hall
UD	154 North Westmark Drive
Dubuque, IA	University of Dubuque
	Dubuque, IA 52001

The address on the left is incomplete, and nobody knows what it means! Is "357" a street address or a room number? What about "UD?" Is that a school? Is it a law firm? Do you know how many UD's exist in the United States? (*Google* it and find out. It's a bunch!). "Dubuque, IA" is clear enough, but there is no zip code. An employer could very easily interpret this incomplete information as an indication of your abilities, and your resume could end up in the company shredder. If another job seeker's resume is as good as yours, but that person has complete contact information, which one would you guess will get the call?

If you live on campus, you should consider providing your permanent, home address as well.

Objective

Stating your career objective is very difficult, and it could be time consuming. However, the investment in time and effort is well worth it. The objective that you state should truly represent you and your actual career goals and not be a worn-out, overused statement that sounds good but says nothing. If you were the person reading the resume, how focused and motivated do you think the person who wrote this objective is: "To get a rewarding and challenging position that would allow me to work with people." How would *you* evaluate that statement? Make your statement represent *you*.

The Career Services Web site at the University of Dayton (careers.udayton.edu) suggests that a well-written objective answers two basic questions for a prospective employer. The first question is, *"What position is the applicant looking for?"* The second question is, *"Is the applicant clear about the opportunities this company has for people with his or her qualifications?"* The answers to these two questions will assist you to write a statement that is meaningful to the employer and one that will help you focus on what you really want in a job and career. Here are a couple of clearly stated and significant objectives:

- To enter the advertising industry as a copywriter with the long-term goal of becoming an account executive.
- To obtain a position as a design engineer with potential to move to project administration.

So take the time to give some thought to this critical question. Some career consultants also mention that, while the general objective must be a true and clear statement of what you are looking for, your actual statement should be adapted to the kind of company you are interested in and the specific opportunities available with that company.

A clear, descriptive resume will accurately illustrate your career goals, education, and experience.
© javarman, 2008, Shutterstock.

Education

You should include the names and addresses (at least include the city and state, or country) of all schools attended. If you are still in college and looking for a job or an internship, provide information about your high school (honors, activities, sports, and other details that you think are notable), as well as information about colleges (or other schools) you have attended.

Be sure to include information about college majors and minors, certificates, and specialized training. Include the date that you received your diploma or degree, as well as an accurate name for the degree. If you are not sure of the correct name, contact your academic department office or the office of the dean of the college or school. Get it right! If you have not received a degree yet, include a *realistic* projected date that you will receive the degree.

Don't forget to mention other kinds of training or special classes you might have taken. This can include, but is certainly not limited to, software training, military training, first aid or life-saving classes, and other kinds of training.

Employment History

List your past and current positions in chronological order. Most people prefer to list the most recent positions first, and then move back in time in reverse chronological order. Include all the necessary information in this section. You should provide the name of the company, an accurate address and telephone number, the dates that you worked for this company, the name of your immediate supervisor, any specialized training you might have received, and a description of your duties.

Descriptions of your past jobs should be clear, descriptive, accurate, and *honest.* We have all had jobs that we might look at as silly, meaningless, or maybe even demeaning. This is a very common situation, especially when you are trying to establish a career or while you are attending school. *That is nothing to be ashamed of.* At least you had a job and you were becoming more independent as you were moving ahead. Lots of people take survival jobs to get through school or to cope with challenging circumstances. So there is no need to make jobs sound more important than they actually were. In fact, if you do try to make them sound more important than they were, you are doing a disservice to yourself and to the job. It can also cost you some serious credibility points with a prospective employer. So don't try to oversell it. Here's an example from a person describing a summer job at a local diner:

Bad Job Description	**Good Job Description**
Server (in a restaurant)	**Server**
• Simultaneously managed numerous patrons and restaurant operations in a fast-paced environment.	• Satisfied customers by taking accurate orders and providing fast, efficient service.
• Increased general sales and revenue through evocative selling and targeted product marketing.	• Increased receipts through suggestive selling techniques
• Flourished in a cooperative team environment to maintain fluid business operations.	• Prospered as a member of a team

If you were a waitress, say so! If you had a job pumping gas, don't say you were a "fuel injection specialist." Just say you pumped gas! Although "retail commodities relocator" sounds responsible and significant, it would probably be more honest to say that you delivered packages on your bicycle. If you made hamburgers at Mickey's, you were not a "chef." If you worked at a grocery store, and your main job was to walk around the aisles pulling items to the front of the shelf or replacing sold-out items, just say that in your description. Don't say, as one of our students did, that you are an "ambient replenishment opportunity consultant."

Putting It Together

We have included a model of a very basic resume layout for your consideration (Appendix 2). However, there are templates available for resumes in many word-processing software packages that you can easily access. You should also check out your school's job placement center or office of career services for resume help.

Remember that if you misrepresent yourself, you're setting yourself up for future complications. If you say that you have skills or abilities that you don't really have, and you get a job that demands the use of those skills, that's trouble. Avoid ethical problems: Don't try to be somebody that you are not, and don't lie on your resume.

When you are done creating your resume, you are not finished. *Proofread it* for errors. As an added check, ask someone who is good with details to proofread it, too. A great resume will end up in the trash if you spell the company name wrong or list your position as club president twice. You can also follow the provided links to Web sites with resume advice and templates for your use.

WHAT SHOULD THE COVER LETTER LOOK LIKE?

Every time you send out a resume to apply for a position, send a **cover letter** along with it. The cover letter contains information regarding who (or at least which office) at the company should receive the resume and specifically what job you are applying for. This letter also gives you an opportunity to highlight parts of your resume so you can help readers focus their attention on information you consider to be the most important.

Not sending a cover letter with a resume is a bad idea. Not only is it an indication of the sender's lack of motivation and enthusiasm, but the company might not be sure what job you are applying for. If they don't know where the resume should go, it could be a good candidate for the trash can. Even if you do enclose a cover letter, another indicator of lack of drive is the failure to adapt your letter to that *specific* company. Taking this extra step can add some extra time and effort to the job application process, but it gives you a great opportunity to give this company some information about what's in your resume and what you have to offer. Here's your chance to tell the screener what exactly you can do for *this particular company.* Don't be shy! It is also a good idea to demonstrate a little knowledge about the company. You already did your research, so be clear about why you chose this company.

Consider that this letter is the first impression that you will make with this company. Do *not* allow *any* spelling or grammatical errors to get into this letter. It is especially important to not misspell the name of the person to whom you address the letter. Spelling and grammar errors help your materials take the fast track to the company recycling center.

Try to address this letter to a specific person. Do a little research to find out who makes the hiring decision for the job that interests you and address the letter to that person. Tom Jackson says, "Target delivery of your resume precisely. The best resume in the world will not help you unless it gets to the right person."[13]

Appendix 3 to this chapter is an example of a cover letter. As with the resume, don't send it until you *proofread* it.

WHAT SHOULD A THANK-YOU LETTER LOOK LIKE?

As a courtesy to the interview team and the company, and as a way to keep your name and credentials in front of the decision makers, you should send a follow-up **thank-you letter** to the company thanking them for the time they

Take the opportunity to highlight what you can do for the company by writing a personalized cover letter.
© 2008, JupiterImages Corporation.

took with your interview. Send this letter to the specific person or persons who interviewed you, and be sure to include your contact information in case they require more information from you. This is also an opportunity to high-light a strong point (or two) from your resume or interview, and it's a chance to include some information that perhaps was overlooked in your interview that you believe to be important.

On rare occasions (depending on the company), it might be appropriate to send a thank-you letter using e-mail. If you do, make sure that you follow the same rules for structure and language that you would if sending a letter on stationery through the U.S. mail. Resist the temptation to use the same language and structure that you might use when text messaging, instant mes-saging, or e-mailing your friends. Take a look at the following example:

Bad Thank-You Message

TYVM 4 meeting w/ me today 2 talk about the position u have available. I'm excited about working w/ ur company b/c it fits very well in2 my career goals. Can't wait 2 hear from u! :)

Good Thank-You Message

Thank you very much for meeting with me today to discuss the position that you have available. I'm excited about working with your company because it fits very well with my career goals. I'm looking forward to hearing from you!

Please see Appendix 4 to this chapter for an example of a thank-you letter. But what should you do before you send it? That's right—*proofread.*

HOW SHOULD I DRESS FOR AN INTERVIEW?

We can't conclude a section on employment interviewing without mention-ing **appropriate interview attire.** Even though you worked very hard to pre-pare for an important job interview, you will still find yourself at a significant disadvantage if you allow your appearance to speak for you. If you are remembered by a potential employer because of your *appearance,* it's very likely because it didn't work!

The best advice we have heard on how to dress for professional occasions came from an attorney. When asked about appropriate attire for a courtroom visit, the attorney said, "Dress in such a way as to show respect for the court." An employment interview is not the same thing as visiting a courtroom, but the core of the advice is still relevant. *You should dress in such a way as to show respect for the situation, the company you would like to work for, and the interviewer.*

This means that an employment interview is not the place to make your fashion statement. Stick to a conservative look. For this event, you should focus on simple, clean, and tasteful. Remember that anything you do to dis-tract the interviewer takes away from the message you are trying to deliver. So if you have inappropriate clothes, lots of perfume, body piercings and tat-toos, excessive jewelry, or if you smell bad from smoking or lack of personal hygiene, there will be distraction. All the preparation that you do for this interview could be negated if you allow your appearance to take center stage.

We are not going to try to give specific advice on how men and women should dress for this occasion. There is plenty of expert and specific advice available on how to dress for an interview. Consult your school's career center, look at some of the self-help books like *Dress for Success*.[14]

SUMMARY

This chapter looks at the practical application of two kinds of communication situations: *Information Gathering* interviews and *Employment* interviews. While there are many different kinds of interviews, these two are very widely used and we considered them to be the most useful for students taking this kind of college course. However, no matter what kind of interview you participate in, it is critical that you remember that you must play an ***active*** role. You can't be a passive participant and expect to accomplish your goals for the interview.

The Information Gathering interview invites you to take the part of the interview**er** where your primary task is to ask the questions. In that role, you should focus on goal setting, planning the interview, asking good and clear questions, and efficiently recording the information that you gather. A significant challenge in this type of interview is maintaining your focus and keeping yourself in the "here and now" of the interview situation. It is very easy to get distracted and to let your mind wander when the interviewee is answering your questions. Strategies for avoiding distraction are discussed in both interviewing chapters. The Employment interview, on the other hand, allows you to take the role of the interview**ee** and answer the questions. In the responding role, you should focus on getting to know yourself (i.e., your history, strengths, weaknesses, short-term goals, and long-term goals). It's important to "sweat the details," which include accurate and complete information on your resume and in your cover and thank-you letters.

The appendix sections of this chapter contain information that can help you get to know yourself a little better and also help you to make some practical decisions on resume construction as well as writing clear and personable cover letters and thank-you letters. It's important that you take the time to go through all the personal inventories and consider all the templates for writing letters and resumes. You will be very happy you did so when you get to your first interview!

ENDNOTES

1. "An ILA definition of listening," ILA *Listening Post*, 53 (1) (1995).

2. C. Kelly, "Empathic Listening," in R. S. Cathcart and L. A. Samovar (eds.), *Small Group Communication: A Reader* (Dubuque, IA: Wm. C. Brown, 1970). Also R. Nichols and L. Stevens, *Listening to People* (New York: McGraw-Hill, 1957).

3. Nichols and Stevens. Also L. Steil, L. Barker, and K. Watson, *Effective Listening: Key to Your Success* (Reading, MA: Addison-Wesley, 1983).

4. Nichols and Stevens.

5. A. Sillars, J. Weisberg, C. Burggraf, and P. Zeitlow, "Communication and Understanding Revisited: Married Couples' Understanding and Recall of Conversations," *Communication Research* 17 (1990): 500–522.

6. R. Berko, "Test Your Knowledge Here," *Spectra* 10 (1995): 9–12.

7. L. Hugenberg, D. Yoder, S. Wallace, C. Horvath, *Creating Competent Communication*, 4th ed. (Dubuque, IA: Kendall/Hunt, 2005).

8. D. Sellnow, *Public Speaking: A Process Approach* (Belmont, CA: Wadsworth, 2006).

9. F. Wolff, N. Marsnik, W. Tacey, and R. Nichols, *Perceptive Listening* (New York: Holt, Rinehart & Winston, 1983).

10. L. Hugenberg, D. Yoder, S. Wallace, C. Horvath, *Creating Competent Communication*, 4th ed. (Dubuque, IA: Kendall/Hunt, 2005).

11. S. Wallace, D. Yoder, L. Hugenberg, C. Horvath, *Creating Competent Communication: Interviewing*. (Dubuque, IA: Kendall/Hunt, 2006).

12. F. Abel, "Note Takers vs. Non-note Takers: Who Makes More Errors?" *Journalism Quarterly* 46 (1969): 811–814.

13. T. Jackson, *The Perfect Resume* (New York: Broadway Books, 2004), p. 11.

14. J. Molloy, *John T. Molloy's New Dress for Success* (New York: Warner Books, 1988).

REFERENCES

Clayman, S., & Heritage, J. (2002). *The news interview: Journalists and public figures on the air.* New York: Cambridge University Press.

Nichols, R. (1995). *The lost art of listening.* New York: Guilford.

Stafford, L., Burggraf, C., & Yost, S. (1988). "Short and long term conversational memory in stranger and marital dyads." Paper presented at the annual meeting of the Speech Communication Association, New Orleans, LA.

www.annaivey.com; accessed June 10, 2006

APPENDIX 1: PERSONAL INVENTORY FORM

Objective	*Question 1:*	1. What position am I looking for?
	Question 2:	2. What opportunities do companies have for people with my qualifications? (You could adapt this to each specific company.)
	Objective:	3. What is my stated job/career objective?
Education	*High School*	Dates of attendance Date of graduation Course of study? Honors? Special activities?
	College 1	Dates of attendance Date of graduation (or projected date)? Degree earned? Majors? Minors? Special training? Honors?
	College 2	Dates of attendance Date of graduation (or projected date)? Degree earned? Majors? Minors? Special training? Honors?
	Add more schools as necessary	
	Other Training	Type of training Location of training Dates of training Description of skills acquired
Military Service		Branch of Service Dates of Service Highest rank achieved Date of discharge Specialized training Description of skills Description of duties

Work Experience	Position 1 (Most recent)	Place of employment (name) Complete address Phone and fax numbers, e-mail addresses Dates of your employment Your position Description of your duties Name of supervisor
	Position 2	Place of employment (name) Complete address Phone and fax numbers, e-mail addresses Dates of your employment Your position Description of your duties Name of supervisor
	Position 3	Place of employment (name) Complete address Phone and fax numbers, e-mail addresses Dates of your employment Your position Description of your duties Name of supervisor
Special Abilities	Talents Training Other skills	Description Description Description
References	Reference 1	Name Address Phone, fax, e-mail
	Reference 2	Name Address Phone, fax, e-mail
	Reference 3	Name Address Phone, fax, e-mail
Other	Question 1	What got you interested in your college major?
	Question 2	What got you interested in this career?

APPENDIX 2: BASIC RESUME LAYOUT

Local Address City, State, Zip Local Phone Number E-Mail Address	Permanent Address (if needed) City, State, Zip Local Phone Number E-Mail Address
YOUR NAME (centered on the page)	
Career or Job Objective	
Education	**Name of college or university** B.A. or B.S. (or appropriate degree) Major(s): Minor(s): Date of graduation (or projected) **High School**　　Town, State Any honors? Date of graduation
Special Skills	
Experience *Position 1 (most recent)*	Name of company and address Dates of employment Name of supervisor Job title and accurate description
Position 2	Name of company and address Dates of employment Name of supervisor Job title and accurate description
Position 3 *(Use as many as needed)*	Name of company and address Dates of employment Name of supervisor Job title and accurate description
Activities	Personal interests, hobbies, etc.

APPENDIX 3: COVER LETTER EXAMPLE

123 Maple Drive
Dubuque, IA 34567

June 12, 2008

Mr. Robert A. Roberts
Supervising Technologist
Green River Technologies
12345 Westmark Drive
Dubuque, IA 54321

Dear Mr. Roberts,

PARAGRAPH 1

What motivated you to write.
Specific position you are applying for.
How you learned about this position.
What you have to offer this company *(brief but clear)*.
Statement of your belief that your qualifications match the requirement of the job.

PARAGRAPH 2

Your education and training relative to this position.
Your work experiences relevant to this position.
Other experiences relevant to this position.
Statement of *why* you believe your qualifications to be a good match for this job or company.

PARAGRAPH 3

Restatement of interest in this position and organization.
Request for an interview for the position.
Date when you could start.
How you can be reached by mail, fax, telephone, Internet.

PARAGRAPH 4

Thank recruiter or screener for the time to consider your application.
Express enthusiasm for hearing about opportunity to come for an interview.

Sincerely,

Brian Jay

APPENDIX 4: THANK-YOU LETTER EXAMPLE

123 Maple Drive
Dubuque, IA 34567

June 12, 2008

Mr. Robert A. Roberts   [USE INTERVIEWER'S NAME!]
Supervising Technologist
Green River Technologies
12345 Westmark Drive
Dubuque, IA 54321

Dear Mr. Roberts,

Thank you for taking the time on [DATE] to talk with me about the [position title]. I learned a lot about your company and I enjoyed meeting the other members of your staff. It would be my privilege to work with such a terrific team!

After our conversation, I am even more convinced that my qualifications, experience, and career objectives are very well aligned with your requirements for this position. In particular, my [specific experience, education, etc.] match well with your requirements of [state specific job requirements]. This is just the position that I have been searching for, and I am sure that I can make an important contribution to [company name]. I hope your team feels the same way!

[Use this optional paragraph to add any information that you think might have been passed over during the interviewing process.]

Thanks again for interviewing me. I will be happy to provide more information or answer any questions that you or the team might have. I look forward to hearing from you again very soon.

Sincerely,

Brian Jay

APPENDIX 5

The Equal Employment Opportunity Commission (EEOC) Basic Rules Preventing Discrimination in the Workplace

Age

http://www.eeoc.gov/types/age.html

The Age Discrimination in Employment Act of 1967 (ADEA) protects individuals who are 40 years of age or older from employment discrimination based on age. These protections apply to both employees and job applicants. It is unlawful to discriminate against a person because of his/her age with respect to any term, condition, or privilege of employment, including hiring, firing, promotion, layoff, compensation, benefits, job assignments, and training.

Gender

http://www.eeoc.gov/types/epa.html

The Equal Pay Act requires that men and women be given equal pay for equal work in the same establishment. The jobs need not be identical, but they must be substantially equal. Employers may not pay unequal wages to men and women who perform jobs that require substantially equal skill, effort, and responsibility, and that are performed under similar working conditions within the same establishment.

Disability

http://www.eeoc.gov/types/ada.html

The *Americans with Disabilities Act of 1990* prohibits private employers, state and local governments, employment agencies and labor unions from discriminating against qualified individuals with disabilities in job application procedures, hiring, firing, advancement, compensation, job training, and other terms, conditions, and privileges of employment. An individual with a disability is a person who:

- Has a physical or mental impairment that substantially limits one or more major life activities;
- Has a record of such an impairment; or
- Is regarded as having such an impairment.

National Origin

http://www.eeoc.gov/origin/index.html

Whether an employee or job applicant's ancestry is Mexican, Ukrainian, Filipino, Arab, American Indian, or any other nationality, he or she is entitled to the same employment opportunities as anyone else.

Pregnancy

http://www.eeoc.gov/types/pregnancy.html

An employer cannot refuse to hire a pregnant woman because of her pregnancy, because of a pregnancy-related condition, or because of the prejudices of co-workers, clients, or customers.

Race

http://www.eeoc.gov/types/race.html

The Civil Rights Act of 1964 protects individuals against employment discrimination on the bases of race and color, as well as national origin, sex, and religion.

Equal employment opportunity cannot be denied any person because of his/her racial group or perceived racial group, his/her race-linked characteristics (e.g., hair texture, color, facial features), or because of his/her marriage to or association with someone of a particular race or color. The law also prohibits employment decisions based on stereotypes and assumptions about abilities, traits, or the performance of individuals of certain racial groups.

Religion

http://www.eeoc.gov/types/religion.html

Employers may not treat employees or applicants more or less favorably because of their religious beliefs or practices—except to the extent a religious accommodation is warranted. For example, an employer may not refuse to hire individuals of a certain religion, may not impose stricter promotion requirements for persons of a certain religion, and may not impose more or different work requirements on an employee because of that employee's religious beliefs or practices.

9

WHY DO WE USE GROUPS TO SOLVE PROBLEMS AND MAKE DECISIONS?

LEARNING OBJECTIVES

After reading this chapter, you should understand the following concepts:

- A small group is a collection of people who work together either voluntarily or involuntarily to achieve a goal or solve a problem.
- Voluntary groups come together to achieve goals, solve problems, fulfill needs, or simply to connect with others with the same interests.
- Involuntary groups are formed to solve problems, make decisions, or accomplish necessary tasks.
- Groups offer many benefits, but they also have drawbacks, one of which is groupthink.
- Groups typically progress through five stages: forming, storming, norming, performing, and adjourning.
- Your roles in small groups will vary, depending on the group.
- Tools for handling disruptive members include feedback, perception checking, and group contracts.

INTRODUCTION

"I hate group work!"

This statement is often heard when college students are told they will be working in groups to complete projects. The same sentiment is expressed across offices and at work sites every day. "Why can't I just do this project myself?" Dissatisfaction with working in groups is so common that the term *grouphate* was coined to describe the negative attitude toward group work.[1] If people hate working in groups so much, then why are groups so often used? The answer to the question is fairly simple: Groups outperform individuals most of the time, and groups are capable of taking on more complex tasks. In fact, many employers are willing to pay the added expense of operating a group to take advantage of a group's ability to creatively solve problems and to make high-quality decisions.

Why do groups have an advantage when it comes to problem solving?
© 2008, JupiterImages Corporation.

How do individual strengths combine to make a group successful?
© 2008, JupiterImages Corporation.

For most of us, our first exposure to groups was as early as elementary school. Perhaps we were asked to collaborate with other students to complete an in-class activity or to play on a sports team. These early exposures to groups provide us with our first instructions about how to play nicely with others, how to share, and how to get along. The collaborative learning process continues through college, where the skills being taught are more complex (e.g., conflict management, patience, and negotiation skills) and the stakes are much higher (e.g., grades in our major, grades influencing the next school we attend, financial aid, and our future professions). The stakes continue to rise in our careers. Our ability to work effectively with others affects our salaries, our upward mobility, and even our job security.

Television has capitalized on just how difficult it is to work with others, which is evidenced by the number of popular group-based reality shows. Although the subject of these shows is not directly related to the process of building an effective group or team, they do require participants to work within the framework of a group to achieve goals. For instance, teams are formed on one show to achieve business goals such as marketing and selling a product. Each group member is judged by his or her individual contribution, approaches to group collaboration, and decision making throughout the process. The selling point of such shows is not only the completion of the task at hand but also the relationships among group members. There is something enjoyable about watching how group members balance their own goals with the group goals, manage conflicts, and how they are able to succeed, or fail, under such circumstances.

The way we respond to groups, the roles we play, the understanding we bring to them, and the communication skills we use (or fail to use) combine to influence our group experience. Earlier in this book, we discussed the importance of using communication skills to exercise our democratic rights. Effective group communication skills allow us to foster a free flow and thorough discussion of ideas critical in a democracy. Controversial issues discussed in the context of a group can move from divisive arguments to productive dialogues when the proper skills are employed.

The purpose of this activity is for you to reflect on this particular group experience when reading about the skills necessary to effectively work in and manage groups. Use this experience as a reference point while reading this chapter and participating in class activities.

Take a Closer Look

Working in a Group
Think of the last group in which you worked.

- What was the purpose of the group?
- Was the group voluntary or mandatory?
- What was the best part of the group experience?
- What was the worst part of the group experience?
- If you could repeat the group experience, what would you have done differently?

WHAT IS THE NATURE OF SMALL GROUPS?

Stated simply, a **small group** is a collection of people who work together either voluntarily or involuntarily to achieve a goal or solve a problem. But a small group is actually a complex social and communication phenomenon, so let's expand our definition. If we examine how other scholars have looked at small groups, we can gain some additional insight.

Keyton tells us that a small group is three or more people who work together interdependently on an agreed-upon activity or goal.[2] Forsyth says that a group is made up of "interdependent individuals who influence each other through social interaction."[3]

Wallace et al. suggest that a small group is an interdependent collection of persons engaged in a structured, cooperative, often (but not always) face-to-face, goal-oriented communication; each aware of their own and others' participation in the group; and each getting some satisfaction from participating in the activities of the group.[4]

Finally, Beebe and Masterson define a small group as a "group of people who share a common purpose or goal, who feel a sense of belonging to the group, and who exert influence on one another."[5]

As we look at these definitions, let's focus on the important issues:

Small groups in a work atmosphere often form to solve a particular problem.
© Miodrag Gajic, 2008, Shutterstock.

Goal Orientation

The small groups being discussed in this chapter are created to solve problems or make decisions. As such, they are driven by a focus on some goal to be achieved. The more clearly this goal is defined, the more likely the group will be able to find a solution to the problem or make a quality decision. Group goals provide focus and direction for small groups.

Size Matters

A small group consists of at least three or more members. When there are fewer than three members, the communication is dyadic. When the third member is added to the mix, things begin to change. With three or more members, it is possible for factions to form and for subgroups of members to exchange information that is not available to the whole group. Adding more members to the group can be positive because it means that the group will have more points of view to consider when making a decision.

There is a limit, however, to the size of an effective problem-solving small group. What that specific limit is depends, to a large extent, on the individual personalities in the group, the context in which the group is operating, and the nature of the task or problem the group is trying to solve. A group is too large when every member cannot directly communicate with every other member. If you can't carry on a group conversation, then the group

What difficulties would this group likely encounter if it were trying to solve a problem?
© 2008, JupiterImages Corporation.

members cannot be interdependent. Although there is no definitive upper limit, groups larger than twelve seem to have troubles with interdependence, cohesion, and mutual influence.

Interdependence

The product of a small group is greater than the sum of its parts because of the communication interaction and the **interdependence** of its members. People draw energy, motivation, and ideas from each other, and they take advantage of one another's talents and expertise. Members combine their talents and resources, which gives them the ability to solve more complex problems than they could as individuals working alone. As a result of interdependence, groups have the potential to make better decisions than individuals.

Collection of People

A collection of people isn't necessarily a small group.
© 2008, JupiterImages Corporation.

A small group is not just an assembly of individuals, but a dynamic combination of people working together to accomplish some common goal. This shared goal and communication among the members are the major elements that separate groups from random collections of people, and it is responsible for the ability of groups to solve problems. For example, a group of people standing on a street corner waiting on a bus to arrive is a collection of people, but they aren't focused on some common goal. They aren't doing anything but waiting on a bus. They just happen to be doing it in the same place. However, these same people could *become* a small group if they decided to design a bus shelter to make their wait more comfortable or if they tried to figure out a better route so the buses would run on time.

Structure

Even though they might sometimes appear to be chaotic, small groups have structure. Some of the structure is fairly common across nearly every group, like there are usually leaders and there are usually followers. Some structures, however, only emerge in certain groups, and the compositions of those structures depend on the nature of the group task and the individual characteristics of the group members. After the group has been together for a while, these structures become more stable, but they are rarely static. Groups tend to negotiate and then continually renegotiate roles, expectations, cohesiveness, the group identity, the way conflict is managed, and many other structural elements.

WHAT ARE THE TYPES OF GROUPS?

Now and in the future, you will participate in many types of groups; some mediated and some face-to-face, some voluntary and some involuntary. We begin by looking at mediated group participation, followed by voluntary groups, and conclude by examining involuntary groups.

Mediated Groups

Whenever a group meets, but does not meet face-to-face, there is some form of media involved. Mediated groups are becoming more dominant with the emergence of the global economy and the improvement of the communication infrastructure around the world. These groups come in several varieties, including virtual groups (computer mediated), teleconferencing groups (members meet using a telephone connection), and videoconferencing groups (members using a combined video and audio connection).

Virtual groups are among the most widely used. Many groups are using the Internet and its virtual space to substitute for live meetings, and people are voluntarily joining groups that meet solely in cyberspace. *Virtual groups* are a gathering of people using chat rooms, blogs, social networking sites, bulletin boards, Web sites, listservs, or any other form of computer-mediated communication to meet and solve problems, achieve goals, or share experiences. Of course, while many groups continue to meet face-to-face, many use a *mixture* of face-to-face and mediated channels to accomplish their goals.

What advantages do virtual groups offer?
© 2008, JupiterImages Corporation.

The number of companies using virtual meeting space to conduct business is constantly increasing.[6] Meeting online saves time and money spent on travel. It also enables groups to gather at times when it might not be feasible to do so live (e.g., 6:00 A.M. or 12:00 A.M.), it enables groups to transform travel time to time spent on task,[7] and it also encourages shy or reluctant members to participate more openly than they might in face-to-face meetings.[8]

A challenge to virtual groups is the lack of traditional nonverbal communication cues. During a live meeting, a group member may communicate frustration by using a sarcastic tone of voice, a rolling of the eyes, or an unsettled posture. In a virtual meeting, text is often the only channel, so the use of nonverbal cues is limited. This is changing, however, as more and more computers are equipped with video cameras that enable the addition of audiovisual communication channels.

Several Web-based, open-source communities have emerged, starting a revolution in not only in the way we do business, but also in how we work in groups. Many of today's best-known Web-based companies (Google, Amazon, and eBay, for example) are using computer languages and Web servers that are the result of community-developed software that is produced by programmers from all over the world who collaborate in virtual environments. These group members participate, enhance, correct, and contribute to the building of Web tools without ever being together physically as a group.

What communication cues can you see during a live meeting that would be missed in a virtual setting?
© 2008, JupiterImages Corporation.

Voluntary Groups

In many instances, we join groups voluntarily to achieve goals, solve problems, fulfill needs, or simply to connect with others who have the same interests. This type of group comes in many forms, including support groups, volunteer groups, and specialized groups.

What kinds of volunteer groups do you have in your community?
© Christina Richards, 2008, Shutterstock.

Support Groups. Support groups are groups of people who have similar life goals, tragedies, or experiences, who come together to talk, help, and generally support one another. Some examples of these types of groups are Weight Watchers, Alcoholics Anonymous, divorce groups, dating groups, and cancer survivor groups. These groups may be large or small in size and function to help individuals psychologically, emotionally, and at times, physically.

Volunteer Groups. With the increased attention paid to the value of giving something back to the community, many people are joining volunteer groups. For example, some individuals join groups that organize people to tutor public school students, build houses, assist the elderly, or plant trees. These groups are often associated with nonprofit organizations such as the American Red Cross, Habitat for Humanity, and Children of the Americans.

Volunteerism has received much attention over the last decade. This attention has manifested itself into new educational and noneducational requirements. In both compulsory education and universities, there exists a strong commitment, and in some cases, a requirement, for students to volunteer. For example, many high school students involved in International Baccalaureate Programs (a special honors program) are required to complete up to 150 hours of community service. In March 2000, the California State University (CSU) Board of Trustees passed a resolution in support of community service and service learning. The intent was to ensure that all CSU students have opportunities to participate in service learning, community service, or both. Several colleges and universities, such as Cal-State Monterey Bay require their students to complete service learning hours to graduate. (http://www.calstate.edu/csl/facts_figures/servlearn.shtml). It could be argued that volunteering to fulfill a requirement moves this type of group work from a voluntary group to an involuntary group. However, not only are students learning valuable group lessons through the practice, but many of them continue to volunteer after they have met the requirement.

Participation in volunteer work is not limited to academia. In the corporate world, employees are encouraged to participate in volunteer groups. For example, many companies (e.g., Cargill, American Express, Minnesota based ADC) are providing staff specifically designated to manage the company's volunteer efforts such as organizing events like paint-a-thons, promoting volunteer opportunities to employees, and providing grants to nonprofit organizations where employees volunteer. (http://www.minnesotagiving.org) Nationally, businesses may join the Corporate Volunteer Council (http://www.pointsoflight.org/networks/business/cvc/) to find volunteer locations, share effective practices, and address community needs through employee volunteerism.

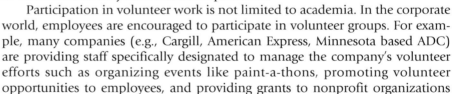

Specialized Groups. Specialized groups are gatherings of people who work in pursuit of a mutual interest. Participation in campus clubs such as the literary club, the future teachers club, or societies like Phi Theta Kappa is voluntary and involves individuals who work toward the achievement of similar goals, such as the advancement of their skills or the opportunity to network. These types of groups include our hobbies (e.g., scrapbooking groups, book clubs), our place in life (e.g., new mothers club, PTA involvement, senior citizen clubs), our own interests (e.g., stock club, chess club, Lions club, Rotary club), or our career interests (engineers clubs, entrepreneurs' club).

Specialized groups, such as local senior citizens, share common interests.
© 2008, JupiterImages Corporation.

Involuntary Groups

Involuntary groups are groups in which we are required to participate. They are often formed to solve a problem, make decisions, or accomplish other tasks. Involuntary groups include academic groups, professional groups, and civic groups.

Academic Groups. These are groups in which you are required to participate to reach academic goals. For example, when you are asked in a class to collaborate with two or more people to write a paper, conduct an experiment, or present a speech, you are participating in an academic group. This type of group can especially be challenging, as individual member's grades often depend on the performance of other group members.

Professional Groups. Committee work in the professional world also requires involuntary collaboration. For example, teachers are required to sit on various committees such as the budget and planning committee, program review, and safety committee. How individuals conduct themselves in these groups can affect their position in the organization in terms of perception of promotability and leadership assessment.

Civic Groups. We participate in civic groups as part of our public or community responsibility. Some civic groups, such as juries, are mandatory if you are selected. Other civic groups are voluntary and perform services for the community, such as Kiwanis Club, the Rotary Club, and a variety of men's and women's clubs.

Volunteer community firefighters provide valuable service to their area.
© 2008, JupiterImages Corporation.

WHAT ARE THE BENEFITS OF GROUPS?

Understanding groups is a bit easier if you understand some of the properties or characteristics that are common to most small groups. Some of these properties are positive and help groups' productivity, and some are not so positive and present a challenge to a group's ability to accomplish its goals. Let's look at the more positive properties first.

Synergy

Synergy usually occurs in situations in which people with a variety of talents and skills cooperate. **Synergy** suggests that the end product of a group's efforts is superior to the product of the individuals working independently. In essence, the sum is greater than the total of its parts. If we were to examine this in terms of a math equation, then the comparison would look something like this:

The sum of the group's efforts	The sum of individual efforts
2 + 2 = 7	2 + 2 = 4

Take a Closer Look

The Pervasiveness of Groups in Your Life
Take time to think about all the groups in which you are currently involved.

· Which groups are voluntary?
· Which groups are involuntary?
· What did you hope or need to accomplish in each group?
· What function did each group serve in your life?

The consequences of a synergistic system can be seen in the group product. A simple and easy way to think of it might be when a light bulb blows out in a very high ceiling. One person working alone is not tall enough to replace it, but two people working together could do it. If one person stood on the shoulders of the other, the goal can be accomplished! In terms of the kind of groups we are concerned with, here's another way to consider synergy. Say you were taking a marketing class and one of your assignments was to market a new line of cell phones to fellow college students. The synergy perspective argues that if you and three others were sent off to complete the task individually, you would not come up with a campaign as comprehensive, innovative, or effective as those who were collaborating in a group. Some of the explanation for this phenomenon can be found in the other properties of small groups.

Pooling Talent

Groups allow members to pool their talents, combining the strengths of each group member. Instead of just depending on the knowledge and skills of a

single member, a group can take advantage of the knowledge and skills of all its members. This means that groups tend to have better collective memories, a variety of expertise, diversity of strengths (and weaknesses), a variety of perspectives (which is essential to group decision making), and more creativity.

Brainstorming

When working with others, ideas are developed further. **Brainstorming** is a free flow of ideas from all participants, and the process can spark initial ideas into new directions and solutions. This process helps to open the group up to original perspectives and ideas with a thinking-outside-the-box mentality. Brainstorm-

What are the advantages of brainstorming in a group?
© 2008, JupiterImages Corporation.

ing can be a powerful tool for creative decision making, but it can also *fail* to be effective if all the members don't participate or cooperate or if the rules for brainstorming aren't followed. Brainstorming will be discussed in a later chapter as a tool for generating a wide variety of solutions to problems.

Complexity

Small groups of people working together are *complex*. This means that a number of individual and independent people have become interdependent and are interacting together in many ways to accomplish some mutually agreed upon goal.[9] If you think of all the ways that individuals are different from each other, and then you think of five individuals working together in a group, the possible combinations of behaviors, conflicts, and outcomes challenges the imagination!

Complex problems often require the expertise of a group effort.
© 2008, JupiterImages Corporation.

Complexity explains why groups of experts are commissioned to solve societal problems, make policy, and to analyze disasters and tragedies. We see this in the form of national think tanks, political or organizational committees, and commissions. This property of groups allows them to provide more thorough, more creative, and high-quality decisions.

Self-Organization

Groups have a strong tendency to organize themselves. As we will explore in this chapter, groups experience phases or stages of development with no guidance from rules or outside sources. Sometimes this kind of organization works very well and allows groups to achieve their goals. But sometimes the organization that emerges does not allow the group to be productive. In these cases (and often when the nature of the problem to be solved demands it), many groups choose to follow established decision-making procedures. We will explore these procedures in Chapter 11.

Adaptivity

Complex, self-organizing systems are *adaptive*.[10] This means that small groups interact with their environments or situations and change or reorganize themselves as needed to be able to accomplish their goals. They have the ability to learn from their experiences and to make appropriate changes in their behaviors or problem-solving strategies. This property allows groups to stay on course or focused even when they face distraction, conflicts, or other difficulties that might otherwise prevent goal achievement.

Dynamic

Small groups do not stand still; they are always moving and changing. They are often unpredictable, messy, and strongly inclined toward disorder. You could even think of it as a goal-oriented, living system that just happens to be made up of other goal-oriented living systems. Successful small groups are able to overcome all the messiness and even take advantage of it by bringing it into a kind of balance that allows goals to be achieved.

Norms

A product of group interaction is a shared standard of acceptable behavior. **Norms** *are shared guidelines for beliefs and behavior.*[11] Norms develop as groups reach implicit agreement that certain behaviors are appropriate and other behaviors are inappropriate. Although there will be some deviance within each group, *norms help establish the group identity* and they are have considerable influence on the behavior of the group members.

Cohesiveness

When a group is cohesive, individual group members feel a connection or attraction to each other. They are motivated by the attraction to each other and by their attraction to the task. Members feel a sense of bonding and they experience a feeling of trust and interdependence. This is important to the group's productivity, as those who have a strong sense of cohesion are generally more productive. It is not clear if high cohesion causes high productivity or if high productivity causes high cohesion. Whatever the case, the two appear to be strongly related. When cohesion gets too high, however, there is a strong potential for **groupthink** to exist, and this condition can prevent groups from making quality decisions. Groupthink will be discussed in Chapter 11.

Take a Closer Look

Group Cohesion

Thinking about one of the groups you listed at the beginning of this chapter, reflect on the following:

- On a scale from 1 to 10, how cohesive was the group? (10 = most cohesive)
- Why did you assign this score to the group?
- How was cohesion built in the group?
- What opportunities were missed to build cohesion?
- If you could change one thing the group did, what would you change?

Companies are aware of the value of group cohesiveness and actively promote cohesion among their employees. Some companies send entire departments to volunteer together, not only to help the community, but also to give those employees an opportunity to bond. Other companies have been known to fund beach parties and picnics for their employees.

WHAT ARE THE DRAWBACKS OF GROUPS?

We have discussed the more positive properties of groups; however, groups also have some properties that present significant challenges to group success.

Time Consuming

Groups can be time consuming. There are many factors that cause groups to be more time consuming than individuals working alone. Groups begin with organizing schedules. We are all familiar with the scheduling nightmare of trying to get a group of people with varying work, volunteer, family, and school schedules to meet. Solving logistics problems with five or six people can be more difficult than completing the task itself. In a later chapter we will discuss ways we can preschedule meetings and use computer meeting space to help us with this challenge.

In general, while group decisions often take up more "person-hours," the overall time for a group decision is usually less than an individual working alone. For example, a five-member group might work on a problem for ten hours. If you do the math, you will see that the total time equals fifty hours. The same problem might take an individual thirty hours. If you are employer who has to pay all these people, you can quickly appreciate this difference! There are two important differences, however. One is that the group solved the problem more quickly in real time (i.e., 10 hours vs. 30 hours), but it cost more. The other difference is that the group is more likely to produce a higher-quality solution than the individual working alone. An employer (who needed this problem solved) will have to make a judgment as to whether the difference in solution quality is worth the difference in price.

Difficult Members

Difficult group members can also prove to be a time drain. They come in many forms and use a variety of strategies that cause the group to stall. Their behavior distracts the group from time spent on task. Cooperative group members may need to complete work not completed by a difficult group member, to mediate aggressive behavior, and to talk through unsupported objections. The group may find that the time required to finish the task is greatly extended. This will be explored in more depth in our discussion of conflict.

Require a Balance of Task and Social Dimensions

Difficult group members can diminish productive efforts.
© Jorge Pedro Barradas de Casai, 2008, Shutterstock.

Fostering the social dimensions in groups leads to cohesion and is good for a group as it works to accomplish its task, in moderation. Take, for example, the situation of Samantha, a straight-A student majoring in sociology. When Samantha attended the first meeting of her Sociology 101 group, she found herself incredibly frustrated. After a two-hour meeting, the group had only achieved one thing: deciding on a topic for the project. The meeting was held at a convenient location near the college. When she arrived, she found group members eating pizza, talking about instructors, and debating recent films they had seen. It was not until the last ten minutes of the meeting that the group decided to chat about the project. When they were finally engaged in meaningful discussion, some group members needed to leave, ending the discussion before it really started. Samantha, who had turned down an extra shift at work to attend the meeting, was more frustrated than ever. What happened here?

This example shows a group that is building cohesion without moderation. This group needs self-discipline or a leader who allows time for building cohesion but also keeps the members focused on the task at hand. A balance of both task and social dimensions is necessary. It is critical that we learn how to be tolerant of the social time groups need, yet still balance it with appropriate task time. In Samantha's case, the group was imbalanced and spent far too much time on the social dimension.

Samantha could have done one of two things to address the situation. First, as soon as she realized the group was taking too much time to socialize, she could have talked to the group leader to request the meeting get started. Second, if the group had no specific or appointed leader, Samantha could have taken control by asking the group members to focus on the task at hand with her for the next hour. She could have softened this request by reminding them that those who were able to stay longer could socialize a bit more after the meeting.

Groupthink

Mentioned earlier, the term *groupthink* refers to a phenomenon that very often results in a flawed decision made by groups whose cohesiveness becomes so strong they stop challenging each other's ideas. Political mistakes have been attributed to groupthink such as the Bay of Pigs invasion, the Watergate cover-up,[12] the space shuttle *Challenger* disaster, and the 2003 space shuttle *Columbia* disaster.[13] This disadvantage to groups will be discussed in more depth in Chapter 11.

GROUP DEVELOPMENT: HOW DO COLLECTIONS OF PEOPLE TURN INTO GROUPS?

Educational psychologist Bruce Tuckman studied group behavior in the 1960s and identified five stages that groups progress through before reaching a point of maximum productivity.[14] An understanding of these stages can help us better manage our own group experiences. Before reading through these stages, take a moment to reflect on the group you described in the beginning of this chapter. Use your memory of that group experience to see whether the group followed Tuckman's stages.

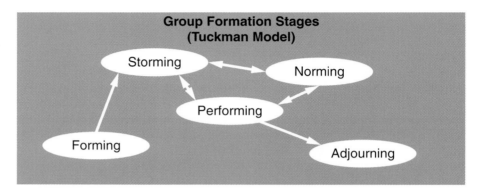

Forming (Orientation)

This initial stage of a group's experience is characterized by a high uncertainty level. Group members are typically quiet and uncomfortable as they attempt to understand the group's goals, member personalities, and overall dynamics. There is an absence of norms of behavior and an absence of clearly defined roles, so there is a lot of uncertainty about how to behave and what to say. The **forming stage** is characterized by group members: (1) attempting to orient themselves, (2) testing each other and the group boundaries, and (3) creating dependence on the group leader or other group members for support during this uncomfortable time. The most important job for the group in this stage is to orient itself to itself.[15] The tension is reduced as members get to know each other better and roles begin to be defined.

What happens during the storming stage?
© 2008, JupiterImages Corporation.

Storming (Conflict)

The **storming stage** occurs as a result of interpersonal struggles and polarization inherent in responding to the task at hand. This is where different ideas often compete for consideration, and group members share and challenge each other's ideas. This tension is also a response to struggles for authority and the direction taken by the group that occurs between leaders and the rest of the group. This stage requires active leadership while the group works out its most important dimensions: goals, roles, relationships, likely barriers, and support mechanisms. But as soon as patterns of authority and communication become fairly stable, the conflict is reduced. Until this time, however, the group can be a very active and stormy place! As you might guess, forming and storming are very time consuming, making up about three-fourths the length of Tuckman's five-step process.[16]

Norming (Structure)

The **norming stage** happens when group cohesion develops, new standards evolve, and new roles are adopted. The group members have become more unified and more organized. A structure is put into place that enables the group to complete the task at hand.[17] The end results of this stage are that roles are clarified and accepted, a team feeling develops, and information is freely shared among group members.[18] At this stage, members try to make decisions by consensus. Hare says that this is when the group becomes cohesive.[19]

Performing (Work)

It is during the **performing stage** that most of the productive work is accomplished. Group roles become flexible and functional, and group energy is channeled into the task.[20] People are getting their jobs done properly, on time, and in coordinated sequence.[21] Research has demonstrated that this is the point of development, later in the group's life, at which most groups are most productive.[22]

Adjourning (Dissolution)

The **adjourning stage** was added by Tuckman, in collaboration with Mary Ann Jensen,[23] and takes us beyond the time that a group remains productive and functional. This phase involves group dissolution. The group has achieved its goals, solved the problem, or is no longer needed. Roles are abandoned, and participants often experience mourning feelings associated with the loss of a relationship.[24] Care should be taken at this stage because several members of this group could very well become members of another group. Failure to properly handle this stage could jeopardize the success of future groups.

GROUP CULTURE: WHY ARE ALL GROUPS DIFFERENT?

Robert Bales found that members of groups cooperate not only to accomplish some task, but also to create a group culture.[25] Through communication with each other over time, a collective personality and a unique group point of view emerge from the interaction.[26] The emerging culture is based on the values and experiences of all the group members, and it expresses a set of values, behavioral standards, and an identity that influence the way the group members make decisions, respond to each other, and interpret information.

For example, a local water utility was receiving comments about a small group of maintenance technicians who installed and repaired fire hydrants in the city. The comments were all very positive and they came from citizens, the fire department, and from supervisors in other city departments. The members of this group made it their goal to make each repair quickly, neatly, and with a high standard of quality. This kind of group culture was not typical of other work groups in the city. The other groups did generally good work, but the standards of this group were much higher than the norm.

How did this happen? All the members of the group were formerly members of other city work groups and shared general the culture of the city utility.

This group found that it actually took less time, but only a little more effort and focus, to do a high-quality job. In addition, the members of the group found that they were getting satisfaction from doing good work! So, in addition to getting a paycheck, they felt good about what they did and they were motivated to come to work and spend the day with the group.

This culture began to develop one day when the group installed a fire hydrant. In addition to the ubiquitous yellow fire plug that we see next to the street, there is always a four- or five-foot pipe reaching below to the main water line. Replacing a hydrant means digging a hole down to the water line, disconnecting the hydrant, and then connecting a new hydrant to the line. When they first started working together, whenever they discovered a hydrant that needed to be replaced, they would call the city office and ask for heavy equipment to be dispatched to dig the hole. The usually had to wait up to two hours for the equipment to arrive and then wait for the hole to be dug. In addition, the use of the equipment made quite a mess in people's yards that was difficult to repair.

One day the crew found a hydrant that required replacement, so they called the city and they were told all the equipment was busy and could not be dispatched. So the crew got out their shovels and began to dig. They were surprised to learn that it took the four of them very little time to dig the hole, and they also discovered that they could do it more neatly than when the heavy equipment was used. They did such a great job that day that the lady whose yard they were digging in brought them cookies and then called the city supervisor to report how happy she was with the quality of the work and the care that was taken by the crew. This experience was only the beginning for this group, who found other high-quality ways to approach their jobs and gained a great deal of satisfaction from working together.

You might think this is a silly example, but the fire departments that depended on the hydrants to work properly when needed and the citizens who retained neat lawns would disagree with you. The city also found that this group made their repairs at lower cost than all the other maintenance crews. They didn't do anything to change the world, but because a culture of quality work evolved in this group, it turned into a true high-performance team.[27]

All groups develop their own unique cultures. Fraternities and sororities, clubs, social groups, and work groups each negotiate their own unique view of reality. The rules that govern your interaction with other group members, your interpretation of events, and the meaning you give to messages and behaviors differ from group to group. The culture of the group provides the frame of reference that tells members how to behave and how to interpret others' behavior.

WHAT SHOULD *MY* ROLE BE IN SMALL GROUPS?

Your specific roles in small groups will very likely be different as you become a member of different groups and as those groups attempt to accomplish different tasks. You and other members in your groups will adapt your behaviors and problems-solving strategies to these different situations. Considerable research has identified typical roles that appear in most groups, and they have been categorized as **task roles, group maintenance roles,** and **individual-centered** (also referred to as disruptive or egocentric) **roles.**

Take a Closer Look

What Kind of Group Member Are You?

One of the critical factors determining your success as a communicator is the ability to monitor and reflect on your own behavior. It is through this process that you can discover communication behaviors and skills that can be improved.

To help you do this, think of the last group you worked in and consider the following:

- What do you believe to be your greatest strength as a group member?
- What was your most significant contribution to the group's goal?
- What do you believe to be your greatest weakness as a group member?
- What two aspects of your participation in groups would you like to improve?

Keep in mind that you can often fulfill more than one role when working in groups, and that the roles you play may change, depending on the group and the group task.

Functional Roles in Small Groups

Earlier we discussed the fact that there are both task and social dimensions to groups. Similarly, the informal roles we play work to fulfill the tasks or the maintenance of our groups. Informal roles differ from formal roles like chairperson, secretary, or sergeant-at-arms because they are not appointed or elected. Informal roles often result from an individual member's personality, knowledge, or talents, or they arise from the problem-solving context itself. Task roles contribute to the group's productivity and are concerned with moving the group toward achieving its goals. Maintenance roles strengthen the group's social and emotional structure and contribute to the group's cohesion. They have a more indirect impact on group productivity than task roles, but are still necessary for group success at making high-quality decisions. Benne & Sheats concluded that for a group to survive and for it to make quality decisions, it must focus on accomplishing its task and it must maintain relationships among the group members.[28] Table 9.1 illustrates a selection of the task and maintenance roles.

Not all group roles contribute to building cohesiveness and solving problems. There are individuals who fulfill *individual-centered*[29] or *disruptive* group roles.[30] This type of role distracts the group or blocks the group from moving forward toward goal or task completion. Individuals exhibiting these roles harm the group's productivity, cohesiveness, and harmony.

Group members who play individual-centered roles might be doing so consciously or unconsciously. Although it is possible that they are trying to prevent the group from accomplishing its goals, it is likely that they just have some strong personal needs to be fulfilled and they use the group to get attention, recognition, or help with their problems. Whatever the cause, the effect is interference with group problem solving. Table 9.2 identifies some specific individual-centered roles.[31]

What role does the man at the end of the table play?
© 2008, JupiterImages Corporation.

TABLE 9.1	Selected Group Task and Maintenance Roles
Task Roles	**Maintenance Roles**
Initiator-contributor: Makes suggestions, considers new ways to look at group problem.	*Compromiser:* Tries to find agreements among conflicting points of view. Could change own position to help mediate conflict.
Information seeker: Focused on finding the facts; asks questions.	*Follower:* Serves as audience for the group; goes along with the other members.
Opinion seeker: Looks for expressions of attitudes and opinions of group members.	*Gatekeeper/expediter:* Tries to encourage participation from all group members.
Information giver: The expert of the group. Provides information based on experience.	*Encourager:* Gives positive feedback to others. The encouragement results in an increase in group members' self-esteem, excitement to complete the task at hand, and confidence.
Coordinator: Finds connections in suggestions and possible solutions; pulls information together into a coherent whole.	*Standard setter:* Expresses or begins discussion of standards for evaluating the group process or decisions.
Procedural technician: This person volunteers to complete tasks, help others, takes notes, distributes information, and takes on additional work.	*Harmonizer:* Always willing to listen. Group members often seek this person out to help soothe nerves, mediate interpersonal conflicts, or solve problems not group-related.
The organizer: This person helps to keep the group organized via scheduling, mapping out courses of action, coordinating efforts, etc.	*Observer/commentator:* Calls attention to the group's positive and negative characteristics and advocates change when necessary.

Source: Benne and Sheats, 1948.

How is this man's role disruptive to the group?
© 2008, JupiterImages Corporation.

Disruptive Roles in Small Groups

Mudrack and Farrell identified **disruptive group roles** that are similar in type and function to the individual-centered roles mentioned above.[32] The following roles fit the disruptive definition, and we suggest some communication strategies to help counteract them.

The Nonparticipant. This is a passive group member characterized by not participating in group activities, consistently missing group meetings, and not completing individual group work. When he does attend a group meeting, he either arrives late or leaves early. There could be many reasons why an individual may be a nonparticipant. Some people are very shy. Their intent may be to be an active group member, only they simply cannot overcome their communication apprehension to the point where they speak up. Others just might not care, do not feel connected to the group, or are bitter toward the group for some reason.

TABLE 9.2	Individual-Centered Roles
Aggressor: Communicates disapproval of ideas, attitudes, and opinions of other group members. Attacks the group and other members.	
Blocker: Takes advantage of opportunities to oppose group plans or procedures. Says he or she wants no part of the group. Expresses negativity.	
Dominator: Manipulates group members and situations; Creates defensiveness with certainty and superiority.	
Self-confessor: Wants to talk about his or her own feelings that are unrelated to the group goal.	
Help seeker: Seems insecure and confused; asks for personal advice.	
Recognition Seeker: Self promoter; wants attention or praise for himself or herself.	
Playboy/girl: No interest in being involved in the group; detached; interested in having a good time.	
Special interest pleader: Separates self from the group; identifies strongly with another group or interest.	

Source: Benne and Sheats, 1948.

Strategy. Regardless of the cause, a constructive way to approach nonparticipants is with encouragement.

- Gently invite them to participate.
- Ask for their opinions, ideas, and help.
- Notice when they do not attend meetings.
- Try to avoid assuming that their behavior is intentional. Rather, give them the benefit of the doubt and make a strong effort to include them.

The Bulldozer. This person takes control of the group without paying much attention to the desires, opinions, or ideas of others. A bulldozer monopolizes conversations, imposes courses of action, and discourages the participation of others. Individuals might bulldoze as a result of (1) a past experience in which they were not listened to or heard, (2) a lack of awareness of *bulldozing*, or (3) a desire to be the group's leader, but without the knowledge of how to approach the role constructively.

Strategy. One way to respond to bulldozers is with an intentional description of group norms. To prevent them from monopolizing the group, set up expectations for balanced participation, such as asking every group member to contribute at least one idea at each group meeting or by using an agenda to impose time limits on any one individual's *floor time*.

The Controller. This group member wants to make all of the decisions for the group. He or she appears to have a self-perception of superiority above the other group members and a belief that his or her ideas and plans are the best. An individual may feel a need to control the group due to insecurity, fear, or hunger for power. Whatever the reason, it is important to avoid making assumptions and to approach this behavior positively.

You can use communication strategies to balance the power in the group. This may be achieved in a variety of ways: by rotating group roles, by assigning tasks by pulling names from a hat, or by creating a meeting agenda. Whichever approach is used, first try to understand the reason for the disruptive communication choices and then do your best to respond in a way that helps the group to continue moving toward its goal.

Some gossip is inevitable in a group, but it can become a problem.
© 2008, JupiterImages Corporation.

The Gossiper. Although some gossip is inevitable in all groups, it becomes a problem when it hurts the feelings of others or undermines the group's goal achievement. An individual may do this to get back at a group member in retaliation, to be popular, to control the group, or to intentionally sabotage the group.

Strategy. Group members should work to create a climate of trust and mutual support when the group is in the early stages of formation. This can be done through increased social time (hosting a barbeque at one of the group member's houses, for example) or by utilizing team-building activities such as paper airplane contests, working through puzzles together, or volunteering to help with a campus club drive.

To respond to the gossiper, constructively confront the person. Discuss not necessarily the content of the gossip, but more importantly, the reason for it. Many times dissatisfaction is expressed in a passive-aggressive fashion. After confronting the group member, use the collaborating conflict management style (see the Interpersonal Communication chapter for additional information about conflict management styles) to unearth the real problem and work toward finding a mutually satisfactory solution.

The Social Loafer. This is one of the most troublesome of group members. The social loafer is an individual who loves working in groups because it means a *free ride* for the project's duration. The loafer does not complete assignments, is generally unreliable, and often submits inferior work. A loafer is often perceived to be someone who simply does not care, is not skilled, is lazy, or is a low achiever. However, some loafers are not lazy at all; rather, they loaf because they can. Other group members allow them to loaf by completing work for them that they do not finish.[33]

Strategy. This is a good time to practice your leadership skills. Most individuals will work when there is motivation to do so. It is important that the loafer feel valued and that his or her contributions are needed and are important. It is critical that other group members *do not* complete the work for them, as this only allows loafers to continue in that role. Instead, loafers can be mentored by being paired with another group member who is willing to mentor. In extreme cases, you can resort to the **group contract** (explained later in this chapter).

What Would You Do in These Situations?

It is the beginning of the semester; you are ready and eager to dive into school, work on projects, expand your mind, and successfully complete another semester, getting closer to achieving your goal of becoming a teacher. You attend your history class and learn that you will soon be placed in groups with four other classmates to complete a semester-long project.

At the next class meeting, you learn who your group mates will be:

- **Candy:** A twenty-two-year-old single mother of two. Candy works part-time, is enrolled in twelve units, and is maintaining a 3.9 G.P.A.
- **Dawn:** An eighteen-year-old freshman. Dawn is not quite used to the college environment and feels a bit lost on campus, in this class, and in the group.
- **Mike:** A twenty-one-year-old water polo player. He is a C student with a very active social life.
- **Kevin:** A thirty-year-old student who is back in school to change careers. He works full-time, is married, and has two children.

The group selects you as the leader. Thus, the onus is on you to organize meetings, motivate individuals, and monitor the group process. You do not mind the role until you run into some difficult situations.

Situation one: Dawn cannot seem to make it to group meetings on time. Your last meeting was across the street from campus at Starbucks and she was responsible for bringing a laptop for the group to begin typing out the assignment. She arrived thirty minutes late without the laptop. The group's frustration is growing and they look to you to solve the problem.

Situation two: Kevin not only completes all of his group work, but does so with perfection. He approaches schoolwork with the utmost professionalism. With this professionalism comes a low tolerance for those who do not approach their schoolwork with the same zeal. Subsequently, Kevin often becomes annoyed and even verbally aggressive with members who do not "pull their weight." He seems to feel the need to control as much of the group work and process as possible so as to ensure a good grade.

Situation three: Mike is the socialite of the group. Everyone loves his personality but loathes his approach to group work. He does not meet deadlines and turns in little to no work. The group members are beginning to feel taken advantage of. When he does arrive to a group meeting, he only wants to talk and socialize, not to work. Kevin views him as setting out to sabotage the group's performance.

Situation four: Candy is a hardworking group member, but simply does not have much time to devote to the group meetings and work. Subsequently, she has very little tolerance for those who arrive to group meetings late, do not spend time on task, or waste the group's time in any way. She is becoming especially intolerant of Mike and Dawn and frequently discusses her dissatisfaction without talking directly to Mike or Dawn.

- How would you characterize the roles these group members play?
- How would you address each of these situations so as to achieve the group's goals while still maintaining cohesion?

(After answering these questions, compare your answers with the discussion later in this chapter about the communication strategies to use with disruptive members.)

How could he convey his disappointment constructively? © 2008, JupiterImages Corporation.

Coping with Disruptive Members

There are a number of strategies we may use to respond to disruptive or egocentric members. In addition to those already mentioned, we have included some strategies for coping with more generalized types of egocentric and disruptive behaviors.

Feedback Sessions.

A **feedback** session is the act of communicating to the disruptive group member how his behavior is affecting the group. Many students who have experienced trouble working in their groups go to their instructor for help. When asked if they have discussed the issue with the troublesome group member, the usual answer is that they have not. Before approaching a supervisor, manager, or teacher, group members should first try to solve the situation using *feedback*.

Negative or corrective feedback is not always easy to give to others. If you are not careful about the manner in which the feedback is given, then relationships could be damaged. However, when used effectively, it is one of the most powerful communication tools available. The feedback process involves the following:

1. *Describe the problem as clearly, neutrally, and specifically as possible.* (See discussion on group decision making for a discussion of description versus evaluation.) Point out the similar interests you have with the group member, such as earning a good grade on the assignment or the satisfaction of a job well-done.
2. *Resist the temptation to place blame.* Instead try to take a *mutual problem approach* in which you use language such as, "How can *we* work to remedy this situation?" The use of *we* shows a sense of mutual responsibility and commitment to solving the problem as a team.
3. *Take ownership of your feelings and avoid blaming or attacking the disruptive member.* This can be achieved by using "I" messages instead of "you" messages.
4. *Stick to one issue at a time.* Bringing up more than one concern complicates the discussion and makes resolution more difficult.
5. *Do not gang up on the disruptive person with the other group members.* Those receiving the feedback need to be sent the message that it is fair, unbiased, and that your goal is *not to criticize*, but to work together to solve the problem.

Perception Checking.

Imagine the following situation:

You are in Athens, Greece, on vacation and decide to go to the flea market, the *plaka*, to buy some souvenirs. You find yourself in a negotiation with a merchant for an item. As you keep insisting on a price, the merchant nods his head from left to right and says "ne." You interpret this as a rejection, are disappointed, and are ready to leave when he interjects and keeps repeating the same phrase "ne, ne." You perceive his behavior to mean "no."

Before leaving the market and missing out on an opportunity to buy a great souvenir, it would be a good time to use some perception checking. You find a translator and go through the perception checking process as follows:

1. *Describe* the behavior: "I am trying to buy this item from the merchant over there. When I offered him a price, he nodded his head from left to right and said 'ne.'"
2. *Interpret* the behavior: "I thought he did not want to negotiate. However, he kept at me. I am not sure whether I have misunderstood his rejection or if I have offended him in some way."
3. *Ask:* "Can you tell me what is going on?"

Through this perception checking and with the translator's help, you find that "ne" means "yes" and his headshaking is, in fact, a sign of confirmation.

You do not need to be in a foreign country to experience misunderstandings like this. When group members communicate with each other, differences in perception occur often. Try using the three-step perception-checking process when you suspect that your perception may be inaccurate.

Utilize a Group Contract. Since we often do not know if we are going to encounter disruptive group members until we are in the middle of a group task, it is wise to use some preemptive strategies to handle problems before they arise. This can be done by writing up a group agreement, or contract, that outlines group norms and consequences for breaking them. Although the contract is usually a preemptive tactic, group members will still misbehave and problems will still come up. So you could draw up a contract even when your group is fairly mature. The contract is something a group should resort to only when all communication attempts fail.

Group contracts should have these elements:

• All group members are involved in the writing of the contract.
• Responsibilities and behaviors expected of all members are clearly defined.
• Consequences for misbehavior behavior are clearly specified.
• All group members sign the contract and receive a copy.

CASE STUDY

What Would You Do?

You have been asked to help out in a freshman class at the local high school. You are responsible for organizing student work groups (teams), introducing the student's group assignment, and monitoring the students as they discuss their approach to the task. Most students in this class are hardworking, motivated, and ambitious. However, there are a few class members who are known to engage in loafing and troublemaking.

You consider your options:

1. Mixing them into the group with the students who are hardworking, knowing that those students will more than likely do the work for them.
2. Speaking with them ahead of time to ask them to be "good" to their group members.
3. Group all the loafers and troublemakers together to work as a team, taking the risk that they will either meet the challenge or fail miserably.

What would you do?

A teacher faced this very challenge while teaching high school. She did not want to burden the hardworking students with the loafers and troublemakers. She did not think it would be fair to the dedicated, hardworking students. This was especially true given the fact that these disruptive students had already been talked to about their behavior, only to have it continue. She opted for the third choice and put them in a group together.

Through this experience, she learned a great deal about these types of troublesome group members who knew they were loafers and troublemakers and responded to the teacher's decision with attitudes reflecting, "How can you put us all together? We will fail." Ironically, they did not fail. As a matter of fact, it was with this project that the teacher was able to get them to work the hardest. They rose to the occasion and completed the task; it met all the requirements, was submitted on time, and helped participants feel better about themselves and the class.

SUMMARY

Though many people remain resistant to working in groups, extensive experience and research show us, again and again, that the product of group collaboration is worth all the effort. Groups are messy, complex, and a constant challenge to control. But we tolerate these conditions because the quality and creativity of group solutions to difficult problems are nearly always superior to solutions produced by individuals working alone. The key to successful and productive small groups is managing the "messiness" and keeping the members motivated and focused on group goals.

The next chapter, "Leadership and Power," is designed to help you gain some insight into how you can influence and manage groups that you belong to. Following that chapter, we provide some specific decision-making steps you can follow to help your group make the best use of its time and produce high-quality decisions.

ENDNOTES

1. S. Sorensen, "Grouphate," paper presented at the International Communication Association, Minneapolis, Minnesota, 1981.

2. J. Keyton, *Communicating in Groups: Building Relationships for Group Effectiveness* (New York: Oxford University Press, 2006).

3. D. Forsyth, *Group Dynamics.* (Belmont, CA: Wadsworth, 1999).

4. S. Wallace, L. Yoder, L. Hungenberg and C. Horvath, *Creating Competent Communication: Small Groups* (Dubuque: Kendall/Hunt, 2006).

5. S. Beebe and J. Masterson, *Communicating in Small Groups: Principles and Practices.* 8th ed. (Boston: Allyn and Bacon, 2006), p. 4.

6. L. Rosencrance, "Meet Me in CYBERSPACE," *Computer World* 39 (8) (February 21, 2005): p. 23–24.

7. A. Cohen, "Virtual Sales Meetings: On the Rise," *Sales and Marketing Management* 155(8) August, 2003: 12.

8. B. J. Carducci and K. W. Klaphaak, "Shyness and Internet Usage," poster session presented at the annual meeting of the American Psychological Association, Boston, August 21, 1999.

9. M. Waldrop, *Complexity: The Emerging Science at the Edge of Order and Chaos* (New York: Simon & Schuster, 1992).

10. Ibid.

11. S. Kiesler, *Interpersonal Processes in Groups and Organizations* (Arlington Heights, IL: Harlan-Davidson, 1978).

12. R. Cline, "Small Group Dynamics and the Watergate Coverup: A Case Study in Groupthink," paper presented at the annual meeting of the Eastern Communication Association, Ocean City, MD, April 27–30, 1983.

13. J. Schwartz and M. L. Wald, " 'Groupthink' Is 30 Years Old, and Still Going Strong," *New York Times*, March 9, 2003, p. 5.

14. B. W. Tuckman, "Developmental Sequence in Small Groups," *Psychological Bulletin* 63 (1965): 384–399. Also B. W. Tuckman and M. A. Jensen, "Stages of Small Group Development Revisited," *Group and Organizational Studies* 2 (1977): 419–427.

15. H. Robbins and M. Finley, *The New Why Teams Work: What Goes Wrong and How to Make It Right* (California: Berrett-Koehler Publishers, 2000).

16. Ibid.

17. B. W. Tuckman (1965).

18. Robbins and Finley.

19. A. P. Hare, *Handbook of Small Group Research* (New York: The Free Press, 1976).

20. B. W. Tuckman (1965).

21. Robbins and Finley.

22. R. F. Bales and F. Strodtbeck, "Phases in Group Problem Solving," *Journal of Abnormal and Social Psychology* 46 (1951): 485–495. Also, A. P. Hare and D. Nevah, "Conformity and Creativity: Camp David, 1978." *Small Group Behavior* 17 (1986): 243–268.

23. Tuckman and Jensen.

24. Ibid.

25. R. Bales. *Personality and Interpersonal Behavior.* (New York: Holt, Rinehart, and Winston, 1970).

26. E. Bormann, Fantasy and Rhetorical Vision: The Rhetorical Criticism of Social Reality. *Quarterly Journal of Speech,* 58 (1970): 306–407.

27. J. R. Katzenback and D. Smith, *The Wisdom of Teams: Creating the High Performance Organization* (New York: Harper Business, 1993).

28. K. Benne and P. Sheats, "Functional Roles of Group Members," *Journal of Social Issues,* 4 (1948): 41–49.

29. Ibid.

30. P. E. Mudrack and G. M. Farrell, "An Examination of Functional Role Behavior and Its Consequences for Individuals in Group Settings," *Small Group Behavior,* 26 (1995): 542–571.

31. Benne and Sheats.

32. Mudrack and Farrell.

33. D. R. Comer, "A Model of Social Loafing in Real Work Groups," *Human Relations* 48 (1995): 647–667. K. Williams, S. Harkins and B. Latane, "Identifiability as a Deterrent of Social Loafing: Two Cheering Experiments," *Journal of Personality and Social Psychology,* 40 (1981): 303–311.

WHAT ARE THE ROLES OF LEADERSHIP AND POWER IN GROUP DYNAMICS?

LEARNING OBJECTIVES

After reading this chapter, you should understand the following concepts:

- Leadership is the ability to influence people; power is the ability to control them.
- Leadership is a cooperative process; task leaders help the group advance toward decisions that will complete the job, while maintenance leaders develop a positive climate and manage conflict.
- Leadership effectiveness depends in part on the style of leadership and how well that style fits in the context of the situation.
- Transformational leaders possess the charisma necessary to motivate followers and evoke change.
- Six bases of power are typical in a small group: legitimate, coercive, reward, expert, referent, and interpersonal linkages.
- Conflict is inevitable in small groups, but it can be useful for helping groups try to solve complex problems. Intrinsic conflict relates to the task facing the group; extrinsic conflict relates to the personal interactions between members.
- Cultural differences can lead to extrinsic conflict, but conflict management strategies can help mitigate conflicts, regardless of cultural differences.
- The way people communicate can create as many conflicts as the ideas they use to communicate, so you should be careful with the words and tone used to express those ideas.

INTRODUCTION

How can my group manage itself to be productive and make quality decisions? That's a very hard question! One way to get some insight is to learn the chapter objectives. Even if you have the best group staffed with very bright and highly motivated members, most groups still need some help. You will have to find ways to help the group coordinate all its efforts, as well as help the members remain civil with each other. After all, the groups we are talking about are challenged with complex problems requiring information gathering,

Groups are challenged with complex problems requiring a coordinated work approach.
© Zsolt Nyulaszi, 2008, Shutterstock.

How does a leader motivate others in the group?
© 2008, JupiterImages Corporation.

analysis, debate, and commitment. All that activity needs to be coordinated to keep the group on track. The members will require occasional motivation and, perhaps, even some discipline. In addition, because this process is rarely completed overnight, the potential for conflict is very high. It's natural for people to become irritated with each other and argue, especially when they spend a lot of time together. We're people; it's what we do! We have to find ways to keep that conflict under control and to use it to help our groups make the best decisions.

To help answer all these questions, this chapter addresses three separate but related topics: leadership, power, and conflict.

ARE POWER AND LEADERSHIP THE SAME THING?

Leadership is the ability to influence the behavior of others. A leader is someone who can use interpersonal *influence* to move people to action. A person exercising leadership uses persuasion to motivate people to action. **Power,** by contrast, is the ability to *control* the behavior of others.[1] Power can be based on legitimate authority or position, access to information, or access and control of desired resources.

The use of power and the use of influence are not the same thing. It is possible to use one without using the other. For example, a group member in a leadership role could be very successful at motivating other members to complete tasks in the effort to accomplish the group goal, but that leader could have no source of power. Conversely, a group member with some form of power (control over desired resources, for example), might be able to control the behavior of other group members, but he or she might not be personally persuasive or motivating.[2]

In reality, many leaders likely use a combination of influence and power to accomplish tasks with groups of people. Good leaders try not to rely on power to motivate people, because a reliance on power damages the motivation and creativity of group members, and it results in flawed decisions and inferior products.

Leadership and power will be treated separately because they are different, but the discussion will emphasize the relationship between the two concepts.

WHAT IS THE ROLE OF LEADERSHIP?

Forsyth says that leadership is a specialized form of social interaction. It is a "reciprocal, transactional, and sometimes transformational process in which cooperative individuals are permitted to influence and motivate others to promote the attainment of group and individual goals."[3] Let's look at the parts.

Reciprocal suggests that leadership is an ongoing process and is defined by the leader, the group members, and the particular situation that the group happens to be experiencing. There is a give-and-take relationship between the leader and the members in which the followers allow themselves to be influenced by the leader. There is no leadership without followers.[4]

Leaders and group members work together in a *transactional* process "exchanging their time, energies, and skills to increase their joint rewards."[5] The leader specifies what follower behaviors are needed to solve the problem and how the group's or followers' needs would be satisfied as a result.[6]

Transformational means that leaders can communicate a group vision that members find appealing. This vision motivates and empowers followers to become leaders themselves and influence the outcomes of group tasks. The leader's task is to make the vision clear to the followers. It asks them to make the group goals perhaps more important than their own individual goals.

As we mentioned earlier, leadership is really a *cooperative* process that uses persuasion instead of power and control. Members with the most influence usually emerge as leaders over time, and they are followed by the other members of the group. Remember that we are talking about the member with the most influence, and not *necessarily* the person who was appointed or elected leader of the group. Finally, leadership should function to help the group to adapt to changing circumstances and remain focused on *accomplishing goals.* Leadership helps to provide the direction that moves the group toward its objectives.

In a give-and-take relationship, followers allow themselves to be influenced by the leader.
© Yuri Arcurs, 2008, Shutterstock.

Influence of a Leader

Leadership is not "built in" to particular people who possess certain personality characteristics. That is, people are not born or destined to be leaders or followers. Instead of leadership being determined by a set of personality traits, we suggest that it depends more on experience and skills that can be learned and developed. Leadership is given or attributed to a person by others in the group. Even though we have suggested that personality characteristics or traits do not determine who has the ability to lead others, personal qualities do seem to affect *perceptions* of leadership.[7]

If your group does have an appointed leader, it doesn't necessarily mean that he or she will be the most influential person in the group. Leadership is not the sole possession of *the* leader. Many members of the group could provide leadership in different areas or at different times as the group progresses through a task. For example, if your group is working on a project related to the responsible use of energy resources, and even though you might not be *the* leader, you could be influential in decision making because you know a lot about the issue, because you are interested in energy policies, or because you belong to an active energy conservation organization. Whenever you influence the course the group takes, or when you help move the group toward the accomplishment of its goals, you have provided *leadership*.

How can you emerge as a leader within your group?
© kristian sekulic, 2008, Shutterstock.

Take a Closer Look

A study by Geier reports that a process of elimination of contenders for leadership takes place in the initial meetings of any group. If you want to contribute to the goals of the group and become a leader, take these steps:[8]

1. *Be informed:* Being uninformed is seen as a negative characteristic that eliminates most contenders.
2. *Participate:* Groups typically judge quiet members as nonparticipative and unsuitable for leadership.
3. *Be flexible:* Try to remain open to new ideas or methods, especially when your ideas or methods are in conflict with group norms or goals, and be willing to compromise.
4. *Encourage:* Encourage other members to participate; don't try to make all the decisions yourself or dominate the discussion

---

What role does a task leader play in a group?
© Répási Lajos Attila, 2008, Shutterstock.

Task and Maintenance Leadership

We talked about task and maintenance roles of group members in Chapter 9. Task roles are oriented toward helping the group accomplish it's goals, while maintenance roles are focused on the social and relational issues that arise whenever people work together.

Consistent with this model, **task leaders** are those group members who help the group with organization and advancement toward making a decision of completing a job. They are sometimes perceived as the leader of the group, but they can also be group members who are influential in a particular situation. Task leaders often *emerge* from the interaction of the group over time, but they could also be appointed or elected by the members. The presence of effective task leadership results in the group spending more time on task and staying focused on specific topics. Groups with leaders have longer attention spans than groups without leaders.

Maintenance leaders focus on relational issues, the development of an open and supportive climate, motivation of members, and conflict management. This type of leader also emerges from the interaction of the group. This function is far more than a cruise director sort of position. Maintenance leaders are critical to quality decision making because they mediate differences of opinion and interpersonal conflicts, maintain a high set of standards for group behavior and contributions, and encourage the participation of all the group members.

Both task and maintenance functions are essential to groups interested in making important decisions or completing complex tasks. Keep in mind these important functions of leaders as you consider the three perspectives on leadership presented in the next section.

Leadership Styles

The **styles approach** to leadership is focused on the behaviors of the leader. McGregor tells us that the behavior of a leader is based on assumptions that he or she makes about the members of the group.[9] These assumptions are divided into two groups, Theory X and Theory Y, which were designed to show leaders two ends of a continuum of leadership possibilities.

Theory X Assumptions
- People don't like to work and require the control of a leader.
- People do not like responsibility and they will resist it.
- People are not creative problem solvers.
- People are motivated by lower level needs such as security, food, and money.

Theory Y Assumptions
- People like to work; it comes as naturally as play to them.
- People are capable of self-direction.
- People are attracted to self-control and responsibility.
- People are creative and imaginative in problem solving and like to make decisions.
- People are motivated by higher-level needs such as recognition and self-actualization.

Theory Y assumes that people are creative and imaginative in problem solving.
© Andresr, 2008, Shutterstock.

The practical application of these assumptions can be seen in the leadership styles: autocratic, laissez-faire, and democratic.[10] Autocratic and democratic leadership capture the ends of the continuum, and those will be the primary focus of our illustration.

The Autocratic Leader.

The **autocratic leader** follows the Theory X assumptions most closely and creates an authoritative atmosphere that is based on direction and control. This type of leader does not solicit follower feedback. Instead, he or she makes the decisions and supervises followers to make sure the task is being accomplished. Members do not communicate much with each other. Instead, they communicate mostly with the leader, and communication is mostly task-related questions. There is very little discussion. An example of autocratic leadership can often be found in military organizations and on the shop floor in factories geared for high-volume production.

The autocratic style normally results in high efficiency and a high quantity of work, but it is low on cohesiveness, creativity, and member satisfaction. Lewin found that groups with autocratic leaders had the highest incidents of aggressive activity and exhibited the most productivity, but only when closely supervised.[11] Additionally, employees who had low needs for independence and were authoritarian performed best under autocratic supervision.[12]

What does the autocratic style of leadership accomplish?
© Dmitriy Shironosov, 2008, Shutterstock.

The Laissez-Faire Leader.

The **laissez-faire leader** is one who takes a hands-off approach to leadership and provides very little direction to those being led. This leader seems to be a nonleader, because he or she does so little to guide the group. He or she abdicates responsibility, delays decisions, gives no feedback, and makes little effort to help followers satisfy their needs. There is no exchange with followers or any attempt to help them grow.[13] This is rarely an effective style.

Why are democratic conditions better when searching for a creative solution?
© Dmitriy Shironosov, 2008, Shutterstock.

The Democratic Leader. The **democratic leader** adopts the Theory Y assumptions and creates an atmosphere of member integration, self-control, and participatory decision making; the input of subordinates is encouraged and is used to make decisions. This type of leadership is most effective with groups who have some knowledge about how to complete the task at hand and are fairly motivated to do so. Followers tend to be motivated by higher-level needs such as self-esteem and job satisfaction. In this case, a leader who is too authoritative will only serve to inhibit the group's creative processes.

The democratic leader facilitates group discussion and participation in the decision-making process. In Lewin's study, groups with democratic leaders had the highest levels of individual satisfaction and functioned in the most positive and orderly fashion.[14] Likewise, employees with a high need for independence and who are not authoritarian performed best under a democratic supervisor.[15]

The strength of the styles approach is its focus on leader behaviors and assumptions made by leaders about followers. Some styles would only be effective in particular situations. For example, the autocratic style should be useful in a factory type setting where work is repetitive and high quantity is expected. By contrast, a group trying to find a creative solution to a complex problem would probably perform better in a democratic condition. The situation, the task, and the composition of the group members will determine what style will produce the best outcomes.

Situational Leadership

Situational leadership assumes that a leader's effectiveness is contingent, or dependent, upon how well the leader's style fits the context.[16] The situational leadership model by Hersey, Blanchard and Johnson argues that leadership effectiveness is built on a combination of task-based and relationship-based behaviors of the leader.[17] The composition of the group will determine what leadership approach will work best. People in leadership positions should first analyze the group, and then implement one of a variety of leadership styles designed to address the situation.

How does a leader effectively analyze the group?
© Tomasz Trojanowski, 2008, Shutterstock.

The primary factors that leaders look for are the ability of members to complete a particular task and their motivation to do so. As we discussed earlier, groups function on two levels: a task level (which is focused on goal achievement) and a relationship level (which is focused on maintaining the group as a unit and motivating members). As such, after situational leaders examine the abilities and motivation levels of followers, they must determine what combination of task and relationship leadership behaviors will work for the group in this situation. Hersey, Blanchard, and Johnson have outlined four leadership styles that consider these issues: telling, selling, participating, and delegating.[18]

1. *Telling.* A high-task and low-relationship approach is used when group members have low levels of ability and low motivation. Groups that are not motivated to perform a task need and expect the leader to be direct in telling them what they should do. Communication is one-way and the leader decides what should be done and how. This leader typically uses a clear, confident, and directive communication style.

2. *Selling.* A high-task and high-relationship approach is used when the members have low levels of ability but high motivation to complete the task. The leader is comparable to a salesperson and works to gain acceptance of a particular course of action by explaining why it is the right or best one to take. The communication used by this leader offers emotional support, and it is motivational, encouraging, and, at times, stern.

3. *Participating.* A low-task and high-relationship approach is used when the members have high levels of ability but low motivation to complete the task. The leader and the group work together to determine what should be done, how, and when. It is similar to the democratic style mentioned earlier. It requires the leader to be less directive, more supportive, and to include the members in decision making. The leader utilizes an open communication style conducive to facilitating discussion, sharing ideas, and encouraging input.

4. *Delegating.* A low-task and low-relationship approach is used when the members have high levels of ability, as well as high levels of motivation to complete the task. This group needs very little guidance or motivation. The leader outlines what needs to be accomplished and the group gets the job done its own way and at its own pace. This requires the leader to use feedback as well as clear communication that fosters a supportive climate, while still maintaining a sense of his or her role as a facilitator. The leader demonstrates confidence in the group by delegating more responsibilities.

The strength of the situational approach to leadership is its focus on member assessment and thinking through what and why a particular leadership approach should be used. For example, we may be more authoritative when a quick response is due and more facilitative when we are working with a mature group and have the time for facilitation. In addition, individuals from high context and collectivistic cultures may not ever use an authoritative (i.e., telling) style, as this approach would cause both leaders and followers to lose face. Please see the cultural discussion later in this chapter.

Transformational Leadership

A **transformational leader** is someone who possesses the charisma necessary to motivate followers and evoke change. Transformational leaders have charisma and vision, provide intellectual stimulation, and inspire their followers:

- They stimulate interest among colleagues and followers to view their work from new perspectives.
- They generate an awareness or a vision of the mission for the group.
- They develop colleagues and followers to higher levels of ability and potential.
- They motivate colleagues and followers to look beyond their own interests toward those that will benefit the group.[19]

Transformational leaders are visionary and inspire followers to achieve higher goals. Lee Iacocca, a transformational leader, joined the Chrysler Corporation in 1978 when the company was on the verge of bankruptcy. From 1979 to 1986, Iacocca was able to turn the company around and make it profitable. Stephen Sharf, who was the head of manufacturing for Chrysler when Lee Iacocca took over, attributed the Chrysler transformation to Iacocca's leadership style. Iacocca is described as someone who knew what he was doing, someone who was well liked, and a person who took charge. Sharf states: "His tremendous self-confidence radiated to whomever he talked to—workers, suppliers, banks, and the government. He was articulate and a motivator. There was no doubt in his mind that he could turn Chrysler around and people began to believe he really could."[20] Iacocca was a transformational leader and a visionary who was able to share that vision with others and transform Chrysler's way of doing business. Lee Iacocca is still regarded as a folk hero because of his leadership and achievements at Chrysler.[21]

Other examples of transformational leaders include John Kennedy, Sam Walton, Steve Jobs, Abraham Lincoln, and Franklin D. Roosevelt.

As with the other leadership approaches mentioned in this chapter, there are some weaknesses of transformational leadership. One is the possibility that passion and confidence may be mistaken for truth and reality. Additionally, the energy these leaders exert can become unrelenting and exhausting because the followers and leaders of this type tend to see the big picture at the expense of the details. However, this approach helps us to understand why some leaders are more successful than other leaders. They can empower individual members to perform beyond their own expectations. This kind of motivation can create strong group identity and often changes the culture of entire organizations.

How to Destroy a Group: Understanding What Not to Do

In order to improve our communication skills, understanding what *not to do* is important. Communication scholar D. M. Hall jokingly suggests eight ways in which a group member should not behave in groups:

1. Never prepare in advance; speak spontaneously. It keeps things on a superficial level.
2. Always take your responsibility lightly. This reduces your anxiety level and increases the frustration levels of others.
3. Never try to understand the group's purposes. This guarantees you'll accomplish nothing.
4. Always do the lion's share of the talking. None of the others have good ideas anyway.
5. Never give credit; hog it all for yourself. The rest love a braggart.
6. Always speak of your many years of experience. This compensates for your lack of ability.
7. Never tell anyone how to do it, else you may lose your prestige and position.
8. Always encourage the formation of cliques. The group can't last long when they begin to fight among themselves.

Have you engaged in any one of these communication behaviors?
If so, what can you do to avoid doing so in the future?

Source: Written by D. M. Hall, summarized by Murk (1994).

You don't need to be born with certain personality traits to be a good leader. You can rise to leadership if you take the time to develop the skills and gain experience. Hackman and Johnson tell us that skill development is a continuous, life-long process. The moment you think you have "arrived" as a leader, the progress stops.[22]

From the discussion of leadership styles and types in this chapter, you should learn that a single leadership type will not always be successful. There is no absolute or formula that will be perfect in every situation. To be a successful leader, you should be able to analyze the task, the context of the task, and the group of people who will be making the decision or working on the task. When you have completed that analysis, you should gain some insight into what kind of leadership approach will be most useful in that situation. However, you should not get comfortable! Groups mature, motivation levels change, and the nature of the task could vary as you move toward completion. You should always pay attention to these changes and be ready to adapt and to alter your leadership approach as needed to best achieve your group's goals.

Good leaders always adapt their approach as the group changes.
© Yuri Arcurs, 2008, Shutterstock.

WHAT IS THE ROLE OF POWER?

At the beginning of this chapter, we defined *power* as the ability to *control* the behavior of others.[23] As you read before, power can be based on legitimate authority or a person's position in an organization, access to information, and access to or control of desired resources. It is possible to use power without being influential (i.e., exhibiting leadership), and it is possible to be influential without using power. The best situation exists when leadership and power are combined: the influential leader who uses power at the appropriate times and in moderation can be very successful at helping groups accomplish goals.

French and Raven identified five foundations of power that are typically used in small groups:

1. Legitimate power
2. Coercive power
3. Reward power
4. Expert power
5. Referent power

This section looks more closely at these five power sources, plus one more—interpersonal linkage.

Legitimate Power

Legitimate power exists as a function of someone's position in an organization. Followers defer to the *authority* carried by the position regardless of who occupies the position. Respect for the individual in the position of legitimate power is not required for control. The higher the position in the organization, the more legitimate power a person typically has. An example of the amount of influence and psychological effects legitimate power can have over an individual can be found in the studies of Stanley Milgram.[24] This series of studies found that people would obey legitimate power even when it conflicted with what they believed to be the right thing to do. The best condition exists when the person holding the legitimate power in the

Is using coercive power an effective way to lead?
© Jaimie Duplass, 2008, Shutterstock.

organization is also respected by the subordinates. In this condition, the power can be used to direct activities rather than to control group members.

Coercive Power

Coercive power could also be called power to punish. Members follow leaders with coercive power because they want to avoid reprimand or punishment. Followers allow themselves to be controlled in order to avoid the punishments or sanction that could be associated with the failure to comply. Such punishments could include criticism, social ostracism, poor performance appraisals, reprimands, undesirable work assignments, or dismissal.

Coercive power ends when the power holder is no longer able to inflict punishment. Unless it is necessary, it is a good idea to avoid the use of this type of power because it is uncomfortable for most people and it can have a negative effect on the motivation and creativity of group members.

Reward Power

Reward power is just the opposite of coercive power. Where coercive power threatens to punish (or remove access to some desired resource) for noncompliance, reward power offers access to some desired resource as payment for compliance. The primary motivation of the follower is to comply with the leader to get the reward. Your teacher could reward you with bonus points for coming to class on a very cold day, or your boss could give you a bonus for completing a project on time or under the budget. Other rewards at your workplace could include pay increases, recognition, interesting job assignments, or promotions.

Like coercive power, this individual's power ends when he or she is no longer able to provide rewards. Individuals with only reward and not coercive power promise fewer rewards than someone who has both coercive and reward power. Likewise, those who possessed coercive power without reward power were more likely to invoke coercive power more frequently.

These first three power bases can be considered as what Porter and his colleagues termed *position power*, which includes power that is granted as a result of a person's position in an organization rather than by the unique characteristics of the individual.[25] Position-based power is an impersonal source of power. It is also granted to those who have supervisory positions.

The last two bases of power identified by French and Raven[26] and one identified by Hocker and Wilmot are forms of personal power.[27] Unlike position power, these are granted based on individual knowledge, skills, or personality. These power bases often transfer from role to role and are used by either supervisors or subordinates.[28]

Expert Power

A person with **expert power** is able to assist the group in reaching its goals because of his or her expertise on a given topic. Group members comply because they don't have the knowledge to complete the task without help.

Followers perceive that the expert has the knowledge to achieve the group's goals. This person can easily lose power if his or her knowledge base is needed for just one subject and if the knowledge is no longer needed or desired.

Referent Power

Referent power is based on the personal liking or respect that one person has for another. The person with referent power is influential because others respect or admire the way he or she does a job or if the power holder possesses personal qualities that others would like to emulate. When people admire you and want to be liked or admired by you, they are often willing to be influenced. You could say that people who have referent power have charisma. As long as followers feel connected with this leader, he or she will exert referent power. If, for some reason, followers' perceptions are altered, then this leader's power is diminished.[29]

A person with referent power is influential because others respect or admire the way he/she works.
© Yuri Arcurs, 2008, Shutterstock.

Interpersonal Linkages

In addition to the five bases of power identified by French and Raven,[30] Hocker and Wilmot identified a power base that comes from the power holder's access to people who control desired resources.[31] The **interpersonal linkage** is power based on who you know and what resources those people control. If your group needs information from a government agency, for example, and you happen to know somebody at that government agency who can get the information for you, then that can be a source of influence. You don't have access to the information, but you know somebody who does!

Power bases give us insight into the reasons that some leaders are effective. Power can be based on one's position in a company, as we see with legitimate, coercive, and reward power. Power such as expert, personal linkage, and referent can be based on one's individual qualities. Any group member can have this kind of power, and it is dependent on the context and task facing the group. When you possess this kind of power, it is essential that you are ethical with its use. You should be aware of the unethical use of power and question it when it comes in direct conflict with your moral and ethical standards.

DOES MY GROUP HAVE TO HAVE CONFLICT?

Just as you can count on the sun coming up in the morning, you can count on the presence of conflict in small groups. Whenever you get two or more people together who are trying to do something, there will be conflict! Even though many of us are quite similar, we still have individual differences that make us unique. We see the world around us in our own unique ways. When we come together as a small group, those individual differences are going to clash to create misunderstandings and disagreements. Conflict!

Conflict involves disagreement over task and procedural issues, over personality and affective issues, and over competitive tensions among group members. It can arise from differences of opinion, incompatible personalities, and even from geographical and cultural differences.

How is group conflict a *good* thing?
© Diana Lundin, 2008, Shutterstock.

Conflict is inevitable in small groups. It is not something that you can avoid. But don't walk away from this discussion with the idea that conflict is always a bad thing. Conflict is a central and essential element for groups trying to solve complex problems. As we mentioned in the previous chapter, one of the primary reasons that groups make better decisions than individuals working alone is the multiple perspectives that group members bring to the table. It is when these perspectives conflict that new ideas, points of view, and solutions are created. This is group synergy in action!

Conflict related to the problem challenging a small group is central to the group's success, but it has a darker side. Conflicts based on personality clashes or competitive group members can be a distraction to groups, prevent the group from thoroughly completing the decision-making plan (discussed in Chapter 11), and even threaten the existence of the group. However, personality-related conflicts can serve a maintenance function. Members of even friendly and cohesive groups get upset with each other now and then. Conflict provides those members with an outlet for hostile feelings, and it can facilitate a close examination of relationships. The bottom line is that if conflict is properly managed, it can be productive on both the task and relationship levels.

As you might have guessed by now, we will be discussing two kinds of conflict: conflict *intrinsic* to the task and conflict *extrinsic* to the task.

Intrinsic Conflict

Intrinsic conflict usually centers on disagreements related to the task facing the group. Intrinsic conflict can take two forms. It can be *substantive conflict*, which involves issues directly related to the content of the decision being made. It is unrelated to personal tensions that might exist between group members. Substantive conflict helps groups achieve their goals. Intrinsic conflict can also be *procedural*, which involves group policies and methods of solving problems. Members could disagree, for example, on what is the best way for reaching agreement.[32] Some members might favor voting, for example, while other members believe that all decisions made by the group should have the complete agreement of all members. To prevent procedural issues from taking too much time, some groups adopt explicit policies that specify member responsibilities and decision making processes.[33] Some groups even adopt standard policies such as *Robert's Rules of Order*.[34] You can see an application of *Robert's Rules of Order* in the section on "Running a Meeting" in the appendix of this textbook.

Young, et al. provide us with a comparison of three standard procedures for reaching decisions: voting, compromise, and consensus.[35] If your group gets stuck deciding how to decide, consider adopting of these procedures as your standard policy. Before you choose one, however, carefully look at the strengths and weaknesses of each procedure. We have ranked them good, better, and best, but all decision making experts might not agree with our assessment.

If your group gets stuck on substantive or procedural differences, then you should consider adopting a policy that will help you resolve or manage them. If intrinsic conflict is not managed well, it distracts from the group working on the task. In addition, it could get out of control and lead to

Standard Procedures for Reaching Decisions

- *Good: Voting.* Voting is quick and it solves the problem efficiently, but it creates a majority and a minority. The majority gets everything it wants, so its members are satisfied and committed to carrying out the decision. The minority gets nothing that it wants, so the commitment level of its members is often low, which results in a lack of motivation to follow through with implementation.
- *Better: Compromise.* In this situation, the members made trade-offs to make the decision. All of the members get some of what they want, and all of the members have to give up something to gain the agreement of the group. The resulting level of commitment is only moderate from all members, so follow through on decision implementation could be weakened. Compromise is not as quickly accomplished as voting.
- *Best: Consensus.* Consensus implies unanimous agreement of all members. Because all the members are satisfied and take ownership of the outcome, commitment to the decision is high and all are motivated to follow through on implementation. Consensus could take a very long time with complex issues. You should also beware that a consensus decision, because it has to please all the members to gain agreement, might not always be the most creative or best decision.

extrinsic conflict. The decision-making plan (DMP) described in Chapter 11 is a comprehensive procedure designed to help you understand and solve complex decisions. The three strategies just described will be very useful as your group navigates its way through the DMP procedure.

Extrinsic Conflict

When most people think of conflict, they are probably thinking of **extrinsic conflict.** This kind of conflict is related to the personalities and relationships between members. It can arise when you *just don't like* another group member, or when some basic incompatibility exists between members that cause tension.

There are multiple causes of extrinsic conflict:

- Recall that group communication implies interdependence among the people. When the communication becomes less interdependent and more competitive, the potential for conflict is high. Group members who are committed to the group's goals (creative solution to the problem facing the group) are at odds with members who are more committed to their own individual goals (promotion, money, job recognition).
- The use of power such as threats and punishments and the poor application of legitimate power by leaders or other members can lead to extrinsic conflict.
- Extrinsic conflict can arise when individuals do not understand the reasons for the behaviors of others. If the reasons are not understood, then the behaviors can easily be misinterpreted and lead to resentment. For example, geographic diversity and cultural differences are often a source of conflict.[36] These will be described in the next section.

- Extrinsic conflict often arises from the ways the members communicate with each other. Sometimes it is not *what* you say but *how* you say it that creates the problem. If communication makes another member defensive, then extrinsic conflict becomes more likely. The final section of this chapter looks at communication that can create defensive climates and strategies that can help you avoid conflict.

- Extrinsic conflict can arise because you just don't like another group member. Maybe he or she reminds you of the kid who broke your pencil in kindergarten or the bully who beat you up. If it's all inside your head, then here's some friendly advice: *It's time to be an adult and let go of it!* If, however, the other person feels the same way about you, you should handle the problem in private. If you and the other member can't resolve these differences, try to agree on a strategy for at least managing your relationship while you are working with the group. If you can both commit to the goals of the group, petty differences can be put aside and maybe you can share a friendly, professional relationship.

As stated before, extrinsic conflict can serve a useful maintenance function. However, unmanaged extrinsic conflict often causes harm to a group. If unmanaged, even minor extrinsic conflicts can turn into major problems. Conflicts that go unresolved or unmanaged generally do not go away. They can "explode," and the group cannot go about the business of making decisions because it is caught up in destructive conflict.

Whatever the kind of conflict that arises in your group, the key to making it work for you is **conflict management**. Some strategies you can use for managing extrinsic conflict include the following.

1. *Do everything you can to encourage cooperation among group members.* Look for opportunities to agree whenever possible. Small agreements can eventually lead to larger agreements and cooperation.

2. *Try to encourage participation of all members.* Approach reticent or shy members in a nonthreatening way and ask for their opinions. Listen to their answers. When they realize that other members listen to them, participation will increase.

Example: Countering Extrinsic Conflict

A group member complains, "Steve is always late for our meetings. He says we meet too far from his house. That really burns me up. Let's throw him out of the group!"

Problem: Extrinsic conflict leads to low member satisfaction, a lack of agreement, the loss of the cooperative climate, low productivity, and even the disintegration of the group. What do you do when you see escalating extrinsic conflict?

Strategy: Individual group members can successfully counteract extrinsic conflict by turning disruptive acts (that would normally escalate the conflict) into constructive contributions.[37] This helps defuse the situation and refocus the attention of each member to the task at hand. You could turn that expression of anger into a constructive suggestion by saying, "Let's meet at *Steve's* house. That way, he can't be late! Besides, we can watch the game on his HDTV and his refrigerator is always full of food!"

3. *Be honest about your intentions.* Don't play games or try to manipulate other members.
4. *Maintain a supportive climate.* Look at the final section of this chapter and be able to recognize the difference between defensive and supportive climates. If the climate in your groups becomes defensive, use some of the strategies suggested to move toward a more supportive, cooperative atmosphere.
5. *Keep the group goals as a priority.* They should take precedence over the individual goals of members.

HOW CAN CULTURAL DIFFERENCES LEAD TO EXTRINSIC CONFLICT?

How has the "digital age" changed the way we do business?
© Yuri Arcurs, 2008, Shutterstock.

Cultural influences have a profound effect on decision quality and the overall decision-making process. Chances are, you have already worked in a group made up of people from a variety of cultural and ethnic backgrounds. If not, get ready! The world is becoming increasingly *flat.* This means that collaboration and competition for jobs is open to people from all over the world, not just those who live near you or even in your country! Instantaneous communication technology in the "digital age" is shaping the way we manage our lives and do business, and that business is increasingly conducted with others around the globe.[38] Because diverse groups are more likely to experience extrinsic conflict than homogeneous groups, we will briefly examine some of the cultural dimensions that affect groups.[39]

If you are aware of the cultural influences on others, and if you are aware of your own cultural influences and biases, you will be better able to adapt to new situations when they present themselves. Instead of moving directly to an extrinsic conflict situation, you should be willing to understand (and possibly explain to others in the group) that the source of your differences is culture related and perhaps not a fundamental interpersonal disagreement.

Geert Hofstede used the term *cultural dimensions* to refer to the common elements or the key issues of a culture that can be studied and analyzed in meaningful ways.[40] Hofstede's value orientations are used to test and understand culture's influence in today's digital world. Some of these dimensions can be directly applied to the small-group context.[41]

Individualism/Collectivism

In **individualistic cultures,** people are taught personal autonomy, privacy, self-realization, individual initiative, independence, individual decision making, and an understanding of personal identity as the sum of an individual's personal and unique attributes.[42] People from individualistic cultures are taught that their needs and interests are just as important, if not more important, than the needs and interests of others. Some examples of individualistic societies are Australia, Great Britain, Canada, and the United States.[43]

Group members from individualistic cultures are most comfortable working on projects alone and have a tendency to do all the work or none at all. This is not because they are uncooperative or difficult. Rather, it is

Group members from individualistic cultures are most comfortable working on projects alone.
© 2008, JupiterImages Corporation.

because they are not socialized to collaborate like those from collectivistic cultures. For individualists, the group experience can be exceedingly frustrating. When an individualist approaches group projects and collaboration with a collectivistic mindset, he or she may find that to put group goals before personal goals is not necessarily a losing position.

Collectivism characterizes a culture in which people, from birth, are integrated into strong, cohesive in-groups.[44] Collectivistic cultures emphasize emotional dependence on groups and organizations, less personal privacy, and the belief that group decisions are superior to individual decisions.[45] They believe in interdependence, an understanding of personal identity as knowing one's place within the group, and concern about the needs and interests of others.

Collectivistic cultures include China, Hong Kong, India, Japan, Pakistan, and Taiwan.[46] Group members from collectivistic cultures experience less frustration when working with group members who also have collectivistic tendencies. This is largely due to the practice they have had collaborating with their own families, friends, and colleagues. Their frustration with groups is more likely experienced when they are collaborating with people who approach group work as individualists.

High Power Distance/Low Power Distance

Power distance is the extent to which the less powerful members of organizations and institutions accept and expect that power is distributed unequally.[47] Individuals from low power-distance cultures believe that inequality in society should be minimized, that all individuals should have equal rights, that power should be used legitimately, and that powerful people should try to look less powerful than they are. Individuals from high power-distance cultures stress coercive and referent power and believe that power holders are entitled to privileges, and that powerful people should try to look as powerful as possible.

Participating effectively in small groups may be more challenging for group members from high power-distance cultures. Likewise, decision-making processes and approaches to conflict resolution are likely to be influenced by the group's power distance level. For instance, conflict management in teams with a low power-distance factor is based on principles of negotiation and cooperation, while in high power-distance teams, conflict is resolved primarily by the power holder.[48] On the one hand, those who come from low power-distance cultures think that group decisions should be made by consensus, should have shared leadership, and that role responsibilities should be based on expertise. On the other hand, people from high power-distance cultures use voting, expect leaders to lead, and are uncomfortable in teams where they are asked to take on more autonomy and responsibility.[49]

Uncertainty Avoidance

Uncertainty avoidance refers to the extent to which risk and ambiguity are acceptable conditions. Hofstede suggests that it is the extent to which the members of a culture feel threatened by uncertain or unknown situations.[50] This is one of the cultural dimensions most problematic for groups.[51] Group members from high uncertainty avoidance cultures interact based on a need

for rules, suppression of deviant ideas and behavior, and resistance to innovation. They are motivated by security, esteem, and belongingness. Some
countries with high uncertainty-avoidance cultures are Greece, Portugal,
Guatemala, Uruguay, and Japan. Low uncertainty-avoidance cultures include
the United States, Sweden, Jamaica, Singapore, and Hong Kong.[52]

Group members from low uncertainty-avoidance cultures are more tolerant of different opinions, prefer as few rules as possible, are more calm and
contemplative, and they are not expected to express emotions. They are better
able to function within a group that is less structured. Such groups are characterized by loose deadlines, undefined roles, few rules, and a high tolerance
for innovation and "outside-of-the-box" thinking. Understanding the uncertainty avoidance tendencies of members can help groups structure a productive decision-making environment. Such an environment would provide a
balance of structure for those high in uncertainty avoidance. They would still
maintain a spirit of innovation and encourage unique approaches to decision
making for those who are low in uncertainty avoidance.

High Context/Low Context

Hall divided cultures into high and low context according to their ways of
communicating.[53] A **high-context culture** uses communication in which
most of the information is either in the physical context or internalized in the
person. To understand high-context communication, one should consider the
content of the messages and the context together. Context is the situation,
background, or environment connected to an event, a location, or an individual.[54] Very little is explicitly stated. High-context communication is typically
indirect, ambiguous, harmonious, reserved, and understated.[55] A **low-context
culture** is just the opposite. The majority of information is stated explicitly.
Low-context communication is direct, precise, dramatic, open, and based on
feelings or true intentions.

When interacting with people who are from a high-context culture, using
communication that is too direct can result in embarrassment or even anger.
Likewise, when interacting with someone from a low-context culture, using
communication that is indirect or implied can result in confusion and frustration because it is perceived that the communicator does not say what he or
she means. For instance, if a North American supervisor is unsatisfied with a
subordinate's sales proposal, the response will probably be explicit and
direct: "I can't accept this proposal as submitted, so come up with some better ideas." A Korean supervisor, in the same situation, might say, "While I
have the highest regard for your abilities, I regret to inform you that I am not
completely satisfied with this proposal. I must ask that you reflect further and
submit additional ideas on how to develop this sales program."[56] The message is essentially the same, but as you can see, the approach is different.

In addition to personal and ideational differences that normally exist
between people, multicultural groups have a high potential for intrinsic conflict based on their different points of view. The potential for extrinsic conflict
is even higher, considering the number of potential misunderstandings and
interpersonal transgressions resulting from the clash of cultural expectations.
An awareness of different cultural expectations will help keep nonproductive
conflict to a minimum and promote the level of communication, understanding, and cooperation necessary for making creative decisions.

High Context Cultures

Japan
Arab Countries
Greece
Spain
Italy
England
France
North America
Scandinavian Countries
German-speaking
  Countries

Low Context Cultures

Source: Hall & Hall (1990)
Understanding Cultural
Differences

Defensive versus Supportive Behaviors

Defensive and supportive climates can be created and maintained with communication behaviors

Defensive Behaviors
1. Control strategies
2. Superiority
3. Evaluation
4. Neutrality
5. Strategy
6. Certainty

Supportive Behaviors
1. Problem orientation
2. Equality
3. Description
4. Empathy
5. Spontaneity
6. Provisionalism

HOW IS COMMUNICATION A SOURCE OF EXTRINSIC CONFLICT?

A frequent source of extrinsic conflict is communication itself. Sometimes it's not what people say that creates the problem but the way they say it.

Control/Problem Orientation

Most of us need to feel we have some control over our lives. So we respond to control with *psychological reactance*.[57] In response to feeling controlled, we do the opposite of what we are told to do. Communication typical of **control strategies** includes statements such as, "You need to be more considerate," "You must stop procrastinating," and "You have to listen to me." Statements like these create psychological reactance and lead to defensiveness, which leads to extrinsic conflict. Gibb says that hidden in attempts to control is the assumption by the controlling person that the other is somehow inadequate.[58] Wouldn't that make *you* feel defensive?

Using a **problem orientation** allows others an equal contribution to the discussion and decision making. It sends the relational message that the other's position, opinions, and concerns are important. When you take a problem orientation approach to interacting with others, they are likely to be more committed to the resolution of the problem. Just as individuals may respond with psychological reactance when feeling controlled, individuals who feel they have a voice in decision making are more likely to commit to the decision's implementation. Statements that illustrate a problem orientation include, "We are in this together," "What can we do to solve this problem?" and "What do you think?"

Take a Closer Look

Sometimes when your group has a competitive environment or spirit, it means that there is a lack of compatibility between group goals and the goals of individual members. What should you do?

Try this: Create a cooperative climate!

Instead of allowing the competitive attitudes of group members to become more intense and inhibit cooperation in the group, try to find something on which all members can agree. Even if the members don't go along with you, discovering these opportunities to agree should push the group climate toward the more cooperative end of the continuum. Agreement tends to be reinforcing in that, before too long, others in the group will begin to "pay back" your agreement with their cooperation. Over time, the environment of your group should become more cooperative.[59]

Superiority/Equality

Communicating **superiority** creates defensiveness by demonstrating that we perceive ourselves to be better than others, and that quickly leads to extrinsic conflict. Superiority is characterized by comments such as, "You do not know what you are doing," and, "I have had more experience with this type of situation; I will handle it." This sends the relational message that the other's opinion is not worthy, his expertise is not valued, or that he is not important.

Equality, by contrast, involves treating others with respect and valuing their thoughts and opinions, regardless of their knowledge about the topic, their status, age, or position. People who *appear* to be of lower status or position are capable of having profound insights. Communication illustrating equality would be, "What do you think?" and, "I never thought of it that way; let's explore this idea together further."

Evaluation/Description

Communicating equality involves treating others with respect and valuing their opinions.
© Répási Lajos Attila, 2008, Shutterstock.

If a communicator appears to be evaluating you, either through tone of voice, expression, or message content, you will likely go into a protection mode. This kind of communication is often perceived as an attack on a person's self-esteem. The person feeling attacked then focuses energy on defense, which draws his or her focus from the problem to be solved. When communicating with others, you should first *describe* before forming evaluations. This is not to say that you cannot evaluate behavior, but before jumping to conclusions, you should demonstrate that you are attempting to understand. Through description, you may create a more supportive climate. To be descriptive is to be factual without offering an opinion.

If you look at the descriptions provided in the box, can you say with certainty that the behaviors indicate rudeness, pushiness, or unfairness? Based on the behaviors described, there *may* be other possible interpretations. Could Kate have not realized she bumped into someone? Or did she softly say she was sorry but was not heard? Could Tom have had an urgent message? Could Stacey have valid reasons for her decision that were, indeed, fair? The answers to these questions are, *maybe*. We cannot be entirely sure without more information. The point is we need to be descriptive if we want to avoid extrinsic conflict by creating a defensive climate.

Take a Closer Look

Kate is rude.	**Tom is pushy.**	**Stacey is unfair.**

Each of these statements is an evaluation. Now, if we were to take the time to describe the behavior that made us conclude that Kate is rude, Tom is pushy, and Stacey is unfair, we might come up with the following descriptive statements:

- Kate bumped into me without acknowledging it. She didn't say she was sorry or excuse herself.
- Tom kept phoning me after I told him I was too busy to talk.
- Stacey didn't give me the opportunity to work on the marketing project.

Neutrality/Empathy

One of the best ways to devalue someone is to respond in a way that communicates a lack of caring. **Neutrality** communicates that you simply do not care about the person or what he or she is saying. Using the supportive strategy of **empathy** means approaching a discussion with the intent to understand the other person's position from his or her point of view. This is not to be confused with sympathy, or responding with how we would feel in a particular situation. To be empathic is to express genuine interest in hearing what others have to say; it is one of the most confirming communication forms. Some examples of empathic responses are, "Kate, you must feel very upset by your layoff," and, "Stacey, I can only imagine how you must feel right now." To respond with neutrality, you might use responses like, "It doesn't matter to me," and, "Whatever you want."

If you want to create and maintain a supportive climate in your group, practice responding in ways that demonstrate that you care and understand.

Strategy versus Spontaneity

To use **strategy** is to communicate that you have a hidden agenda. There is something motivating your communication that is not initially revealed to others. You try to manipulate others in the effort to gain some advantage. Have you ever had someone ask you, "What are your plans Friday night?" And you respond with, "I am free. Do you want to do something?" only to hear, "Oh good, can you babysit?" Somehow, this approach asking us to babysit feels like a trick. Another stereotypical example is the feeling when you walk into a sales presentation. You suspect that everything from the first handshake to the free dinner is carefully scripted to get you to buy something. Your defenses are activated and you begin to interpret everything that is said to you as part of a sneaky plot to buy that time-share in an exotic resort area. Strategic communication is revealed when you feel that people are flattering you for their own personal gain, or using self-disclosure to get you to reciprocate.

Spontaneity is characterized by honesty, directness, and good faith. It is saying: "I really need a babysitter Friday night; if you are free I would greatly appreciate your help." In a spontaneity condition, you probably won't be as suspicious of others and you will take things they say at face value. If they attempt to shake your hand, you can be sure it's an invitation to friendship and nothing else. When you get into the defensive mode, it is easy to misinterpret and start looking for hidden meanings in things that people say.

Certainty versus Provisionalism

People who communicate **certainty** seem to know all the answers. There is nothing they don't know, and they are quite sure about it. We tend to see this dogmatic individual as needing to be right and "wanting to win an argument rather than solve a problem."[60] This behavior communicates to others a lack of interest in their position on an issue. The defensiveness that is created by certainty can be countered by provisionalism. **Provisionalism** means trying to explore issues, look for solutions, and consider the points of view of other group members.

Research tells us that supportive climates not only produce happier and more satisfied group members, but that groups with predominately supportive climates are more productive.[61] When the climate becomes defensive, group members become distracted by the suspicion that they are being manipulated or attacked, the potential for destructive extrinsic conflict is high, messages are consistently misinterpreted, and the group loses sight of the problem to be solved. All the assumptions that we make about groups making better decisions are based on the broad assumption that the members are fully engaged in the solution of the problem. When the attention of the group is distracted from that problem-solving goal, defective decisions will be the result.

SUMMARY

There was a lot of territory covered in this chapter, so we'll try to boil down the answer to the question, "What should I take from this chapter?" First, you should understand that every group member has the potential for leadership. You don't have to be *the* leader to exhibit leadership; you just have to use influence to help the group somehow mover closer to its goals. You should also understand that every group is unique, and that there is no single leadership style or approach that is going to be successful in every group. You will have to understand the functions of leadership, and then you will have to adapt what you know to each particular situation. There are many suggestions in this chapter to help you accomplish this. Look at the leadership styles approach, the situational leadership approach, and the information on transformational leadership to get some insight about how to adapt to your group.

You should also try to understand the bases of interpersonal power and how they can be used as a tool of leadership. Remember that those power bases can be easily abused, especially legitimate and coercive power, and that abuse can prevent your group from accomplishing its goals.

Finally, you should take with you an appreciation for conflict. If you are a member of a small decision making group, conflict can be your best friend and your worst enemy. Conflict related to the task, intrinsic conflict, unleashes the real power of small groups by allowing the clash of divergent points of view. This clash leads to a synthesis of ideas which the group members could not have created if they were working alone. This clash exploits the synergy of the group and makes the solution of complex problems possible.

However, conflict can also be your worst enemy. Extrinsic conflict, related to personalities, can distract your group from its task and even destroy the group itself. Although there are a lot of sources of extrinsic conflict, this chapter explored two common causes: differences in culture (very important in the age of the global economy), and the defensive climates that are created when interpersonal sensitivity is overlooked in conversations. Being aware of the roots of conflict and understanding management strategies can help your group stay together, make complex decisions, and provide all the members with a satisfying experience!

ENDNOTES

1. D. Ellis and B. A. Fisher, *Small Group Decision Making: Communication and the Group Process*, 4th ed. (New York: McGraw-Hill, 1994). Also J. French and B. Raven, "The Bases of Social Power," in Group Dynamics: Research and Theory, ed. D. Cartwright and A. Zander, (New York: Harper and Row, 1968).

2. E. P. Hollander, "Leadership and Power," in *The Handbook of Social Psychology*, 3rd ed., ed. G. Lindzey and E. Aronson (New York: Random House, 1985), 485–537.

3. D. Forsyth, *Group Dynamics*, 3rd ed. (Belmont, CA: Wadsworth, 1999): p. 343.

4. J. Barrow "The Variables of Leadership: A Review and Conceptual Framework," *Academy of Management Review* 2(1997): 231–251. Also E. P. Hollander, and L. R. Offermann, "Power and Leadership in Organizations: Relationships in Transition," *American Psychologist* 45 (1990): 179–189.

5. Forsyth, p. 364.

6. B. M. Bass, (1985). *Leadership and Performance beyond Expectations* (New York: Free Press, 1985).

7. M. Hackman and C. Johnson, *Leadership: A Communication Perspective* (Prospect Heights, IL: Waveland Press, 2000). Also D. Kenny and S. Zaccaro, "An Estimate of Variance Due to Traits in Leadership," *Journal of Applied Psychology* 48 (1983): 327–335; and R. Lord, C. De Vader, and G. Alliger, "A Meta-analysis of the Relation between Personality Traits and Leadership Perceptions: An Application of Validity Generalization Procedures," *Journal of Applied Psychology* 71 (1986): 402–410.

8. Geier (1967). "A Trait Approach to the Study of Leadership in Small Groups," *Journal of Communication* 17 (1967): 316–323.

9. D. McGregor, *The Human Side of Enterprise* (New York: McGraw-Hill, 1960).

10. K. Lewin, R. Lippit, and R. K. White, "Patterns of Aggressive Behavior in Experimentally Created Social Climates," *Journal of Social Psychology* 10 (1939): 271–301.

11. Ibid.

12. V. H. Vroom, *Some Personality Determinants of the Effects of Participation* (Englewood Cliffs, N.J.: Prentice Hall, 1960). Also W. W. Haythorn, A. Couch, D. Haefner, P. Langham, and L. Carter, "The Effects of Varying Combinations of Authoritarian and Equalitarian Leaders and Followers," *Journal of Abnormal and Social Psychology* 53 (1956): 210–219.

13. Peter G. Northouse, *Leadership Theory and Practice*, 2nd ed. (Thousand Oaks, CA: Sage, 2001).

14. Lewin, Lippit, and White.

15. Vroom; also Haythorn et al.

16. Northouse.

17. P. Hersey, K. Blanchard, and D. Johnson, *Management of Organizational Behavior: Leading Human Resources*, 8th ed. (Upper Saddle River, NJ: Prentice-Hall, 2000).

18. Ibid.

19. B. M. Bass and B. J. Avolio, *Through Transformational Leadership* (Thousand Oaks, CA: Sage, 1994).

20. S. Sharf, "Lee Iacocca as I Knew Him; He Was Certainly the Right Man at the Right Time," *Ward's Auto World* (May 1, 1996).

21. J. Smith, "Lutz for Chairman? His Leap from Ford Fuels Talk about Iacocca Succession," *Ward's Auto World* (July 1, 1986).

22. Hackman and Johnson, p. 358.

23. Ellis and Fisher; French and Raven.

24. S. Milgram, "Behavioral Study of Obedience," *Journal of Abnormal and Social Psychology* 67 (4) (1963): 471–478.

25. L. W. Porter, A. Harold, and R. Allen (eds). *Organizational Influence Processes* 2nd ed. (New York: M. E. Sharpe, 2003).

26. French and Raven.

27. Hocker, J., and Wilmot, W. *Interpersonal Conflict*, 3rd ed. (Dubuque: Brown, 1991).

28. Porter et al.

29. Ibid.

30. French and Raven.

31. Hocker and Wilmot.

32. Forsyth.

33. C. Houle, *Governing Boards: Their Nature and Nurture* (San Francisco: Josey-Bass, 1989).

34. H. M. Robert, *Robert's Rules of Order, Revised Edition* (New York: Morrow, 1971).

35. Young et al.

36. R. Moreland, J. Levine, and M. Wingert, "Creating the ideal work group: Composition effects at work," in *Understanding Group Behavior: Small Group Processes and Interpersonal Relations*, ed. J. Levine and M. Wingert (Mahwah, NJ: Erlbaum, 1996).

37. D. Gouran, Principles of counteractive influence in decision-making and problem-solving groups," in *Small Group Communication: A Reader*, ed. R. Cathcart and L. Samover (Dubuque: Brown, 1992), 221–235.

38. T. L. Friedman, *The World Is Flat* (New York: Farrar, Straus and Giroux, 2005).

39. Moreland et al.

40. G. Hofstede, *Cultures and Organizations: Software of the Mind* (London: McGraw-Hill, 1991).

41. E. Würtz, "A Cross-cultural Analysis of Websites from High-context Cultures and Low-context Cultures," *Journal of Computer-Mediated Communication* 11(1)(2005), http://jcmc.indiana.edu/vol11/issue1/wuertz.html (accessed May 28, 2007).

42. A. F. E. Darwish and G. L. Huber, "Individualism vs. Collectivism in Different Cultures: A Cross-cultural Study," *Intercultural Education* 14 (1) (2003): 47–57.

43. A. Baron and R. Byrne, *Social Psychology* (Boston: Allyn and Bacon, 1997).

44. G. Hofstede and H. M. Bond, "Hofstede's Culture Dimensions: An Independent Validation using Rokeach's Value Survey," *Journal of Cross-Cultural Psychology* 15 (4) (1984): 417–433.

45. Darwish and Huber, pp. 47–57.

46. Baron and Byrne.

47. G. Hofstede, *Culture's Consequences: Comparing Values, Behaviors, Institutions, and Organizations across Nations* (Thousand Oaks, CA: Sage Publications, 2001). Also M. Mulder, *The Daily Power Game* (Leiden, Netherlands: Martinus Nijhoff, 1977); and Hofstede.

48. M. Deutsch, *The Resolution of Conflict: Constructive and Destructive Processes* (New Haven, CT: Yale University Press, 1973).

49. T. M. Paulus, B. Bichelmeyer, L. Malopinsky, M. Pereira, and P. Rastogi, "Power Distance and Group Dynamics of an International Project Team: A Case Study," *Teaching in Higher Education* 10 (1) (2005): 1–14.

50. Hofstede.

51. S. Van Hook, "Cross-cultural Variances in Team Effectiveness: The Eastern European Experience," http://wwmr.us/teams.htm (accessed Febuary 4, 2007).

52. Hofstede.

53. E. T. Hall, *Beyond Culture* (New York: Anchor Press/Doubleday, 1976).

54. Würtz.

55. W. B. Gudykunst, Y. Matsumoto, S. Ting-Toomey, T. Nishida, K. Kim, and S. Heyman, "The Influence of Cultural Individualism-collectivism, Self-construals, and Individual Values on Communication Styles across Cultures," *Human Communication Research* 22 (4) (1996): 510–543.

56. Y. Choe, "Intercultural conflict patterns and intercultural training implications for Koreans," Paper presented at the 16th Biennial World Communication Association Conference, Cantabria, Spain, 2001.

57. S. S. Brehm and J. W. Brehm, *Psychological Reactance: A Theory of Freedom and Control* (New York: Academic Press, 1981).

58. J. Gibb, "Defensive Communication" *Journal of Communication* 11 (1961): 141–148.

59. Gouran.

60. Gibb, p. 79.

61. C. Tandy, "Assessing the Functions of Supportive Messages," *Communication Research* 19 (1992): 175–192.

REFERENCES

B. M. Bass and B. Avolio, *Through Transformational Leadership* (California: Sage, 1994).

B. M. Bass and Steidlmeier, "Ethics, Character, and Authentic Transformational Leadership," From the Center for Leadership Studies, School of Management. Binghamton University, Binghamton, New York, http://cls.binghamton.edu/BassSteid.html (accessed May 24, 2007).

J. A. Bonito and A. Hollingshead, "Participation in Small Groups," in *Communication Yearbook 20.* ed. B. Burleson (Thousand Oaks, CA: Sage, 1997).

F. Bowers, "Terrorists Spread Their Messages Online: A Growing Number of Al Qaeda Websites Offer Instructions for Kidnapping and Killing Victims," *Christian Science Monitor* (July 28, 2004): 3.

R. A. Cooke and J. Kernaghan, (1987). "Estimating the Difference between Group versus Individual Performance on Problem-Solving Task," *Group and Organizational Studies,* 12 (3) (1987): 319–342.

F. E. Fielder, *A Theory of Leadership Effectiveness,* (New York: McGraw-Hill, 1967).

J. R. French Jr. and B. Raven, "The Bases of Social Power," in *Studies in Social Power* ed., D. Cartwright (Ann Arbor, MI: Institute for Social Research, 1959), pp. 150–167.

T. L. Friedman, *The World Is Flat* (New York: Farrar, Straus and Giroux, 2005).

J. Gardner, *On Leadership* (New York: Free Press, 1989).

M. Hackman and C. Johnson, *Leadership: A Communication Perspective* (Prospect Heights, IL: Waveland Press, 2000).

E. T. Hall and M. R. Hall, *Understanding Cultural Differences* (Yarmouth, ME: Intercultural Press Inc., 1990).

W. Haythorne, A. Couch, D. Haefner and L. Carter, "The Effects of Varying Combinations of Authoritarian and Equalitarian Leaders and Followers," *Journal of Abnormal and Social Psychology* 53 (1956): 210–219.

P. Hersey and K. Blanchard, *Management of Organizational Behavior: Utilizing Human Resources* (6th ed.) (Upper Saddle River, NJ: Prentice Hall, 1982), 248.

D. Katz and R. L. Kahn, *The Social Psychology of Organizations* (New York: Wiley, 1978).

D. Kenny and S. Zaccaro, "An Estimate of Variance Due to Traits in Leadership," *Journal of Applied Psychology* 68 (1983): 678–685.

D. Kipnis, "The Use of Power," in ed. L. W. Porter, R. Harold and R. Allen *Organizational influence processes* (2nd ed.). (New York: M. E. Sharpe, 2003).

K. Lewin, R. Lippit and R. K. White, "Patterns of Aggressive Behavior in Experimentally Created Social Climates," *Journal of Social Psychology* 10 (1939): 271–301.

R. Lord, C. DeVader and G. Alliger, "A Meta-analysis of the Relation between Personality Traits and Leadership Perceptions," *Journal of Applied Psychology* 71 (1986): 402–410.

C. MacDonald, "Street Gangs Take Turns in Cyberspace," *Boston Globe*, Metro/Region, July 18, 2004, p. B-10.

R. D. Mann, "A Review of the Relationship between Personality and Performance in Small Groups," *Psychological Bulletin* 66 (4) (1959): 241–270.

M. W. McCall Jr. and M. M. Lombardo, *Off the Track: Why and How Successful Executives Get Derailed,* (Greensboro, NC: Centre for Creative Leadership, 1983).

S. Milgram, "Behavioral Study of Obedience," *Journal of Abnormal and Social Psychology* 67 (4) (1963): 471–478.

P. J. Murk, "Effective Group Dynamics: Theories and Practices," paper presented at the International Adult Education Conference of the American Association for Adult and Continuing Education, Nashville, TN, 1994.

P. G. Northouse, *Leadership: Theory and Practice* (3rd ed.) (New York: Sage Publications, 2003).

M. S. Poole, "Procedures for Managing Meetings: Social and Technological Innovation," in R. A. Swanson and B. O. Knapp *Innovation meeting management,* ed. (Austin, TX: Minnesota Mining and Manufacturing, 1991).

L. W. Porter, A. L. Harold and R. W. Allen (eds), *Organizational Influence Processes* (2nd ed.) (New York: M. E. Sharpe, 2003).

W. Schutz, *The Interpersonal Underworld* (Palo Alto, CA: Science and Behavior Books, 1966).

S. Sharf, "Lee Iacocca as I knew Him; He Was Certainly the Right Man at the Right Time," *Ward's Auto World* (May 1, 1996).

D. C. Smith, "Lutz for Chairman? His Leap from Ford Fuels Talk about Iacocca Succession," *Ward's Auto World* (July 1, 1986).

R. M. Stogdill, "Personal Factors Associated with Leadership: A Survey of the Literature," *Journal of Psychology,* 25 (1948): 35–71.

R. M. Stogdill, *Handbook of Leadership. A Survey of Theory and Research* (New York: Free Press, 1974).

V. H. Vroom, *Some Personality Determinants of the Effects of Participation* (Englewood Cliffs, NJ: Prentice Hall, 1960).

V. Wall and L. Nolan, "Small Group Conflict: A Look at Equity, Satisfaction, and Styles of Conflict Management," *Small group behavior* 18 (1987): 188–211.

11

How Can My Group Make Decisions?

LEARNING OBJECTIVES

After reading this chapter, you should understand the following concepts:

- Decisions of consequence involve four circumstances: choice, action, consequences, and commitment.
- The prescriptive approach to decision making is logic based and focuses on how groups should make decisions. The descriptive approach is research based and focuses on how they actually do make decisions.
- The decision-making plan combines logic with reality and thus includes recognition of coping patterns, through which humans reduce stress.
- The decision-making plan is a seven-step strategy for making quality decisions: Identify the problem; study the problem; establish criteria for a solution; generate solutions; test solutions against criteria; deliberate; and implement a solution.
- Groupthink can undermine the positive qualities of a group if the group members agree with solutions that have not been adequately investigated in order to avoid conflict. Therefore, it must be prevented.

INTRODUCTION

The previous two chapters are designed to prepare you to make decisions through having a clear understanding of the processes and characteristics of small-group communication. This chapter is designed to help you understand the specific structure and challenges of the decision-making process and to provide you with a practical set of instructions to guide your group to a quality decision.

WHAT ASSUMPTIONS ARE MADE ABOUT GROUP DECISION MAKING?

Before we begin to explain and describe decision-making approaches and strategies, it is important that you understand the critical assumptions that we are making about the nature of decision making. Assumptions, in this case, can be considered the foundation on which the descriptions and explanations of decision making are based.

KEYWORDS

decisions of consequence
choice
action
consequences
commitment
history
current situation
goal
obstacles
solution
prescriptive approach
descriptive approach
reflective thinking model
decision-making plan
conflict model
coping patterns
unconflicted adherence
unconflicted change
defensive avoidance
hypervigilance
vigilance
defective decision
groupthink

A jury decision can have a huge impact on the lives of others.
© Nikolay Titov, 2008, Shutterstock.

Decisions of Consequence

This chapter on decision making will focus on what Janis & Mann call **decisions of consequence**.[1] Decisions of consequence generally are not concerned with trivial and unimportant decisions such as "What should I wear today?" or "What movie should we see?" Instead, this kind of decision is concerned with the more important life decisions such as "Should I buy this house?" or "Should I take this job?" Decisions that you will be making about your business should also be treated as decisions of consequence, because they involve the potential gain (or loss) of a lot of money, or they might even affect the livelihoods of a large number of people. Other examples include public policy decisions, as well as a jury deciding the fate of a defendant in a court case. Decisions of consequence have effects on people's lives, and the consequences of those decisions are often difficult to handle.

People making decisions of consequence must be in a position to act on the decisions. That is, they must be able to follow through in such a way as to meaningfully effect change. Your group can decide that the people on Earth should, in fact, set up a base on the Moon so that we can eventually travel to Mars. It's a good policy debate, and it's certainly timely! Your group could send your reasons for supporting space travel to agencies who are empowered to make the actual decision and who are in a position to carry it out. But your group is in no position to send people into space, and the group will face no consequences if the decision is a poor one. It will be hard to argue that this was a decision of consequence!

Requirements for Decision Making

A decision requires that at least four circumstances exist: choice, action, consequences, and commitment. In the problem you are trying to solve, you must be able to make a **choice** among at least two (or more) viable alternatives. If there are no realistic alternatives, then there is really no decision to be made. Second, decisions require that a course of **action** be taken to implement the decision. If no behavior or course of action is needed, there is no real decision being made; the group is merely expressing opinions or debating for its own sake. Third, a real decision of any importance involves **consequences** resulting from the decision. The action taken by the decision maker(s) will have an effect on the decision maker(s), other people, and/or their environment which sometimes result in the necessity of making more decisions. Finally, decisions require **commitment** to the course of action selected and the decision maker(s) must be willing and able to follow through with the plan, even if negative consequences are experienced.

Basic Model of Decision Making

The strategies for making quality decisions of consequence that are discussed in this book are based on the following simple model.[2] Any decision will have a **history** of events leading up to the current situation, which should help decision makers understand why the situation exists. The **current situa-**

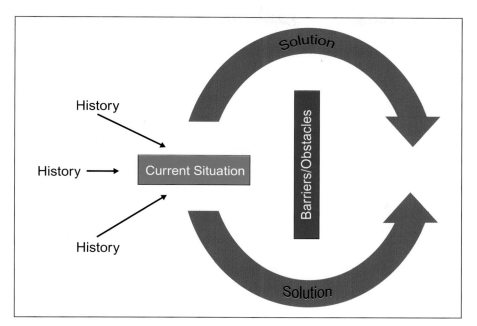

Figure 11.1
Basic model of decision making.
MacCrimmon, K., & Taylor, R. (1976).

tion describes the present status, which could be unsatisfactory and in need of some modification. The **goal** is a desired state that decision makers would like to reach. What would a satisfactory situation look like? This future satisfactory state might not be the same as the current situation. If not, this supplies the reason for the decision makers to make a decision. The **obstacles** are those factors, barriers, or constraints preventing movement from the current situation to the desired goal state. A **solution** supplies the course of action that allows the obstacles to be overcome and the goal realized.

Even though this is a very simple and basic model, it shows a strategy for breaking down a decision into manageable parts and help decision makers better understand how to solve the problem. Please see Figure 11.1 for an illustration of the model.

WHAT APPROACHES ARE USED IN DECISION MAKING?

There are at least two significant points of view about decision making. The two that we will consider are the *prescriptive* approach and the *descriptive* approach. The **prescriptive approach** is logic based and is focused on how groups *should* make decisions. Prescriptive models of decision making involve a set of steps that, if followed correctly, should lead to a quality decision. The **descriptive approach** is research based and is focused on how groups actually *do* make decisions. Descriptive models of decision making typically describe a process that emerges naturally from the interaction of group members. There are lessons to be learned from each perspective, so we will briefly examine both.

How is the prescriptive approach to decision making like following a recipe?
© 2008, JupiterImages Corporation.

Prescriptive Approach

Groups following the prescriptive approach typically use a set of steps to help them solve problems. The steps are based on logic or on research about how groups *ought to* make decisions. A cookbook is an example of a set of prescriptive steps used to accomplish something. If you follow all the steps in the proper order, you can bake a cake or create a perfect bowl of chili. Likewise, if groups can follow the prescribed steps of a decision-making model, they should be able to make a quality decision.

This set of directions for decision making can be used in a wide variety of applications, but they are not always a perfect "fit" for every group and for every problem that groups might face. So you should not make the assumption that a particular prescriptive model, or *cookbook*, will always be successful. You might encounter a situation where the group, or the problem being faced, or both might require that the group find its own way and let a decision emerge from the interaction.

The prescriptive approach to decision making is based on some assumptions:

- There is a "best" way to structure decision making.
- The decision-making process is primarily linear, so it should follow a sequence of steps. The steps should be followed in order, and no steps should be skipped. Failure to follow the sequence of steps will result in a flawed or inferior decision.
- Because it is a logical process, emotional behavior is disruptive to decision making. People are capable of the level of detachment necessary to make quality decisions.
- Decision making is a rational process, which means that people can be unbiased and capable of processing large amounts of information. The more information that can be obtained about a problem, the better the decision outcome.

Although using these methods to make decisions can be practical and efficient, Ellis and Fisher suggest that they can also limit the creativity of group members.[3] Groups will likely finish the job and reach a decision, but there might be little group imagination used in the solution. The prescriptive approach also assumes that people will behave and process information rationally and without emotion, which brings up this predicament: Members of decision-making groups are *people*, and people typically behave emotionally and in a nonrational way. When a group is faced with a decision, it actually has two problems to solve: one is the task itself, and the other is managing the social and emotional issues of group members. If you need detached and completely rational decision makers who are capable of knowing and critically evaluating large amounts of information without bias, don't choose *people* for your group! Hire a staff of computers! Humans do not always have the capacity to know and understand all the alternatives and possible outcomes for complex decisions, even if they had the resources and time necessary for a thorough search.

In spite of some shortcomings, prescriptive models of decision making have been quite useful to groups making decisions of consequence. They have limitations, but they can help groups to coordinate their activities, focus their members on goals, and organize discussions. Prescriptive models can help groups make quality decisions.

A widely used example of a prescriptive approach is Dewey's (1933) **reflective thinking model.**[4] This model is based on the premise that a group must adequately understand a problem before it can be solved. The model directs decision makers to follow these steps:

1. Define and limit the problem.
2. Analyze the problem: causes, current status, goals, obstacles, and solutions.
3. Suggest solutions.
4. Evaluate solutions and select the best solution.
5. Implement the best solution and evaluate the consequences.

Characteristic of prescriptive models, Dewey's model proposes a series of steps that must be followed in order, beginning with a definition of the problem. Following a model such as reflective thinking will coordinate group activities so that all members are doing the same thing at the same time. An explanation and extensive application of the reflective thinking model can be found on the companion Web site for this book.

Descriptive Approach

Based on data collected from the observation of real-life decision-making groups, the descriptive models attempt to illustrate how groups actually *do* make decisions. While the prescriptive models provide a series of task-related steps to follow, the descriptive approach combines task and social activities in the explanation of how groups progress through decisions. The descriptive models are based on the following assumptions:

- A natural process of decision making exists. It emerges over time and in a fairly standard way from the interaction of decision-making groups. Groups do not necessarily need to have an organized procedure to follow.
- Decision making is not a strictly linear or sequential process. Groups often move ahead and then revisit past ideas in a very nonlinear way. The members then modify the ideas again and again until they are satisfied with the outcome.[5]
- Decision making requires an interdependence of the task and social dimensions existing in groups. Social interaction is not a distraction (as suggested by the prescriptive approach), but it is essential to problem solving.
- External constraints, such as time limits and availability of resources, are minimal.

Three of these assumptions are in contrast to the assumptions made by the prescriptive approach. The descriptive approach assumes that decision making is not linear or sequential, that a prescribed set of steps will *not* improve decision quality of a group (and it might even inhibit creativity of the members), and that the social dimension is an essential part of the process. The fourth assumption typically creates controversy: For the descriptive models to work properly, the group should have unlimited resources and as much time as necessary to solve the problem. In the real world, that is usually not possible. Groups operate as parts of larger organizations or systems that have constraints. Finally, while the descriptive models describe and explain the essential nature of the social aspects of the process, there is no direction in the models to give structure to or guidelines for decision making.

Examples of descriptive models include Tuckman's phases (forming, storming, norming, performing, and adjourning)[6] discussed in Chapter 9, and Fisher's Phases of Decision Emergence.[7] Fisher's phases report the activity of a decision-making group as members meet each other and work their way through a decision. The phases are briefly summarized in the following box according to the general patterns of communication in each phase.

Fisher's Phases of Decision Emergence

Phase One: Orientation

Members are getting acquainted.

Neutral and nonevaluative statements are exchanged.

Members' attitudes are explored; tentative statements are made.

Conversation involves mostly clarification and agreement.

Ambiguity arises (as members get to know each other and the problem to be solved).

Primary tension is experienced until rules are established.

Phase Two: Conflict

Argument and disagreement emerges (over decision proposals).

Statements unfavorable to decision proposal are made.

Members' attitudes polarize, leading to disagreement and conflict.

Ambiguity and tentativeness disappear.

Task-related tension builds.

Phase Three: Decision Emergence

Attitudes converge on decisions (decisions are made).

Primarily interpretive statements are made.

Neutral and ambiguous statements are reinforced.

Dissent is reduced.

Phase Four: Reinforcement

The decision is reinforced or bolstered.

Dissent is diminished.

Cohesion and satisfaction builds.

Favorable interpretive comments are made.

Group unity is affirmed.

The descriptive approach, even with its various shortcomings, provides us with valuable insight into group development and gives us a realistic view of real-life decision-making processes. Taken together, the prescriptive and descriptive approaches to decision making provide insightful but incomplete explanations of the processes that decision-making groups actually experience. A more constructive and practical model would account for human limitations as well as to provide enough task-related direction to guide a group when it is uncertain about what to do. The decision-making plan is designed to address both issues.

WHAT IS THE DECISION-MAKING PLAN (DMP)?

Ellis and Fisher suggest that prescriptive approaches help avoid inefficiency, help focus the group on common issues, and coordinate the efforts of members of the group toward a common activity.[8] A prescriptive plan for decision making can be useful and productive, and can be applied in a great many different situations. It is sometimes true that having a structure, *any structure*, is helpful to groups that might not be able to self-generate the organization or structure necessary for approaching complex decisions of consequence. However, some groups find themselves stifled by the imposition of a structure that doesn't fit the character, personality, or composition of their particular group. For that reason, the structure described here is not guaranteed to work in all situations. It will, however, provide inexperienced or even experienced group members with a path to follow if the group finds itself going nowhere. This structure is called the **decision-making plan** (DMP).[9]

How can structure help groups struggling with a complex decision?
© 2008, JupiterImages Corporation.

The steps in the DMP are based, in part, on Dewey's reflective thinking model. Many scholars and decision-making practitioners have expanded Dewey's original steps into what has become known as the *standard agenda*, so it is there that we begin to build our plan. However, we have included additional steps and assumptions that we believe will give you a solid guide to follow for making complex group decisions.

For example, the DMP differs from other prescriptive models in that it recognizes that *humans* will be making the decisions and not a totally rational and nonemotional machine. One of our major assumptions, based on the work of Janis and Mann, is that decisions are made under conditions of *uncertainty*.[10] This means that a decision maker can never be absolutely sure of a decision's outcome. One of the goals of decision making, therefore, is to reduce that uncertainty. Conditions of uncertainty result in *anxiety* (a fear of the unknown) which impairs the ability to make decisions. Along with coping with weighing the facts to make a good decision, group members must also cope with not knowing if the decision they make will be a good one. Too much anxiety can completely disable many groups. Sometimes groups get so worried about the outcome of a decision that they just can't function. Too little anxiety, by contrast, does not promote good decision making because groups are not sufficiently motivated to perform a vigilant search and appraisal of alternatives and to take the proper or necessary action. As hard as it might be to believe, the presence of *some* anxiety is positive and contributes to productivity.

How do you cope with the fear of making an incorrect decision?
© Velychko, 2008, Shutterstock.

A secondary influence on the creation of the DMP is Janis and Mann's *conflict model*, which employs a *combination* of approaches to decision making. The model combines the logical prescription to problem solving while taking into account that emotional, not-always-rational humans are making the decisions. The emotional aspects of decision making are addressed by describing the ways that people deal with the anxiety that comes with making important decisions. As a prelude to the decision-making plan, we examine the emotional strategies that real people use when making real decisions.

Coping Patterns

If humans experience anxiety, they will attempt to find a way to reduce it. Because decisions are made under conditions of anxiety, the **conflict model** suggests five ways people make decisions to reduce anxiety. These are referred to as *coping patterns:*

1. **Unconflicted adherence** indicates little or no anxiety related to a decision. The current situation appears compatible with the goal (or the obstacles are not perceived to be serious), and there is no risk involved with continuing the current course of action. In effect, this is a decision to do nothing.

2. **Unconflicted change** involves somewhat more anxiety because the current situation is not compatible with the goal. The group sees a need for some action, but adopts the first alternative that presents itself that meets the requirements of the goal. This strategy uses an inadequate search and evaluation of possible solutions, so the *best* solution is *probably* not found.

3. **Defensive avoidance** is associated with moderate to high anxiety. The current situation is not compatible with the goal, and the group sees a need to take *some* action. But all available alternatives appear to have undesirable consequences. In this case, groups respond by distorting information, procrastinating, attempting to pass responsibility to someone else, or completely avoiding thinking or talking about the problem.

4. The **hypervigilance** coping pattern involves *high anxiety*. The current situation is not compatible with the goal, so action is required. It is believed that a satisfactory solution exists, but there is not enough time to search for and evaluate alternatives. As such, the group perceives that it must make a *snap decision* and responds to this pressure by quickly and indiscriminately examining as much information as possible. The result is information overload and the group operates in a state of *panic*, resulting in inadequate evaluation of information.

5. The **vigilance** coping pattern is the best of all possible strategies. The current situation is not compatible with the goal, so the group perceives there is a need for action. The level of anxiety is high enough to motivate a thorough search for alternatives, but not high enough to impair decision making. There is enough time to search for and evaluate solutions. This coping pattern is the *only one that promotes a quality decision* because all of the necessary steps can be followed correctly. The assumption of the model is that *all* the other coping patterns lead to flawed decisions.

High anxiety can cause a group to make a snap decision under pressure.
© 2008, JupiterImages Corporation.

Whenever possible, decision-making groups should try to maintain this ideal condition of vigilance. The group needs to consider and carefully assess its coping strategies, identify the patterns, and make adjustments to get as close to the vigilant condition as possible. Stress is always present, so it is very helpful to make an assessment of just how you and/or your group is handling the stress and how it might be affecting your ability to make quality decisions. Therefore, part of the problem challenging the group is actively and explicitly assessing the stress levels to maintain a high level of vigilance. You can visit the companion web site for additional information and web links.

Steps in the Decision-Making Plan (DMP)

Janis and Mann supplied us with a plan for understanding the *emotional* dimensions of decision making. The second part of the DMP is a seven-step strategy for the *task* dimension of the problem.

Step 1: Identify the Problem.   It is important to define the problem as specifically as you are able. This is a step that many groups either pass over quickly or completely ignore. Ellis and Fisher suggest that you try to phrase the problem as a question.[11] Hirokawa and Salazar say that you should try to identify the causes, symptoms, and history of the problem.[12] It is also essential to limit the scope of the problem. You should not define the problem in such a general or extensive way that your vision of the problem becomes restricted or that the problem will not allow a distinct solution.

During this step, group members should pose questions about the nature of the problem to the person who brought the problem to the group's attention and to each other. You should not be satisfied until you have adequate clarity about what you are being asked to accomplish. If you do not have a clear definition of the problem, it is very unlikely that you will find a quality (or any) solution.

Step 2: Evaluate the Problem.   In this step, the group gathers information to aid in understanding the causes of the problem as well as past attempts at solving it. This step is really the "meat" of the decision-making process. It is very easy to jump right to the solution steps without a careful factual search and appraisal of the current problem. Hirokawa points out that the more effective groups do not move quickly to the generation of a solution.[13] Instead, they are patient and spend the necessary time analyzing and studying the problem. Figure 11.2 presents the actions your group should take during this step.

Step 3: Establish Criteria for a Satisfactory Solution.   After clearly defining the question or problem, determine what goals you have for a solution. What do you want a solution to do? In addition, your group should decide on the criteria that you will use to recognize satisfactory decision proposals and reject proposals that are unsatisfactory. Keyton suggests that the more criteria that the group generates for evaluating solutions, the more comprehensive and practical the decisions will be.[14]

Ellis and Fisher recommend that a group's activity focus on the following five actions during this step:[15]

1. Decide what a "best" solution should look like.
2. What should be included in a best solution?
3. What would *not* be included in a best solution?
4. What *specific* standards should be used to evaluate any solution?
5. What would a reasonable, but less than *best*, solution look like? This suggestion calls for the development of a *Plan B* solution, because a best solution might not always be possible. The clear definition of a Plan B will also help with evaluation and second guessing the primary solution.

Use wording such as, "Any solution must/should . . .".[16] This wording will focus the group's attention on *outcomes* of decisions.

> ## The Decision-Making Plan (DMP)
>
> 1. Identify the problem.
> 2. Study and evaluate the problem.
> 3. Establish criteria for a satisfactory solution.
> 4. Generate alternative solutions.
> 5. Test solutions against established criteria.
> 6. Deliberate about commitment.
> 7. Implement the solution.

When you make a choice to buy something, you evaluate what features it has compared to the list of features you want.
© 2008, JupiterImages Corporation.

FIGURE 11.2	Evaluating the Problem
A. *Gather facts.*	Examine the history of the situation. What previous decisions have led to this decision? Was the most recent decision a bad one? Did the situation change in a way that challenged the previous decision?
B. *Determine how the problem might relate to other issues.*	How complex is the current situation? What else might be affected by the changes you might make in the current situation? Will the changes have an economic impact? A physical impact? Will changing the situation undermine some larger or overriding goal of the group or organization?
C. *Determine what is wrong with the current situation.*	What is the specific challenge to the current course of action? Why is the current situation not satisfactory?
D. *Determine what barriers block the path to a solution.*	What obstacles must be overcome to allow the goal to be reached? If the current situation is not satisfactory, what prevents the situation from being satisfactory? Is funding a barrier to reaching a solution? Time? Logistics? Is there a lack of expertise or information that is blocking the path to the goal?
E. *Come to a decision on a clear statement of the question or problem.*	After completing the investigation and evaluation, then write a specific statement of the problem and any barriers that prevent a solution.

Example: Using Specific Criteria

Your friend's car is worn out, and repairs are no longer cost-effective. To aid him in the search for a new car, he has established specific criteria for evaluating possible solutions:

- Any new vehicle should seat four people comfortably.
- Any new vehicle should be able to tow a 2000-pound trailer.
- Any new vehicle should have adequate cargo-carrying capability for travel and sports activities. The golf clubs must fit!
- Any new vehicle should be powered by an alternative fuel source.
- Any new vehicle should, if possible, have four-wheel-drive.

As our friend examines the vehicles on the market, he evaluates each according to the established criteria. The vehicles (solutions) that meet the criteria are chosen for inspection and test drives, and vehicles that do not meet the criteria are eliminated from further consideration.

Step 4: Generate Alternative Solutions. Many groups are tempted to skip Step 4 and adopt the first reasonable-sounding alternative that comes to mind. This leads to the *unconflicted change* coping pattern that was described earlier, and typically results in a flawed or lower-quality solution. This step primarily consists of *brainstorming* and creating a list of possible solutions.[17] Evaluation of possibilities is *not* a priority in this step. The goal is the creation of a broad list of alternatives.

Many prescriptive models of decision making combine our Step 4 and Step 5, asking groups to discover *and* choose solutions at the same time. We keep these two steps separate because they are performing *two distinct functions*. In Step 4, the goal of the group is to survey potential solutions and make a large list of those possibilities. It is in Step 5 that these alternative solutions are evaluated. Some solutions are retained for further evaluation, and those solutions not meeting the criteria (established in Step 3) are discarded.

It is critical that the group take the time to make a substantial list of solutions. If you skip over this step, or if you don't spend the necessary time completing this step, you will likely reach a less-than-optimal solution because you didn't investigate the full range of potential solutions.

Brainstorming Procedures

Define the problem.	If you have followed the decision-making plan, you should already have a clear and explicit definition of the problem.
All members of the group must participate.	Group members stimulate each other to generate ideas they might not think of on their own. If a group member does not participate, not only are those ideas lost, but the stimulation of other group members by those contributions is also lost.
No criticism of ideas is permitted.	Criticism can weaken the ability of group members to stimulate each others' ideas. The goal of brainstorming is to generate a large list of possibilities. Critical evaluation will be done by the group after the brainstorming session.
Members must listen carefully to each others' ideas.	If members' ideas are going to stimulate ideas in each other, then each member must listen closely to what other members are saying. There is a temptation to become absorbed in your own thinking process as you try to come up with additional ideas.
Post the ideas.	It is often helpful to post ideas where everyone can see them. If the ideas are readily available, they can continue to stimulate new ideas among the group members.
Be patient!	Brainstorming takes time. Yoder suggests that your group should brainstorm for at least five minutes for every group member. This number can change, depending on the type and complexity of the problem being considered.

Yoder advises that brainstorming is a valuable method for generating ideas to aid group decision making.[18] The interaction among members stimulates creativity and produces ideas that a single person would likely not generate alone. When done in an open, evaluation-free climate, group members are able to say whatever they wish. When the group concentrates on the quantity of ideas rather than quality, and when they are willing to risk suggesting outrageous ideas to stimulate each others' thinking, brainstorming can significantly improve the quality of group decisions. A more detailed explanation of brainstorming is available on the companion Web site. An alternative strategy to brainstorming is the *nominal group technique* (NGT), which can also be found on the companion Web site (Delbecq & VandeVen, 1971; Delbecq, VandeVen, & Gustafson, 1975).

Step 5: Test Solutions against Established Criteria.

The group evaluates *all* alternatives according to the criteria established in Step 3. If an alternative meets the criteria, it is retained for further examination. If the alternative fails to meet the established criteria, it is removed from any more consideration.

The group should then examine the alternative solutions that met the criteria and choose what appears to be the *best* solution. If no alternatives meet the criteria, the group should return to Step 4 to gather more possible solutions. If the group decides that all possible alternatives are unattractive or negative, it could get caught in the defensive avoidance coping pattern, as described by Janis and Mann. If, however, a solution is chosen at this time, the group should move ahead to Step 6.

Step 6: Deliberate about Commitment.

We imported this step completely from the Janis and Mann model of decision making.[19] It is a very useful step, and leads to considerable success in group as well as individual decision making.

When the group deliberates about commitment, it should try to project into the future to see if it can live with (that is, commit to) the decision it has made. The group should try to anticipate potential consequences of the decision and formulate strategies to cope with possible negative feedback. If the group thinks it can cope with the consequences of its decision, especially the negative consequences, it can adopt the course of action and inform others about its decision.

A group that does a good job of anticipating the consequences of its decision builds in a kind of invulnerability to *negative feedback* concerning the decision. As such, the group should have less trouble coping with the consequences. For a group that did not adequately examine the consequences and risks of implementing the solution, however, the negative feedback comes as a surprise. This surprise usually constitutes a challenge to the decision.

To illustrate this idea, consider that our car shopping friend in the earlier example might decide to purchase a particular vehicle. As with all choices, there will likely be some positive and negative aspects related to this choice. One criterion was that the vehicle should be capable of towing at least 2,000 pounds. Although the new vehicle will tow a trailer, the towing weight limit is 1,500 pounds. This limit means that our friend can still tow most of the things that he normally tows, but he will have to find a new way to tow his boat to the lake when he wants to go fishing. Our friend will have to project a short time in the future to anticipate how that inability to tow the boat will affect him and his family. If he anticipates and understands this consequence, and if he decides that this negative is offset by the many positives, then he can commit to the decision. When the purchase is made and the time comes to take the boat to the lake, our friend will know it was coming and will be better able to cope with this consequence while feeling no regret. If he had not anticipated this consequence, the "surprise" of a lower towing weight could amount to a challenge to the purchase decision. The challenge might cause regret with the decision, or even force him to consider selling the vehicle and starting the search over again.

A handy tool for helping your group anticipate potential consequences is the *Decision Balance Sheet.*[20] The balance sheet helps you consider four types of consequences for decisions of consequence: gains and losses for yourself; gains and losses for significant others; self-approval or disapproval; and the approval or disapproval of significant others.

Decision Balance Sheet

Gains and losses for self:

Includes all the practical consequences of the decision related to your own objectives. The vehicle purchase gains might be that the car is affordable, gets good gas mileage, and came with a trailer hitch. The losses might be that the car's towing limit is lower than expected and that the alternative power source is hybrid and not a "plug-in" electric.

Gains and losses for significant others:

Includes all the practical consequences of the decision related to the goals of other people significant to the decision makers. The vehicle gains in this category include seating for the whole family, rear-seat air bags for safety, and DVD player to entertain back-seat riders. Potential losses might include the lack of complete flexibility on trips to the lake because the vehicle will not tow the boat.

Self approval or disapproval:

Moral standards, ego issues, and elements of self image that could be related to this decision. Many American men have a standard of "masculinity" that they believe should be reflected in the vehicle they drive. Does a hybrid vehicle present the image of manhood strongly enough to support the driver's self-image? Another potential positive consequence is self-approval for reducing fuel consumption and the amount of emissions into the atmosphere.

Approval or disapproval of significant others:

The potential approval or disapproval of reference groups or significant others. Will the family approve of this vehicle selection? Will the driver's friends approve? Will others give approval for reducing fuel consumption and the amount of emissions into the atmosphere?

The better job you do at completing the balance sheet, the more likely your group will be to commit to the decision, even in the face of negative feedback. To the extent you anticipated the negative feedback, your commitment will remain strong and your decision will survive any challenges. Failure to be patient and fill out the balance sheet completely leaves the decision makers open to unanticipated negative consequences that could represent a significant challenge to your commitment and to the decision itself.

Step 7: Implement the Solution. When a group has found the solution to a problem, the members must commit to the solution and must implement the solution. Very often, implementing a solution means asking questions and making more decisions about how to accomplish successful implementation. Here is a list of questions appropriate to this stage:

- What will the solution look like when it is in place?
- What tasks do we need to accomplish to implement the solution? Write down the tasks in the sequence that they should be accomplished.
- What resources are required to implement the solution?
- How much time will be needed?
- How will the group divide up the labor of members to implement the solution?

Then, at every step of the implementation, gather and evaluate both positive and negative consequences and feedback.

WHAT IS GROUPTHINK?

Making a good decision requires that groups *completely* execute the DMP or whatever quality decision-making strategy that they decide to use. To the extent that you *do not* study the problem, make a thorough search and evaluation of alternatives, deliberate about commitment, and collect feedback during the implementation stage, you have made a **defective decision**. Another cause of flawed decision making is *groupthink*, which is associated with an incomplete search and evaluation of alternatives, as well as some factors concerning the relationship among group members.

Groupthink is the tendency of group members to avoid conflict and to express agreement with their group even when a proposed solution has not been adequately investigated or critically analyzed. Groupthink manifests itself in strong pressure to conform to the will of the group and motivates members to avoid disagreements with the proposal, and to avoid questioning weak evidence or unsupported arguments. An alternative is selected by the group, or by the group leader, and all the members "fall in line" behind the alternative.

We stated in an earlier chapter that conflict should be encouraged and not avoided when making decisions in a group. The clash of diverse ideas is one of the primary strengths of small groups, and it is absolutely essential to quality decision making. Although it is true that too much conflict can stifle a group's ability to be creative and productive, too little task-related conflict usually results in defective or flawed decisions.

In some *highly-cohesive* groups, the motivation to maintain the relationships in the group can be more important than the necessity of making quality decisions. This is especially true if the group is caught up in defensive avoidance (where the hope of finding a satisfactory solution is low). In this case, group members strongly support a decision proposal with very little searching or deliberation.

Groups with powerful leaders seem to be especially susceptible to groupthink. Members do not want to disagree with the leader. Instead, all members express enthusiastic agreement.

How do you avoid groupthink?
© 2008, JupiterImages Corporation.

Determining If My Group Is Experiencing Groupthink

How do we know when a group's cohesiveness has shifted from something that helps the group make better decisions to something that causes a group to make defective decisions? Janis[21] found eight symptoms of groupthink.

1. *Illusion of invulnerability.* This is a collective view that the group is incapable of making bad decisions. The group has unwarranted confidence and supports high-risk decisions and behaviors.
2. *Belief in inherent group morality.* Group members do not challenge the ethical consequences of a decision or of the group's actions.
3. *Collective rationalization.* Group members discuss reasons why their decision is the best course of action while discounting opposing evidence and warnings. These warnings might influence group members to reconsider their assumptions.
4. *Out-group stereotypes.* Group members view any opponents to be inferior by stereotyping them as weak, misinformed, or unqualified to challenge their decisions.
5. *Self-censorship.* Individual concerns are not voiced for fear of rejection, ridicule, or embarrassment by the group. As such, members play down the importance of their own doubts about the chosen course of action.
6. *Illusion of unanimity.* Group members truly believe all individuals agree with the decision, even when they have not made attempts to examine the situation from multiple perspectives. There is a belief that silence indicates consent or approval.
7. *Direct pressure on dissenters.* Members are pressured to agree. This may come in the form of direct threats (e.g., loss of job or position) or indirect pressure (e.g., hints of rejection). Dissent is *not* expected from members loyal to the group.
8. *Self-appointed mindguards.* Individuals perform the function of protecting group members from information that does not support the decision.

These symptoms strongly relate to some high-profile poor decisions that have affected public opinion, resulted in lost jobs, and even cost lives. In February 2003, the Space Shuttle *Columbia* exploded over Texas while reentering the atmosphere. All seven crew members died. NASA was criticized for giving in to pressure to keep the space program funded by pitting shuttle flights and the associated risks against political and economic pressure to keep the program visible to hold the public's interest.[22]

The structure of NASA's organization set the stage for groupthink to occur. NASA provided bonuses to independent contractors for on-time delivery. This resulted in an unwillingness to discuss problems or to raise flags that might slow a project. Additionally, investigators found the *Columbia* mission management team was unwilling to say anything potentially negative about the mission and failed to investigate suggestions that the foam insulation could cause serious damage to the spacecraft, which was later found to be the cause of the accident. The transcripts from the investigation show evidence of a team that was both isolated and isolating. The NASA middle managers in the mission evaluation room, where engineering issues during flight are resolved, were found to be reluctant to raise issues of importance. It was concluded that

The structure of NASA's organization has resulted in instances of groupthink.
© 2008, JupiterImages Corporation.

there was pressure to overestimate the success of the shuttle, and there was a culture of management that rationalized risks against political and economic factors. This indicates that the disaster could have been prevented.[23]

Another example of groupthink occurred during the 2004 presidential election year. At that time, CBS news aired a story critical of presidential candidate George W. Bush's military record. The report was later found to be incorrect. Many were at a loss to explain how this could happen in such a reputable news organization. The subsequent investigation revealed that those in charge of checking facts and ultimately authorizing such a report suffered from many symptoms of groupthink.

Preventing Groupthink

So how do we prevent this from happening in our own decision making? Janis has suggested strategies for avoiding groupthink:[24]

- *Assign a devil's advocate.* Give a group member license to pick apart the group's decision. Ask the devil's advocate to examine the decision from an opponent's point of view and have fun with tearing it apart. Ask the other group members to think about the questions raised by the devil's advocate and discuss them as a group.
- *Leader should avoid stating a position.* Individuals tend to conform to a strong group leader's position. This makes sense if the leader, for example, is also your boss. Who wants to disagree with the person who controls decisions about your future promotion, future raises, hiring and firing? Thus, the leader, whether the boss or not, should refrain from stating his or her position until all other group members have shared. This is meant to help free the decision from bias.
- *Hire an unbiased outside expert to evaluate the decision.* Companies often use outside experts to help them understand the impact of a decision or to assure them that a proposed course of action will, indeed, be the best. This is also true of companies who hire research firms to conduct focus groups with employees to better understand the impact of their policies from their employee's perspectives, or educational institutions who hire researchers to interview students enrolled in special programs or majors.
- *Split the group.* Another strategy is to split the group into two or more subgroups, with the each subgroup working to solve the problem. The solutions are then brought forward for evaluation and selection by the group as a whole. This is comparable to Donald Trump's reality TV show *The Apprentice.* In this show, competing teams work on business-related tasks and bring forward their ideas to the "boardroom," where Trump and his executives decide which approach is the best.
- *Encourage questioning and challenge others.* There are many ways we can encourage questioning and respectfully challenge each other's ideas. We can set up a climate where all questions are welcomed and appreciated. This is not accomplished by simply making the statement, "There's no such thing as a stupid question;" rather, it is accomplished by the manner in which the question is received and responded to. To respond with understanding, appreciation, and encouragement is to send the message to the group as a whole that constructive criticism is an acceptable practice.

Example: The CBS 2004 Election Year Faux Pas

It was the 2004 presidential election year, and news organizations were in a mad rush to print the hottest stories about the two top contenders, George W. Bush and John Kerry. CBS news had the "scoop," so they assumed, on George W. Bush's military record. News producers and executives approved the airing of the Wednesday, September 8, edition of *60 Minutes,* but quickly found they had made the wrong decision to do so.

After the report was found to be erroneous, an independent investigative panel concluded that the CBS producers and executives failed to meet basic journalistic standards. In looking at their decision making, we see each symptom of groupthink.

Those Involved:

Dan Rather: Anchorman

Mary Mapes: Story producer

Josh Howard: Executive producer of *60 Minutes Wednesday* (Mapes's supervisior)

Mary Murphy: Senior broadcast producer (Mapes's supervisor)

Andrew Heyward: President of CBS news

Groupthink Symptoms Demonstrated by the CBS Team:

Illusion of Invulnerability: Dan Rather failed to check facts, and failed to attend meetings where his input may have prevented the report. Additionally, he misrepresented the findings of a document expert, and was found to have mischaracterized some of the corroborating evidence. Rather's illusion of invulnerability was evidenced by his overconfidence and blind reliance on a team he perceived to be incapable of making a mistake.[25]

Belief in Group Morality: The source of the story, Bill Burkett, demanded many perks in exchange for his information. These perks left the appearance of conflicts of interest between CBS and its informant.[26] Additionally, phone calls were made by Mapes to the senior adviser to democratic presidential candidate John Kerry that were later considered to be "a clear conflict of interest."[27] The CBS team was making ethically questionable decisions that were left unchallenged by other teammates.

Collective Rationalization: During the investigation, the investigators blamed the segment's airing on a "myopic zeal" among staffers, who were all determined to be first with the story.[28] In other words, the staff members were so focused on the goal, they failed to critically analyze the process, the facts, and the behaviors of other group members.

Out-Group Stereotypes: Mapes dismissed the fact-checking experts' worries in an e-mail to her boss, Howard, concluding: "I think these people are nuts."[29] Mapes's statement indicates she viewed her perceived opponents to be inferior and uninformed, even if they were experts.

Self Censorship: Heyward gave explicit instructions to his deputies not to let the program's staff "stampede us in any way."[30] By doing this, the CBS news president was sending a clear message they were not open to criticism.

Illusion of Unanimity: Individuals involved in the steps to airing the program blindly trusted Mapes without checking facts or talking to each other.[31] Inaccurate press statements were issued vowing the then-secret source of the documents was "unimpeachable."[32] There was no thoughtful discussion and analysis of the story. This led to a perception of unanimity about the reliability of their main source, and a perceived unanimity about whether the story should air.

Pressure on Dissenters: With increasing pressure to air the story before other networks, individuals in the newsroom felt a strong need to just get the story aired.[33] Given these conditions, a group member who might have expressed skepticism would suffer the consequences.

Mindguards: Mapes received multiple reports of concern over the authenticity of the evidence. All were ignored.[34] By ignoring these concerns, Mapes served as the group's mindguard. She was protecting them from what she alone regarded as unimportant information.

SUMMARY

To begin, hold on to the concept of a *decision of consequence*. If you are dealing with a less important decision, then you should not expend the time, expense, and energy needed to use the tools that are supplied in this chapter. If the decision that challenges your group passes your test and qualifies as a decision of consequence, then you should be ready to use the tools.

You should have a clear view of what a complex decision looks like. You should be capable of breaking any decision into its component parts (history, current situation, goals, barriers, and solutions) and using those components to enhance your understanding of the challenge. When you have reached that understanding, you should be able to apply the seven steps of the decision-making plan and guide your group through a thorough search and evaluation of available alternatives, deliberate about commitment, and then implement your solution.

You should also be aware of the social complexities involved in group decision making. Remember that giving a problem to a group adds to the difficulty of finding a solution. The payoff, however, is that groups can take on much more challenging problems than individuals working alone, and that they are capable of making creative, quality decisions. Responsible group members must always focus on the task, and they must pay attention to social issues, especially those concerning conflict and groupthink, which can lead to defective decisions.

Now you know how to make small groups work for you. You will see that it's worth the trouble!

ENDNOTES

1. I. Janis and L. Mann, *Decision Making: A Psychological Analysis of Choice, Conflict, and Commitment* (New York: The Free Press, 1977).

2. K. MacCrimmon and R. Taylor, "Decision making and problem solving," in *Handbook of industrial and organizational psychology*, ed. M. Dunnette (Chicago: Rand McNally, 1976).

3. D. Ellis and B. A. Fisher, *Small-group Decision Making: Communication and the Group Process* (New York: McGraw-Hill, 1994).

4. J. Dewey, *How We Think: A Restatement of the Relation of Reflective Thinking to the Educative Process*, 2nd ed. (Boston: D.C. Heath, 1933).

5. T. M. Scheidel and L. Crowell, "Idea Development in Small Discussion Groups," *Quarterly Journal of Speech* 50 (1964):140–145.

6. Bruce Tuckman, "Developmental Sequence in Small Groups," *Psychological Bulletin* 63 (1965):384–399.

7. B. A. Fisher, "Decision Emergence: Phases in Group Decision Making," *Speech Monographs* 37 (1970):53–66.

8. Ellis and Fisher.

9. S. Wallace, "The Decision Making Plan," in *Creating Competent Communication: Small Group Decision Making*, ed. S. Wallace, D. Yoder, L. Hugenberg, and C. Horvath (Dubuque, IA: Kendall/Hunt, 2006).

10. Janis and Mann.

11. Ellis and Fisher.

12. R. Hirokawa and A. Salazar, "Task Group Communication and Decision Making Performance," in *The Handbook of Communication Theory and Research*, ed. L. Frey (Thousand Oaks, CA: Sage, 1999).

13. R. Hirokawa, "Communication and Problem Solving Effectiveness II," *Western Journal of Speech Communication* 47 (1983):59–74.

14. J. Keyton, *Communicating in Groups: Building Relationships for Effective Decision Making* (New York: Oxford University Press, 2006).

15. Ellis and Fisher.

16. K. Young, J. T. Wood, G. Phillips, and D. Pedersen, *Group Discussion: A Practical Guide to Participation and Leadership* (Long Grove, IL: Waveland Press, 2001), p. 115.

17. A. F. Osborn, *Applied Imagination* (New York: Scribner, 1963).

18. D. Yoder, "Brainstorming," in *Creating Competent Communication: Small Group Decision Making*, ed. S. Wallace, D. Yoder, L. Hugenberg, and C. Horvath (Dubuque, IA: Kendall/Hunt, 2006).

19. Janis and Mann.

20. Ibid.

21. I. Janis, *Victims of Groupthink*. (Boston: Houghton-Mifflin, 1972).

22. C. Ferraris and R. Carveth, "NASA and the *Columbia* Disaster: Decision-making by Groupthink?" Paper presented at the annual convention of the association for business communication, 2003.

23. Ibid.

24. Janis (1972).

25. J. Rainey and S. Gold, "How CBS' Big Story Fell Apart," *The Los Angeles Times* (January 16, 2005). Retrieved January 21, 2005 from Newsbank Info Web. Also, "Sitting between Fiasco and Fallout," *Washington Post* (September 22, 2004).

26. Rainey and Gold.

27. Kurtz.

28. J. Cook, "CBS News Fires 4 in Erroneous Bush Story." *Chicago Tribune*, January 11, 2005.

29. Rainey and Gold.

30. Kurtz.

31. Ibid.

32. Rainey and Gold.

33. Rainey and Gold; also Kurtz.

34. Rainey and Gold.

REFERENCES

A. Delbecq and A. VandeVen, (1971). A group process model for problem identification and program planning. *Journal of applied behavioral science VII*, 466–491.

A. Delbecq, A. VandeVen and D. Gustafson, (1975). *Group techniques for program planners*. Glenview, IL: Scott, Foresman.

12

AUDIENCE: WHO ARE YOU COMMUNICATING WITH?

LEARNING OBJECTIVES

After reading this chapter, you should understand the following concepts:

- You must assess your audience and the context in order to communicate effectively.
- General communication goals include information giving, persuasion, and expression.
- Specific communication goals include adoption, discontinue, and continuance.
- Audience analysis is the process of gathering demographic and psychographic information about your audience.
- Context creates expectations of what type of communication will be taking place.
- Effective speaking involves adapting to the audience, sometimes in the middle of a presentation.
- Using strategies to help the audience listen will make your presentation more effective.

INTRODUCTION

In your lifetime, the importance of understanding your audience so you can achieve your goal has been made clear. As a child, you may have noticed which adult or sibling was most likely to give in to your whining when you wanted something. You found that some people were more likely to listen to your complaints or needs than others were, and you discovered when and how that listening occurred. Once you reached school age, you realized that tattling on another was not always seen as a positive social response from your teacher's or peers' perspectives. You paid attention to the ideas your teacher suggested for getting along with others, so you began to develop negotiating skills with your classmates. In middle school, friendships evolved based on interests and abilities; you lost some friends and gained others. You began to think more seriously about your eventual career, so you started noticing and showing interest in people holding those jobs. In high school, your abilities to "read" a teacher were more refined, so you figured out how to attain your desired grade. You displayed interest, took chances on answers (if you felt your teacher likes people who respond), did the extra credit, joked around (or kept silent). You also started to hone in on appropriate avenues

KEYWORDS

general goals
information giving
persuasion
expression
specific goal
adoption
discontinue
continuance
audience analysis
demographics
age
culture
socioeconomic status
gender
psychographics
belief
values
motives
attitudes
communication context

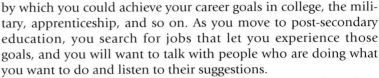

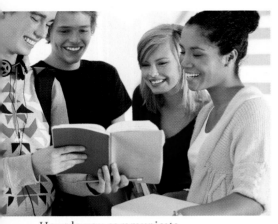

How do you communicate when you're with a group of friends?
© Yuri Arcurs, 2008, Shutterstock.

by which you could achieve your career goals in college, the military, apprenticeship, and so on. As you move to post-secondary education, you search for jobs that let you experience those goals, and you will want to talk with people who are doing what you want to do and listen to their suggestions.

This need to assess the audience and the context, based on your goals, is essential to success in life. When your evaluations and assumptions fail, your goals are not achieved. When you ignore adapting your ideas to your audience, or if you're incapable of listening to their responses, you will not be able to engage them in your message. You can't predict how they'll respond to your ideas. You know the drill: Your false assumptions about your significant others' parents result in your saying things that horrify them, when all you wanted to do was to please. You do not get your perfect job, because on the interview you represent yourself in a way that disqualifies you, or you fail to listen to the questions being asked. You confuse someone when giving directions because you assume that he knows the same landmarks that you do.

You've already learned about the kinds of knowledge a critical thinker needs: organized knowledge (what you believe), skill knowledge (your grasp of how to do something), and understanding, where you add skill to belief in order to create insight (that clear realization of the depth of a complex situation). In this chapter, you will need to employ all three, because you will be introduced to the strategies for analyzing and adapting to your audience. You'll learn about the importance of goal setting, what to consider about the demographic and psychographic elements of your listeners, the role that context plays in message construction, and how to help your audience to use effective listening as they receive your message.

WHAT COMMUNICATION GOALS SHOULD I CONSIDER?

When preparing your message, you will have both general and specific goals that you will want to teach through your communication.

General Goals

Communication can be thought of as addressing one of three general goals (or general purposes), each answering the basic question, "Why am I talking about this issue/topic for this specific audience and occasion?" Every communication event, whether it is an interpersonal, small group, interview, or public address situation, requires you to determine your goal. You might be pursuing comprehension (information-giving), influence (persuasion), or emotion or value-sharing (expression). Think of **general goals** as the primary purpose of your communication. Although any communication context or event may have elements of all three, there are fundamental differences that will guide the kind of message you create.

Information Giving. **Information giving** means communicating data or beliefs in order to develop understanding and awareness. Your goals here should be reception, comprehension, and retention on the part of your audience. Perhaps you have found yourself explaining how you chose your major or the career you are preparing for; that's providing information. When you give someone directions, you are informing by detailing the routes and milestones the person should look for. In the same vein, if you try to explain the problems that exist in a certain proposal, you are aiming for an understanding of the issues (and not necessarily trying to fix them—at least not yet). All of these primarily involve the goal of information giving.

Persuasion. The goal of **persuasion** is to influence the audience; it is much more complex than information giving, yet it also involves reception, comprehension, and retention. But persuasion adds the dimension of acceptance to its goal. When you persuade, you attempt to influence people to change something about the way they think or behave. If you want your friend to practice safe sex, you might give data about rates of STDs and HIV, but your goal is beyond understanding or knowing those data—you want your friend to make a change in behavior. As another example, think about a job interview you went on. You offered information about your past education and occupational experiences, but you went beyond those details to share why you should be the one hired. There may have been many others competing for that job, but you wanted to convince that employer that you were the one who most fit the company's needs. Finally, when proposing a change in the way a meeting is run, you might explain how past meetings have been ineffective, but additionally, you will suggest a means for altering the meeting protocol. In persuasion, you seek audience change.

When you are explaining procedures your goal is to inform your audience.
© Diego Cervo, 2008, Shutterstock.

Expression. **Expression** is sometimes called value-sharing or emotional communication. When your goal is expression, you are seeking an outlet to convey your feelings or values to your audience. For our purposes, expression as communication is goal-oriented; when you speak your mind or reflect on some emotion or value, your goal should be to create in the audience the same state of mind. Think about some time when you were angry, and you just needed someone to listen to how you were feeling. In the end, did you only want the person to listen to you, or did you want that person to identify with your emotional state? Did you want that person to suggest some means of relieving that anger? Beyond the interpersonal need to share, there are many special occasions for public address where expression is the goal. Listening to a eulogy at a funeral, we want to reflect on a deceased person's life and the ways he affected our lives. We go to a commencement address to hear about how the graduates have succeeded in their goal and are embarking on a new journey. When giving someone an award, we celebrate in her achievement. None of these is "simply" expressing emotion; in each case, we are attempting to create an emotional communion within the audience.

What kind of message do you expect to hear from those who speak at a graduation ceremony?
© Stephen Coburn, 2008, Shutterstock.

Your general purpose is naturally constrained by the occasion or context, which we'll consider later in this chapter. A meeting where you are proposing a change in a procedure probably requires persuasion. A commencement would seem to suggest an expressive message. Lecturing in the classroom is supposed to be informative. But these general goals are relative. Is news as informative as it purports to be? How about scientific reports? Are their intentions only to capture audience understanding, or do they have an additional goal of affecting the way the audience acts? When your professor shares information with you, does she choose stories that reflect her personal experience that perhaps are expressions of values or emotions as well?

When considering your general goal, keep in mind the initial question: "Why am I talking about this issue/topic for this particular audience and occasion?" This will guide you. Your general goal must be considered as you begin to construct your message.

Specific Goals

A **specific goal** (or specific purpose) answers the question, "Where do I want this audience to be at the end of my message?" You can think about specific goals as being one of three types: adopt, discontinue, or continue.

Adoption. If your goal is for your audience to adopt your message by the end of your speech, *you want them to take on something new.* Examples would be if you want them to grasp some new data, to learn about something they have never heard of, or to take on a position they never considered. In each case, the goal of **adoption**—of taking on a belief that was not considered before—is your target. For example, you might want to persuade the audience to boycott a particular company because of its policy toward migrant workers. The audience is likely not to have a prior position on this issue, and your specific goal for them would be to adopt a negative attitude toward the company and to not buy its products. Or, you might be telling someone about a brand-new product on the market: you are introducing something novel, and at the end of your message, your friend will have acquired new information. To *adopt* does not mean to replace some already-held conception; as a goal, it is the creation of something new.

Discontinue. If you want to *replace* something your audience already believes with something else, you would have the specific end goal of **discontinue:** you want your audience to end one belief (or behavior) and to replace it with another. For instance, say your friend does not like amusement park rides. She says that she is never going to Disney World, because she would not go on the rides. If you told her that at Disney World there are historical and animal exhibits, international restaurants, and a host of nonride activities, she might change her mind about visiting the place, replacing her conception with a new one.

Continuance. As a specific purpose, **continuance** means that you want to supplement, or add on to, what the audience already knows, without denying previous knowledge. Consider a coach who exhorts her lacrosse players to work harder. The athletes already know that practice will improve their game, but hearing motivational phrases or getting new timing goals might present them with greater awareness of what they can achieve. You have experienced continuance all through your academic career as concepts have gotten more and more complex. When you were younger, you might have learned a simplistic view of history, but as you took more courses, you learned more than just names and dates and a

How does a coach motivate a player to keep trying?
© Scott Milless, 2008, Shutterstock.

simple cause or two: You understood economic, social, political, and philosophical foundations for historical events. Learning about the death of a president not only reviews historical fact; it also supplements those facts with details not known when the events occurred. When faced with an audience that already has some knowledge, continuance means that you have to create added value in your message.

Goal setting is important for a communicator; without clear goals, your message may fail, or your audience might not be able to engage in their own critical thinking. In later chapters, you'll see how these goals can be developed in specific communication contexts. However, you're probably thinking that you do have so much to share, but you need someone to share it with! That is where your audience comes in. You have to know who they are and why they're part of the communication event before you can reach your goals. That involves audience analysis and adaptation.

FOR WHOM AM I PREPARING THIS MESSAGE?

In communication, the audience is always the central concern. Your audience—whether it is one person, a small group, or many people—takes precedence over you and your message. Without considerable thinking about the audience, you cannot strategically develop any idea. You have to consider your listeners' perspectives in order present your views in a way that will make sense to them. This fundamental belief in the *centrality of the other* will guide all the choices that you make as you consider your communication goals, discover your evidence, and construct your message.

It might be useful to think of your audience as an imaginary construct. You might be able to guess how someone thinks based on past experience, but you do not know exactly how any other human will react at a certain time or place when given a message. Humorists don't know how comedy club patrons will take to topical humor. Filmmakers are never sure what audience their film will reach. Politicians can develop messages to constituents that may fall flat. Teachers can slave over lectures that fail to inform. Advertisers can pitch products that have unexpected success or unanticipated failure. Faced with that reality, you could just give up and move somewhere that would never require you to communicate again. That probably is not practical. So what should you do?

The process of **audience analysis** is the gathering of demographic and psychographic information about your audience. Such an analysis will allow you to make reasoned judgments about your message receivers, whether they are single listeners or large groups, strangers or friends, hostile or supportive. The extent to which you will perform audience analysis will likely be proportional to the formality of the communication context. When you are talking with friends, you probably know a lot about them, can guess how they will react, and are able to tailor your message and language without really thinking too much. But more formal communication contexts require greater thought. If you're going on a job interview, you should learn about the interviewer, the company and its policies, and even questions that interviewers like to ask. You do this because you want to prepare your responses so they are tailored to that listener and context.

How can a teacher design his message to effectively reach his students?
© PhotoCreate, 2008, Shutterstock.

The same is true in group decision making and public address: Your preparation must involve consideration of those you are going to talk with. Without that preparation, you will likely end up with a less successful message, simply on the basis of a poor choice of words, lack of the right evidence, organization that does not make sense to your audience, or even a poor impression on a personal level by dressing incorrectly. In audience analysis, you gather information about the audiences' demographics, psychographics, and situation in order to predict reactions and to guide strategic decisions as you develop the message. When you engage in audience analysis, you are adding to your understanding, one of the bases of knowledge so important to critical thinking.

Audience Demographics

Demographics refers to a broad class of population characteristics such as age, gender, ethnicity/race, and socioeconomic status. How do you know the composition of your audience? Some of those demographics are easy to discern: You'll know if a person is male or female, young or old, Caucasian or Asian, and so on. Say you wanted to give an informative speech about computers to an audience comprised of individuals fifty years of age or older. What might you assume based on this demographic? Although not true of all individuals over the age of fifty, you might think that people in this age category experience higher levels of anxiety when faced with technology. Also, this population may be less adept at troubleshooting and mastering new software. Now, imagine your audience is composed of all twenty year olds. What might you assume about this audience? This audience has grown up using computers and is probably more knowledgeable and confident about computers than the previous audience. Would you give the same speech to each audience?

What should you know about the people who will be in your audience?
© Junial Enterprises, 2008, Shutterstock.

In Chapter 3, you gained some research and questioning skills. You could supplement your own initial knowledge by requesting information from whomever asked you to speak or by querying others who have appeared before that group or similar ones. Knowing who your interviewer is, who will constitute the panel that is reviewing your proposal, who will be represented at the PTA board meeting, or who will be in your audience for your speech will help you to develop your content and message strategies. Over the years, researchers have developed general conclusions that might help you in your analysis. Some of these generalizations are presented here.

Age. **Age,** the first demographic, can be an important factor in considering how someone might react. Age may impact the way the audience receives your information; we know, broadly speaking, that someone's interest will vary with age, as will that person's ability to comprehend and to listen. Think about how different you were when you were struggling to figure out "who you are" (usually in the teen years), versus your concerns now for establishing yourself professionally and developing lasting relationships. As you age and become part of the sandwich generation, you find yourself worried about your children *and* your parents, not to mention your career. With age, mortality, retirement, and physical changes begin to take a greater prominence.

When you communicate, an awareness of the audience's age can guide you in developing content that is appropriate to the interests or needs of that group. Cognitive functioning changes with age, also. This means that you might have to define terms differently, or significantly change your language. A simple example is the use of the word *heroin*. A child might hear the word *heroin* and think you are talking about a female superhero (a *heroine*, but the word is said the same way); a teen might hear the word and think "party drug." Our attention spans, experiences, and contexts all change as we age. Superman has been around since the 1930s, so depending on who your audience is, that image might relate to a 1938 Marvel Comics figure, George Reeves (who played the Man of Steel from 1953–1957), Christopher Reeve's movie portrayal beginning in 1978; the *Lois and Clark* (1993–1997) or *Smallville* (2001–2008) television shows, the film *Superman Returns* (2006), or the multiple cartoon rebirths.[1] This generational identity gives generations shared perceptions about events, images, and people. Making sure that your supporting materials relate to the age of your audience surely will impact their ability to understand your point.

Also, it is important to know that cultural differences in the perceptions of age may influence your approach to the audience. In Chinese culture, for instance, the elderly are shown great respect. This can be seen in two Chinese proverbs, "Don't underestimate experienced people, old people still may have great ambitions and potential" and "To succeed, consult three old people." Pueblo Indians have a saying, "Cherish youth, but trust old age." Knowing this cultural perception may prevent you from telling your audience (if there are many cultures represented) that you should reject an item or object because it is old or out of date!

Ethnic or Racial Composition. As a communicator in our multicultural society, you will encounter a wide variety of audience members with differing ethnic or racial backgrounds. The concept of **culture,** meaning "a community of meaning," also figures in. Some members of the audience may have common backgrounds with you; others may not. Some may be fluent in your language, while others may be less familiar with slang and culturally grounded ideas or words. Different cultural groups share different values (individualism versus collectivism, the roles of males and females) and approaches to life roles.[2] It may help you to consider these differences so that you can be rhetorically sensitive as you develop your ideas and avoid potentially offensive terminology, concepts, or attitudes, because you need to treat your audience with respect and fairness. As you think about your audience, think about your cultures. Are there values that center you, but that your listeners do not share? It is important to note the changes that immigrants have brought in the last fifteen or so years. According to University of Michigan demographer William H. Frey, in 1990, only seventeen states had populations composed of at least 5 percent immigrants, compared to twenty-nine states in 2005. Frey contrasted traditional immigrant magnet states (California, New York, Florida, Texas, New Jersey and Illinois) with the rapidly expanding new immigrant destinations of North Carolina, Tennessee, Georgia, Nevada, Arizona, Iowa, Nebraska, and Colorado, where the immigrant population has grown 200 percent or more between 1990 and 2005. According to Frey, the foreign-born attracted to these destinations are likely to be more recent U.S. arrivals, are less well-off financially, and are more likely to be undocumented than those who reside in traditional magnet states. With increasing immigrant growth and the sharp contrast between immigrant minorities and the existing state residents, attitudes toward immigration in the new state destinations are different from

How can you design a message that will be well-received by everyone in your audience? © 2008, JupiterImages Corporation.

those in traditional magnet states. Frey found that 57 percent of those existing state residents in new destination states felt that levels of immigration should be decreased, compared to 47 percent of those in traditional magnet states. In the new destination states, 72 percent opposed three-year work permits for illegal immigrants, compared to 55 percent in traditional magnet states.[3] If you are aware of value differences, you can avoid ethnocentrism, or the belief that your own group or culture is superior to all other groups or cultures. Even though you cannot know everything about your audience's ethnic and cultural composition, your goal should be to design a message that is targeted and respectful.

Socioeconomic Status. Socioeconomic status includes occupation or profession, education, and income level. Occupations and professions are important, because the type of work someone does often indicates a broad range of interests and concerns. Also, being a member of an occupational group may mean that the person has adopted many values associated with that profession; business executives may look at tax regulations differently than steelworkers; teachers will likely consider educational issues differently than plumbers. Closely tied to occupation might be educational attainment, because education influences people's ideas, approach to issues, and skills. Higher-paying jobs usually indicate higher levels of educational attainment. People with different educations know different terms, or they may have considered issues in broader ways. Education level probably influences how people think, their values, and what they earn. A higher level of education in your audience may allow you to use specific language, but they might also expect greater depth in evidence. This might be essential in that job interview; if you do not know the correct terms for that employer, you might find yourself talking yourself right out of that job. If talking to someone with a lower level of education, you might need to clarify points with more illustrations and examples. Income also affects how people perceive life in many ways; obviously, it affects how people eat, live, and spend. But income also influences choices that people make: travel destinations, leisure activities, brand names versus generics, paying for medicine or for food. Income is omnipresent in our lives.

Gender. Gender is another important concern, yet, in a sense, it is a changing demographic. Although past researchers focused on differences between men and women, the contemporary importance of gender analysis now focuses on gender styles. In fact, some research shows that differences in gender behaviors are learned rather than biological, and the differences are often minimal.[4] There are some specific language differences that might impact the audience's expectations:

1. Women tend to use more intensifiers and hedges than do men. Intensifiers modify words. ("This is *really* important.") Hedges modify words by softening or weakening them. ("This *might* be of interest to you.")
2. Women ask questions more frequently than men, gaining more information or determining how others feel about the information.[5]

You might not think these differences are significant, but if they have judgmental consequences, then they are. Mulac suggests that audience members perceive female and male speakers differently based on their language use.[6] According to his research, female speakers are rated higher than men on social status, being literate, and being pleasant. Males are perceived as being more dynamic: They are seen as stronger and more aggressive. These judgments are all based on perceived language differences.

Other demographic elements that might play a role in your analysis could include religion, political affiliation, marital status, or even geographic location. In sum, when developing your message, it is important to gather as much information as you can about your audience, because that data will give you the basis for assumptions about their orientation, involvement, and interest toward your topic. A demographic analysis will also lead you into your next area of audience analysis: that of psychographics, or the audience's key beliefs, values, motives, and attitudes.

What strengths as a speaker do you think this woman possesses?
© dasilva, 2008, Shutterstock.

Audience Psychographics

Kenneth Burke said, "You persuade a man only insofar as you can talk his language by speech, gesture, tonality, order, image, attitude, idea, identifying your ways with his."[7] You have to go beyond what you can see and attempt to discover how the audience might perceive you and your topic so you can design the most effective message. For example, think of what you did last weekend. Now, think of what you might tell one of your parents about the weekend versus what you'd relate to one of your close friends. Chances are, the messages would be different because you would tailor what you say, how much you say, the examples you use, and the amount of information you disclose. Audience **psychographics** involves the audience's cognitive elements: how they think, value, and tend to act.

Beliefs.   Beliefs, the first cognitive element, constitute what your audience knows. A **belief** is your perception of reality, and it describes your conception of something. A belief reflects how confident you are about something, of the validity of a statement. Thus, your knowledge about the existence of a supreme being or Bigfoot are beliefs. When someone mentions a belief in Champy, the Lake Champlain monster, that level of validity for the existence of such a creature is his belief. Your beliefs also include the meanings that you attach to words. How you define *faith,* for instance, might be very different from someone who observes different religious practices. In communication, we face this all the time; it is not unusual for someone to assume that a communication major is involved with broadcasting, because that is what others tend to think communication is all about. Beliefs range in their strength; there are some things that you know with all the conviction you have, and other beliefs that you are less sure of. Beliefs, those ideas that are your sense of reality and truth, allow you to function, and they form the basis of your ability to comprehend and understand. Beliefs constitute the three kinds of knowledge covered in Chapter 3: organization, skill, and understanding.

Does this photo prove the existence of the Loch Ness Monster to you?
© Chris Harvey, 2008, Shutterstock.

Values.   A second concern of psychographics is **values,** which are enduring judgments or standards about what is good or bad. Values guide and evaluate your personal conduct and interaction with others. They help you to determine what is right and wrong, and they give your life a sense of meaning. They are a set of conceptions based on beliefs, but they are much more difficult to change because they are enduring. You have personal values (I need to be honest), cultural values (we Romanians think a good meal is essential), social values (pornography is tasteless), and work values (the customer is always right). Some values tell you how to act every day; these are called *instrumental values* (you should be honest, altruistic, cheerful, caring). Some values point you toward desired end goals; these *terminal values* could be voiced as having a successful career, achieving salvation, creating a stress-free life. Understanding key audience values will direct you to the types of examples you might use, the points you might argue, or the clashes you will face with your listeners. You have judgments about what television shows are appropriate for children (no violence, no adult situations, no loud music), or what constitutes a good class (held between 10 A.M. to noon twice a week, no pop tests, and a funny teacher). Your beliefs and values interact; the definition of what constitutes violence will affect your judgment of it.

Motives. Motives, the third aspect of psychographics, underlie both beliefs and values. **Motives** are the drives, urges, or needs you have. Psychologist Abraham Maslow classified motives into five developmental levels, with the satisfaction of physiological needs (food, water, sleep, sex, shelter) most important to fulfill, then safety and security, with social esteem and self-actualization (approval from outside sources, belonging, and growth) needs being lesser in urgency. According to Maslow, the most basic needs must be satisfied before successively higher needs can emerge. Maslow's research indicates individuals have needs that motivate them to do things. The first four of these needs were termed *deficiency* needs and are mandatory for humans to meet for survival. The fifth was termed *growth* need, which is a need that continually shapes our behavior. Maslow explains this theory and each of the five needs using a pyramid (see Figure 12.1). He argues that we first strive to meet the needs listed at the base of the pyramid, and that as those needs are met, we work to meet the next need.

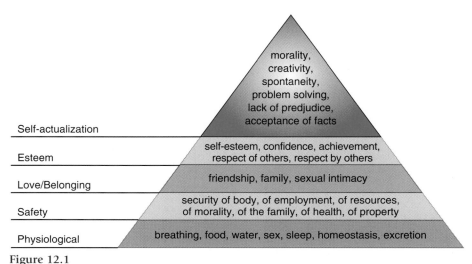

Figure 12.1
Diagram of Maslow's hierarchy of needs, represented as a pyramid with more primitive needs at the bottom.
SOURCE: A. H. Maslow, *Motivation and Personality* (2nd ed.) (New York: Harper & Row, 1970).

Physiological needs include things like food, water, sleep, sex, and shelter. An audience who feels their ability to meet these basic needs is threatened (e.g., access to healthful food, or loss of job or wages) will be motivated to prevent the threat. Once our physiological needs are reasonably met, we then move to *safety needs.* This includes the need to feel safe on a personal level (our bodies are free from harm), a community level (we feel safe walking from our front door to our cars or the bus stop), and national level (we feel reasonably safe from the threat of terrorism). A speech about the dangers of Aspartame or high-fructose corn syrup in processed foods appeals to the audience's safety need. Showing how consumption of foods with these additives could increase risks for health complications may motivate audience members. Our need to have people we connect within our lives and to feel that we belong and are accepted by these people is called *belonging needs.* The cellphone commercial stating, "Don't be left out! Get your new camera phone today!" is an example of appealing to our belonging needs; the ad intends to motivate us to buy the newest camera phone—not because we need one—but because we may be "left out" if we do not get one. *Esteem needs* refer to our need to be acknowledged and respected by others. Finally, *self-actualization* involves striving to challenge ourselves and improve. For nearly 20 years, the Army targeted young adults with "Be All That You Can Be" in its recruiting campaign aimed at the audience of over 20 million Americans between the ages of 18 and 24. The fact that you are reading this textbook is testimony to the fact that you are working on self-actualization. By appealing to the physiological, safety, belonging, esteem, or self-actualizing needs of your audience, you can increase audience members interest in and desire to listen to your speech.

Audience-centered communication will link the message with something already desired by the intended audience. Knowing what drives your audience, understanding their needs, will allow you to establish that link. If, for instance, you are selling a new kind of whole-grain pretzel, you need to know if your audience is concerned about fat or salt (physiological and safety needs) or bring something new to a party (social needs). That knowledge would help you to decide what pretzel aspects you want to highlight in your advertising. Would it be the health value of your product, or would it be the buzz that the consumer would create at the next party when she shows up with something so new?

Attitudes.   Finally, **attitudes** are predispositions to respond to others, ideas, or events in a particular way. Attitudes are built on our beliefs and values, and they cause us to lean toward something (or to lean away from it). For instance, if we hold a positive attitude about saving money, we are likely to use grocery coupons. The belief is that a coupon is a way to save money. You *know* that. The value is the "good worth" of saving. The attitude is the leaning toward the behavior of clipping and then using coupons when you shop. Your attitudes are formed based on your motives, beliefs, and values. A simple example shows this relationship: Your values say that stealing is a bad thing. You know (belief) that all Martians steal. Your attitude is, "I do not want a Martian moving into my neighborhood." Let us take a more down-to-earth example: you feel that arguing is a bad thing (value). Your brother-in-law holds conservative political views and you do not (beliefs). You decide that talking about politics is better to be avoided because otherwise, a fight will ensue (attitude).

Audience Psychographics

Beliefs	Your perception of reality; Describes your conception of something
Values	Enduring judgments or standards about what is good or bad
Motives	The drives, urges, or needs you have
Attitudes	Predispositions to respond to others, ideas, or events in a particular way

Psychographics refers to the classification of the audience's beliefs, opinions, and interests. Psychographic analysis will lead you to an understanding of your audience's potential reaction towards you, your message, and the occasion. For instance, if the audience does not know much about your topic, then it is likely they do not have strong beliefs, values, or attitudes. That may suggest that you should stick to pretty basic information sharing, give them background details, and do not attempt to persuade, because people might be more resistant to decision making on things they do not know about. When developing any message, you should take time to think through who you are talking to, what they already know about your topic, what their feelings are about the topic, and why they are listening to the speech. Once you have sized up your listeners through demographic and psychographic analysis, it will also help to understand elements of the speaking situation or context.

IS THE COMMUNICATION CONTEXT IMPORTANT?

Communication context or situation is the final aspect of audience analysis. This involves time of day, location, setting, and occasion, or purpose, of the event. Depending on the communication context, your audience will have differing expectations. Think of the different perspective sitting in a classroom provides, versus sitting in a movie theater. What do you expect in terms of interaction, message, and behavior? Does sitting around a conference table generate a different type of discussion than instant messaging? If you hold an important discussion at the end of the day, does that impact others' abilities to listen? What kind of language and images are appropriate in a wedding toast versus a eulogy, or an evaluation interview versus a counseling session? In addition, the context may determine the strategies you choose in creating the message. Where is this communication event taking place? When? How many people will be involved? Will you need any additional presentational materials, and will there be the opportunity to use them? Where will the audience be in relation to me? Who else will be talking? Are there any special circumstances that I need to acknowledge? Understanding the audience's expectations toward the context can impact how you plan and deliver your message.

This initial presentation of goals, audience, and communication context gives you a sense of the dimensions that successful communication involves. Although you might have a great idea to share, a failure to figure in the audience's needs or the contextual limitations can lead you to failure. A simple example of this frequently happens in many classrooms. The instructor will finish what she thought was a well-crafted lecture, replete with examples, and a student will raise his hand and say, "Is there anything important we should remember for the test?" While the instructor internally rolls her eyes, an honest contemplation of her initial audience analysis might tell her that the next time, she needs to highlight "important" ideas more, perhaps by saying, "This will be on the next test," or "This is simply an example; does someone else have another?" In that way, she will engage the audience differently. That leads us to a simple question: Once we have done our audience and context analyses, how can we practice audience adaptation?

HOW DO I USE MY AUDIENCE AND CONTEXT ANALYSES TO ADAPT MY MESSAGE?

How do instructors adapt to their audience of students?
© 2008, JupiterImages Corporation.

Effective communication is targeted at a specific group of listeners, their beliefs, attitudes, values, motives, experiences, culture, and context. If you are a Web designer, you want your site to appear on the appropriate search engines that your target audience uses. You have to consider keywords and phrases that they most likely will be searching for. Otherwise, your site may never get its message out to the desired audience. In business, if you don't want any customers, be sure to ignore your target audience. Don't worry that you're trying to pitch hair replacement services for middle-aged people in a teen magazine, or the latest toddler fashions to members of the AARP. Your target audience doesn't really matter, does it? Knowing your target audience is crucial to any successful campaign, and the same is true for any successful communication event. You know that you have to identify and learn about your audience before beginning any work on your message. But learning about the audience isn't enough; you have to adapt your ideas to them in order to achieve success.

Audience adaptation flows from the discoveries you've made during your audience and context analyses. When you adapt, you present your message in a way *that will best fit the audience's beliefs, attitudes, values, and motives in order to create shared meaning.* This means that you have to work on adjusting your message in terms of the structure, evidence, tone, and approach appropriate for the specific audience. You do this because you want to become an audience-centered speaker.

Audience adaptation happens before you speak and as you are presenting the message. If you've considered how the audience is likely to respond to your ideas, then you'll construct a message that attempts to meet those concerns. However, you have to be able to adjust your message as you progress if you discover that the approach isn't working. One important concern is that you remember that you shouldn't let the audience cause you to abandon your idea or goal. A good audience analysis shows you their position and lets you consider how best to impact them, whether that is providing new information or adding to their knowledge base or attempting to influence them. Perhaps it's a misstatement to call this audience adaptation, because what is really going to happen is that you will adapt yourself (your ideas, organization, delivery, and supporting materials) so that you can achieve your message purpose.

Prespeech adaptation comes as you prepare the speech. Keep your audience in mind; what did you discover about their beliefs and attitudes? Do they know much about your subject, do they agree with your position? Are there terms that you'll need to explain, or will one type of evidence likely be of greater interest or cause a stronger impact than another? This premessage adaptation allows you to predict and anticipate the responses you're going to get. That will suggest strategies for structuring your ideas and for delivering the message, which we'll explore in upcoming chapters. In essence, prespeech adaptation means that you put yourself in your audience's position as listener, and then you design your message to meet what you've discovered.

Even the most strategic plans have to be adjusted when you discover that what you anticipated hasn't occurred. When you shop, if the kind of bread you need isn't there, do you go without out and decide to remain hungry? If you're on vacation and it rains, do you just stay in your room and sulk that all of your plans have been ruined? No matter how much you plan, sometimes things don't happen as you had predicted, and if you still want to achieve your goal, you have to revise. You might find that the context has changed (the room is smaller or less equipped, the time allotted has been cut). The audience might indicate through nonverbals (or verbal questions) that some point you're making isn't clear, or they don't understand how you're using a term. For instance, if you're in an interview, you might have prepared a series of answers to anticipated questions, only to be asked something different. You might have expected to meet only the human resources director, only to be escorted to the staff break room and invited to sit down and talk. If you freeze or fail to rise to the challenge, your "I'm the one to hire" message will fail.

How do you prepare for questions in an interview?
© 2008, JupiterImages Corporation.

Adaptation Techniques

Here are some common adaptation techniques that can be utilized either premessage or during the event.

Create Common Ground. *Create common ground* with your audience by showing how you all share some common values, ideas, or experiences. On a job interview, you would change your style of dress and appearance to reflect the employer's style. In the same vein, as you are talking, you could find something in the interviewer's office (or dress, or language style) that allows you to create identification, the association with or assumption of another person or group's qualities, characteristics, or views. The same techniques exist in small groups and public speaking contexts; you can use "we" and "us" terms rather than impersonal ones, for example, to indicate sharing. Think about the difference in creating closeness with the following statements:

People are challenged to find simple ways to recycle.

We are challenged to find simple ways to recycle.

The latter sentence creates a bond between speaker and audience; the former simply points out that someone "out there" is impacted.

Create Goodwill. Consider ways to *create goodwill,* that feeling that the audience senses you care about them. If you can focus on their experiences by relating to some event that they've recently lived through (you discover this in audience analysis), or if you mention or quote from an important figure in their culture, they'll know that you've put some thought into their perspectives. Another goodwill technique is to demonstrate engagement or involvement, shown through attentiveness. Use verbal and nonverbal behaviors to illustrate that you think the other's messages and feelings are important. Attentiveness can be shown nonverbally by looking directly at the listener, moving closer, nodding your head, or leaning forward. Looking away or disinterested, lack of eye contact, looking at your watch, positioning your body away, or a blank facial expression all express a lack of attentiveness to the other person's message. Interpersonally, engagement can be shown verbally through short phrases such as, "I see," "Go on," "I understand," and "Uh-huh." You indicate that are interested in the message, you are focused on the transaction, and you want the person to continue communicating with you. Simple goodwill tactics tell the other person that you are engaged and that you want to share in creating meaning with them.

Use Rhetorical Questions. The *use of rhetorical questions*, asking for a mental response, signals to the audience that their thoughts are valuable, and their input is needed for this message. Even though you're not really requesting a verbal or physical response, by asking the audience to participate, you're involving them. If the question is worded strategically, the audience will know that you've studied up on them, too!

Obviously, *a well-designed message*, complete with a variety of supporting materials, structured in a logical way, helps with premessage adaptation designed to engage listeners. But you can't be stuck on following exactly those supports. Despite your best plans, what if you discover that the audience doesn't understand one? Do you forge ahead, or do you add some explanation? What if you find that you need to add an extra illustration or ask for one from the audience? Can you do that? You'd like to stick with your organizational plan, because it has provided the bones of your message, but you may need to sacrifice one of the points in order to meet any challenges you face.

Watch for Feedback. Finally, you should *watch for feedback* from the audience. Their nonverbal cues (head nodding, eye contact, puzzled facial expressions, leaning forward in their seats) can indicate how well they're receiving your message. A prespeech adaptation has given you a sense of what kind of language is appropriate and maybe even what kind of delivery is expected (Will you be expected to have presentational aids? Will you sit or stand? Will you use electronic projection?). But your nonverbals may have to be adjusted based on what you see from your listeners. You may need to speak more slowly or more loudly; you may need to review a slide you had planned to pass over; you may need to move into the audience to break away from the front. You'll sense that these behaviors are necessary if you're aware of the feedback your audience sends you.

What does her expression indicate about the message she's receiving?
© 2008, JupiterImages Corporation.

Strategies for Helping the Audience Listen

In Chapter 3, you learned about the important role that listening plays in our lives, how it plays an essential part of our ability to think critically. You learned about barriers to listening and were given some ideas about what you could do to improve your own listening habits. Remember, though, that the listener only plays half of the role in the communication event; the sender plays the other half. That suggests that there are some strategies you could consider that would aid your audience as they work on their successful listening behavior. These listening strategies can come before or during the message.

Ask Direct Questions. *Ask direct questions of the audience* if you feel that something is unclear. Checking to see if they've missed key information may take a bit of time, but if they don't grasp one idea, your entire message may fail. In a perfect world, your audience analysis would have given you an accurate picture of the audience's knowledge and attitudes, but remember, most of us don't listen well. If they've missed something essential, it may not be because they don't already know it; it may be because a listening barrier is in the way.

Omit Unnecessary Information. Be flexible enough to *omit information* your audience doesn't need. Sometimes you discover that the audience is more familiar with your ideas than you thought (perhaps they recently heard a report on the topic), so you have to change the level of the information you currently have. You may have the right information but it may be "pitched" at too high or too low a technical level. If, for instance, you had planned to do a product-design presentation to your work group and members of the financial affairs office show up, the terminology that you use might shift. Change the level of your examples; technical ones may miss nonspecialist audiences.

Use Retention Devices. *Employ retention devices* to help in remembering. We simply are limited with the amount of information we can keep hold of. Research shows, for instance that when presented with a series of unrelated sentences and asked to remember the last word of each sentence, people can remember, on average, 2.805 items. Similarly, in a dynamic, conversational listening task where people must remember a series of related questions and respond to them, they can remember and respond to 2.946 items.[8] You'll learn more about this suggestion when you read about creating informative messages. A few retention techniques include repetition, acronyms, and chunking. Repeat key ideas through a summary, saying something like, "There are three points for you to consider." An acronym (an abbreviation also known as initialism) is usually made from the initials of the words it represents, such as FBI (an acronym for the Federal Bureau of Investigation). In chunking, you group ideas into categories. This means that you may have to have shorter main points, or focus on less than you'd like to, simply because you don't want to overwhelm your audience. Remember, information overload is one of the barriers we all face.

Strengthen Connectives. It may be difficult for listeners, especially ones who aren't actively engaging in the process, to follow the connections between the main ideas of your message. You can make these connections much clearer by adding transition words and by echoing key words more accurately. *Connectives* are covered in detail in the chapter covering organizing strategies.

Control Your Delivery. *Manage your delivery style* during the speech. Remember, you may be facing listeners who are easily bored, who daydream, who have short attention spans—all of which means that they may need to be kept alert by physical and vocal delivery. Make sure that your speech isn't boring to the ear or to the eye; consider what presentational aids might keep your ideas front and center. Subtle changes like these can assist in your audience's listening ability. These strategies are discussed in Chapter 3.

IS THERE ANYTHING ELSE I SHOULD CONSIDER ABOUT AUDIENCES?

Audience analysis and adaptation can be complicated by a host of other factors, including the distinction between captive and voluntary audiences. A *captive audience* didn't choose to hear a message; they're required to. If you are told to listen to an on-campus address, if you are compelled to attend in-service training sessions, or even if you're stuck watching commercials that interrupt your favorite television show, you are a member of a captive audience. Because a captive audience hasn't made the choice to be present at your message, you probably will have to motivate them to listen. They also bring multiple reasons for coming, none of which might meet your purpose. You may have to adapt your ideas to a broader range of beliefs and attitudes. The good news is that when you have the chance to speak with a captive audience, you may be energizing listeners who otherwise never would have considered the topic or ideas. A *voluntary audience* comes together out of choice; they have a reason to hear the message. This need or reason could be professional or personal, but the key is that the audience comes with a reason that ostensibly meets your purpose for speaking. When speaking to a voluntary audience, you might be "speaking to the choir," or talking to people who already know and agree with the message. Your approach can't be to simply echo what they already believe; you will have to take them someplace new, but at the same time, you must meet their expectations. If you can determine if your audience is captive or voluntary, you'll have a better grasp on your strategic choices of topic, purpose, organizational approach, supporting material, and delivery.

What if you have to give the same message to more than one audience? What if you have a report to be given to experts and technicians that also will address administrators or executives in the same audience? This is a tough one—if you speak to the lowest common denominator of understanding, you'll likely end up with a message that will insult the majority of listeners. But if you don't address that lowest level, you lose that segment of your audience. What to do? Most would advise you to go for the majority of your audience and sacrifice that minority that needs more help. However, be sure to define important terms and jargon (it's better to insult those who know than to confuse those who don't). If nothing else, you could prepare background information for them to review prior to your message, in an attempt to catch them up a bit. That would signal some premessage adaptation to them.

Adapting to an audience is essential; even the most well designed speech will fail miserably if it's not adapted to the audience.

SUMMARY

Being a critical thinker stretches your internal interests into a desire to share ideas with others. You communicate to create community. You have to consider the goals that you want to attain with others, and you have to analyze your audience and context in order to determine what might be impacting them during this interactive process. You've already learned about the importance of goal setting, You've learned to ask questions about the demographic and psychographic elements of your listeners, the role context plays in message construction, the importance of audience adaptation, and how to help your audience to use effective listening as they receive your message. If you consider all of these strategic elements, you'll be well on your way to becoming an audience-centered speaker. You'll keep the audience at the top of your mind in every step of message production and presentation. This fundamental belief in the "centrality of the other" will guide all the choices that you make as you consider your communication goals, discover your evidence, and construct your message. Now you are ready to put strategy into action. Let us consider the various contexts that communication operates in, and you will see how critical thinking is fundamental to making strategic decisions.

ENDNOTES

1. PopCultureMadness.com, "Superman history," http://thesupermanmovie.com/ (accessed July 14, 2007).

2. One way to learn about cross-cultural value systems is to seek out surveys. The international Social Survey Programme (*http://www.issp.org*) presents survey results from 38 nations, posing the same set of questions to a representative sample of citizens. Questions such as the role of government, national identity, family, and religion are presented.

3. William R. Frey, "Immigration Goes Nationwide, Heightening Public Interest," University of Michigan News Service, March 28, 2006. *http://www.umich.edu/news/index.html?Releases/2006/Mar06/r032906* (accessed July 15, 2007).

4. Julia T. Wood and Kathryn Dindia, "What's the difference? A dialogue about differences and similarities between women and men." In *Sex differences and similarities in communication: Critical essays and empirical investigations of sex and gender in interaction,* ed. Daniel J. Canary and Kathryn Dindia, (Mahwah, NJ: Lawrence Erlbaum Associates, 1998), 34–36.

5. Anthony Mulac, "The Gender-linked Language Effect: Do Language Differences Really Make a Difference?" in *Sex differences and similarities in communication: Critical essays and empirical investigations of sex and gender in interaction,* ed. Daniel J. Canary and Kathryn Dindia, (Mahwah, NJ: Lawrence Erlbaum Associates, 1998), 133–34.

6 Ibid., p. 147.

7. K. Burke, A Rhetoric of Motives. (Berkeley: University of California Press, 1969; Original work published 1950).

8. L. A. Janusik, "Researching Listening from the Inside Out: The Relationship between Conversational Listening Span and Perceived Communicative Competence," *UMI Proquest: Digital dissertations,* 2004. Available at http://www.lib.umi.com/dissertations.

How Should I Construct My Message?

LEARNING OBJECTIVES

After reading this chapter, you should understand the following concepts:

- If your ideas and message are disorganized, your communications will be as well.
- Selection is a decision strategy of determining your topic and purpose, meeting the audience's needs, and choosing the proper supporting evidence.
- Once the topic is selected, the general purpose of a speech will guide all other decisions. The specific purpose will narrow the focus to what you want to accomplish from the speech.
- Evidence should be relevant, accurate, and appropriate for the audience, and it should be presented truthfully.
- Sequencing strategies help you organize the message into a logical order of introduction, body, and conclusion.
- The body of the message contains the main points and is developed first.
- The introduction motivates the audience to listen and prepares them for the subject.
- The conclusion should close the speech with an effective, appealing summary.
- Connectives create a dynamic flow between the sections of the speech.

INTRODUCTION

I enjoy making baked goods for my family. I know where every ingredient, recipe, and utensil is in my kitchen, and I can bake pretty efficiently (even if not always successfully). I have several books that tell me how to bake elaborate to simple things, and I even have a folder on my computer that is filled with baked goods yet to be tackled. There are pictures of completed pies, delicious-looking cakes, and yummy cookies to inspire me. When planning to spend an afternoon baking, I make sure I have all the needed ingredients, prepare and measure them, and line them up in the order in which they'll be needed. I set aside time to do this all. Even the most complicated baking project seems uncomplicated once I have everything laid out, and my planning and organization give me some sense of control over the eventual outcome.

KEYWORDS

selection
topic
audience interest
speech purpose
informative speech
persuasive speech
ceremonial speech
general purpose
specific purpose
evidence
main points
chronological order
spatial order
categorical (topical) order
cause-effect order
comparison and contrast
problem-solution order
Monroe's motivated sequence
attention step
need
satisfaction
visualization
action
primacy
recency
specificity
introduction
thesis statement
initial summary
speech preview
final summary
conclusion
connectives
transitions
signposts
previews
internal summary

How can you expect to accomplish anything when your surroundings are in complete disarray?
© 2008, JupiterImages Corporation.

However, in the chaos of my home office, a different scenario exists. Although I write all the time, the process is often made more painful because of the disarray I attempt to work in. Usually, I know the task I have to complete: Write a report, develop a lecture, create some slides, construct a test. I know the general materials that need to go into those, and most of the time, I'm pretty sure I have a sense of what the end result product should look like. Although I sort of know where most things are, I usually end up wasting time looking for long-lost papers buried in stacks. To begin my project, I sit at the computer and stare, stuck from the start without a coherent plan. I have good intentions to file papers where they need to go (witness all of my folders), but somehow, everything seems to end up in heaps. My computer desktop has icons galore, and while I can eventually find the folder I've put work into, guessing what I've named something has to come first. When faced with complicated projects, I have wasted hours looking for a book or document that I know is here somewhere, in some electronic or hard-copy form. Books surround me, leaning in haphazard piles. At my feet are various blank CDs and DVDs, along with a printer, a jumble of cords, pencils and markers, and some old computer disks. Eventually, because I can't find anything or something falls over on me, I'll have to stop working and straighten things up before I can continue in my stumbling way.

Do you notice a difference between my baking structure and my office organization? The similarity is that doing something and thinking about something probably require the same discipline. Both require strategic planning and goal setting. You have to be motivated to engage in both, and it would be nice if you enjoyed the activity. The difference is that although I like both baking and writing, my structural deficiencies in my office make writing much more painful than it has to be.

Now, let's imagine that we all believe that strategic planning is desirable; I seem to do it when baking, don't I? I know that it will help in understanding, finding, developing, and relating information. Strategic planning gives organization and form to thinking and doing. How could I employ that structure on my writing missions? Before starting a project, I could jot down a quick summary of what I have to accomplish. That should give me a sense of the materials I'll need to gather. Setting some time goals never hurts; I'm not really good at all-nighters, and sometimes I can stress over details that really aren't that important. I could decide to reorganize my office: Papers could be filed in neatly labeled drawers or boxes; books could be shelved alphabetically or by topic. I could decide that only the left wall will be used for bookshelves. I could rearrange my computer desktop into well-designed folders, with clear headings that follow a specific pattern. I could move off anything that wasn't currently in use and store it off my computer. All the clutter on the floor could find a new home in the closet, on specific shelves designed for office use. I could buy a desk organizer that holds pencils and pens, clips and markers, so that they weren't all over the desk and floor. Come to think of it, any one of those strategies would probably help me to have a more structured office and successful writing program!

A neat office atmosphere makes it more inviting to get down to work.
© terekhov igor, 2008, Shutterstock.

The same organizational strategies are true for communicating. Thinking and doing are both harder when you, your ideas, and your materials are disorganized. You learned about the audience in Chapter 12. Considering their demographics and psychographics will help you to design a message that will fit their needs. The context can impact the ideas that you develop, because if you're expected to inform but instead decide to entertain, for instance, your poor context analysis will leave the audience feeling cheated. Once you have a sense of audience and context, you'll move to the next steps of topic selection and goal setting, gathering evidence, and structuring the message. Determining your goal for the audience is essential, because that will guide you in making some decisions about the direction your message should take and the evidence you must gather. Once you have considered those necessary elements, you can structure your message.

When you have ideas or issues that you want to share with others, there's a choice among several decision strategies that can help you and your audience. You just have to learn which ones to choose and how to use them, and which contexts call for certain approaches. *Constructing any message can be accomplished through the two primary decision strategies of selection and sequence of ideas.* As you impose coherence on the jumble of data that you'll be gathering, you'll apply these strategies and will become a more effective communicator.

WHAT TWO DECISION STRATEGIES AID IN CONSTRUCTING MY MESSAGE?

Two decisions strategies work together to help you construct a message. The first is selecting your topic, its purpose, and its supporting evidence. The second strategy is organizing your message in an efficient sequence. Let's look at how to use these strategies effectively.

Decision Strategy 1: Selecting Your Topic, Purpose, and Evidence

The concept of selection suggests that you have choices to be made from a range of options. In communication, **selection** involves determining your topic and purpose, meeting the audience's needs and expectations, and recognizing the kinds of supporting materials that you will use to build the message. When you read about critical thinking earlier in the text, you discovered that the selection of stimuli is necessary and typical of our perceptual process. As you take in all the data that bombard you, you can't make it all relevant; there's just too much there to process, and it's difficult to structure it in a meaningful way. You choose to focus on the stimuli that you define as important to the task at hand.

You can't process too many pieces of information at one time.
© GeK, 2008, Shutterstock.

Stop and pay attention to the variety of stimuli around you right now. Is there is noise from other people, the TV or music source, or even environmental noise such as a fan blowing or a siren in the distance? Did you notice them until you stopped to listen for them? Are you paying attention to only the ideas that are highlighted in this text in some way, or are you just reading the examples? Did you look at the objectives listed for this chapter? Have you ever considered how you approach a text? Are you marking in the text, taking notes, or rereading paragraphs over and over again because you aren't really focusing? Have you developed an effective way to make the words significant and able to be retained?

What stimuli are impacting you, and which ones are you ignoring? The same need to make certain stimuli relevant, immediate, or intense exists for your audience. As the speaker, you have to help that audience to focus on the important stimuli—those you have chosen to highlight for them. That means you have to select topic, purpose, and supporting materials.

Speakers are most often asked to talk about their specific areas of expertise.
© Dmitriy Shirohosov, 2008, Shutterstock.

Selecting a Topic. The starting point in selection is to determine your **topic.** On the face of it, this seems pretty challenging: You might be asking, what do I know that would be interesting to anyone? You can answer this question in several ways. Many times, of course, you are asked or told to speak on a specific topic. You're asked for a progress report, you're told to explain how to do some process, someone inquires about an experience you've had. When that happens, topic selection has been taken out of your hands. After college, you will mostly be invited to speak on topics related to your work or your passions. Speakers are nearly always asked to speak in areas of their expertise, be it gardening, geography, radiation, or radio frequency identification. Even on those occasions, you'll find it necessary to narrow the subject so you can meet the needs of the audience and the context. Sometimes, the occasion or issue determines the topic, like when you're giving a nomination speech, a wedding toast, or the introduction of a speaker. But on those occasions where you have complete freedom in selecting the subject, there are some simple guidelines you can use that should help to erase the majority of your worry.

Topic selection should begin with you. What do you care about? What interests you? What do you know something about? If you don't feel the topic is important, it's likely that you won't be able to make the audience feel any differently. You might think that telling college students about the importance of creating a burial plan is a "good idea," but if you really don't believe that it's true, then find something else to talk about. How about creating a speech about the difference among different types of life insurance policies? Can you competently lay out the pros and cons? If not, choose again. If you are taking a history class at the same time you are taking your speech class, why not speak about the significance of some historic event you are already studying? If you enjoy reading a particular blog, consider the emerging role of blogging as a topic for your speech. Remember, however, that not only do you have to be interested and have some degree of expertise, but you also have to make sure that you make the audience the target of that message. You shouldn't be speaking just to hear yourself do it! Filter that topic through a fast audience analysis (you'll flesh this out more once you've settled on your subject).

That notion of **audience interest** is also an initial challenge. Keep in mind that others are interested if what they're hearing gives them new, useful information; if it provides a solution to something that concerns them; if it relates to their own experiences; or if it shows a connection to what they know and something new. As a speaker, each of us has an ethical obligation to bring the audience something of value, to challenge listeners by sharing something they do not already know, or to ask listeners to rethink something they are familiar with. Unlike our grade school "what I did on my summer vacation" speeches, a speech to an adult audience must offer something of value to the listener. An interesting phenomenon is that sometimes, audience interest can actually be a detriment. If you're presenting the company's plan for budget cuts, it's pretty likely that the employees will have a vested interest. However, the threat that they feel when they hear "budget cuts" can actually weaken their ability and desire to listen to the ideas you intend to present. Their unique bias may create a block to effective listening. In another scenario, interest might be determined by the audience's sense that what they're hearing is or is not worth their time. How many meetings do you go to grudgingly, feeling that you have better things to do? What if you had to listen to a speech about how make a peanut butter and jelly sandwich? Think about what it would be like to sit and listen to such

Is your speech one that others will think worthy of their time and attention?
© Dmitriy Shirohosov, 2008, Shutterstock.

a speech. Would you consider it worth your attention and time? Even if you have never made a sandwich before, you probably do not need a six-minute speech to describe the process, unless some really unique spin is put on the description. A speaker in this situation fails to honor the audience by ignoring the value of their time and ignoring if they would be better off after hearing the speech.

Finally, you should not only avoid topics that waste audience members' time and attention, you must also be sure that your topic doesn't harm or intentionally misinform. Carefully weigh the impact of examples and ideas that could reinforce negative stereotypes or slander others. Knowingly including false or misleading information in a speech is unethical and should be avoided. Just as harmful is selecting a topic because it seems funny without considering how audience members might be affected. Although it might seem humorous to give a speech on how to get drunk fast, for example, it would be ethically irresponsible and it could be highly offensive to a classmate who lost a friend or family member to binge drinking. Use language that respects others: Avoid demeaning, sexist, or racist words. As a speaker, you must exercise your opportunity to speak responsibly.

Now that you have an idea of the guidelines for determining a good topic, how do you select one? Sources of topics exist within public issues you care about (immigration reform, global warming, big box stores' impact on local retailers); they can come from personal experiences you can open up to the audience (the time you got a flat tire can become "how to change a flat," or your camping fiasco could relate tips for safe camping); or they might be stimulated by media exposure (ideas present in news magazines, interviews that generate awareness). In all honesty, if you spend a bit of time brainstorming about the ideas that catch your attention, you'll probably be faced with the task of narrowing the field to the best one for this audience and situation.

The Role of Speech Purpose. I attended church last week, as I normally do. The sermon surprised me, though. Rather than hearing a homily that enlightened or stimulated me, I listened to a report on the church's finances. I felt uncomfortable as the service progressed, although I couldn't really figure out why, since the rest of the rituals included all the usual elements of songs, prayers, and readings. So what caused my discomfort? It was that the purpose of the sermon was compromised: I expected one thing and was given something else.

Speech purpose is a statement of a goal and the desired audience response. It usually is determined by the audience and the occasion: Why were you asked to speak? Think of purposes as having two dimensions: general and specific. The general purpose is the broad, overall speech goal. Traditionally, we perform one of three general purposes in speaking: to inform, to persuade, or to entertain. An **informative speech** is one whose goal is to produce shared understanding, to increase knowledge, to cultivate appreciation, or to develop skills or abilities. A **persuasive speech** involves the process of social influence in order to influence beliefs, values, attitudes, or actions of others. **Ceremonial speeches** reaffirm common values and strengthen ties among a community. The first two purposes are covered in Chapters 15 and 16; the third can be found on the companion Web site.

Your **general purpose** will guide all the choices to come: what evidence or supporting materials you'll gather and use, how you'll structure your ideas, and even the delivery techniques you'll employ.

The second dimension of speech goal setting lies in determining the specific purpose. Your **specific purpose** states precisely what you hope to accomplish in your speech: What response do you expect from your audience? What is it that you want the audience to know, believe, do, or feel by the end of your message? The specific purpose is a limitation placed on the audience's focus that develops your general purpose.

When formulating your purpose statement, here are a few strategic guidelines. A well-planned specific purpose contains one distinct idea worded in terms of the desired audience response. For example, if you said, "To persuade my audience to volunteer their time with the Red Cross and to learn more about marrow donation," you'd have different general and specific purposes working here. Either you can persuade your audience to volunteer, or you can inform them about marrow donation. It is impossible to reach both purposes in one speech. Second, your specific purpose should match your general purpose. If your general speech purpose is to persuade, your specific purpose can't be "to tell my audience about the negative effects of cigarette smoking." Third, you should word your specific pur-

How do you attempt to persuade someone to act in a specific manner?
© Tomasz Trojanowski, 2008, Shutterstock.

Take a Closer Look

Let's consider a few simple examples to show how the general purpose dictates what the specific purpose will be.

If your general purpose is to *inform*, then your specific purpose would be:

1. To create awareness in my audience about the services provided by the American Red Cross in our community
2. To demonstrate to the audience how to choose among cell phone plans
3. To describe how recycling saves the environment

If your general purpose is to *persuade*, then your specific purpose would be:

1. To convince my audience to donate their time to the upcoming Red Cross blood and bone marrow drive
2. To recommend to the audience that they select Verizon's cell phone plan
3. To urge my audience to participate in campus recycling

pose as a statement, not a question. A question doesn't tell the audience about the response you're seeking from them: "Do we need capital punishment?" isn't as directive as, "The state should revoke its statue permitting capital punishment." Finally, your specific purpose statement guides your speech focus in terms of time: Can you really achieve your goal in the time allotted? Could you "explain about golf" in a five- to seven-minute speech? How would you need to refine the focus of this specific purpose?

Think of the selection of general and specific purposes as the step that provides you a target: Where do you want to be by the end of the speech? That answer will guide the formation of your speech purpose statement. If you have a clear idea of your direction, then the next element of selection can be achieved. You're ready to start gathering evidence.

Collecting Evidence. In Chapter 3 on critical thinking, you learned about the various categories of evidence or supporting material (examples, statistics, testimony, narratives, and analogies) that a speaker can consider. During the selection stage, you'll employ *knowledge gathering*, identifying the evidence you will need to reach your communication purpose of information giving, persuading, or expressing value. Rather than repeating the categories, let's think about how your own cognitions work. Why do you believe the things you do? Do you know how to search Internet databases? Why do you have the attitudes you hold? Do you feel that the draft should be reinstated, or that people should buy only American goods? How about the things you value; where did those judgments come from? Why do you believe that your football team is the best, or that the worst role

We learn by sharing our experiences with friends.
© Galina Barskaya, 2008, Shutterstock.

models for young girls are found in Hollywood? All of these views come from someone or something in your life that gave you evidence from which you built your perspectives. Most of these pieces of evidence came to you from an external source: a friend who shared a personal experience, a teacher who explained a concept, a Web site or television show that exposed you to something new, a poll that revealed national trends, or even the comparisons that your parents made between your life and theirs. All of these contributed to the convictions that you hold. In the same way, when you select **evidence**, or supporting materials, you will make decisions about what kinds of cognitions (beliefs, attitudes, and values) you hope to create in your audience.

Some of the cognitions you want to support in a message are pretty fundamental; you can use your own experience or a friend's narrative to explain what you mean, and the audience will see the similarities with their own way of thinking. However, other ideas will require more compelling supports from credible external sources; your personal statement just isn't enough. Why should we believe your claim that the school mascot should be changed because it is a racist symbol? Why should we agree that the town should sell a plot of land to a developer in order to improve the tax base? You have to support these claims or assertions with evidence that helps to solidify (or prove) them in your audience's frame of reference. Evidence is necessary because it helps to prove your point, and it helps to make your ideas more valid.

You can gain acceptance from a wider group of people when you support your ideas with evidence beyond your own word. When you support your statements with external proof, you can show that it's not just your opinion that is being given. You can show that you are not alone in your

Where do you go to research for evidence about your topic?
© Damir Karan, 2008, Shutterstock.

line of thinking. Take a simple example: You want to inform your audience of the dangers of young adult depression. You might be brave enough to share your own personal experience (a narrative) with your listeners, but they could just as easily dismiss you as being an exception. But when you bring in statistics from the American Psychological Association demonstrating the increased suicide rate among young adults, and then you follow it up with testimony about undiagnosed depression from the surgeon general and the campus psychologist, and cap it off with a list of depression symptoms for your audience to compare with their own feelings, your speech will be made believable and acceptable to a wide-ranging audience.

You know that the evidence created by examples, statistics, testimony, narratives, and analogies can amplify, clarify, personalize, capture attention, visualize, aid in retention, and link ideas in any message. Here are a few reminders about the selection of supporting materials:

- *Represent the evidence truthfully.* Do not present a hypothetical illustration as a real one, for example, or present only part of a piece of testimony. You might remember that in October 2005, Oprah Winfrey named as her book club selection *A Million Little Pieces*, author James Frey's nonfiction memoir of his vomit-caked years as an alcoholic, drug addict, and criminal. In January 2006, following the discovery of Frey's "embellishment" of the facts of the narrative he had depicted as all true, Oprah castigated him on her hour-long show for the lies he had told.[1]
- *Make sure that your evidence is clearly relevant to the point you're making.* If you were giving that speech about young adult depression and only gave statistics for mental illness in postwar veterans, the statistics would fail.
- *Present accurate evidence; check your examples, testimony, and statistics to make sure you have not misspoken or left anything out.* Cite the sources for your evidence. Make sure that those sources are credible and will have meaning for your audience. Former Secretary of State Colin Powell was reminded of this guideline when he admitted in September 2005 that information he gave to the United Nations in a February 2003 speech was flawed. He told Barbara Walters that he had relied on information he received at Central Intelligence Agency briefings. "There were some people in the intelligence community who knew at the time that some of those sources were not good, and shouldn't be relied upon, and they didn't speak up," Powell said. He called his prewar speech to the United Nations accusing Iraq of harboring weapons of mass destruction a "blot" on his record and admitted, "I'm the one who presented it to the world, and (it) will always be a part of my record. It was painful. It is painful now."[2]
- *Make sure the evidence is appropriate to the audience.* Does the analogy fit their knowledge level? Can they understand the quotation?

Early in the process of message creation, you have to gather supporting evidence. How do you know when enough is enough? There really is not a quantifiable statement to be made here, so let's just say this: Gather more than you think you will need. You'll have the opportunity to limit the range of evidence after you structure your speech. Remember, *selection* means that you determine your topic and purpose and begin to amass your supporting materials to help your audience to achieve your goal. It's in the next process step of sequence that you'll start to structure the ideas that you've selected.

Decision Strategy 2:
Using Sequencing Strategies

Imagine you are planning to do some shopping for a new cell phone, a new pair of shoes, and some food for the family dinner. Your time is important to you, so you want to be efficient. You've done some Internet searches to find out current national prices on the phone and shoes, but you really want to buy local. However, your funds are limited, so you want to conserve gas and do all the shopping at once. This will require several stops, because you want to compare prices locally, too. How will you organize your trip? You could plan your trip based on what you are most excited to buy, or you could focus on the most important items first. You might plan your trip based on a particular route that is efficient. You could plan your trip based on the order of "greater need," so you pick up food for dinner first and the new cell phone last. While you plan your mission, you would think about how to accomplish all of your objectives in the time available and with the limited resources you have. The sequence choices you make give progression and order to your day.

Organization is essential for many tasks, including a successful shopping trip.
© iofoto, 2008, Shutterstock.

Organizing a message is much like organizing a shopping trip. It will involve reviewing your goals, considering your audience, and several strategic choices. When you organize, you can pull your evidence, analysis, and ideas together from the fragmented pieces you've gathered. Creating order from these elements then allows you to figure out their best sequence. What's the best progression of ideas for your purpose, audience, and occasion? You can determine the relationships between the "big" ideas and the ones that are subordinate to them. In addition, effective organization should help you and your listeners to achieve shared meaning; ideas will be clearer, easier to follow, and less complicated to remember. Finally, clear organization will reflect favorably on you; your audience will perceive that you have prepared and given thought to what you want to say, and your credibility should be enhanced.

Remember what you learned about perception in an earlier chapter? We all try to structure perceptions in order to make sense of them. If you've never been to a flea market, the stimuli of antiques, collectables, clothing, farm goods, people, and food will assail you. You have to decide which stimuli to keep or to abandon, which are more important than others, and even where to turn your attention first. That organizational sorting and arranging is based on your personal reasons for going to the flea market in the first place. Was your purpose to see what was out there? Were you on a mission for that perfect lamp? Did you hope to find some organic vegetables? Did you just want to see what a flea market was? Those purposes guide how you structure your walk through the flea market and will help you to make sense of the stimuli that you're receiving. Now think about presenting a message to others. You're going to give them stimuli in the form of ideas and evidence. You want them to perceive those stimuli in a specific way so shared meaning will be established. That means you need to arrange the stimuli for the audience so that they have a better chance of perceiving through your lens.

How you structure ideas should be based on the needs of the situation and audience. Those analyses will have given you a sense of their knowledge level and interest. Now you must strategically decide how to put your evidence and ideas into a progression that will meet those findings. The most basic step in developing your organization is to think of the three basic parts of sequence: introduction, body, and conclusion. But we're going to take a twist here and consider them out of order!

HOW DO I CONSTRUCT THE BODY OF THE MESSAGE?

The body of your message is the "meat" of the content. It's where the audience will learn the most, will be given the most evidence, or will be given arguments to influence them. As a result, it's the most important part of your message, and it should also be the longest. If you structure the main part of the speech first, developing the introduction and conclusion can be made much easier.

Importance of the Main Points

The **main points** are the ideas generated by your specific purpose; they divide your message into manageable units for you to present and your audience to consider. They need to be selected carefully and arranged strategically to meet your purpose. How do you decide what main ideas to consider for inclusion? Your specific purpose provides a simple starting point: it tells the audience what you expect of them. Let's take the earlier example of this informative specific purpose: to create awareness in my audience about the services provided by the American Red Cross. What kinds of questions could you ask yourself to determine how best to develop that awareness? Consider these for a start:

- What is the Red Cross's purpose?
- What is the history of the Red Cross?
- What does the audience already know about the Red Cross?
- Who are the people in my community involved in Red Cross activities?
- Who receives benefits from the Red Cross?
- Is there a difference between the national Red Cross services and local ones?
- Does the Red Cross have divisions?
- How does the Red Cross raise money?

Now, you can see that there is no way you could answer all of these in one speech, considering the time it would take to adequately answer each question. Learning the history of an organization is a speech unto itself. The question about what the audience already knows is answered by your audience analysis; it's possible that you'll find out they've never heard of the Red Cross, so you need to start pretty basic in your speech. You probably also realize that some of these questions don't really relate to your specific purpose, since it's a focus on services provided by the Red Cross. Would it be important to know the difference between the national Red Cross services and local ones? That lets you eliminate several questions, and end up with maybe two or three:

- What is the Red Cross's purpose?
- Who receives benefits from the Red Cross?
- Does the Red Cross have division?

If you inspect these questions, you'll see that even they can be further divided. "Who receives benefits from the Red Cross?" could be split into something like, "How does the Red Cross help meet emergency needs from natural disasters?" and, "How does the Red Cross help meet emergency needs from accidents?" You can carry out this exercise until you feel comfortable with the main points you think are important in order to meet your purpose. Then you can add depth to those main points by including the supporting materials you have gathered.

Generally, the guidelines suggest dividing your specific purpose into between two and four main points; this is enough to be specific and focused and still meet a gamut of time limits. Remember: Your main points must be directly relevant to your specific purpose; if they're not, you either reconsider and refine those points or rethink your specific purpose. In addition, you would like to have a balance among the main points. You don't want to load up most of the information under one point and have the other two be entirely subordinate. If, for instance, you wanted to change your specific purpose to a more in-depth look at the Red Cross overall, you might want to talk about what services it offers, what values it represents, and how it is funded. If you find yourself spending the majority of your time detailing the services the Red Cross offers, then you can go back and restrict your specific purpose. Maybe your specific purpose is better stated as "to learn about the Red Cross organizations' outstanding (or unheralded) services." In that case, your main points could be disaster services, blood services, and health and safety services. If you can create parallel wording in the structure, that can help the progression and retention of ideas. The example about natural disasters and accidents is created in parallel structure. Compare that with two points that say, "The Red Cross gives help in natural disasters" and, "If there's a local emergency the Red Cross is there." Similarly, the three services are easy to create in parallel wording. Once you've settled on some possible main points (they still can be refined), you're ready to decide on their order.

Your speech topic may answer how a volunteer group helps those who've suffered a natural disaster.
© Wendy Kaveney Photography, 2008, Shutterstock.

Sequencing Choices

As with the shopping trip scenario, there may be many "right" ways to organize your ideas, deciding what to do first, second, and last. A list of organizational patterns could go on forever, because we arrange our perceptions through our own experiences and needs. However, there are some simple, standard patterns that you can use as you help your audience to take meaning from your message:

- **Chronological order** *structures ideas according to time orientation.* It is used most often when explaining how to do something or how something occurs, since order of activities is critical. An example of chronological order would be an informative speech about the history of the World Wide Web would discuss its evolution from the 1980s to today. You can structure time order from the past to the present or vice versa. A speech on weight clubs in your community could start with the current state of affairs, then move backwards to the origins.
- **Spatial order** *arranges your main points in terms of their place or position.* Think about how sometimes we explain ideas in terms of how they're related to each other by location. Describing how Hurricane Katrina devastated the Gulf Coast could easily move from the impacts in Louisiana

to Mississippi to Alabama. Another example would be a speech that identifies the various component pieces connected to create the Web, starting with your home computer. If you wanted to focus on global impacts of some issue and move closer to the audience's immediate context, that would also be spatial order: Uncontrolled pet population growth affects our nation, our state, and our community.

- **Categorical** or **topical order** *is the "natural" or "relevant" organization pattern.* As you think about your main points, they seem to fit best in this way. There is no required order other than what you impose. If you wanted to talk about the three impacts that social networking sites have had on interpersonal communication in the twenty-first century, what topical order would you use in discussing the ideas of privacy, job search, and politics?

- **Cause-effect order** *is used to show a relationship between a source and its outcomes.* You could also reverse the order and show how some effects can be traced back to their origins. Explaining how an animal became endangered could be shown by the causes of habitat depletion, pesticides, and invasive competing species, for example. The key is that you must be able to demonstrate that such a causal relationship exists.

- **Comparison and contrast** *structures ideas by showing that there is a similarity and/or difference of your topic with something the audience already knows.* You could explain how the changes the Internet has created are similar to the changes brought about by television's introduction, for example. Since your audience has always known television, its early impact may surprise the audience. You may have to decide whether to focus on only the differences or the similarities, or both. This is shown in a topic such as immigration issues of the early twenty-first century are both similar and dissimilar to those of the early twentieth century.

- **Problem-solution order** *structures ideas by pointing out a dilemma and offering (or supporting) its potential remedies.* If you use this structure, you must first demonstrate that a dilemma exists, that it's serious, and that it affects your audience. Then you are able to move into the potential solutions, perhaps even focusing on one resolution. Perhaps you feel that the allocation of special event tickets to currently enrolled students should be changed. The first main point you'd make is the extent of the problem: how ticket allocation is inefficient and how ticket allocation is unfair. You would then suggest a means for resolving this problem: Ticket allocation should be tied to class standing. The problem-solution order is quite common in advertisements. You are exposed to a problem you hadn't been aware of (you are alone and lonely, you have no opportunity to meet potential mates, you have no sense of how to talk to members of the opposite sex). Then, as if by magic, Dating Site X can resolve those issues by helping you to meet hundreds of compatible potential mates in your area, and they'll even coach you in how to fix your communication style.

If you assert that an animal became endangered because of habitat depletion, you need to demonstrate the cause-effect order.

© 2008, JupiterImages Corporation.

Finally, there is **Monroe's motivated sequence,** developed by Professor Alan H. Monroe in the 1930s. This organizational pattern, used mostly in persuasion, combines logic and psychology, because it models the human thinking process and motivates the audience to action. When you read it, you may see it as an extension of the problem-solution order, but it does much more. The motivated sequence consists of five major steps: attention, need, satisfaction, visualization, and action. In the **attention step,** you want to cause the listeners to focus tightly on you and your ideas. This step comes in the introduction of the speech. The next three steps constitute the body. **Need** demonstrates to the audience that a serious problem exists that demands change. Potentially, four elements are covered:

1. *Statement:* a clear, concise statement or description of the problem(s)
2. *Illustration:* one or more detailed supports that picture the need for change
3. *Ramification:* any additional data to show the problem's extent
4. *Pointing:* convincing demonstration of how the need directly affects this group

Remember, in the need step of the body, you try to create in your audience an uncomfortable state that they will want to alter.

Satisfaction proposes a plan of action that will solve the need. Three elements should be covered:

1. *Statement:* Briefly state your plan.
2. *Explanation:* Clarify the details of the plan (who, what, when, where, how much).
3. *Practical experience:* If possible, give an actual example of how this plan has worked effectively elsewhere, or how this belief has been proven correct by others.

The third part of the body (or fourth step of the motivated sequence) is **visualization,** where you picture for the audience what the world will be like if your plan is adopted. This step projects the audience into the future to intensify their desire for change. You may visualize in one of three ways:

1. *Positive method:* Describe conditions as they will be if your advocated action is accepted. Each motive appeal and problem from the *need* step should be answered.
2. *Negative method:* Describe adverse conditions that will prevail in the future if advocated belief/action is not accepted. Describe unpleasant conditions that will result.
3. *Contrast method:* Combine the negative and positive approaches.

It's important to remember that the visualization step must stand the test of reality. The conditions you picture must seem probable. The visualization step should be a logical counterpart to all of the ideas brought up in the need

Take a Closer Look

If you have utilized the motivated sequence correctly, the audience will respond in a fashion somewhat like the following:

ATTENTION: Audience response will be, "I want to listen."

NEED: Response will be, "Something ought to be done. I can't live with things the way they are now." Or even, "I didn't know it was so bad. What can I do?"

PLAN: Audience will say, "This plan sounds like it will solve the problem."

VISUALIZATION: Reaction will be "I can see how I'll benefit" or, "Gee, without this solution, things will get worse."

ACTION: "I will do this."

Example: Five Ways to Organize a Speech about HIV/AIDS

Imagine that you plan to present a speech about HIV/AIDS. The speech design will influence the aspect of HIV/AIDS that you will discuss.

Match each of the following five speech designs with their associated purpose statement.

1. Chronological
2. Topical
3. Spatial
4. Logical
5. Compare/contrast

A. To inform the audience about the latest HIV/AIDS treatments

B. To demonstrate for the audience the process of how HIV becomes AIDS

C. To inform the audience about the causes of HIV/AIDS and its effect on the world's population

D. To compare and contrast the magnitude of the HIV/AIDS epidemic in South Africa and India

E. To inform the audience how HIV/AIDS spread, beginning in Africa and moving east

Answers: (A. 2, B. 1, C. 4, D. 5, E. 3.)

step. Finally, the last step is **action,** where you urge the audience to do a specific, definite act. You want to give them specific information on how to accomplish this action, so that they will know how to commit themselves. One caution: Asking your audience to "think about this" isn't an action! What behavior do you want them to do?

Integrating My Evidence with My Main Points

As you make the selection of your order, you'll begin to arrange your supporting materials. Main points are nothing without the evidence that clarifies them. But how exactly do you organize your evidence within your main points? What if you have a great set of statistics, a quote or two, and an example, all of which support the first main point? What goes first? Sometimes, the answer is based on the same structural choices as the body: you might move chronologically through your evidence, for instance. In some cases, you can use the principles of primacy and recency to guide you. **Primacy** arranges ideas in terms of how convincing they are, moving from most important to least important. The belief is that by putting the most important first, you will compel the audience to believe what comes after. **Recency** is the opposite; it moves from the least convincing to the strongest. You might use this technique when you have some simple examples that lead naturally to a major example, for instance. With recency, the last thing heard is the one that is best remembered. Finally, you might choose to arrange by **specificity;** you could start with a general illustration and move to a specific one, or vice versa. You could present national statistics, regional ones, and end on local ones.

Because you probably have gathered more supporting materials than you really need, here is when you start to edit. You'll want to use your audience as your guide: What examples, statistics, testimony, narratives, and analogies will help them to achieve meaning? Which ones fit into the time limits you're facing? Are there some that are easier to explain than others? Do some require additional explanation through presentational aids? There is no magic number of supporting materials that any one point should have; that's totally dependent on your purpose, your audience, and your context.

You need to determine which supporting materials you ultimately use for your speech. © Amihays, 2008, Shutterstock.

WHAT GOES INTO A COMPELLING INTRODUCTION?

You now know about the structural choices to be selected from as you create the body of your message. You are able to start adding in evidence that augments and clarifies those main points. But sequencing isn't just about creating a pattern for the body. You have to develop the entire package of the message, which also includes a welcoming, compelling introduction and a reinforcing conclusion that establishes psychological closure.

The opening remarks made that provide the audience with initial message orientation is the **introduction.** This starting part of your message serves two important purposes: It motivates the audience to listen, and it prepares them to focus on the subject. You can meet these purposes by setting the stage through some strategically considered statements. Remember, you probably won't develop your introduction until you've already put the body of the speech together. Once the latter is done, you can then set up the introduction to reflect what will follow. How do you launch a speech? You do it by gaining attention, revealing the topic, suggesting to the audience a reason to listen, establishing credibility, and previewing the body through an initial summary.

Gaining Attention

You have probably heard the famous maxim, "You never get a second chance to make a first impression." That's certainly true about presenting a message. The first thing you say should capture the audience's attention; if you fail to establish that focus from the start, there's really no need to continue. Think about what captures your interest. Is it something creative? Something unique? Something surprising or unexpected? Popular television shows often begin with a powerful dramatic moment, perhaps the portrayal of a crime or a unforeseen circumstance. This "hook" is used to capture viewers' interest so that they do not switch the channel. This isn't a new idea. In 1947, Elmer Wheeler was one of the best-known salesmen of his time. Among the gems that he shared about initiating a sale were statements like, "Your first 10 words are more important than your next 10,000," and you must "Excite 'em, annoy 'em, or startle 'em, all in the first ten seconds."[3] His advice is good: Use your opening lines to capture your listener so he wants to hear what you have to say. Some popular approaches to capture an audience's attention are as follows:

- *Relate a narrative or anecdote.* Everyone likes to hear a riveting story. This may be accomplished in one of two ways. You could share a narrative, which is a story about someone else. You might share an anecdote, which is a story about yourself. If the story is told with conviction, it can capture the audience's imagination.

- *Create a hypothetical situation.* If you ask the audience to imagine something, they can be transported into a specific place, with accompanying emotions and images. We all like to imagine, but be sure to ask the audience to conceive of something they can realistically picture. Asking an audience composed of eighteen- to twenty-two-year-olds to imagine they are through with college, married with two kids, and contemplating a career change is a bit of a stretch. The audience may struggle to imagine finishing college, let alone anything beyond that. It would be better to ask this audience to image something within the realm of their current life, another reason to analyze your audience. Also, when you let the audience think of themselves in another place, be sure to bring them back to the present and your message. If your speech was about the advantages of taking a cruise and you asked us to see ourselves relaxing on deck, umbrella drink in hand with no cares in the world, we might just decide to stay in that daydream, rather than come back to the present.

- *Ask a series of rhetorical questions.* Rhetorical questions do not require the audience to answer aloud or by a show of hands. The answers are implied or are meant for audience members to think about. This mental participation can be very effective in creating immediate involvement. A speech talking about genocide in Darfur, for instance, could easily begin with the query: Do you know where Darfur is? Are you aware of the mass killings that are being perpetrated there? Do you know when you first heard about the crisis? The pitfall to avoid with this type of attention-getter is asking a question that is not thought-provoking or that should really have been asked as part of the audience analysis. An example of a question that should have been asked as part of a class survey would be, "How many of you are registered to vote?" It is not a rhetorical question and it certainly is not thought-provoking. A more effective rhetorical question to ask would be: "How many of you have thought about your voting rights being revoked? Would this threat motivate you to exercise those rights?"

- *Startle with some surprising information or statistics.* The Internet has enabled us to gather interesting statistics at the click of a button. Opening a speech with a startling statistic or shocking information can startle the audience into wanting to learn more. For example, you could begin a speech about the dangers of distorted body image with some shocking facts such as these. The average U.S. woman is 5'4" and weighs 140 pounds, whereas the average U.S. model is 5'11" and weighs 117 pounds. Young girls are more afraid of becoming fat than they are of nuclear war, cancer, or losing their parents. The "ideal" woman—portrayed by models, Miss America, Barbie dolls, and screen actresses—is 5'5", weighs 100 pounds, and wears a size 5.[4]

- *Use a thought-provoking quote.* It's not unusual to find an authoritative or memorable statement by someone else that fits into your speech. This can even add to your initial credibility, because that quotation will resonate with what you're about to say. The guiding principle to using such quotes is to be sure they are indeed interesting, related to your topic, and linked to the purpose of your speech. A quote such as, "Experience is a hard teacher because she gives the test first, the lesson afterward. And in the end, it's not the years in your life that count. It's the life in your years," by Abraham Lincoln can be a great way to interest an audience about speeches, ranging from financial planning to pursing a dream career.

- *Use humor.* A funny story, relevant joke, or witty comment can help to relax your audience, and ease any sense of anxiety, especially on subjects where they disagree with your position. But there are some pitfalls to consider with this attention getter. A joke can be offensive in its language or in the way it pokes fun at other groups (e.g., age, gender, ethnicity). If this is the type of joke you would like to share, it is not appropriate and is unethical to use. Also, some witty comments or jokes are grounded in cultural knowledge and a clear understanding of the language in which they were developed. If you are faced with an audience whose members are from diverse cultural backgrounds, you may run the risk of them not "getting" the punch line. Finally, to employ the delivery required to tell a joke well, the speaker must be at ease at the beginning of the speech. For novice speakers, this can be challenging.

- *Share some information counter to the audience's beliefs.* This could be in the form of stating a truth that was typically accepted but recently shown to be false. For example, many people believe senior citizens to be helpless, yet a recent *Los Angeles Times* article revealed that senior citizens are not as vulnerable as we might think. The article titled "U.S. Tourists Kill Mugger, Costa Rica Says," recounts an unfortunate incident in which a man who pulled a .38 caliber revolver on a group of senior citizen tourists was killed when the group jumped on him in self-defense.[5]

- *Refer to the occasion.* Sometimes, you'll be asked to speak at some special event or occasion, such as a holiday, a professional conference, or even graduation. It's appropriate to say something like, "I'm honored to be part of this celebration with you," and then continue with a reference to the event.

- *Play a short video or audio segment.* People respond well to visual messages. To do this well, however, remember that this will cut into your speaking time. The last thing you should do is play three minutes of video for a six-minute speech. Your message content is the important thing, not your introductory audio or video. Thus, for a six- or seven-minute speech, the use of a video segment should be fifteen to thirty seconds, tops. It is important to explain to the audience what they will be watching and what they should look for. Imagine for a moment that you are an audience member and the speaker begins his speech by walking over to the DVD player and playing a clip from *The Terminator.* You have no idea why you are watching the film but you sit back and enjoy the action. After the clip, the speaker says, "I am here to talk to you today about violence in the media." In this example, the speaker failed to set up the visual so that it motivated the audience to listen. The speaker should have begun by stating, "I am going to show you a clip from the film *The Terminator.* Count how many violent acts you see." You would know why you were watching the clip and would engage in the set task. After playing the clip, the speaker follows up by stating, "There were a total of fifteen violent acts performed in fifteen seconds. Watching such violence desensitizes us to real life violence in our communities." By explaining the clip and linking it to the speech, the speaker has created a compelling attention getter.

How would you toast the bride and groom?
© Shanta Giddens, 2008, Shutterstock.

Whatever attention-getting technique you choose to use, your attention getter should establish interest, should be relevant to the message, and should prepare the audience for the thesis statement about to come.

Revealing the Topic

After capturing your audience's attention, you want to clarify for your audience exactly what you will talk about. This is achieved by providing a clear and simple **thesis statement** (or topic sentence, or central idea), which announces in one sentence what your speech is about. It's not the same as your specific purpose statement, but it certainly echoes that focus. If your specific purpose was "to create awareness in my audience about the services provided by the American Red Cross in our community," then your thesis statement could be: "A simple rule of thumb is that you should be able to say it in one breath, and it answers this question: 'If I were to ask to give one focused sentence that introduces the subject of my speech, what would that be?'" Few things frustrate listeners more than sitting through a speech attempting to figure out what you are talking about.

Moving the Audience to Listening

Consider how your information could possibly impact the listeners. Could it save them money or time? Do they lack of information or perspective? Why not give your listeners a reason to listen? By listening to your speech, they could be improving their understanding for another course or important life issue. Your audience analysis will help to reveal what reasons might motivate your particular audience to listen. You know about how and why we fail at listening, and you have some strategies for helping your audience to overcome those barriers. Keep all those elements at the center of your message preparation.

To be audience-centered means to find a way to add value to your audience's lives through your speech. It means giving your audience more for their money. It means connecting your speech topic with the needs of the listener. Remember Maslow's hierarchy of needs that you read about in Chapter 12? There is the basis of your reflection: What needs can I connect to early on in my speech? The audience should not have to work to see the link between their needs and the topic you have chosen. The link should be obvious in the introduction. This is analogous to sales training. Salespeople are taught to answer for customers the question, "What's in it for me?" (W.I.F.M.). In other words, the audience is silently wondering, "Why should I buy your product?" If the salesperson tells us what we gain from the purchase, then she motivates us to listen further to her sales pitch. You can create this reason to listen by showing the audience that what they're about to hear impacts them directly. You don't have to spend a great deal of time on this idea, but you do have to give the audience direction on why the topic is worth listening to. This could be something as simple as a statement saying, "You might not own this, but you probably know someone who does," or, "You might not think that what happens here is part of your life, but your tax dollars are going to support this effort." Part of creating a compelling introduction is telling the audience what they have to gain by listening. When you do that, you show them that you've thought about their perspective, and you have their best interest at heart.

Establishing Credibility in the Introduction

You've already read about the concept of ethos or credibility. You know that it's the audience's perception of you, seen through the lenses of character, intelligence, goodwill, and charisma. By helping the audience consider why they should listen, you have established a sense of goodwill. Another way to increase people's motivation to listen to your message is by offering a statement of your expertise. People are certainly interested in what Steve Jobs or Bill Gates has to say about technology, but why should they believe you? By offering a bit of information about how you are knowledgeable on the subject you have chosen, you boost your credibility, increasing the chance that your audience will listen to your ideas. Your competence might be built on personal experience and firsthand knowledge, or it might come from classes, reading, or even the experiences that others have shared with you.

For example, if you have trained show dogs as a hobby for ten years, tell your audience about your experience in a speech about caring for pets. If your have recently learned about the risks related to nano-technology through a chemistry class, share that in a speech about nano-technology. If you have volunteered during an emergency or given blood at a Red Cross center, then tell your audience your experience as you discuss American Red Cross services. A credibility statement in the introduction may be as simple as telling the audience about the amount of research done to prepare the speech: "Over the past couple of months, I have read numerous articles, books, and interviews about the Red Cross's history and services." When you help your audience to perceive you as believable, you are also giving them the opportunity to identify with you. If they think that they're like you and the topic is important to you, then by extension, it's also important to them.

Previewing the Body through an Initial Summary

The **initial summary** or **speech preview** forecasts what main points are about to come in the body. You want to let the audience know what the main points include so that they have a perspective on what to focus on. You're telling the audience what you're about to tell them, providing an initial listening guideline. But an initial summary can do more than that. Not only does it preview what's to come, but it can serve as a reminder to you, too. By telling your listeners that you plan to cover the ingredients, process, and cautions of making mortar, you review for yourself one last time where you're about to go. In a similar fashion, that initial summary serves as a bridge to the first main point in the body; it signals that the main content (body) of the speech is about to come. The initial summary is typically presented at the end of your introduction and should flow naturally from your thesis statement. In the speech about the American Red Cross, it might sound something like this: "Today I will explain three major services offered by the Red Cross in our community: disaster relief, health services, and military support services." This preview should be short, specific, and easy to understand. Avoid the temptation to state your preview as a question; an initial summary should state clearly what the speech will cover and the order in which it will be covered.

The tone and direction of your message are established when you create an effective introduction. This is done by gaining attention, revealing the topic, suggesting a reason to listen, establishing credibility, and previewing the body through an initial summary.

HOW DO I CONCLUDE THE SPEECH?

If you did a good job in the introduction, you set the stage for your audience to listen. The end of the speech should wrap up your ideas through a final summary and create closure for you and the audience. Have you ever read a book or gone to a movie that left you unsatisfied at the end? Do you recall one of those times when you weren't sure that it was over? This **final summary** helps the audience recall the main points, improving overall recollection and comprehension. You could signal the coming end with a simple review of your main points. In the Red Cross example, it might appear like this: "You've learned today about the services provided by our American Red Cross, which include disaster relief, health and safety, and military family services." An effective **conclusion** gives the audience one last time to hear your main points. By this time, you've now repeated your main points three times: first in the initial summary, then in the body, and now in the final summary. The final objective of the conclusion is to *close the speech* as powerfully as you began. Two important pitfalls to avoid: Don't assume that you'll "know" how to end the speech when you're done (the "lightning will strike me" approach) and make sure that it's really the end. One mistake speakers make is that they assume some inspirational ending will come to them as they're speaking. It doesn't happen. You need to know what your final statements will be, and you need to practice them so you wrap up with direct eye contact and strong delivery. Equally irresponsible is saying, "In conclusion," and then not concluding. We've all suffered through speakers who use that signal one or more times but then continue to drone on.

So how do you create closure? How do you end a speech? In the introduction, you try to capture the listeners' attention with a *hook*. Any of those techniques could be employed again in the conclusion. If you began by hooking the audience with a story, your closing might offer the moral of the story. If you started with thought-provoking questions, you might wish to return to those questions and offer answers, or you might ask the audience to reflect again on their answers. You could use the conclusion for a final appeal or challenge to the audience, telling them what response you expect from them. The key is to create a sense of closure in the same way that a well-written novel or movie leaves the audience feeling complete or satisfied.

HOW DO I USE CONNECTIVES TO BRIDGE MAIN IDEAS?

Now you have explored the most obvious structural aspects of sequence: creating an introduction, body, and conclusion. There is one more sequencing strategy to consider as you craft your speech: How do you connect those three structural elements into a seamless yet dynamic message? Unlike an interpersonal dialogue, where you can jump from topic to topic and still share meaning, in a speech you have to link the main ideas through connectives.

Connectives create the dynamic flow of a speech and help listeners to remember and to recognize where they have been and what to expect next in a speech. They are a subtle aspect of speechmaking that can turn a good speech into a great speech. The most common kinds of connectives are transitions, signposts, internal previews, and internal summaries.

Transitions consist of phrases or key words that we use to link ideas; they're typically used to bridge "big" ideas in a speech, such as a link between introduction and body, between main points, or between body and conclusion. A transition usually signals that one idea is done and the speech is moving to something new. Examples of transitions are phrases such as, "As I move to the next point . . ." or, "The final idea I want to make is . . ." Even "in summary" is a transition.

Signposts alert the audience to something important about to come; think of them as pointing a spotlight on an idea. "What you should remember is . . ." and, "The only thing that you should know is . . ." are signposts. So are numbers (*"the first cause* of obesity is . . ." They warn the audience of the importance of the next remarks.

Previews do just that: They give the audience a prompt or advanced warning that movement is about to occur, but they do it in a bit more detail than signposts or transitions. They can serve the same function as your initial summary did in the introduction, except on a much smaller scale. An example would be, "In order to understand the problems of the dangers of parasailing, we need to know first about equipment and then about the process."

Finally, an **internal summary** reviews what has just happened; it is the opposite of your internal preview. It reminds the audience of what they just heard in a preceding point, and it allows the audience to understand how new information connects to previous information. By saying, "Now that I've covered the equipment used in parasailing . . ." you have reminded the audience what they should have heard.

These connectives are very subtle, and what's important is the movement that they'll supply to your message. They're the last part of sequencing that should be considered as you work on your speech. When you use connectives well, you can bridge gaps between and among ideas, adding to the unity of your message.

The decision strategy of sequencing allows you to arrange your ideas and evidence for the audience so that they have a better chance of grasping and sharing your meaning. How you structure ideas should be based on the needs of the situation and audience. The most basic step in developing sequencing is to think of the three basic elements of organization: introduction, body, and conclusion. Each of these elements has specific functions, but each allows you to use your own creativity in adapting your structure to your audience and purpose. You strategically choose among organizational patterns so you can achieve your intended result. Then you add in your supporting materials to flesh out those ideas. Connectives are considered last, because they function to join ideas; they tie the main points into one cohesive whole.

SUMMARY

You've learned throughout life how important organization is in all sorts of ways. You may have been taught how to arrange your books and toys when you were young, or you quickly found that they were lost. Your middle or high school locker could easily become a black hole if you didn't impose some structure on what folders went where. How often do you lose your keys or cellphone? When you finally find them, don't you promise yourself that you'll put them in a place you can always find them? Why do you take notes? Can't you just listen to what your teacher tells you, without having to write

Established Rules for Outlining

Speeches are typically written as outlines, not essays. An outline not only helps to organize ideas, it also makes moving information easier. The outlining process begins with the planning outline, then progresses to a formal outline (the outline you turn in to your instructor), and ends with the development of a key word outline (a.k.a. a speaking outline).

With a well-developed planning outline, a speaker can easily visualize, in order, the ideas to be discussed. This makes it easier for the speaker to ensure the ideas are adequately clear and supported.

Here are some basic principles of outlining:

- *Follow consistent patterns of symbolization for main and supporting points.* For example, main points could be numbered with Roman numerals, while supporting points are capital letters.

- *Indent supporting points to indicate that they are related to the main point.* In our example, points A and B are subpoints of point I.

- *Use full sentences to articulate the information you plan to present.* The goal is to create a clear, succinct planning outline that does not leave the wording of important points to chance.

- *Make sure the organization of the points is logical.* Choose an appropriate pattern of order, based on the purpose and audience.

- *Construct a speaking outline that is a condensed version of the formal outline.* This will keep you from reading the outline when making the speech.

Figures 13.1 and 13.2 show how a formal outline and speaking outline should look.

Formal Outline:

I. The American Red Cross provides disaster relief services.
   A. The Red Cross supports families displaced by fires.
   B. The Red Cross supports communities hit by natural disasters.
II. The American Red Cross offers health services.
   A. The Red Cross provides baby sitter training.
   B. The Red Cross provides CPR and first aid training.
III. The American Red Cross offers military services.
   A. Red Cross offers veterans financial and support counseling.
   B. The Red Cross helps families connect with military personnel abroad.

Figure 13.1
Formal Outline

Key Word Outline:

I. The ARC provides disaster relief
   A. families displaced by fires
   B. communities hit by natural disasters

(Delivery Directions: Pause Here)

II. The ARC offers health services
   A. Baby sitter training
   B. CPR and first aid training

(Delivery Directions: Pause and Show Visual Aid #1 here)

III. The ARC offers military services
   A. financial and support counseling for veterans
   B. helps families connect with military personnel abroad

(Delivery Directions: Don't rush through the conclusion!)

Figure 13.2
Key Word Outline

ideas down? Are you that person who just can't go grocery shopping or pack for a trip without a list? All of these questions reveal the nature of organization: It compels you to configure stimuli into a meaningful structure that will help you to understand and to remember.

Effective message organization begins with careful consideration of your audience, situation, topic, and purpose. Whether your purpose is to inform or to persuade, you can utilize the same decision-making strategies of selection and sequence to construct your speech. The introduction, body, and conclusion each serve important purposes. The introduction attracts attention, develops audience focus on the topic and the speaker, and provides a preview of main points to come. The body presents the main ideas that meet your specific purpose, supported by a variety of evidence that interests the audience and increases shared meaning. The conclusion reminds the audience of the main points and challenges them to act on what they've heard.

A well-planned speech, like a structured office or a well-thought-out trip, allows you to complete your goals, avoid backtracking, and remain audience-centered in presenting your message.

ENDNOTES

1. http://www2.oprah.com/tows/pastshows/200601/tows_after_20060126.jhtml (Oprah after the show). (accessed April 1, 2008).

2. "Powell calls pre-Iraq U.N. speech a 'blot' on his record," http://www.usatoday.com/news/washington/2005-09-08-powell-iraq_x.htm (accessed November 23, 2007).

3. Wheeler, E. *Tested public speaking*, 2nd ed. (New York: Prentice Hall, 1949), p. 35.

4. "Shocking Statistics: Beauty of a Woman," http://www.colorado.edu/studentgroups/wellness/NewSite/BdyImgShockingStats.html (accessed November 23, 2007).

5. "U.S. tourists kill mugger, Costa Rica says," *Los Angeles Times* (February 23, 2007), A10.

How Do I Deliver a Message?

LEARNING OBJECTIVES

After reading this chapter, you should understand the following concepts:

- Effective delivery involves both verbal and nonverbal message management, tailored for the intended audience and content.
- Speeches can be scripted, memorized, impromptu, or extemporaneous, depending on their purpose.
- Effective verbal delivery involves using volume, rate, pitch, pause, articulation, pronunciation, and dialects to engage the audience.
- Effective physical delivery involves proper use of eye contact, facial expression, gestures, movement, and attire.
- Presentational aids add dimension to your delivery and help communicate your message.

INTRODUCTION

What comes to mind when you read the following passages? After you've read them, try listening to them online. Does what you get from the message change?

> Nineteen years ago, almost to the day, we lost three astronauts in a terrible accident on the ground. But we've never lost an astronaut in flight. We've never had a tragedy like this. And perhaps we've forgotten the courage it took for the crew of the shuttle. But they, the *Challenger* Seven, were aware of the dangers, but overcame them and did their jobs brilliantly.

—Ronald Reagan: The Space Shuttle "Challenger" Tragedy Address
http://americanrhetoric.com/speeches/ronaldreaganchallenger.htm

> What we need in the United States is not division; what we need in the United States is not hatred; what we need in the United States is not violence and lawlessness, but is love, and wisdom, and compassion toward one another, and a feeling of justice toward those who still suffer within our country, whether they be white or whether they be black.

—Robert F. Kennedy: Remarks on the Assassination of Martin Luther King, Jr.
http://americanrhetoric.com/speeches/rfkonmlkdeath.html

KEYWORDS

effective delivery
impromptu
SPREE method
PPF method
apples/oranges method
simple 6 method
extemporaneous (extemp) speech
volume
rate
pitch
pauses
articulation
pronunciation
dialects
eye contact
facial expression
gestures
movement
presentational aids
three-dimensional presentation aids
two-dimensional presentation aids
multimedia presentations
three T method

I—I feel it an honor to be here to come and say a final goodbye. I grew up in the South, and Rosa Parks was a hero to me long before I recognized and understood the power and impact that her life embodied. I remember my father telling me about this colored woman who had refused to give up her seat. And in my child's mind, I thought, "She must be really big." I thought she must be at least a hundred feet tall. I imagined her being stalwart and strong and carrying a shield to hold back the white folks. And then I grew up and had the esteemed honor of meeting her. And wasn't that a surprise. Here was this petite, almost delicate lady who was the personification of grace and goodness. And I thanked her then. I said, "Thank you," for myself and for every colored girl, every colored boy, who didn't have heroes who were celebrated. I thanked her then.

—Oprah Winfrey: Eulogy for Rosa Parks
http://americanrhetoric.com/speeches/oprahwinfreyonrosaparks.htm

These words offer you a glimpse into important moments in American history. What would happen if you were to read those words aloud, standing in front of your friends or class? Would you get the same response, be able to do it in the same way? Of course not! You don't have the same delivery style as any of these speakers; their tone, their pauses, their voice, and even their movements are unique to them. In the same way, you can develop your own delivery style that can effectively add dimension and depth to the message you develop.

Effective delivery usually is the result of a conversational style that blends energy, naturalness, and straightforwardness. Some occasions call for a more formal, manuscript-delivered presentation, but most of us will deliver messages that are more informal. That doesn't mean that you don't have to do a run through or two; in fact, good delivery is the result of preparation, training, and practice. **Effective delivery** *involves both verbal and nonverbal message management, tailored for the intended audience and context.* In this chapter, you'll be exposed to strategies for effective verbal and nonverbal delivery and the use of presentational aids to reinforce your message. You'll also learn a bit about the natural effects of communication apprehension on delivery. Just keep in mind that if you're successful, your delivery won't call attention to itself; the message will still be the most important thing the audience takes away.

Develop your own style to effectively add dimension and depth to your message.
© Jaimie Duplass, 2008, Shutterstock.

WHAT METHOD OF DELIVERY IS MOST APPROPRIATE?

You have four different choices to make for your overall delivery plan: all involve a decision about the extent to which the written word will play in your speech.

Scripted

Some speakers like to deliver prepared remarks from a manuscript. This is especially true when exact language is crucial, such as in diplomacy issues or for a commencement address before a large audience. It is common for heads of state to speak from a manuscript in order to ensure accuracy in their messages. In these cases, word-for-word delivery is essential. Time limits may also play a role in the use of a manuscript; a candidate who purchases a one-minute spot needs to nail down that time. However, most of us do not find ourselves in these unique situations.

Using a manuscript might seem like an easy way to present your speech, but it can also have drawbacks. Crafting a manuscript takes an inordinate amount of time; you find yourself concentrating on word choice and sentence development in a way that you wouldn't do in other forms of delivery. Written and spoken language are essentially different; the way you write in long sentences with complex structures doesn't work well in the spoken form, where brief phrases and even incomplete sentences are more natural. Speaking from a script limits the speaker to only those comments prepared in advance. You don't have the chance to stray from the prepared remarks, and if an audience member seems confused, you can't elaborate. It is common for new speakers to make the mistake of just reading from a manuscript, leading to a drop in eye contact and vocal variety. If you do look up from the manuscript, it's easy to lose your place. A manuscript requires you to make the words "come alive" through vibrant vocal delivery, and that requires skill. It's very easy to find yourself reading *at* the audience through a manuscript, rather than talking *with* them.

What should you expect if you feel a scripted speech is appropriate for your occasion? Be sure to practice out loud so that you don't falter over words. Pacing must be timed perfectly; you don't want to pause in the wrong place, and you don't want to rush through the speech. Consider vocal tone: how can you emphasize words so that they sound conversational rather than scripted? Create a manuscript that is easy to read in larger print so that you can still develop and maintain eye contact; you want to be able to move off the script to look at the audience, even though you are tied to the words. Roger Ailes, a political media consultant, suggests that if a manuscript is called for, you should type your words in short, easy-to-scan phrases on the top two thirds of the notes so you don't have to look too far down.[1] A manuscript doesn't have to mean boring the audience with a monotonous tone, lack of eye contact, and stilted pacing; it does mean, though, that you'll have to work hard to overcome those pitfalls.

Memorized

At some point, we have all probably been expected to memorize a speech or poem. Perhaps it was the preamble to the Constitution or the Declaration of Independence; maybe it was a poem or a prayer. You may have wondered why you needed this skill; after all, there is little call for long, memorized, complex speeches, and the effort you put into memorizing was painful. It's safe to say that while you might admire someone who can spout off long speeches from memory, it's probably not something you'd want to do yourself. However, the ability to memorize short passages still has its place in presentations. Memorization is a useful strategy to use for short speeches such as toasts, introductory remarks, or award acceptances. Even small portions of a speech where specific wording or language is important can utilize memorization. You just need to practice over and over, making sure to work on vocal variety as you do the words from rote memory.

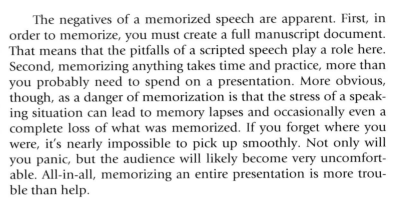

The negatives of a memorized speech are apparent. First, in order to memorize, you must create a full manuscript document. That means that the pitfalls of a scripted speech play a role here. Second, memorizing anything takes time and practice, more than you probably need to spend on a presentation. More obvious, though, as a danger of memorization is that the stress of a speaking situation can lead to memory lapses and occasionally even a complete loss of what was memorized. If you forget where you were, it's nearly impossible to pick up smoothly. Not only will you panic, but the audience will likely become very uncomfortable. All-in-all, memorizing an entire presentation is more trouble than help.

Memorization is effective for short speeches, such as accepting an award.
© 2008, JupiterImages.

Impromptu

What would you do if a television reporter cornered you to get a response about an incident that just happened, an issue that's in the public eye, or a comment about the weather? If you're able to give a competent immediate response, you could be on the evening news! Even if that scenario doesn't hold much appeal, your ability to think and speak on your feet is essential in life. Meetings, interviews, unexpected reports, instructing or supervising others, and participating in general conversation all require the ability to organize thoughts quickly and delivery them effectively.

Speaking **impromptu** means talking about a topic with little or no preparation. Mark Twain said, "It usually takes me more than three weeks to prepare a good impromptu speech,"[2] and he was probably correct. Most of the time when we speak "off the cuff" or say a "few words," we do so in situations where we've given thought to the issue we're about to speak on. So, you might find yourself doing an impromptu speech at a community meeting when your opinion is sought, when your boss asks you to report on some incident, or when you're at a social function and a toast is called for.

A spur-of-the-moment or impromptu speech doesn't carry the same expectations of perfection as might a scripted or memorized speech. An audience usually is more forgiving in an impromptu speech because they understand you haven't had hours or days to prepare. However, that doesn't mean that you need to go into an impromptu situation stone cold. If you're in a meeting or listening to a presentation, take notes of the major points; this activity will likely cause you to consider your own opinion. If time allows you to do so, jot a few notes or outline of the points you want to make in case you're asked to respond.

Let's imagine that you've been asked for impromptu remarks of a minute or two. You need to be spontaneous and demonstrate your quick wit. What quick strategies can you call on?

If you do nothing else, make a note of how you want to open and conclude your remarks; remember, the first thing and the last thing the audience hears may be that which sticks with them. Make sure you understand what you've been asked to remark on, and make sure you answer it. Then structure the body of the message with two or four points, using some simple strategies:

An audience understands that an impromptu speech has not been carefully prepared.
© Yuri Arcurs, 2008, Shutterstock.

- The **SPREE method** offers four points: State your Position, provide your Reason(s), Explain by experience or example, End with summary.

- The **PPF method** utilizes Past, Present, and Future as the main points. You can say something like this: We used to do this . . . but now we find ourselves doing this . . . and in the future we'll need to do this . . .
- The **apples/oranges method** begins by acknowledging that "there are two sides to this argument . . ." and then state the positions: One position says this, the other says that. End by giving your position on the issue.
- The **simple 6 method** uses the common questions of who, what, when, why, where, and how as the main points. Don't try for all of them, but use them to structure ideas and to jog your memory.

When delivering an impromptu speech, there are a few pitfalls to avoid. Don't apologize for a lack of preparation. If it's truly an impromptu occasion, give the best effort you can on short notice. When you offer an excuse, you damage your credibility. Focus your delivery on strong eye contact and vocal variety; you can't do much more. Don't ramble; stick to those main points, give some support, and make it short and sweet. You don't want to be accused of talking without saying anything.

To really speak effectively, you'd like to be able to prepare in advance. Even if you don't have that opportunity, you can still provide your audience with a clearly organized, brief message that makes a point. After all, you do impromptus all the time—you have ample chances to experiment with developing an effective strategy for their presentation.

Extemporaneous

You might hear people confuse impromptu and extemporaneous methods; often, people think they're one and the same. However, an **extemporaneous (or extemp) speech** is one that is carefully planned and practiced, that works from an outline or series of notes yet leaves room for message adjustment, and that maintains a conversational style.

The key to extemp is that outline of ideas. From it, you can adapt the words to the audience as they listen. The advantages of an extemp speech arise from the best of the other three methods. You can write out key ideas, as in a scripted speech. You can commit some lines (key data, phrases, quotations) to memory so word choice is exact. You can remain spontaneous and adapt to the audience and the occasion as you speak, just like in an impromptu. In addition, the extemp speech encourages you to use a conversational style, one that sounds spontaneous even though it's been well thought out and practiced.

How do you prepare an extemporaneous speech? Create an outline of main ideas and say it out loud. As you do, consider the amount and kind of supporting points you're developing, along with the purpose and time of your speech. Then think, am I saying too much or too little? Do my ideas coherently flow? Do I know the supports well enough to be able to present them in an interesting yet clear fashion? How are my introduction and conclusion? Next, revise that outline into a speaking outline, keeping the amount of written material minimal. Practice the speech all the way through, using only the outline. You may forget a few supports the first couple of times, but that's OK—keep going! Your goal is to keep yourself focused on the ideas of the speech, not the perfection of the words or the delivery. If you plan to use presentational aids, bring them into practice. After several run-throughs, you'll find that you are able to get through the ideas and their supports pretty

A combination of styles may work best to present your message.
© ORKO, 2008, Shutterstock.

well by thinking, not by checking your notes, and then it's time to work on delivery. Watch for eye contact by recruiting an audience of family or friends, or even watch yourself in a mirror. Record the speech if possible; listening to yourself (or watching on video) can point out distracting mannerisms. The key is that you must practice more than once; a single practice is a recipe for catastrophe. By giving yourself time to think the speech through, you'll find your confidence growing.

Although each of these speaking styles is described separately, in reality, a combination of styles might be used in any given public speech or other communication situation such as an interview or meeting. You might consider memorizing a portion of the opening so that you can engage your audience without notes or other distractions. This lets you make strong eye contact with audience members and truly hook them into the speech. The body of a speech might involve the use of brief notes in an extemporaneous style. A question and answer session after a presentation resembles impromptu speaking, requiring a person to respond "in the moment." In meetings, you're called upon to offer your opinion on a plan: that's the place for an impromptu. Interviews are extemporaneous in the sense that you can plan and rehearse answers to questions, but you don't exactly know the directions those questions will take.

Remember: No one is born a great speaker. Effective public speaking takes practice, regular practice. The great thing about presenting a message is that, like riding a bike, when you can do it well, you can always do it well if you follow the same pattern of preparation, practice, and presentation.

WHAT STRATEGIES MAKE UP EFFECTIVE DELIVERY?

Do you want a surefire way to bore your audience to tears? To ensure audience members lose interest and drift away, stand in one place, never look up from your notes, use gestures minimally, and speak rapidly in a low-pitched, monotonous voice. Assuming that boring people isn't your goal, if you want to help the audience attend to, hear, and understand your message, you need to consider how to incorporate nonverbal delivery strategies.

Effective nonverbal delivery is critical in the success of any communication effort. This is true for any communication situation, whether it's interpersonal or small group, public or mediated. Effective delivery is a combination of verbal and nonverbal tactics, so factors such as eye contact, posture, vocal quality, and facial expression will play a major role in the audience's ability to listen and to follow your ideas. Even the presentational aids that supplement your words and nonverbal presence are aspects of effective delivery. Earlier in this chapter, you were told that a conversational style of delivery is the most desired, but you're probably thinking about more specifics, such as, "What do I do if I can't breathe?" or "What happens if my hands are shaking?" or "Is it OK to move around a little?" In order to impact the audience in a positive way and to answer those questions, let's consider some of the elements of effective vocal and physical delivery.

HOW DO I SPEAK TO CREATE UNDERSTANDING?

Have you ever met someone in person that you've spoken to on the phone many times? Was the image that you initially had skewed from his actual looks? Did you think he was older or younger than in reality? Was he taller or shorter? Did he dress as you thought he did? Were you shocked to learn that he was a she? Based on vocal cues, we do predict people's age, occupation, status, ethnicity, appearance, and a host of other things. Effective vocal delivery involves volume, rate, pitch, pauses, and the trio of articulation, pronunciation, and dialects, each of which can play a very important part in creating images and impressions. It's important that you present your ideas by using vocal delivery that enhances understanding and interest.

Volume

Volume means projecting your voice loudly enough so that it can be clearly heard by those in your audience. Just how loudly you must speak depends on the room size, the audience size, and the amount and type of background noise. It's likely that your voice sounds louder to you than to your audience, but by watching your audience and adjusting to their feedback (leaning forward, looking puzzled, wincing), you can adjust the volume of your voice so that everyone in the audience can hear. If you have a soft voice, you don't want to cause your audience to strain to listen. They might decide it's not worth their effort. A quiet voice might require the use of electronic amplification, but realize that if you use a microphone awkwardly, the audience could interpret this as ineptness on your part. Your volume can also be manipulated for effect. Sometimes raising or lowering the volume can communicate importance or draw in the audience and emphasize a point. The key is to be aware of your volume and to adapt it according to your audience and setting.

How can you use the volume of your voice for effect in your speech?
© 2008, JupiterImages.

Rate

Rate is the speed at which you speak. The normal rate of adult speech has been estimated to be between 120 and 150 words per minute. What matters is not how many words a speaker can get out, but how many (well-chosen) words are understood by the listener. People talk so fast because others around them do this, because they think erroneously that others will not take the time to listen to them, and because they do not realize the listeners are struggling. Speaking quickly doesn't mean you're unintelligible, however, and you can consider how using rate as a delivery strategy can enhance understanding.

Changing the speed of delivery to coordinate with different elements of your speech is one way to maintain audience interest. Varying your rate can improve the audience's ability to attend to your speech. You might start with a fast-paced, attention-getting story and then slow down as you reveal the topic and preview your main points. However, a study in 2000 found that speaking too quickly causes the audience to perceive you as tentative about your control of the situation.[3] A monotone rate, one that does *not* change, will lead your audience members to lose interest and make it more difficult for them to listen and learn from your message.

Pitch

Singing involves the alteration of the voice to produce the melody. That modulation of your voice is something you can also employ in effective delivery through awareness of pitch.

Pitch is your voice's intonation; how high or low in range your voice sounds to another. Your typical pitch is the range that you use when you're conversing normally, and in natural conversation, vocal pitch rises and falls and often helps listeners to understand a message. Your pitch may give others a perception of your mood and can show your enthusiasm for the topic or audience. Normally, women's voices are pitched higher than men's because women's vocal cords are shorter. However, individuals of each sex may display wide variations due to difference in physical structure. But keep in mind that no matter what nature supplies you for pitch, you still can manipulate it for strong effect.

 In some cultures, inflection plays a major role in changing the meaning of words. Many of the languages of Southeast Asia and Africa are tone languages, meaning that they use pitch to signal a difference in meaning between words. In some of these languages, word meanings or grammar elements like tense depend on pitch level. Words can take on totally different meanings depending on their tones. In Mandarin Chinese, for example, the word *ma* means "mother" when spoken in the first tone, "hemp" when spoken in the second tone, "horse" in the third and a reproach in the fourth.[4]

Typically, our pitch in the United States goes higher when we ask a question and drops when we make a declaration of fact. Try the following activity. Say the following sentences, adding emphasis by raising your pitch on the italicized word each time.

This is a great class.

This *is* a great class.

This is a *great* class.

Now try it with a question mark at the end:

This is a great *class?*

Notice how the meaning shifts, depending on the emphasis of the words.

You can use this stress or inflection when you want to highlight a point, but don't overdo it. You might want to record a conversation with friends or family members and listen to changes in pitch to see what meanings you're suggesting. However, while it can assist you by underlining enthusiasm or importance, pitch change isn't a strategy you want to overdo.

Pauses

Pauses add emphasis and impact to your speech by stopping your message briefly. Where and how you pause in your speech can have a dramatic effect on meaning. Pauses can be used to stress a point, to gain attention, to create a transitional effect, and to allow you time to think and catch up. They often are necessary for your listener just to think about what you've just said. Read the following line: "Woman without her man is nothing." Now think about possible ways to interpret those words. Through strategic pausing, the message meaning could be very different. Read it two more times, pausing at the commas:

Woman without her man, is nothing.

Woman, without her, man is nothing.

How you decide to deliver that line, including pauses, is critical to the message you communicate. Listeners do not "see" the commas in your speech; they must "hear" them through your strategic use of pauses in delivery

Vocalized pauses such as "um," "like," "you know," "stuff like that," or "Uhhhhh" detract from your speech. These involuntary fillers or bridge sounds are understandable in their way, because they are unintentionally included by speakers in order to maintain control. You are uncomfortable with silence, so you fill it up with sounds. These do not function in the same way that intentional pauses do. In fact, they detract from meaning, rather than enhancing it. To avoid vocalized pauses, try this easy test: Call yourself and leave at least a one-minute message about an upcoming assignment. Then listen to your voice mail and count the number of vocalized paused in your message. Give it a try. How many vocal pauses do you count? How do they impact your message? Are you surprised by the frequency of your vocalized pauses? The bottom line is, most of us find vocalized pauses to be annoying; you can eliminate them by paying attention.

Vocalized pauses will detract from your meaning, not enhance it.
© 2008, JupiterImages.

Articulation, Pronunciation, and Dialects

Articulation is the physical production of a sound clearly and distinctly. **Pronunciation** is saying a word in an accepted standard of correctness and sound. While the two are interdependent, they are not the same. You can articulate a word clearly but still mispronounce it; for instance, if you say the "s" in the word *Illinois*, you're articulating the sounds but pronouncing it wrong! An example of misarticulation comes from Ohio, where students sometimes say *fur* when they mean "for" and *doin'* instead of "doing." Because some words sound similar, they require the speaker's careful articulation to avoid audience confusion. Consider, for example, the difference between *persecution* and *prosecution,* or the difference between *asking* someone and *axing* someone. It's not uncommon to mispronounce words, because you may not know how to say it correctly. Alphadictionary.com offers a list of the 100 most mispronounced words in English, which includes *athlete* (some people say "ath-a-lete"), *card shark* (the correct words are "card sharp"), *escape* ("excape"), and *herb* (" 'erb").[5]

Articulation and pronunciation are further confounded by **dialects,** which are regional or ethnic speech patterns that have variations in grammar, accent, or even vocabulary. The United States has four major regional dialects: eastern, New England, southern, and general American. There are also many ethnic dialects, including African-American English, Hispanic English, Cajun English, and Haitian English.[6] Your dialect has been shaped by your background, and it has meaning for those who share it. However, if you're speaking to an audience who doesn't share your dialect, you would want to avoid regionalisms that point out your differences. We're all familiar with those: Do you drink pop or soda? What goes on ice cream: jimmies or sprinkles? When grocery shopping, do you use a buggy or a cart? When washing your car, do you attach your outside hose to the spigot or the faucet? What you should keep in mind is that a distracting dialect may cause listeners to make negative judgments about your personality or competence.[7] This can be an important consideration if you're a nonnative English speaker, because

---

Take a Closer Look

What strategies can you use to impact dialect, articulation, and pronunciation?

- Watch your audience's expressions to see if they seem to understand or if they look confused.
- Define your terms.
- Make sure you pronounce names or technical terms correctly.
- Slow down so you can articulate more clearly.
- Avoid regional words that may not mean the same thing elsewhere, or use both terms (yours and the local one) to show that they're synonyms.

All of these can aid you in avoiding confusing your audience with the way you say ideas!

---

your dialect, along with articulation and pronunciation, may be an additional barrier.

Your vocal delivery is unique; no one sounds exactly like you (which is why the FBI uses voiceprints in its investigative work). You have the ability to impact the audience by strategically using aspects of vocal delivery that you can control.

Your delivery can create emotional connections with your audience.
© 2008, JupiterImages.

HOW DOES MY PHYSICAL DELIVERY AFFECT UNDERSTANDING?

In Chapter 4 you learned about nonverbal communication, the messages you deliver with appearance, movement, posture, eye contact, facial expression, and use of space and objects. Your nonverbal messages can assist audience members in interpreting the verbal message, or they can distract from that understanding. You know the phrase, "Actions speak louder than words." When you consider physical delivery, keep that in mind: An audience expects that good communicators will present their ideas clearly and in an interesting fashion. Your delivery can create (or destroy) emotional connections with your audience. If your nonverbal delivery contradicts what you're saying, the audience will more likely believe the nonverbal rather than the verbal. Think about shaking your head no side-to-side while saying in a flat voice, "I really had a good time tonight." What message will really be believed—the words or the nonverbal one?

How you present yourself nonverbally is vital to your success as speakers. Effective physical delivery allows a speaker to develop immediacy with an audience and involves eye contact, facial expression, gestures, movement, and attire.

Eye Contact

Eye contact is the direct visual contact made with another person. Ralph Waldo Emerson said, "One of the most wonderful things in nature is a glance of the eye; it transcends speech; it is the bodily symbol of identity."[8] The significance of eye contact tells us about meaning in various cultures. Some cultures feel that strong eye contact demonstrates interest and respect in the other person. Conversely, other cultures hold that (especially when you are young) you should not look at others in the eye when speaking, or you'll show disrespect. Some Latin American and Asian cultures show respect by avoiding the glance of authority figures. In the United States, we value meeting another's eyes, because it is seen as demonstrating honesty. People in Brazil engage in intensive eye contact; here, we'd consider it staring.[9]

But since you're in an American classroom, let's consider why eye contact is seen in the United States as important for at least two reasons.[10] First, it creates a strong connection between listener and speaker. Audience members who feel more connected likely will listen more closely. Second, the speaker is able to gather feedback from audience members if eye contact is frequent and effective. Generally speaking, the longer the eye contact between two people, the greater the intimacy is developed.[11]

What strategies can you employ to meet your audience's gaze comfortably? Try looking briefly from one person to the next (you can even think about a "pattern" of gaze, from one corner to another, one row to an adjacent one). This scanning can let you acknowledge individuals without ignoring others. If you are sitting around a table, make sure you share eye contact with everyone in the group. Look for friendly people; conversely, if you're in the audience, smile at the speaker, for encouraging that person can create a pleasant interaction. If you see audience members looking at you with interest, leaning forward and seeming eager for more, you can assume that you are connecting with your audience. If, on the other hand, you see people nodding off or staring at your overhead with confused expressions, these are good indications that a problem should be corrected. By watching the feedback offered by your audience through eye contact, you can make corrections and improve your speech in the moment. Consider the type and amount of notes you use. Generally, the guideline would be to speak from an outline or a key word page, but if you feel you must use more, then make sure your notes are clear, large, and numbered in case you drop them. Effective eye contact tells the audience that you have confidence in yourself and care about their ability to understand your message.

Facial Expression

Another way that you can display concern for the audience and passion for the subject is through your face. Research tells us that your face plays an essential role in expressing your thoughts, emotions, and attitudes.[12] Through your face, you have the initial opportunity to set the speech tone, even before you open your mouth. Think about it: when you don't like some kind of food, you probably make a face. That expression tells others how you feel about that morsel! The movements of your eyes, eyebrows, mouth, and facial muscles can build a connection with your audience.

Just like eye contact, your culture may dictate the kind and amount of **facial expression** you will display. For example, Koreans, Japanese, and Chinese do not usually show outward emotion through their faces, and in fact, may have learned to mask their emotions. Some Native American groups use far less facial animation than do other North Americans. Research also suggests that

Speakers must be alert to the cultural norms of the audience.
© 2008, JupiterImages.

men and women use different facial displays.[13] In other cultures, people expect great animation when they speak, and they expect others to be similarly expressive. As a speaker, you need to be alert to the cultural norms of your audience.

Unfortunately, under the pressure of delivering a group presentation, many people solidify their expression into a grim, stone face, grimacing instead of smiling. Try to soften your face right from the start: when you greet the audience, smile! This is how you'd start a conversation with another, because you'd want to begin by establishing a warm, positive relationship. The same intent probably holds true for a speech. A relaxed smile to start your speech will help create a connection with the audience, perhaps even develop a closeness with them. You probably won't want to smile throughout the entire presentation, because your face should mirror your message. While figuring out how to "hold your face" isn't the most important delivery strategy you can employ, you need to make sure that your facial expressions are consistent with your words. Try taping yourself to discover your expressions just to make sure they're not contradicting your words.

Gestures

Those accustomed to a reserved style of greeting would expect the same of a speaker's gestures.
© 2008, JupiterImages.

Gestures include movement of your head, arms, and hands that you use to emphasize, to reinforce, or to illustrate ideas. You probably don't even notice your gestures when you're in a relaxed conversation, but when you are giving a speech or presenting an important message in a group, you may become very self-conscious. Not everyone is naturally expressive with their gestures; they may not use their hands, cock their head to the side, or even shrug their shoulders to express some feeling. Some speakers try to get rid of their hands by putting them in pockets; others fidget or play with things.[14] As with other delivery techniques, cultural influences impact gestures. For example, Arab and Italian cultures expect a great deal of animation; German and Japanese expect a reserved style.[15] You can see this in how we greet others: Do we shake hands? Do we bow? Do we place our hands crossed on our chest?

Gestures can be used to reinforce your message, such as holding up fingers to reinforce the spoken words *first, second,* and *third.* Gestures can also be used to add emphasis to words; pounding one's fist on the podium demonstrates conviction or emotion.

If you're not sure what to do with your hands, then think about where you will place them during the speech: Are you going to be playing with notes? Giving a podium a death grip? Playing with keys in your pocket? When you stand, do you naturally do it with your arms crossed in front of you? What message does that send? Honestly, gestures will probably take on the form of your normal conversational style, and it really doesn't matter so much if you use many gestures or not. What does matter is *how* you use those gestures. They should support your message, not detract from it.

Movement

Movement involves the positioning of your entire body as you speak. By moving closer to the audience, a speaker removes the physical and psychological barriers that distance him or her from the audience. What does a podium, lectern, or table do to that space? Does it impact the trust that the audience might be feeling? The more willing you are to move toward the audience, the more attentive the audience becomes and the more similarity they feel with you.

You have probably experienced this with a professor who greets you as you enter, calls students by name, makes frequent eye contact with students, and moves among them throughout the class session. Contrast this to the classroom with a teacher who remains tied to notes behind the podium, paces nervously at the front of the room, and flashes up slide after slide with little or no attempt to the audience. Which would you prefer? What message are you taking from each of these instructors?

Posture also is an aspect of movement; slouching probably signals a lack of enthusiasm on your part. Sitting down while giving a formal presentation probably doesn't work, either, because it's too informal; this is unlike giving a short impromptu to a small group seated around a table, where standing would seem presumptuous. Purposeful movement not only creates a connection, but it can signal changes in the speech. You can change position or location by moving a step or two; that not only shows confidence, but it demonstrates that something "new" has happened in your message.

Purposeful movement creates a connection and can signal changes in the speech.
© 2008, JupiterImages.

Consider how you will approach and leave the front of the audience; how will you establish yourself, how will you end? By approaching in a confident fashion, your audience will perceive you as someone to listen to. If you start "packing up" and shuffling notes before your message is finished, your message may be lost and your credibility damaged. Developing speakers should "fake it until they make it," meaning that even if you do not feel confident, you should try to appear confident. By standing tall, looking at your audience, and moving with purpose, you are able to convey a sense of confidence that positively impacts how your audience views.

Distracting movement is aimless. If you move around the room constantly, you may be creating a burden on your audience: they have to follow you and try to maintain eye contact. You'll likely end up with people tuning out; no one enjoys watching someone else pace. Shifting back and forth on your feet suggests nervousness. If you move so that you're blocking the screen you're using, or if you find yourself placing your back to the audience so you can look at something behind you, you're signaling a disinterest in the audience. How can you perceive their feedback, how can they hear you, and what happens to your eye contact?

How can you develop purposeful movement? Again, taping yourself doing a speech is a good way to see how others perceive you. But you can also watch others (professors, peers, public figures) to see how they move; these models might provide you some positive ideas on what to do, as well as pointing out negatives to avoid.

Attire

Your personal appearance makes that first impression. An unkempt, untidy speaker suggests that the message that is about to come will also be lacking in polish or disorderly. If you fiddle with your hair or glasses, wear a hat that shades your eyes, play with jewelry, or wear something distracting (clothes, hair, makeup), your audience will be sidetracked by that rather than being focused on the message. Students often ask if they have to get dressed up when they give their speech. The answer is, of course, that it depends on what

Your appearance should help you feel confident and comfortable.
© Yuri Arcurs, 2008, Shutterstock.

impression you wish to make on your audience. Think about what nonverbal messages your attire or appearance makes as you speak. Does your appearance reinforce or contradict your message? If you're trying to enhance your credibility on a topic, is it appropriate to wear something that indicates your identification with that issue (uniform, school tie, name badge, etc.) Typically in most situations, you'd dress a bit more formally than your audience, but you should be comfortable in what you wear. Your appearance should help you to feel confident, and it should boost your credibility with the audience.

Vocal and physical delivery surrounds your message; they help the audience to form initial impressions about the kind of person you are. The way you sound and the way you look can suggest confidence and concern or incompetence and unreliability. Your speech's impact is strongly impacted by how you deliver it. Having something important to say should take precedence, but saying it poorly will impact the audience's acceptance of your ideas. Good delivery presents your message in an interesting, clear way. One other group of strategies that can supplement your vocal and physical delivery involves the use of presentational aids. Let's examine how they can complement your message delivery.

HOW CAN PRESENTATIONAL AIDS AFFECT DELIVERY?

TV Guide selected NBC's Tim Russert's use of the dry erase whiteboard (November 7, 2000) on which Russert predicted "Florida, Florida, Florida" would be the pivotal state in the 2000 presidential election results, as number 68 of the "100 Most Memorable TV Moments" in history.[16] When Russert turned to a Tablet PC for election 2004, bloggers took note.[17] Why is the aid that the commentator used notable? Because Russert's use of presentational media demonstrated the advantages of this supplemental delivery strategy.

Presentational aids are any items developed for reinforcing a message. These include objects, models, charts, drawings, graphs, videos, and photographs. The importance of visual representations is reflected in common sayings across many cultures. A Saudi Arabian proverb says, "Believe what you see and lay aside what you hear." The Chinese are familiar with, "I hear and I forget, I see and I remember." In Nigeria, they say, "Seeing is better than hearing." Traditional American sayings are, "Seeing is Believing" and, "A picture is worth a thousand words." So what exactly are the advantages of presentational aids?

Advantages to the Speaker and Audience

Presentational aids add a dimension to your delivery. First, they help us to communicate clearly. If you are discussing an object, you can show it or a representation. If you're citing statistical trends, you can picture them. If you're explaining a technique, you can demonstrate it. All of these examples show that you can make your information more vivid to the audience by adding a visual element to your message. Hands-on instruction, math manipulatives, graphing, and recording data make learning easier for the visual and tactile learners, according to education researchers.[18] You may have been the recipient of such instruction, because you learned math more easily when you could see the number in a different way. The audience can see a sequence of events or process, so an actual demonstration or a series of visuals will reinforce how those procedures work.

Second, presentational aids can create and maintain interest and attention. Think of the difference between a newspaper, a textbook, and a web page. Which one springs to mind as having the most visual appeal? Where words might lack interest, a well-placed presentational aid can grab the audience's attention.

Third, presentational aids can help your audience to remember. Research tells us that in addition to aiding your audience's understanding, a well designed aid will reinforce ideas. Researchers estimate that you remember 10 percent of what you read, 20 percent of what you hear, 30 percent of what you see, and 50 percent of what you hear and see simultaneously.[19] Your memory might also be engaged by your presentational aids as they remind you of important aspects of your message.

Fourth (but not the most important reason to use them), some speakers feel that by using a presentational aid, the audience will focus on it rather than on them. You have to recall that an aid is only a supplement to you and your message; it won't speak for you, but it can be there to complement your ideas and your delivery.

Bob enjoyed these benefits of presentational aids when he chose to give a speech to his college classmates on how to hit a baseball. He included a baseball bat that allowed him to effectively demonstrate how to grip the bat, to hold it back off the shoulder, and to swing it properly. The bat also was comforting to him, as hitting a baseball was something he knew well. Although he was not menacing with the bat, it did give him a feeling of being in control and in power. For him, the presentational aid choice helped him communicate his message and feel more confident doing it.

> ## A Closer Look
>
> Review your presentational aids. Do they
>
> ❏ Help clarify understanding?
> ❏ Create interest?
> ❏ Enhance memory and retention?

Types of Presentational Aids

You have a wealth of aids to choose from; that selection depends on your purpose, your ability to create the aid, the context you'll be speaking in, and your ability to use the aid successfully. Let's put the types into three categories: three dimensional, two dimensional, and multimedia.

Three-dimensional Presentational Aid.

Three-dimensional presentational aids include people and other animate creatures, objects, and models. Ask yourself from the very start if there is another way that you could illustrate your point rather than employing something living, simply because there are pitfalls to their use that could be avoided fairly easily. Using *actual animate creatures* (people, pets, etc.) can be tricky. However, if you wanted to show how to style hair, demonstrate how certain tae-kwon-do moves work, or illustrate dance steps, then having a real person there might be fruitful.

Simple thought can make this easier on you and your model: Don't ask for spur-of-the-moment volunteers, don't bring that person up until needed, and make sure the person understands that she is simply a presentational aid, not your partner in delivering the message.

Animals require even more planning: You can't control their behavior most of the time in front of an audience, and it's easy for that creature to become the center of attention, even when it's not playing a role in the message at that moment. In addition, many creatures are difficult to see from all audience vantage points. Out of respect for you and your audience, think long and hard about using an animal as a presentational aid. You might think that it would be unique or more realistic to show the creature, but what if you have audience members who have fears or allergies, or what if the pet gets stressed out by the experience? Stories of "bad animal speeches" are legend in speech classes: the student who brought a live piranha in a zip-lock bag, which started to leak as the fish tried to attack the speaker's hand through the bag; the "how to bury your pet" speech, where the person brought in an actual dead rabbit he killed that morning; the speech about fear of snakes, accompanied by a burlap bag with two rather large boas in it, which, when shown, promptly sent the front row diving from their seats. Generally, it's better to consider other ways to illustrate or demonstrate your points, rather than using animate creatures, simply because the negatives likely outweigh any advantage you would get from them.

Objects can be either the actual item or a representation of it. Objects create interest because they're something the audience can see, hear, touch, and maybe even taste. We can respond to the real thing when we see it, because that tangible presence brings the idea to reality. The example of the baseball bat earlier in this section shows the use of an object. There are simple keys to using objects: Make sure that it's large enough to be seen, but not so large that you can't manipulate it (move, carry, etc.). Showing how to do a card trick may not work if you're not using a regular deck of cards: How do you perform that task with a normal deck? Make sure that there is no danger involved in the object's use (the swinging of a baseball bat could have tragic consequences in a classroom!). Practice how you will use the object, and keep it out of sight when you're not using it so that it doesn't become a focal distraction.

Models are useful when you can't bring the actual thing in but you want to help the audience visualize the object in a three-dimensional way. You can't show how to cut a real person's hair (think about those shaking hands holding scissors in front of an audience), but you can do the process on a wig. You can't bring a helicopter to class to explain why it flies, but you can bring in a model. Again, the use of models is pretty simple: Make sure it's large enough to be seen and practice its use.

Two-dimensional Presentational Aids.

Two-dimensional presentational aids make up the most commonly used category in speeches. These include images such as drawings, photographs, maps, graphs, charts, and overhead transparencies, to name a few. Because of an increased availability of electronic projection equipment in classrooms, conference rooms, and meeting places, images are nearly expected by contemporary audiences as the part of any presentation. Most of these can be developed through presentation software such as PowerPoint, which will be discussed after a brief review of the types of two-dimensional images you can utilize.

Two important cautions should be considered from the start. You must keep in mind the relevance of the image to your message. This is true for all types of presentational aids, but because images are so readily available, many speakers tend to go overboard in their creation. Second, you must ensure that proper permissions have been sought if the images used are protected by copyright or a trademark. Just because it's available on a Web site or in a book doesn't mean you can automatically use it for your own pur-

Two-dimensional presentational aids are commonly used in speeches. © 2008, JupiterImages.

poses. Nearly every article, picture, photo, and cartoon is protected by copyright. Educational use of an image might be allowed in a single use, small audience situation. Repeated use of an image, even for educational purposes, might be a copyright violation.[20]

Drawings are inexpensive, can be designed for your exact needs, and are easily constructed with presentation software, so you don't have to be a master artist to create them. Simple drawings with large, dark lines are more effective for audience presentations than are detailed images. *Photographs* provide greater reality than drawings, but small detail is likely to be difficult to see, even when projected. Enlarging photographs to poster size is possible but relatively expensive (remember, ask yourself how necessary the photo is to your audience's understanding your message). Additionally, you don't want your speech to become a travelogue of "and then there's this," so you need to keep photos to a minimum, and make their impact strong. *Maps* share the size issue with photos; the detail on them is often difficult to see from an audience perspective.[21] Ali gave a speech to familiarize his classmates with his home country of Algeria. He was aware that helping them to picture Algeria's world location would be an essential part of the message. Ali found an image of Algeria in the *World Fact Book*, a resource available through www.cia.gov, which he incorporated into a PowerPoint presentation. In his speech he described where Algeria is located on the African continent and how Algeria was nearly three and a half times larger than the state of Texas. Using the visual aid shown here, along with his comparison to Texas, he was able to make his audience quickly understand both the country's size and location.

Graphs are representations of statistical data; while many in your audience might not understand numbers, they can grasp their meaning when shown visually. Bar graphs, pie graphs, line graphs, and picture graphs are able to show trends and relationships. Because most computer software programs have the ability to translate data into graphs, this is an easy way to include data in your message. The use of graphs can make information visually clear, something spoken numbers might not do. However, remember that the graph does not speak for itself. You must explain in words what the audience should be seeing.

Charts, like graphs, summarize information. They are easy to use in different formats: Flipcharts (large pads of paper on an easel) and whiteboards are inexpensive and low tech. However, because you often have to be writing while talking, their appearance is often unprofessional (not straight, hard to read), and speakers are prone to misspellings. Can you really think, talk, and write simultaneously in front of others? Won't you lose eye contact when you turn to write? The best charts are simple; their words use parallel structure or balanced points; their letters are large and bold. Don't overuse color (many colors might make the audience feel like you're enthralled with that new box

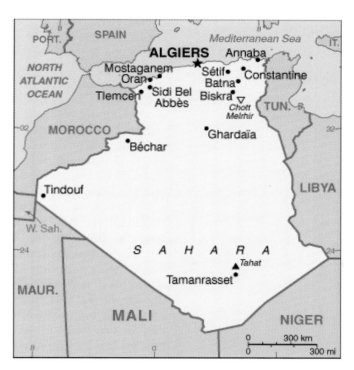

SOURCE: *http://www.cia.gov/cia/publications/factbook/geos/ag.html* (Accessed April 2, 2006)

Graphs serve to make information visually clear to the audience.
© 2008, JupiterImages.

of crayons). The audience needs to see a simple, plain image. Because presentation software is readily available, it's better in most cases to create a chart before you speak. However, if you're in a situation where an ongoing discussion requires writing while the message is being given, consider having someone else do the scribing for you.

Overhead transparencies are the precursor to contemporary electronic projection, using a plastic sheet called a *transparency*. Special markers are required for their creation, or you can usually print on them from a copy machine or home printer. This type of aid is simple to create, doesn't require you to dim the lights, lets you continue to face the audience while the transparency is projected, and can be developed prior to the speech but still allow you to add detail while speaking.

There are universal rules for the creation and use of all two-dimensional presentational aids. You should always practice their use, especially if you're going to be writing on them as you speak. If possible, go to the place where you'll be presenting and make sure that you can put the image's projector and image within easy view of the entire audience. Keep your images simple; bullet points and words or phrases are more effective than long sentences and paragraphs that will cause the audience to want to read. Watch your font size; what looks big to you when you're creating on your kitchen table or laptop may be tiny when projected. A simple rule of thumb is to use 32–36 point type for titles, 24 point type for subtitles, and 18 point type for the rest of the text. You want to use a simple font rather than a fancy, decorative, or specialized font. For example:

Times New Roman 24 point looks like this.

Brush Script 24 point looks like this.

Kuenstler Script Medium 24 point looks like this.

Imagine seeing this projected; which would satisfy your need for clarity and ease of recognition? Last, don't show your presentational aid until it's necessary, and when it's not, cover it up or insert a blank image. Again, you want to control the audience's focus on the message, not the image.

Many of these two-dimensional aids can be developed through graphics presentational software. Such software offers you a means to present information clearly and with visual interest, and they don't require great amounts of time or expertise on your part. Software allow you to create a uniform and distinctive look; save work as you prepare it; establish progression and timing of ideas; and offer the audience a printout or electronic copy for later use. Presentation software such as Microsoft's PowerPoint, Apple's Keynote, Corel Presentation, Astound Presentation, and Lotus Freelance Graphics all allow their users to include two-dimensional images, words, sound, and animation in a presentation. Remember, though, that the software shouldn't dictate

Guidelines for Using PowerPoint

- Limit the number of slides.
  - Rarely are more than five visual aids necessary in a speech. Remember that the visual aid is used primarily to clarify only when words are not enough.
- Simplicity is important.
  - PowerPoint can do many gimmicky things. It was created by people who wanted to show how much the program could do with no regard if it was good for speaking.
  - Avoid sounds and use the same transitions and animations throughout the speech.
- Use only photographs, charts and drawings in the presentation.
  - Do not list your main points. Do not type that which can be said.
- Include a blank black slide at the front and back of all content slides.
  - The blank black slides serves two purposes.
    - It allows the speaker to hide the content slides when not being used in order to keep the audience focused on the speaker.
    - It allows the speaker to remain in front of the screen without being blinded by the projection light and without the light shining on the speaker's face, causing a distraction.
- As with other audiovisual aids, the speaker should be familiar with the content.
  - The speaker should not talk to the screen while the slide is being projected.
- Speakers may look, briefly, at the slide to gain their bearings, but they should maintain eye contact with the audience as much as possible. Pointing to the slide's content may be necessary to ensure that the audience's attention is focused on the correct area of the visual aid.
  - The speech is about you—not the software.

(Reprinted by permission of Professor Corey A. Hickerson.)

what you talk about; it's just a tool for supplementing delivery. Nor should you let special effects such as transitions, music, animation, and video clips attached to slides overwhelm the audience with needless images. PowerPoint is probably the most familiar presentational software and is the industry leader[22] so let's consider guidelines for its use.[23] Dr. Corey Hickerson developed a simple list of "how to's" that you can employ.[24]

One last caution about relying on any electronic creation: Equipment might not work the way you want. Have a backup plan, such as overhead transparencies or a handout ready, just in case. Remember, if something can go wrong, it likely will!

Multimedia Presentational Aids. **Multimedia presentations** involve the combination of sound and sight to create interest and excitement, along with information that is best presented in an audiovisual format. When played via CDs, DVDs, flashdrives, or laptops, audio and visual materials are easily combined into a professional-looking package. For example, if you are giving a speech about the music of the recording artist Prince, incorporating some sound clips might help your audience appreciate and understand the artist more fully. The danger of clips, music, and Web sites is that the audience may be conditioned to use these products in a passive fashion. If you're inserting multimedia in a speech, you want to get the audience to use these media in an active way, as a means to enhance clarity. The same cautions you've read for other presentation aids apply here. Make sure that what you're showing is really necessary; a movie clip might be interesting, but is it meant to be shown as a snippet for a supporting detail? A projected Web site might have too much detail on it to serve as a complement to your speech. CDs, DVDs, and flashdrives can give you a quick way to retrieve audio or visual information, but the temptation may be to put too much on them because of their storage capacity.

When using any multimedia source, make sure you introduce and explain it first, so the audience knows what to be looking or listening for. From a practical perspective, avoid playing an audio track while you are speaking. It might seem like a cool idea to play music as a background to your spoken message, but in the end, the audience will struggle to hear you because they can't listen to both the audio track and you at the same time.

If you don't know how to use the software, then multimedia will take a great deal of time to learn to use effectively. Make sure you're familiar with how to move forward in the presentation; how will you continue the information? Just like any technology, there's always the chance for breakdown or system incompatibility; have a backup plan in place. What will you do if everything falls apart? Remember, use multimedia presentation aids in a sparse fashion so you're not overwhelming the message. Many speeches have been dampened by unsuccessful attempts to use multimedia that did not work at all, did not include audio, or was not visible due to lighting limits or projection problems.

Using Presentational Aids Strategically

The three categories of presentational aids (three dimensional, two dimensional, and multimedia) offer you a range of ways to supplement your ideas. All cultures seem to recognize the value of visual expression accompanying verbal ideas, and they've become an anticipated part of business and academic life. But just because presentational aids are possible doesn't mean they have to be incorporated into a speech. Ask yourself if you learn better when you read something, when you see something, or when you do it? Different learning tasks require different techniques, don't they? The same holds true for presentational aids; some are more effective in representing specific ideas than are others. At the same time, there are many messages we present verbally that don't have "obvious" visuals, so we need to encourage the audience's understanding with additional presentational aids. The skillful use of any aid has become an expectation in our world, and you should consider their inclusion in your message preparation.

While each category has its own strategies and pitfalls, there are some general guidelines for you to consider to avoid the ineffective and enhance the effective.

Prepare in Advance. *Prepare your presentational aids in advance, and practice with them in the same way.* You need to have the resources and time necessary to create clear, memorable, and effective presentational aids. If you prepare in advance, you have a greater chance to make sure your information is accurate (no words are misspelled, ideas aren't missing or organized in a confusing fashion). You also need to be able to practice with them in "real time," as you would when giving the presentation to your audience. Practice helps you focus on the spoken message and augment it with your visual message, as opposed to the other way around. Second, practice is essential to successfully using aids when speaking. Taking time to practice with your presentational aids, whether they are three dimensional, two dimensional, or multimedia, will increase your confidence and readiness for the actual speaking situation.

Keep It Simple. *Keep your presentational aids simple.* Remember, it's the speech, not the dazzling graphics or multiple images, that matters. Too often speakers add transition features, animations, and sounds to a presentation that add little to their message effectiveness. In the same vein, avoid incorporating too many backgrounds or transition sequences just because they are trendy or exciting. You want attractive features that will ensure audience members will see your visual aid, but you want them to focus on your ideas, not the other way around.

The rule of thumb to employ is that you should include in your presentational aid only those things needed to make your point. Obey the 3×5 rule, which means that no more than three words and five lines or five words and three lines should be on any one slide or transparency. Essentially, this means you should not write out whole sentences or paragraphs for the audience to read. Instead, short phrases should be used to provide a visual reinforcement of the spoken message. Clutter is out; clarity is in. Intricate, detailed, and complicated ideas don't belong on a presentational aid; that's counter to the purpose.

You also need to consider color and font, as discussed earlier. Color can add energy and focus to a presentation, but it can also serve as a interruption to thought. Selecting foreground and background colors that are high in contrast will help text and images to be easy to see.[25] Television producers select cool background colors, such as blues and greens, because they create less strain on viewers' eyes. Similarly, careful attention to font selection can also impact clarity and visibility. Too much font variety can be distracting; you might use two (one for the title, the other for the rest), but in any case, you want to use a block-type font that is easier to read. The number and use of images is also important, as crowding a slide with pictures, especially animated ones, can quickly turn an effective presentation into a distracting one.

Make It Visible. *Make sure your presentational aids can be seen.* Your well-thought-out and well-designed presentational aid is worthless if the audience can't see it. That seems obvious, doesn't it? In most instances, modern corporate boardrooms and classrooms are designed to ensure audiences will be able to clearly see the visuals when projected. But not all speaking venues are designed for that purpose, so a little bit of planning can help. One strategy to use is the "floor" test. If using a nonprojected presentational aid (three-dimensional, some two-dimensional), create your visual aid and then place it on the floor in front of you. From a standing position you should be able to read the words and see all images in adequate detail. If you can, they probably will be appropriately visible when projected. If not, then corrections are necessary. Practice with the projected images, and make sure you're not standing in front of the screen. You don't want to be blinded by the light, and you don't want to cast a shadow.

Display It Selectively. *Display the presentational aid only when it's complementing your verbal message.* If a presentational aid is visible, it will be looked at by someone in the audience. That may mean that person isn't listening to you because she is admiring the artwork, wondering what you're going to be doing with it, or thinking that she could do something better. Cover three-dimensional objects or keep them out of sight. If using a flipchart, keep the blank page up until you need to point out the visual aspects. Slides can be blacked out, or you can insert a plain one into the presentation. You don't want to distract your audience by an unnecessary or ill-placed display.

The same goes for the use of sound. Avoid incorporating sound with your visual aids unless that feature improves understanding of your message. Sure, many presentational software programs can add neat sounds like cars screeching to a halt or the sound of a camera shutter clicking, but why would you do that? Before incorporating multimedia features into your presentation, ask yourself, "Will this feature help my audience understand my message?" and, "Can I use it without creating distraction?" If not, then don't incorporate the feature.

Control It. *Control your presentational aids; do not be controlled by them.* When using presentational aids, it is easy to be a slave to the tool. Instead of using the aid to help communicate an idea, the aid becomes the message. Audiences sometimes pay more attention to the background style or transitions used in presentational software slides than the intended messages. Sometimes speakers speed up their presentations to avoid allowing the screen saver to activate. A common mistake made with the best of intentions was made by a speaker who thought he would use the "timing" feature in Power-Point. Unfortunately, his timing in the live presentation was different from his practiced timing (as it should be if a speaker is responding to the feedback of an audience). The result was a slide presentation that appeared possessed by a demon, bent on destroying his presentation.

This strategy is a reminder that you should talk to your audience, not to your aid. It's pretty easy to lose eye contact when utilizing an actual object or a projection, and your audience probably is looking at that aid, too. The message is the important item here, not the means by which it is being presented. A simple way to avoid this downside of using presentational aids is the **three T method.** First, Touch (or point to) the place you want the audience to focus their attention. Second, Turn your face to the audience. Third, begin Talking.

With thought, preparation, and effort, presentational aids will enhance your delivery in an added dimension. Although they're not always required, they provide an appeal to multiple senses. Presentational aids can increase message clarity, interest, and retention. They can enhance your credibility when used effectively. Conceived of poorly, designed inaccurately, or used ineffectively, they'll frustrate or bore your audience. You have a tightrope to walk here: you want to enjoy the advantages of successful presentational aids and avoid the consequences of poor design and use. You should always base your strategic choice on this basic question: Will the effective use of presentational aids enhance my speech purpose?

> **Three T Method**
>
> 1. Touch (or point to) the focal point
> 2. Turn your face to the audience
> 3. begin Talking

SUMMARY

This chapter has focused on how your message is impacted by elements other than the content of spoken words. Effective delivery involves management of both verbal and nonverbal messages. Delivery should be tailored for the intended audience and situation. Effective verbal delivery considers volume, rate, pitch, pauses, and the trio of articulation, pronunciation, and dialects. Good nonverbal delivery involves appropriate eye contact, facial expression, gestures, movement, and attire. Presentational aids should reinforce and clarify the verbal message. Effective verbal and nonverbal delivery constitutes another strategic element in effective communication.

Roger Ailes summed up the importance of what he called the "composite you" as he explained the importance of communication elements beyond the message:

> "You are the message." What does that mean, exactly? It means that when you communicate with someone, it's not just the words you choose to send to the other person that make up the message. You're also sending signals about what kind of person you are—by your eyes, your facial expression, your body movement, your vocal pitch, tone, volume, and intensity, your commitment to your message, your sense of humor, and many other factors.

> The receiving person is bombarded with symbols and signals from you. Everything you do in relation to other people causes them to make judgments about what you stand for and what your message is. "You are the message" comes down to the fact that unless you identify yourself as a walking, talking message, you miss that critical point.
>
> The words themselves are meaningless unless the rest of you is in synchronization. The total you affects how others think of and respond to you.[26]

ENDNOTES

1. Roger Ailes and Jon Kraushar, *You Are the Message: Getting What You Want by Being Who You Are* (New York: Doubleday, 1995), p. 37.

2. *http://www.brainyquote.com/quotes/quotes/m/marktwain100433.html* (accessed August 27, 2007).

3. K. J. Tusing and J. P. Dillard, "The Sounds of Dominance: Vocal Precursors of Perceived Dominance during Interpersonal Influence," *Human Communication Research* 26 (2000), 148–171.

4. D. Deutsch, T. Henthorn, E. Marvin, H. Xu, "Perfect Pitch in Tone Language Speakers Carries over to Music," (Nov. 9, 2004), *http://www.aip.org/148th/deutsch.html* (accessed Sept. 1, 2007).

5. "The 100 Most Often Mispronounced Words in English," alphaDictionary.com, *http://www.alphadictionary.com/ articles/mispronouced_words.html* (accessed Sept. 3, 2007).

6. For information on American dialects, see, for instance, the American Dialect Homepage, *http://www.evolpub.com/ Americandialects/AmDialhome.html* (accessed Sept. 3, 2007), and "Varieties of English, Language Samples Project," *http://www.ic.arizona.edu/%7Elsp/index.html* (accessed Sept. 3, 2007).

7. Mary M. Gill, "Accents and Stereotypes: Their Effect on Perceptions of Teachers and Lecture Comprehension," *Journal of Applied Communication Research* 22 (1994), 348–361.

8. World of Quotes, Ralph Waldo Emerson, *http://www.worldofquotes.com/topic/Eye/1/index.html* (accessed Sept. 4, 2007).

9. See, for example, R. Axtell, *Dos and Taboos around the World*, 2nd ed. (New York: Wiley, 1990); and L. Samovar and R. Porter, *Communication between Cultures*, 4th ed. (Belmont, CA: Wadsworth, 2001).

10. Steven A. Beebe, "Eye Contact a Nonverbal Determinant of Speaker Credibility," *Speech Teacher* 23 (1) (Jan. 1974): 21.

11. For more information about the importance of eye contact, see, for instance, J. B. Bavelas, L. Coates, and T. Johnson, "Listener Responses as a Collaborative Process: The Role of Gaze," *Journal of Communication* (September 2002): 566–580.

12. Paul Ekman, Wallace V. Friesen, and S. Tomkins, "Facial Affect Scoring Technique: A First Validity Study," *Semiotica* 3 (1971).

13. L. Samovar, *Oral Communication: Speaking Across Cultures* (Los Angeles, CA: Roxbury, 2000), 102.

14. For more information about gestures, see, for instance, G. Beattie and H. Shovelton, "Mapping the Range of Information Contained in the Iconic Hand Gestures that Accompany Spontaneous Speech," *Journal of Language and Social Psychology* 18 (4) (1999): 438–462. Also J. Cassell, D. McNeill, and K.-E. McCullough, "Speech-Gesture Mismatches: Evidence for One Underlying Representation of Linguistic and Nonlinguistic Information," *Pragmatics & Cognition* 7 (1) (1999): 1–33; M. Gullberg and K. Holmquist, "Keeping an Eye on Gestures: Visual Perception of Gestures in Face-to-face Communication," *Pragmatics & Cognition* 7 (1) (1999): 35–63; A. Kendon, "Do Gestures Communicate?: A Review," *Research on Language and Social Interaction* 27 (3) (1994): 175–200; A. Melinger and W. J. M. Levelt, "Gesture and the Communicative Intention of the Speaker," *Gesture* 4 (2) (2004): 119–141; J. Streeck, "Gesture as Communication I: Its Coordination with Gaze and Speech," *Communication Monographs* 60 (4) (1993): 275–299 and J. Streeck, "Gesture as Communication II: The Audience as Co-author," *Research on Language and Social Interaction* 27 (3) (1994): 239–267.

15. Samovar, 103.

16. 68. Tim Russert Tallies the Vote (11/7/00) Decision 2000, "TV Guide and TV Land present the 100 Most memorable TV moments," *http://www.tvland.com/originals/100moments/page2.jhtml* (accessed Sept. 4, 2007).

17. "Election 2004 geekery: Tablet PCs are the new whiteboards" Peter Rojas, Engadget, *http://www.engadget.com/2004/11/02/election-2004-geekery-tablet-pcs-are-the-new-whiteboards/* (accessed Sept. 4, 2007).

18. Susan C. Jones, "Memory Aids for Reading and Math," Final Report U.S. Department of Education's Christa McAuliffe Fellowship (1991).

19. M. Patterson, D. Dansereau, and D. Newbern, "Effects of Communication Aids and Strategies on Cooperative Teaching," *Journal of Educational Psychology* 84 (1992): 453–61.

20. Indiana University's Copyright Management Center, *http://www.copyright.iupui.edu/fairuse.htm* has a good discussion of what constitutes fair use and the limits of using materials. (accessed Sept. 5, 2007).

21. Most libraries have online databases of maps, images, and other media. Check with your research librarian for assistance. See, for example, Images, maps, news sources, and other media, Virginia Tech University Libraries, http://www.lib.vt.edu/find/othermedia.html.

22. For an opposing view, see Professor Edward Tufte's, "PowerPoint is Evil," in *Wired* on line at *http://www.wired.com/wired/archive/11.09/ppt2.html*. There is ample information about the construction of PowerPoint slides. See, for example, N. Amare, "Technology for Technology's Sake: the Proliferation of PowerPoint," *Professional Communication Conference*, 2004. IPCC 2004. Proceedings. International Publication Date: 29 Sept.–Oct. 2004.

23. *http://office.microsoft.com/en-us/powerpoint/default.aspx* is the main Web site for PowerPoint, including tips and training points (accessed Sept. 5, 2007).

24. Corey A. Hickerson, Ph. D., Assistant Professor of Communication Studies: James Madison University.

25. For a discussion of the use of color, Microsoft PowerPoint has a brief discussion on choosing the right colors at http://office.microsoft.com/enus/powerpoint/HA010120721033.aspx.

26. Ailes, p. 25.

WHAT SHOULD YOU KNOW ABOUT AN INFORMATIVE MESSAGE?

LEARNING OBJECTIVES

After reading this chapter, you should understand the following concepts:

- Delivery strategies are important for presenting an informative message.
- Descriptive speeches involve sharing definitions, using investigative questions, and using imagery to help listeners remember what you said.
- An effective briefing is a concise overview that gives listeners the key points of a more detailed report.
- An expository speech explains how to do something.
- A narrative speech tells a story to communicate ideas, inspire, and entertain.
- Credibility is essential for conveying an informative message that listeners will believe.

INTRODUCTION

Imagine this: As someone who is interested in conservation causes, you begin thinking about potential speeches you could give about water conservation issues. Consider the different directions your messages could take:

Message One: Description of Water Projects Worldwide

Did you know that while 70 percent of Earth's surface is covered by water, 97.5 percent is salt water and only 2.5 percent is fresh water? In addition, 1.2 billion people are without access to safe drinking water. This translates to one out of five people worldwide who don't have nontoxic potable water.[1] As a result, several projects exist worldwide to attempt to impact these alarming numbers. I'd like to tell you about three of them.

Message Two: How to Use Water Wisely

Fred has lived in his house for five years, but lately he's noticed that his water bill seems to be rising abnormally fast. He calls the water company ready to

What strategies could you suggest in a speech about how to reduce your water bill?
© paulaphoto, 2008, Shutterstock.

complain about rate hikes, but they tell him they've not changed the usage price in three years. This makes Fred wonder: Is his family to blame for the bills? Are there strategies he could use to change the amount of water his family uses, so the bill will be reduced? He thinks about that leaky kitchen faucet, how much he waters his lawn to keep it golf-course green, and how his kids leave the water running when they brush their teeth. His investigation leads to a new way of living for Fred's family; one that's not difficult to manage, but one that shows budgetary results. You might wonder if there are similar steps you could take to save some money, along with reducing your own bill. Those are some strategies I'll suggest to you in my speech today.

Message Three: Educate about Impacts of Reduced Governmental Funding

Here in the United States, our water supplies are threatened by agricultural runoff, increased use of pesticides and forest clearcutting, and pollution. Recent federal proposals call for the relaxing of clean water standards, including allowing increases of mercury pollution from power plants. These plans also reduce funding to water conservation and pollution-prevention programs. While we invest billions of dollars in highways, airports, and other infrastructure programs, the administration has proposed cutting the EPA's clean water funding.[2] We need to be better educated about the current level of governmental funding and what that may mean to our future.

We've all shared information with others in one form or another. Maybe you briefed co-workers of a project's status, clarified what you meant by a technical term, shared information with relatives about the condition of a sick family member, listened to a parent or grandparent share a story from their past, or shared your perspective on needed improvements to something at home or work. We have to contribute information in order to effectively participate in social situations, our professions or workplace, and in civic contexts. Each of these communication situations requires sending and receiving informative messages.

An **informative message** is one whose goal is to produce shared understanding, to increase knowledge, to cultivate appreciation, or to develop skills or abilities. As the definition suggests, informative messages instruct, clarify, update, educate, illuminate, and/or enlighten listeners. Through informative communication, we become more knowledgeable, gain new insight and new information, and understand complicated issues and feelings more fully.

Let's explore some of the types of informative messages you encounter, along with strategies for developing them. Each of these informative speech types and strategic tips may be employed regularly in social, civic, and work-related contexts.

WHAT TYPES OF INFORMATIVE MESSAGES MIGHT I CONSIDER? WHAT STRATEGIES ARE IMPORTANT?

The Descriptive Speech

Think about how often in your day you are asked to describe something: whom do you admire, what your class was like, what you thought of a movie, why you like a certain kind of food, where your favorite vacation spot is, what your progress is on a project, why you use a term in a certain way, when you expect to complete a task. Your answer, whether brief or extended, represents a descriptive speech. A **descriptive speech** attempts to clarify information or to create understanding through vivid language. You want your audience to develop a meaningful image of an idea, term, situation, feeling, and so on, with the intent of having them "get your picture" by the end of the speech. As you are about to see, language strategies are particularly useful to consider when creating a descriptive speech.

Take a Closer Look

Strategies for Descriptive Speech

Strategy 1: Sharing Definitions
Denotative definitions provide the dictionary definition of a word in terms if its class and distinguishing features.

Amplifying techniques expand on the denotative definition to provide greater meaning:

- Explication: Defining terms in the definition
- Comparison/contrast: Relating the word to another word
- Synonyms: Relating a term to another term with the same meaning
- Antonyms: Relating a term to another term with the opposite meaning
- Example: Giving a specific use of the term
- Enumeration: Listing members of the class that distinguishes the term
- Etymology: Explaining the origin of the word
- Negation: Describing what the word is not

Strategy 2: Using Investigative Questions
Leading question words guide speakers in describing a subject.

The key questions are *who, what when, where, why,* and *how.*

Strategy 3: Using Imagery
Imagery uses vivid language to appeal to the senses, making it easier for listeners to remember the topic.

- Visual imagery: Paints a mental picture
- Tactile imagery: Elicits thoughts about how something feels to the touch
- Auditory imagery: Suggests sounds
- Olfactory imagery: Suggests smells
- Gustatory imagery: Suggests taste
- Kinetic imagery: Elicits feelings of movement

Strategy 1: Sharing Definitions. A main language strategy used to create understanding is sharing **definitions**: concise, simple statements that explain what you mean by a word or expression. You might think that "everyone" knows what a term means, but that is often not the case. Think of simple common sayings, such as, "Close, but no cigar." Can you explain what it means? Do you know why that phrase came into being? Perhaps by explaining in the old days, cigars were given out as prizes at carnivals, you can help your audience better understand the phrase.

An example from a Texas speech class demonstrates the need for definition. A west Texas student delivered a speech about clearing the range for cattle. His northern-born-and-bred teacher had never experienced such activity, so she was very interested. However, confusion soon set in, as the student described the need to "pull mesquite." He described all sorts of suggestions, including herbicides, napalm, improving the soil (mesquite apparently prefers poor soil), and digging it up by the roots. Unfortunately for the student, the instructor thought he was talking about *mosquitoes* and spent the majority of the speech wondering in awe about the size of Texas bloodsuckers that needed such desperate means of control. The instructor didn't know what mesquite was, let alone how or where it grew. Had the student begun the speech by defining mesquite as "any of several usually spiny trees or shrubs that often forms dense thickets,"[3] much of the confusion could have been erased. It wasn't just a matter of *how* something was said, but *what* was meant by it that would have resulted in clarity of description.

Defining a concept doesn't have to take a great deal of time, and there are several definitional strategies you can use. The most common type of definition is the use of a **denotative definition** (also known as formal or dictionary definition), consisting of three parts:

1. *Term or item.* This is the word to be clarified.
2. *Class.* The general group to which a word belongs is its class.
3. *Differentia.* Distinguishing features, qualities, or characteristics make this term different from others in its class.

 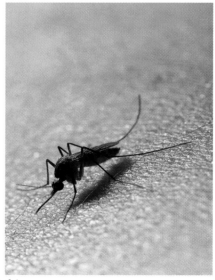

Mesquite and mosquito . . . two very different things.
© EuToch, 2008, Shutterstock.   © Chia Yuen Che, 2008, Shutterstock.

The more narrow you can get when developing the differentia, the less chance there is for audience confusion. Differentia usually combine **intension** (a list of attributes/characteristics that something must have to be properly labeled as this term) and **extension** (examples of actual instances of the term in use). So, for instance, scissors (term) are a cutting instrument (class) for paper or cloth consisting of two blades, each having a ring-shaped handle, that are so pivoted together that their sharp edges work one against the other (differentia).[4]

However, sometimes a denotative definition doesn't quite give the clarity that you seek. You can then use amplifying techniques that extend the definition. Each of these is a method of sharing connotative meaning, or the personal attributes you attach to the term. With **explication,** you simplify or further define other terms in the denotative definition. Let's say you have defined "apprehension" denotatively as "the faculty or act of apprehending, especially intuitive understanding; perception on a direct and immediate level."[5] You may need to follow up with a simple explanation of what words like *faculty* or *apprehending* mean in this context.

Another amplifying technique is **comparison/contrast;** you show how the term is similar or different to closely related terms the audience might know well. You demonstrate this every time you describe one of your classes by matching it up with another. **Synonyms** amplify your term by presenting another term having the same essential meaning, such as hurricane and tropical cyclone. **Antonyms** define your term by presenting another term having an opposite meaning: Freeze and boil are antonyms. You might choose to give an example, which is a specific instance of the word: A team mascot such as Brutus Buckeye helps to inspire fan spirit. **Enumeration** as an amplification technique lets you list all the members of the class to distinguish this one term (the grocery list approach). The word *style* can mean fashion, manner, behavior, typeface, sort, a slender tube, the slender part of a pistil, and so on. The **etymology** of a word explains the current meaning of the term based on the historical meaning or origin. Gravitas is from the Latin *gravitas*, "heaviness, seriousness," from *gravis*, "heavy, serious."

Hurricane or tropical cyclone? Does it matter what you call it?
© Gregory Pelt, 2008, Shutterstock.

Finally, the last amplification term is **negation,** which defines by saying what your term *is not;* you would use this when you want to stipulate new or specialized meaning that the audience is unfamiliar with. When rock hounds use the word *jargon,* they're not talking about slang. They're referring to a colorless (or pale yellow or smoky) variety of zircon.

No matter what techniques you use in defining your term, by clarifying your meaning and use of words, you'll show the audience concern for their understanding.

Strategy 2: Using Investigative Questions. A second strategy to consider when creating a descriptive message would be to answer the questions *who? what? when? where? why?* and *how?* All of these questions may not apply specifically to your message, but they can give you guides as to the depth of information that you might want to give. If you were asked to describe yourself, for instance, you could say *who* you model yourself after, *what* it was like to fail in a task and *how* you overcame that, *when* your least favorite time of life was, *where* you go when you need to escape, *why* you chose your major, and or *how* you view some current event. Each one of those

The more detailed the description of how the dish is made, the better chance you have of making it correctly.
© Tonic Valing, 2008, Shutterstock.

prompts provides a different image to the audience, and each is more than they might learn by a simple demographic recital.

Strategy 3: Using Imagery. Finally, descriptive speeches call for vivid language. **Imagery** uses words and phrases that appeal to the senses (sight, touch, smell, hearing, and taste). By providing the audience visual, tactile, auditory, olfactory, gustatory, or kinetic experiences, you ask them to participate. The difficulty in speaking is that you don't want to become too literary. Remember, written words and spoken thoughts are different.[6] However, you can easily employ imagery in description. *Visual imagery* attempts to picture something; you can refer to color, size, or location. *Tactile* (touch) *imagery* elicits thoughts about texture, temperature, or feeling. *Auditory imagery* suggests sounds (pitch, volume, tone). *Olfactory imagery* reminds us of smells, where *gustatory* calls up tastes (sweet, sharp, bitter). *Kinetic imagery* evokes movement: speed, height, stillness, and so on. You don't have to get fancy with imagery, but a specific descriptive phrase such as, "You want the roux to be the texture and color of dark molasses with no black flecks," rather than saying, "Make the roux brown and thick," might make the difference between great crawfish étouffée and inedible smothered crawfish.

Of course, organizing a descriptive speech is also important. You're trying to make something clearer or to enhance interest; how you structure those ideas is critical. Sometimes, the definition techniques that you've chosen will also dictate your structure; you move from formal, denotative meanings to informal, connotative ones. You move from simple example to extended illustration. You begin with the origin of a word or concept to its current meaning or status. As you read each of those, you can see employing one of the methods described in Chapter 13.

You'll probably find yourself using some of these descriptive language strategies as you develop more complex messages. The techniques used in a descriptive speech can be employed in other informative or persuasive speeches, because you may need to set up some common ground through definition or explanation before you can do anything more complex. However, if your primary goal is to develop a clearer image of an idea in the audience, then focus on the language strategies just described.

The Briefing

According to *The Concise Oxford English Dictionary*, a **briefing** is "a meeting for giving information or instructions."[7] Most likely, this is a term most people encounter only when they enter the work force. For some, their first exposure to a briefing is a military one. For others, their new boss asks them to "brief" the department on progress toward the objectives of a team project. Our nation's chief executive receives numerous briefings each day on topics ranging from domestic issues such as education and the economy or the impacts of a natural disaster like Hurricane Katrina to international efforts such as relief to victims of war and natural disasters. The White House then provides press briefings daily so that the public can remain informed on those issues and our government's perspective on or approach to them. Even if you don't work in the White House, learning how to give a briefing is a beneficial skill.

An effective briefing is an overview: a concise message summarizing or addressing a single issue or problem. The purpose of a briefing is to summarize the key points, saving listeners time and preparing them for more detailed information to come, either verbally or in written form. Sometimes, a briefing might include an opportunity for the speaker to address questions from the listener in an effort to ensure clear and accurate communication.

A briefing serves to summarize key points of a topic.
© Kiselev Andrey Valerevich, 2008, Shutterstock.

Briefings have different purposes. Students give briefings in class when they report on service learning activities. Law students' briefs develop a short summary and systematic analysis of the case that describes the parties, identifies the issues, reports what was decided, and analyzes the reasoning behind decisions made by the courts so that the class can discuss the case further. Professional briefings, such as a strategic planning review, usually accompany a longer original document that the executive or group members haven't had time or access to read. They will include an executive summary, which is a one-page bulleted list of speaking points that are further supported with additional documentation or reports. For example, a grocery chain might use a briefing to identify the main issues for entry into a new market region. Family life involves numerous examples of briefings that give information or instruction. A cell phone call to a sibling or parent that shares results from the day's events or the outcome of sporting event can be considered an informal briefing. The same strategic briefing approaches that help you to be successful with family members can be applied to other contexts.

No matter the audience, the most important aspects of a strategic briefing are clarity and conciseness. A simple way to imagine your briefing is through the three P's.

How often do you call a friend or family member for a "briefing"?
© Michael Krinke, 2008, Shutterstock.

1. **Procedure points** highlight policies that have to be introduced, clarified, changed, or reinforced.
2. **Progress points** describe or clarify steps that have been taken or priorities to be established.
3. **People points** draw attention to issues affecting family or team members.

By considering the three Ps, you may determine that one takes precedence over the others and should be the primary focus of your briefing. You could also decide that all three would constitute the speaking points to be covered, sharpening your focus.

When creating an effective briefing, you want to build understanding, create retention opportunities, and stimulate action. This means that your main message(s) should be clearly stated and reinforced. Your organizational structure depends on your purpose. If you're detailing a process, then chronological is most appropriate. If you're explaining the impact of an event, then perhaps topical works better.

Examples should be concise and descriptive, but not overly vivid. Language should be specific, and you should avoid technical terms or jargon. You should have prepared answers; anticipate any questions that might be likely, and make sure your answer is aligned with the message you just gave. If you don't have an answer, promise to get back to the questioner later, and follow through. But don't use a question-and-answer (Q and A) session as the conclusion of your briefing; that's a different message entirely. You should have a conclusion created for the briefing and then move into a Q and A. You can see examples of questions and consider strategies for managing them in Chapter 7.

Remember, though, a briefing is by design a short summary; use it to call attention, to review progress, to call for action, but not to give full-blown description.

The Expository Speech

Another informative message often used in business and education is the expository, training, or *how-to* speech. An **expository message** focuses on teaching a person a process or skill or describing how some process occurs/ happened. A person's first day on a new job often involves learning how to do aspects of the job in a particular way. Perhaps you've worked for a fast-food chain or retail store; it is likely that you've spent time watching training videos or working through online computer-based training activities that are in large part **how-to presentations.** The topics might include how to greet a customer, how to clean up a hazardous chemical spill, how to rotate stock on the grocery store shelf, or how to complete an employee performance evaluation.

Maybe you'd be interested in knowing how a package gets from source to destination, or how money gets circulated; you'll never actually do those tasks yourself, but knowing how the process works is of interest. Sometimes, you have to explain to someone how something happened. Imagine describing to your insurance agent just how your car got so damaged. All of these messages are expository.

Organizing an expository speech typically follows a chronological form. This simply means that when you explain how to do something or how something occurs, you follow time order. Think of it like making a cake or your favorite batch of cookies. You don't start by putting the ingredients in the oven. The order of priority follows a logical time sequence. First things go first and second things second, and so on. In a speech about cleaning up a hazardous spill, the first thing might be to alert others of the danger and to prepare for the clean-up by putting on the appropriate mask, eye protection, gloves, and coveralls. Without taking this first step, any subsequent step could be fatal and would certainly increase risk of personal injury.

If you're providing instructions about how to make some food item, you have to begin with a list of ingredients; there's nothing worse than starting to bake and finding out halfway through that some spice is needed that you don't have! Then you have to explain what and how to mix, how long to bake, how to plate and ice the cake, and so on.

When explaining how some process occurred (for instance, how Hurricane Katrina was born), you have to start with the place (a narrow area of tropical ocean), with a specific kind of temperature and wind, and so on. If you fall out of the chronological order, it is likely that your instructions will fail.

The other important strategy for expository speeches involves the use of language structural techniques such as mnemonic devices and transitions. They're about the most delicate language skill to develop for speaking, but they help to keep your audience focused and involved, and they move the instructions along. When done well, these can also assist the audience in retaining the instructions. Moreover, they may help to keep you on point, too!

A **mnemonic device** is a method you use for enhancing memory—both yours and the audience. The first language tactic, **alliteration**, involves the repetition of initial or matching sounds in neighboring words. You might be familiar with the tongue-twister "Peter Piper picked a peck of pickled peppers," but this isn't exactly the type of alliteration you might find useful. However, earlier in this chapter, you were exposed to the three Ps of an effective briefing: procedure, progress, and people. The repetitive *P* sound can create a memory peg for the audience. Other examples include the consonants in the four Cs of buying a diamond (cut, color, clarity, carat weight) or the four Ps of marketing (product, price, place, and promotion). Alliteration could be something as simple as "lefty loosie" to remember which way to turn a screwdriver.

You might remember to use the four Cs mnemonic devices when choosing a diamond. © Stephen Lynch, 2008, Shutterstock.

Another device is to use parallel structure. **Parallel structure** occurs when you use the same pattern of words to show that two or more ideas have the same level of importance, such as saying, "*Gather* ingredients, *mix* dry materials, *add* wet materials, *fold* into pan, *bake*, and *finish*." Each of these initial verbs help to move the ideas from step to step.

You might create an **acronym**, a word abbreviated in such a way that it creates a new word or phrase so that something (a concept or a process) is easy to remember. The "ABCs of CPR" describe the main points of rescue breathing: airway, breathing, circulation. If you were trying to remember the primary spectrum light, you'd probably recall ROY G. BIV: red, orange, yellow, green, blue, indigo and violet. FOIL is used in math to remember how to multiply two binomials; first, outside, inside, and last.

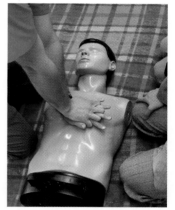

When you learn CPR, you use the ABCs. © Prism_68 2008, Shutterstock.

Acrostics create that memory by using the first letter of words to create a sentence. You learned the treble clef lines by "every good boy does fine (or *deserves fudge*)" and the mathematical order of operations by "Please Excuse My Dear Aunt Sally" (parenthesis, exponents, multiply, divide, add, subtract). As you're reading this, you're probably recalling such mnemonic devices from your past; when was the last time you dragged them up from your memory? That's the point: Once you give your audience a solid memory peg, they're more likely to remember the process you described.

Finally, don't forget **connective transitions.** They're the most subtle part of speaking, as they develop movement from point to point and create a seamless message. You've already learned about them in Chapter 13, so consider how you might employ transitions like "the next point is" or "in conlusion."

The expository message is one that you are exposed to daily: how to get someplace, how to do some task, how something happened. When you create one, remember the keys of chronological order and specific language use to create memory.

The Narrative Speech

Perhaps you've heard the story of how William S. Harley and Arthur Davidson started an American phenomenon in a 10×15-foot wooden shed back in 1903. These two men, later aided by brother Walter Davidson, created a product that continues to be sought over 100 years later.[8] Theirs is a story of personal sacrifice, determination, innovation, and imagination. The tale of the Harley-Davidson company is an American story, yet similar stories exist for many other companies and families throughout the world. These stories communicate powerful messages about sacrifice, misfortune, success, and family. Such stories are the personal narratives of our work, our lives, and our families.

A **narrative speech** tells a story that organizes our perceptions of the world, preserves our history, lets us experience other's lives or cultures without being there, entertains and engages us, promotes creativity, and connects each person involved in listening to the story. An effective speaker is one who can present a narrative that others can accept and that transcends differences in culture and experience. Before learning some strategies for developing narratives, you need to know what constitutes an effective one.

You've probably noticed that several of the chapters in this text begin with or include a story about someone's communication experience; our choice to do this reflects Walter Fisher's Narrative Paradigm, which says that humans are storytellers.[9] Fisher tells us, in essence, that we are more persuaded by a good story than by any other kind of communication. Robert Rowland echoed Fisher, reminding us that the idea that people are storytellers has been used in disciplines as diverse as history, anthropology, psychology, biology, and theology.[10] John Lucaites and Celeste Condit commented on "the growing belief that narrative represents a universal medium of human consciousness."[11] Fisher said that narratives are important because there are "ideas that cannot be verified or proved in any absolute way. Such ideas arise in metaphor, values, gestures, and so on."[12] According to Fisher, we experience the world as being filled with stories, and we have to choose from among them based on "good reasons." These "good reasons" are determined by biography, culture, and history.

Fisher defined *narrative* as a symbolic action: "words and/or deeds that have sequence and meaning for those who live, create, or interpret them."[13] If you agree with this definition, all communication is a narrative; it's a form of social influence. It isn't fiction or nonfiction; when you give an excuse to a parent or a partner for being late, when you read the headlines on the Web, when you watch a newscast, you're involved with narratives, all of which are shaping your reality. Narratives constitute our lives.

We make decisions about what narratives we'll accept and reject based on what makes sense to us, what Fisher calls *good reasons*. If you watch *Entertainment Tonight* or *Access Hollywood*, you are presented with stories about celebrity behavior. Often, those

Narratives constitute our lives and shape our reality.
© 2008, JupiterImages Corporation.

narratives compete with stories in other tabloids or as told by the celebrity herself on a talk show. If you serve on a jury, you're presented totally opposite narratives of a crime: Who did what and why are not the same as seen through the eyes of the defense or prosecution. You have to decide which story to believe, and you do this by using an internal set of criteria called **narrative rationality,** our standard for judging which stories we should believe and which we should ignore. It is formed from two aspects, coherence and fidelity.

Coherence is the narrative's *internal* consistency: Does the story "hang together" by having all the points there, or are aspects left out or contradictory? You can see coherence by asking yourself about the flow (do the plot elements follow each other in a way you understand?), characters (are the people in the story believable?), and material (does this story seem to agree with other similar stories?). As an example, the film *Pulp Fiction* doesn't follow a traditional chronological flow, nor do all the characters interact. There are individual chapters involving some but not all; the timeline shifts. When a narrative skips around or characters seem to disappear and then suddenly reappear without explanation, you may judge its coherence as lacking.

Fidelity, the other aspect of narrative rationality, is the *external* standard for judging the truthfulness of a story. You probably got caught by your parents when you were younger, simply because some detail of the story you were giving as an explanation didn't ring true. Maybe they'd pursue the truthfulness by asking, "Now, if I called your friend's mom (or your teacher, or the storekeeper), would s/he say the same thing?" Fisher says that we judge fidelity by employing **good reasons**: a set of values that let us accept a story as true and worth acceptance. These good reasons include questions about facts (does anything seem to be omitted or distorted; does the narrative address significant or important issues of this case?) and values (are the values present appropriate? What would happen if I went along with those values? Are those values validated by my experience, and do they represent my ideals?).

Do you remember your parents ever catching you in a lie as a child?
© Patricia Marks, 2008, Shutterstock.

Consider a couple of examples of narratives and Fisher's concepts, before you reflect on how narrative plays a role in your own communication behavior. The epic tales of Harry Potter, Luke Skywalker, and even Shrek the Ogre

Example: Michael Vick Involves Fans in an Unexpected Narrative

In August 2007, former Atlanta Falcons quarterback Michael Vick was charged with several federal crimes involving illegal dog fighting. Vick first denied involvement, and then he later represented himself as bankrolling a dog-fighting ring, assisting in the testing of dogs, and participating in the killing of inferior dogs. He also said that he did not gamble by placing side bets on any of the fights, nor did he receive any of the proceeds from the purses that were won by "Bad Newz Kennels," which he owned.[14]

Those hearing about the indictment were faced with many challenges: Would someone so talented and rich be engaged in such horrific behavior? Was Vick targeted by the federal prosecutors because of race or fame? How can someone who was a role model fall so far? How long had this behavior been going on? What should be done?

Each of these questions reflect narrative rationality: at the start of the narrative, Vick supporters said

that the indictments were unfair and we shouldn't be quick to judge; the Falcons and companies for whom Vick did endorsements took a wait-and-see stance. However, as the narrative unfolded through the revelations made by indictments, endorsement companies dropped Vick, the Falcons and NFL suspended him, and Vick struck a plea agreement that landed him with a felony conviction.

The narrative wasn't simply about one person; it became much more—about values (animal cruelty and race), the fall of a hero, and the revelation of an entire subculture in America of a "sport" called dog fighting. Fans had to choose whether to keep Vick memorabilia, support him, pray for him, or use him as an example of how we take down heroes and the power of redemption. The narrative took place in the media, the corner store, and athletic fields.

Do the stories that you read as a child still influence you today?
© digitalskillet, 2008, Shutterstock.

are all narratives that challenge our notions of coherence and fidelity. Do the events in the narratives seem to "ring true" to us? Are the characters believable? Do they stand for values to which we can relate? Do the stories seem to be congruent with our expectations based on other stories? Are there elements that have been left out, or that leave us wondering? Can you relate to elements in the narrative? In what way?

Every night the evening news brings us narratives, some with greater depth of description, some with less: the stories of fires and floods, of heroism and despicable acts, of political issues and arguments. Legends, fables and folktales are at the heart of most cultures. From *Aesop's Fables* through the stories of the Han Chinese, Native American First People legend and Kumeyaay stories to Appalachian Jack tales and Russian folk tales,[15] we've all been told narratives that provide a glimpse into the past. These stories tell us about traditions and philosophies, crafts and foods, ways of living, and great battles and fearsome creatures.

Religious texts are filled with stories replete with values, heroes and villains, morals and ethical choices. You may view these stories in another way now than you did as a child, since your narrative rationality has become differently focused, but it's likely that these same narratives still play a role in your life. At the basis of Fisher's paradigm is the idea that we live in a world filled with stories, and as we choose among them, we experience life differently.

So what are the strategies for developing a narrative? They're pretty simple, and you've lived with them all of your life. You've developed your narrative rationality standards, and as you create your own narratives to share, keep those ideas of fidelity and coherence in mind.

Narratives provide listeners with a sense of action or drama by developing a plot, characters, dialogue, vivid descriptions, and narrative tension leading to resolution. When you develop a narrative, it must enhance the audience's experience, understanding, or appreciation of a person, event, or concept. Your story should connect to something within the audience's lives. The introduction must establish a context and pull the audience in from the start. You could set details or character descriptions, place the story in a larger context, or even tell the audience what the moral or outcome will be. As the narrative unfolds, remember chronological construction: Give description and don't ramble. The story must have coherence and fidelity, with characters, a plot, and values that make sense to listeners. The conclusion should leave a lasting impression with your audience. It should make the significance of the narrative clear to the audience.

Emotional sincerity and personal involvement are essential. A good storyteller employs vivid language choices and expressive delivery; both lend interest and animation. You've learned about techniques for language imagery earlier in this chapter, and Chapter 4 exposed you to effective delivery techniques.

Narratives often give detail to ideas that are shared from generation to generation. Stories develop characters and plots that help us make sense of sometimes difficult and unrelated ideas. They help to bridge difference in age, culture, gender and distance. Narratives stir emotions and generate interest in the minds and ears of listeners. We live in a world filled with narratives.

HOW IMPORTANT IS CREDIBILITY?

At the start of this chapter, you learned that informative messages instruct, clarify, and/or enlighten listeners. Through informative communication, your audience becomes more knowledgeable, gains new insight and new information, and understands complicated issues and feelings more fully. You can provide all the basic information to successfully create a well-developed informative message, but if you lack credibility, you will not be believed, nor will your information. Remember, credibility is developed through character, intelligence, goodwill, and charisma *as perceived by your audience.*

It is likely that you've had a teacher that you just didn't believe. Maybe that teacher contradicted something you learned before, didn't explain something clearly, used words you didn't understand, or told stories that were off topic. When informing, you are essentially acting in that teacher role, so you want to avoid those pitfalls. You can create a well-structured message and work on your language use, but are there other details you should consider?

Let's review some suggestions for you to try to enhance the audience's impression of your credibility and that of your message. Be prepared. Have a well-organized, well-supported message, and be flexible enough to alter it if needed. Be ready to answer questions competently. Use language that is adapted to the audience; you do not want to insult them by talking down, but if you have any doubts about their ability to comprehend your message, be sure to define, describe, and illustrate with examples. If you share group affiliation (because of your age, location, educational or work experiences, cultural background, or organizational membership), be sure to incorporate those affiliations into your message if appropriate by referring to them or using supporting materials that will reinforce them. Credibility is a changing factor, based on a number of perceptions. The only constant is that credibility exists within the mind of the audience, and your listeners or readers attribute character, intelligence, goodwill, and charisma based on their own unique perceptions.

Establish your qualifications to speak on this topic. Do you have experience? Is this your major? What you're trying to do here is show why we should listen to you in the first place. As you develop your ideas, be sure to share information accurately from credible sources. Credibility of sources can be established by reviewing the credentials of the information (or its source), including who said it, when they said it, and where it appears. This is as important in an educational setting as it is in any business environment. When you back yourself up with other credible sources, it enhances the audience's perceptions of whether or not to believe you; you're not the only one forwarding this idea. If you're defining something, you can easily cite the dictionary source that provided the original denotative meaning. If you're giving cautions in a process, there's probably a guidebook that you used at some point that reminded you of them. If you're explaining how an event got to the present point, why not provide testimony from those involved? If you fail to share accurate and credible information beyond yourself, you'll quickly be revealed for the shallowness of your contributions. Speakers who fail to acknowledge sources are charged with plagiarism, as you learned earlier in this text. Citing sources of evidence and using sources that the audience already accepts can add to your credibility.

Totem poles are used as narratives by Native Americans to help communicate important tribal stories.
© Ieva Geneviciene, 2008, Shutterstock.

You must also make sure that what you are saying is accurate when communicating an informative message, since such messages are often repeated. Misinforming a person either "accidentally" or intentionally has serious implications. If your audience is well informed and picks up on the misinformation, your credibility will be diminished, and your message will have lost its impact. On a more serious note, business people who knowingly share inaccurate information are quickly removed from positions of significance to ensure that they cannot harm the organization or its people. Alternatively, if the listener repeats the misinformation, more people are lead astray. If you forget to mention one step in a process, leave out one ingredient, or misspeak about a person involved in a narrative, you're deceiving the audience. Imagine the impact of one piece of misinformation shared in one speech to a group of twenty people who share that information with four other people, who share the information with two of their family members. In this scenario, 260 people are misled by one ill-informed or perhaps unethical speaker.

The creation of a credible persona is not easy. In fact, it carries some peril with it. When you open yourself up to others by sharing your ideas or values, you are taking a risk. What if others do not agree? What if they find your ideas to be ridiculous or wrong? When you attempt to establish yourself as someone to believe (in order to inform), others might think you lack expertise or are trying to come off as a know-it-all. Can you show that your point of view is believable, along with demonstrating that you should be perceived as a reliable authority? Because credibility is an essential factor in communication, it is worth the risk. There are some fairly simple, straightforward strategies that you can use to enhance your audience's perception of your credibility.

SUMMARY

What should you remember about creating and presenting informative messages? When you give an informative message, your listeners become more knowledgeable, learn new information, and/or gain a greater appreciation about some idea. A variety of informative messages exist: they seek to educate, train, describe, critique, or facilitate the sharing of information. In each case, the goal of the message exchange is to increase understanding between sender and receiver.

ENDNOTES

1. Global Green USA, http://www.globalgreen.org/programs/water/index.html (accessed August 10, 2007).

2. Global Green USA, http://www.globalgreen.org/programs/water/day.html (accessed August 10, 2007).

3. "Mesquite," *Dictionary.com*, http://dictionary.reference.com/browse/mesquite (accessed August 26, 2007).

4. "Scissors," Dictionary.com, http://dictionary.reference.com/browse/scissors (accessed August 26, 2007).

5. "Apprehension," Dictionary.com, http://dictionary.reference.com/browse/apprehension (accessed August 26, 2007).

6. There are all sorts of literary figures of speech you can see, such as metaphor, irony, hyperbole, and so on. However, these probably don't come quickly to mind while you're speaking. It's more likely that you'd find these useful when writing. Keep in mind that spoken language is simple rather than complex, concrete rather than abstract.

7. http://www.askoxford.com/concise_oed/briefing?view=uk AskOxford.com Oxford University Press, 2007 (accessed August 22, 2007).

8. "History of Harley-Davidson," Harley-Davidson Company, http://www.harley-davidson.com/wcm/Content/Pages/ H-D_History/history_1900s.jsp?loc=en_US (accessed August 26, 2007).

9. W. R. Fisher, *Human Communication as Narration: Toward a Philosophy of Reason, Value, and Action* (Columbia: University of South Carolina Press, 1985).

10. R. Rowland, "On Limiting the Narrative Paradigm: Three Case Studies." *Communication Monographs,* 56, (1989): 39–53.

11. J. L. Lucaites, and C. M. Condit, "Reconstructing Narrative Theory: A Functional Perspective." *Journal of Communication* 35, (1985): 90.

12. Fisher, 19.

13. Fisher, 58.

14. Michael Vick Statement Excerpts. Washington Post.com. Saturday, August 25, 2007; Page E10. http://www.washingtonpost.com/wp-dyn/content/article/2007/08/24/AR2007082402081.html?hpid=topnews (accessed August 26, 2007).

15. http://www.chinapage.com/story/story.html
http://www.firstpeople.us/FP-Html-Wisdom/sitemap.html
http://www.kumeyaay.com/
http://www.mwg.org/production/websites/jacktales/resources/appalachian_scholars.html
http://russian-crafts.com/tales.html

WHAT IS PERSUASIVE COMMUNICATION?

LEARNING OBJECTIVES

After reading this chapter, you should understand the following concepts:

- Persuasion is a process of social influence, involving the preparation and presentation of messages that affect others' beliefs, values, attitudes, and actions.
- Informative communication goals differ from persuasive goals, and it is important to recognize the differences.
- There are three types of persuasive propositions: claims of fact, value, and policy.
- Every speech should have one level-one goal and one level-two goal.
- The social judgment theory, cognitive dissonance theory, and elaborate likelihood model are three models that theorists have used to describe how persuasion influences audiences.
- Credibility, reasoned arguments, and emotional appeal are essential to effective persuasion.
- Flaws in a persuasive argument include defective evidence, defective arguments, and misused language.

INTRODUCTION

When the national collegiate football polls come out in the summer, declaring this team or that team the preseason number one, do you agree? When a television infomercial shouts that you need this new weight-loss solution, do you pull out your phone or log on to the Web site to buy it? When hearing a claim by a political party that it is the one to protect American values, do politicians associated with that party get your vote? Have you ever participated in a boycott, protest march, or fundraising drive? The choices you made in all of these cases were the result of persuasion.

Persuasion involves influence, attempting to get someone else to see or do things our way. But the word *influence* is too simple for this complex phenomenon. **Persuasion** is a process of social influence, involving the preparation and presentation of verbal and nonverbal messages to others to influence their beliefs, values, attitudes, or actions. First, it involves social influence; the person being persuaded has the choice to accept or to reject the message. She can decide whether the strategies should influence her choices.

Do you take a salesperson's advice when you buy clothes?
© 2008, JupiterImages Corporation.

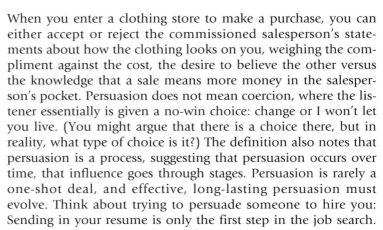

When you enter a clothing store to make a purchase, you can either accept or reject the commissioned salesperson's statements about how the clothing looks on you, weighing the compliment against the cost, the desire to believe the other versus the knowledge that a sale means more money in the salesperson's pocket. Persuasion does not mean coercion, where the listener essentially is given a no-win choice: change or I won't let you live. (You might argue that there is a choice there, but in reality, what type of choice is it?) The definition also notes that persuasion is a process, suggesting that persuasion occurs over time, that influence goes through stages. Persuasion is rarely a one-shot deal, and effective, long-lasting persuasion must evolve. Think about trying to persuade someone to hire you: Sending in your resume is only the first step in the job search. You will probably have a call-back, will hopefully get an interview, and then may negotiate the job. When we persuade, we prepare and present both verbal and nonverbal messages. You can influence others by a look as well as with a piece of data. Persuasion may involve symbols as well as symbolic acts. Imagine that you have been pulled over by a state highway patrol officer for exceeding the speed limit. What will you say or do? You might look repentant and admit your error, offering an apology. Maybe you will be defiant and refuse to show your registration, saying that you were just keeping up with the flow. Perhaps you break down in tears, throwing yourself on the officer's mercy. The definition says that when we persuade, we attempt to influence (to alter, reinforce, or create) beliefs, values, attitudes, or actions in others. So all of your police-response strategies are kinds of persuasion, but the success of each one depends on some intricate aspects. That depth of influence explains why persuasion is so complex and takes time.

Underlying this definition are some other essential considerations. Persuasion has an *instrumental orientation*, meaning that it is goal-oriented with goals that are potentially multifaceted. You might be attempting to influence beliefs, values, or even policies that others have. *Persuasive contexts* are important. As with most communication acts, where and when a message is delivered is important. An infomercial is different from a Web site pop-up; a personal plea is not the same as hearing a political speech in an auditorium rally. Finally, while the listener can choose whether and how much to be influenced, you as the persuader have the ability to strategically create a message that is effective in that influence. Persuasion is not just about the reasonableness or emotional impact of a message; it also involves the listener's perception about the credibility of the source, as you will see.

What would you tell a police officer who stopped you for speeding?
© 2008, JupiterImages Corporation.

ARE THERE DIFFERENCES BETWEEN INFORMATIVE AND PERSUASIVE GOALS?

As you have already learned earlier, communication serves many different purposes. When you construct a strategic message, it is important for you to consider what your goals are, and where you want to take the audience. Before we look at how you create strategic persuasion, it is important to consider how persuasive goals differ from informative goals, since these are the two kinds of messages you will give most often.

First, *informative communication clarifies, whereas persuasion urges choice.* Consider the role of an instructor. His mandate is to offer information so that the material becomes more comprehensible to the audience. Although you may already know something about the topic, the instructor's informative communication tries to help you understand it on a more complex level. Perhaps you will learn about the symptoms of depression in a psychology class. As opposed to the instructor, the persuader comes with the goal of choice: She wants you to take ideas and do something with them. That "doing" might be believing in a different way (changing your mind about people who suffer from depression), or it might be deepening your conviction (getting you to believe that you can make a change in your life to overcome depression).

An instructor's role is to inform so students understand subjects on a more complex level.
© 2008, JupiterImages Corporation.

A second distinction is related to the first: *where informative communication teaches, persuasion leads.* Consider this as a different role the source plays. If someone asks you for directions, you are expected to dispassionately offer the turn-left-here details. A persuader is also an expert, but her job is to move the listener. If you were trying to persuade someone of the best route, you might say that there are three different ways to go: one offers greater scenic views, one passes shopping areas, and the third, your favorite, is the most time efficient.

Third, *where informative communication stresses understanding, persuasion does that and more: it adds the arousal of emotions.* As you will shortly learn, the impact of pathos, or emotional appeal, is a hallmark of persuasive strategy. The networks' evening news is supposed to be presented by impartial journalists who present the details of the day; Jon Stewart's *The Daily Show* may also cover those stories, but his ironic or sarcastic slant is designed to influence the way you perceive what happens in the world.

Finally, *informative communication calls for little audience commitment; persuasion requires it.* The audience for an informative speaker simply needs to receive the information; the source has no sense of whether the audience accepts it. As a persuader, you are consumed with a desire for commitment and approval. You want to see that your listener can use your message for future thought or upcoming action.

News journalists present the details of the day in an impartial manner.
© Florian ISPAS, 2008, Shutterstock.

You might be thinking that there seems to be overlap on these two goals: Certain newsgathering organizations decide to cover a story in one way (or ignore it totally), while others provide a different slant. Is that informing or persuading? What if you provide a friend with statistics about the links between skin cancer and excess suntanning? Are you simply attempting to provide her with some enlightening data, or are you attempting to get her to stop using the tanning booths? What about the choices your instructor makes in thinking about course materials? When he tells a story to illustrate a point, does it come from his own value-laden experience, and might that be more influential, rather than being just a means of providing the wisdom of his discipline? In use, there is a fine line between informative and persuasive communication. The speaker's intent is the primary distinction here: What is the goal that the speaker has for the audience?

Persuasive skills come into play when you're trying to sell a product or service.
© Teze, 2008, Shutterstock.

WHAT ARE THE TYPES OF PERSUASIVE CLAIMS?

Since this is a chapter primarily about persuasive public speaking, the focus will be on the speaker's task, but most of the fundamental aspects of public speaking can also be applied to other persuasive endeavors, such as interviewing for a job, pleading your case to another, creating an ad, selling a product or service, or designing a persuasive Web site. You already know that persuasion has an instrumental orientation. When you persuade, you do so with a strategic end result in mind. You can probably guess that persuasive speaking is a complex task, but it is a bit simpler when you think about it in terms of types of persuasive claims and their accompanying goals.

A **claim** serves the same purpose as a thesis statement in an informative speech: it represents the desired end result of the speech, the main idea that you want the audience to assume. Claims are also referred to as *conclusions* or *propositions*. Think of it this way: A conclusion is what you want the audience to reach by the end of your speech; a proposition is what you want them to accept. Just as there were different types of informative messages, the same is true in persuasion. There are three types of persuasive claims:

1. Claim of fact
2. Claim of value
3. Claim of policy

A **persuasive claim of fact** attempts to create a belief in an audience. Remember, a *belief* is your personal conception of reality—what you think "is." You might have beliefs about the existence of a supreme being, the existence of the Loch Ness Monster, or what the term *abortion* means. Those constitute your *facts* or *beliefs* (see Chapter 12). The goal of a claim of fact is to get your audience to think of something in a new way, or to get them to conceive of something they had never thought of before. You are attempting to create a shared reality. For example, a speaker might propose, "Nuclear power is an alternative form of energy to oil." The speaker is not just giving information about what constitutes nuclear power; he is trying to get you to see that it is an alternative to another form. A communication professor may find himself explaining the discipline as "not just an offshoot" of English, but rather as an ancient discipline with its own theories, strategies, and skills. A speaker wants you to make his reality into your reality when offering a persuasive claim of fact.

A **persuasive claim of value** goes beyond creation of reality. It attempts to get the audience to accept a judgment based on certain criteria. Using the nuclear power example, a speaker might say, "Nuclear power is the most efficient form of energy." If you are going to accept that claim, then you and he have to agree on what *most efficient* means. If you try to persuade another individual that Tom Hanks is the best actor of his generation, you are making a claim of value. How do you judge what a *best actor* is? Is it defined by the number of Oscars won, box office receipts, variety of roles, or number of films in a certain period? These become criteria by which "best actor" can be both understood and judged. When a friend asks you for an opinion about a class you took, you do not just repeat what was on the syllabus; you offer value judgments about the excellence of the professor, the importance of the book, the helpfulness of the assignments—or just the opposite. But when you make that claim that this is a "good" class, you are doing it on the basis of some value judgments on criteria that help to center you.

A **persuasive claim of policy** argues what should be done by the audience. Policy claims focus on the *oughts* or *shoulds* in our lives. You should not use tanning booths, you should have your pet spayed or neutered, you ought to dump your significant other, you ought to go see this movie starring Tom Hanks, you should vote for candidate X. Policy claims focus on future actions that the listener should consider; they are based on a foundation of shared beliefs and values. Once the speaker has gotten you to believe that nuclear power is an alternative to oil and that it is the most efficient form of energy, he can then attempt to persuade you that "the state should invest in nuclear power plants." This progression of claim of fact, to value, to policy illustrates another of the basic ideas about persuasion: it is rarely a one-shot opportunity. Persuasion takes time to develop; your persuasive goals may have to be incremental to get the desired end.

What kind of an argument might someone make if they are advocating nuclear power?
© Kristin Smith, 2008, Shutterstock.

WHAT DO I NEED TO DEVELOP PERSUASIVE GOALS?

Let us look a bit deeper at these types of persuasive claims to examine their instrumental orientation. Consider a two-tiered approach to persuasive goals. The speaker has goals for the overall effect of the speech; the speaker also develops a specific goal for the audience. Every speech should have one level-one (or general) goal and one level-two (or specific) goal.

Level-one Goals

Level-one (general) goals might be considered the broad, overall goals of the speech. As the message creator, what is it that you hope to accomplish? Based on your audience analysis, what do you know about your audience that impacts the choices of rhetorical strategies you will use? It might be easy to think of level-one goals as being based on your perceptions of the audience at the start of your speech.

To Convince. If your goal is to **convince,** then you want to change the way your audience thinks or believes. You begin with the assumption that the audience disagrees with you, or perhaps they know nothing about your topic. For instance, what if you wanted to develop a speech that said, "Excessive suntanning is harmful." That is a claim of value, and you think that most people in your audience see nothing wrong with tanning booths or laying out in the sun. You want to influence them to change their minds.

To Stimulate. A goal to **stimulate** assumes that the audience already agrees with you, but you want to strengthen that conviction because it is built on a shaky foundation. "The Shroud of Turin is the burial cloth of Jesus" would be a claim of fact. The audience probably has heard of this Shroud, but perhaps they have not thought about why they believe or agree with you. You want to cement that

How does a coach heighten players' desire to win the game?
© Amy Meyers, 2008, Shutterstock.

agreement by heightening their belief. Speeches to stimulate are the ones coaches give before a game and at half-time; the team already wants to win, but the coach needs to stoke that fire.

To Actuate. Finally, the level-one goal to **actuate** means "to move to action." You are not satisfied with simply making the audience feel stronger in their belief; you want to get the audience up off their feet and doing something. "You should not purchase music with racist or sexist lyrics" is a policy speech where you assume the audience agrees with you but they are not doing anything about that agreement. By the end of your message, you want to push them to action.

Level-two Goals

Level-two (specific) goals mesh with level-one goals by providing a definitive, explicit goal for the audience. Think of these as specifying where you want the audience to be in mind or action at the end of the speech. What's the desired end result? You learned about three of these specific goals in Chapter 3 about critical thinking, but they are so essential to your creation of persuasion that a brief review and addition are important here.

To Adopt. To **adopt** means that you expect the audience to take on something new. A goal to adopt would assume that the audience does not know what you are talking about or isn't currently doing what you propose. The policy claim "Bravo Company should be fined for dumping unused baby formula in third-world countries" is an example of the level-two goal to adopt. Your level-one goal would be to convince, because it's likely that the audience is ignorant about the issue. You want them to adopt a position that gets them to agree with your suggested policy.

To Discontinue. The goal to **discontinue** suggests the replacement of one idea or policy with another. Suppose you wanted the audience to agree to raise the drinking age to twenty-two. It's probably safer to assume that most people in your college-age audience will disagree. This would mean that your level-one goal is to convince. But what will you propose as an alternative? When you attempt to discontinue, you try to get the audience to abandon one way of thinking or behaving in favor of another.

To Continue. A goal to **continue** this speech is needed because you sense the audience's enthusiasm is flagging. It is usually paired with the level-one goal to stimulate. Now, you need to give them something specific to focus on to energize them again. Self-help groups use this message with frequency: You have not taken a drink (or a drug, or a hot fudge brownie sundae) for six months, so keep up the good work! You need to remind the audience why they started something in the first place, and you need to figure out a way to keep them on the right path.

To Deter. Finally, a level-two purpose to **deter** might be a bit unusual, for it means "to influence to stop something before you begin it." The anti-drug program D.A.R.E. has this purpose. Fifth graders probably do not know much about drugs and alcohol (to convince), and D.A.R.E.'s goal is to influence them through appeals to stop that behavior before the children reach middle school and are faced with decisions about alcohol or drugs.

When you consider your goals, you are not only thinking about your general purpose (level one) for speaking to this group, but also the end result (level two) you expect to reach with that audience. When you consider your goals, they should guide you in terms of the type of speech you need to give. More importantly, your goals will help you to strategize about what will form the content of your message. But before you can begin to strategize, you need to know as much as you can about your audience.

As explained in Chapter 12, part of the way you can work on your audience's perception and willingness to accept your claim is to have your own picture of them in order to target them most effectively. Because the individual members of your audience will possess her or his own blend of demographics and psychographics, it is probably impossible to really construct an accurate picture of the group. But the very nature of communication requires that you address people as though they are a known entity. Therefore, you need to be able to form some generalized beliefs about people and how they might react to your message and to you. A good message is audience-centered; your message needs to demonstrate in its content, organization, and language that you have placed the highest interest in the audience's needs and reactions.

Why is it important to know as much as you can about your audience?
© Igor Karon, 2008, Shutterstock.

HOW DO THEORISTS DESCRIBE THE PERSUASIVE PROCESS?

Different theorists have discussed how persuasion actually works in influencing an audience, and you may have never thought about how influence has an effect on your daily life. Let's consider three theories that provide differing perspectives on the persuasive process. The **social judgment theory** suggests that attitude change is mediated by a judgment process, and it also supplies a way of thinking about how to persuade others.[1] In essence, people compare incoming persuasive messages to their present points of view. **Cognitive dissonance theory** says that dissonance resulting from inconsistent beliefs, attitudes, or behaviors is an uncomfortable feeling that motivates people to try to reduce it.[2] The **elaboration likelihood model** attempts to explain how people's attitudes are formed and influenced.

Social Judgment Theory

Social judgment theory says that people do not evaluate messages based on their merit alone; instead, their beliefs and attitudes are reference points for deciding whether to accept or to reject the persuasive message. Put simply, the success of persuasion is the end of a process when you compare your position to that of the persuasive message. This theory first suggests that we have core beliefs and values, called **anchor positions,** which serve to center our thoughts. Imagine being in a small boat out in the middle of a lake. Before fishing, you toss out the anchor that will keep you in the same stable

Your anchor positions will keep you centered, much like an anchor holds a boat in place.
© Kokhanchikov, 2008, Shutterstock.

area. Although your boat may move a bit, you will essentially stay put. That is what core anchors do. Second, according to this theory, we have **judgment categories** (latitudes or zones) that we use to evaluate incoming persuasive messages. Our opinions cannot be represented as points along a continuum, because we have degrees of tolerance around our positions. These latitudes include *the latitude of acceptance* (the range where incoming persuasion agrees with our core beliefs), the *latitude of rejection* (the zone where incoming messages deny something we believe or value); and *the latitude of noncommitment* (a neutral zone, where either we have no core anchors to judge the incoming message by, or we do not know enough to make that judgment).

As an example, let us say that you feel higher education is essential to a successful life. This anchor is made up of beliefs about what constitutes higher education (post-secondary), as well as some values about what makes up success. Your friend suggests that you take a special class that the community college is offering on emerging electronic technologies. Although you will not get academic credit for the class and it will cut into your limited free time, you put that message into the latitude of acceptance, because it agrees with your notion that higher education is valuable. But what if that friend comes to you and says that he thinks you should drop out of the classes you are taking this term, because they are a waste of time and you can make better money as a reality show cast member? That message will likely fall into your latitude of rejection; what your friend is telling you negates your beliefs in higher education and the definitions of success.

The next concept in the social judgment theory is about **ego-involvement;** it refers to the importance of an issue to you. You might be able to determine high ego-involvement by several characteristics:

- It includes membership in a group with a known stand (social conservatives, for example).
- Your latitude of noncommitment is nearly nonexistent (things are either accepted or rejected; there is no middle ground).
- You care deeply about the topic, and it's tied to your self-concept.

For example, for an adoptive parent, issues about adoption such as adoption law, adoption discrimination, and adoption costs are very important. The adoptive parent is ego-involved and may even have studied the topic more thoroughly than necessary for his own personal involvement. When that person hears stories about disrupted adoptions, adoption fraud, changing state adoption laws, or single-parent adoption, there is no middle ground for him. He knows where he stands, and why. In contrast, he may not be nearly as concerned with issues involving gun rights, legalizing marijuana, or forest clear-cutting. A person might be highly ego-involved with one issue but not involved in others. We are all susceptible to ego-involvement. Criticize a friend's parents or family, ridicule the way a girlfriend thinks, or make a disparaging comment about a new hairstyle, then wait for the ego-involvement to become apparent.

Social judgment theory suggests that persuasion works because we tend to make incoming information fit our judgment categories. These *distortions* of information are called assimilation and contrast effects.

An **assimilation effect** is said to occur when a person perceives the message to advocate a position closer to his or her own position than it actually does; the person minimizes the differences between the message's position and his position. For example, you might perceive the candidate from your political party as having the same attitudes as you do on issues of restarting the draft, school funding, and immigration reform, even though the person has made policy statements on those issues that don't really reflect what you think should be done. You minimize the distinctions between your position and your candidate's because you think that someone from your party must think like you, and you feel that policy statements are more political than personal on her part.

A **contrast effect** occurs when a person perceives the message as advocating a position further away from his position than it actually does; the person exaggerates the difference between the message's position and his own.[3] In the political example, this would be where you "push away" the ideas from a candidate from a different party, even though they're very similar to yours, because you can't believe that someone from that other party could think anything like you do.

Two important findings can be gathered from social judgment theory. First, if people judge a message as within their latitude of acceptance, they adjust their attitudes to accommodate it. This results in a positive persuasive effect. The most persuasive message is the one that is most discrepant from the receiver's position but still falls in his or her latitude of acceptance. Second, if a person judges a message to be within the latitude of rejection, she may adjust her attitude away from it.

This impact is complicated even more: For individuals with high ego-involvement, most messages that are aimed to persuade them that fall within their latitudes of rejection have the opposite effect, called the **boomerang effect**. By hearing something that is perceived as negating your position, you are made to feel even stronger about your position, rather than the desired persuasive effect of changing your mind.

How does the assimilation effect occur when you are comparing a politician's views to your own?
© 2008, JupiterImages Corporation.

Tips for Persuasion under the Social Judgment Theory

For some practical persuasive advice, the social judgment theory suggests these three tactics:

1. *For maximum influence, select a message right on the edge of the audience's latitude of acceptance.* Change cannot occur in the latitude of rejection. When you hear a message that you place in this zone, you will either stop listening to it or respond to it in a negative way.

2. *Persuasion is a gradual process, consisting of small movements.* You will not be able to move your listener from rejection to acceptance, but maybe you can move the listener from rejection to noncommittance (and a willingness to learn more) and then toward acceptance. If your audience does not know much about your topic or if the topic is a new one, then stick to basic information; you cannot move them until they have a perspective. Relate your ideas to things that are already familiar, and show them that this topic is relevant to them. If your audience is negative toward your topic, you may need to modify your position. Seek that common ground, and show that your points are relevant to their beliefs and attitudes, rather than to your own. You cannot expect your audience to undergo massive, immediate change. That happens only in the movies or by a miracle!

3. *Ego-involvement is essential to consider when persuading.* Take, for example, going to a parent–teacher conference. As soon as the discussion revolves around their child, it is likely that the parents will feel very strong ego-involvement. These reasonable people may change their behavior or attitudes when the teacher mentions anything that sounds remotely critical of the child. Why is this? Your child is an ego-involving issue; she reflects on your parenting, your family structure, and your ability (not to mention hers). Almost anything negative the teacher says is likely to fall into the latitude of rejection. It is also likely that if the parents distort anything the teacher says, the distortion will be contrast and not assimilation. Contrast will cause the parents to perceive negative teacher comments as being much worse than they really are.

Would skiing win out over working in your internal battle over what to do?
© 2008, JupiterImages Corporation.

Cognitive Dissonance Theory

Cognitive dissonance theory is based on the assumption that people need to see themselves as consistent in their thoughts and actions. When there is an inconsistency between cognitive elements (perceptions, beliefs, values, motives, and attitudes) and behavior, dissonance occurs. Think of dissonance as disharmony, stress, an uncomfortable feeling of being out of balance. We do not like living with inconsistencies in our lives; we prefer to be in balance. This theory suggests that competing cognitive elements will require something to change to eliminate the dissonance, and that is where persuasion comes in.

Say, for instance, that you have a project due at work on Monday, but you are invited to go skiing over the weekend. You feel dissonance because completing the project is important to your career, but skiing is really tempting fun. You must decide to do one or the other, but you consider the two sides. On one hand, completing the project will be tiring; you will be locked in your office all weekend; you are not sure if you have all the data you need; you do not want to disappoint your boss. On the other hand, you do not want to miss out on a ski weekend. Skiing is great exercise, which you really need; you desperately need a break; maybe you will meet someone new on the slopes. How do you deal with the dissonance created by this stressful dilemma?

According to dissonance theory, you have several choices.

- You could change your beliefs or attitudes about one of the choices (skiing becomes a dangerous physical activity rather than great exercise).
- You could add additional beliefs to one side of the equation (skiing is really expensive).
- You could make one of the choices seem to be less important than you originally did (your job will not be lost if the project is a day late).
- You might distort or misinterpret the information involved (you could claim that you did not know the project was due *this* Monday).

Cognitive dissonance is a fact of daily living. Let us look at another example. You are asked for your position on changing the immigration laws. On one hand, you acknowledge the mostly positive impact that immigrants have had on our nation. Your own grandparents were immigrants to the nation. You realize the economic influence they have. You work alongside people who have immigrated. On the other hand, you think that people who have come to the United States illegally should be deported; they have broken the law. You resent the fact that some immigrants resist learning English. You feel that your tax dollars are being used to support people who do not pay taxes.

To relieve this dissonance, you could reject the belief that tax dollars are being misused; you could remind yourself that your friend's adopted children were immigrants, and it took them three years to get here, but it was done legally, adding new beliefs to the mix; you could distort your beliefs about how many illegal immigrants there really are; you could seek out more information that supports one side or the other. In any case, the theory suggests that you will have to come down on one side or the other. Dissonance may be eliminated by reducing the importance of the conflicting beliefs, acquiring new beliefs that change the balance, or removing the conflicting attitude or behavior. In sum, dissonance occurs when you must choose between attitudes and behaviors that are contradictory.

As a communicator, you can employ dissonance theory to influence your audience. You might be able to create that dissonance and then help the audience to "solve" it by giving them ideas that support your position. This is the basis of most ads. You are told that a large number of people die needlessly because they are thrown from their cars for lack of a seatbelt, but this car has automatic seatbelts that stop that. You are reminded how little kids use too much toilet paper, resulting in stopped-up toilets and waste; however, buying this special toilet paper with marks on it will teach children how much to use. You are alarmed by statistics on the growing number of melanoma deaths, but your concerns are allayed by using this sun block lotion with SPF 50. Your audience will change by reorganizing their beliefs, attitudes, values, or actions because they cannot live with the imbalance they are feeling. You will have successfully persuaded!

Elaboration Likelihood Model

The elaboration likelihood model (ELM) attempts to explain how attitudes are formed and changed and how a person is influenced or persuaded.[4] This provides you with a third way to understand how theorists view persuasion. According to this theory, an individual's motivation toward change is developed through thought traveling through one of two routes. The **central route** suggests that people think actively about the message, evaluating information and weighing it against what they already know. To process a message centrally, the audience has to be motivated to respond and to think critically. **Elaboration** involves cognitive processes such as evaluation and recall. We use the central route to scrutinize ideas, determine their worth, and contemplate possible consequences. When people are motivated and able to think about the content of the message, elaboration is high. Your unique cognitive responses to the message determine the persuasive outcome (i.e., the direction and amount of your attitude change). If you're faced with a decision on buying a high-end product such as a car or a house, it's likely that you'll take time to list pros and cons, check out others' opinions, and take your time before you spend your money.

How much time would you take to decide to buy a big-ticket item such as a house?
© 2008, JupiterImages Corporation.

The **peripheral route** is used when we do not think about the message very much and are influenced more by the nonargumentative aspects of the message; this is low elaboration. It offers a way to accept or reject a message without any active thinking; you make quick decisions by relying on a variety of cues such as surface message features (the way a person looks, the number of supports given rather than their quality) or judgment heuristics (rules that guide thought, such as, "Professors know what they are talking about, so I should believe her").

This is typical of advertisements using celebrity endorsers; the hope is that you'll buy the product because someone you admire is using it. You don't think about the cost, your need, or any other important consideration. You want to be like that person, and by using that product, you will be one step closer. Persuasion can also occur with low elaboration. The receiver is not guided by a critical evaluation of the message, as happens in the central

Elaboration Likelihood Model

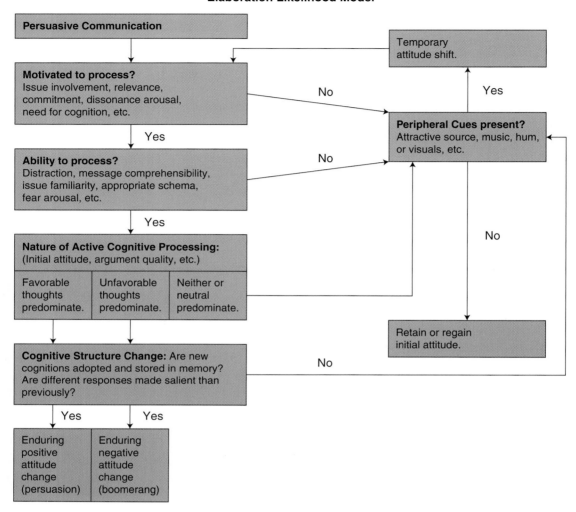

route; instead, the receiver decides to employ a decision rule that makes thinking simple.

As a speaker, you must determine whether the receivers are motivated to listen to the message and how much elaboration is likely to occur. Motivational factors could include the personal relevance of the message topic (ego-involvement), a person's need for information to think about and ability to examine that information, and factors such as the presence or absence of time pressures or distractions. One of the ways to motivate your listeners to take the central route is to make the message personally relevant to them. Fear can work in making them pay attention, but only you keep it moderate and give them a solution. Consider those ads that suggest you need a certain kind of energy drink, where someone just like you is pictured dragging through the day starting at about 2:00 P.M., just when you're supposed to be getting a project finished or meeting with an important client for a crucial presentation. Then the friendly announcer suggests that you could avoid that horrible scenario if you drank "High Energy Revitalizer," which costs under $2.00 per drink and is available in drink machines or your local convenience store. The end of the ad shows that person downing a delicious can of the drink, and minutes later she's no longer tired, the project gets completed, and the client loves the presentation! The ad moves you from fear to solution to visualizing success, all in thirty seconds.

ELM explains the differences in persuasive impact produced by messages that have a large amount of information and compelling reasons, as compared to messages that rely on simplistic reaction to some issue, situation, or thing. The key variable in this process is involvement: how willing and able to elaborate the audience member is. Is he willing to put in the effort required to critically consider the issue being advocated and its supporting materials? When elaboration is high, the central persuasive route is likely to occur. Conversely, the peripheral route is the likely result of low elaboration.

ELM helps us to understand why and when messages and self-motivated efforts are more or less likely to lead to influence. Keep it in mind when you are puzzled by your audience's reaction to your well-thought-out ideas. Maybe they are just using the peripheral route to thinking they have developed: They're saying to themselves, "If a college student is saying that, it can't possibly be true."

There are many communication theories that explore how persuasion occurs. Social judgment, cognitive dissonance, and elaboration likelihood are three that show you the importance of influencing the audience by the information you develop in your message. Persuasion is not linear; you do not really change someone else. Instead, you give that person reasons to change himself in the direction you desire. Let us consider some persuasive strategies that you might employ.

WHAT PERSUASIVE STRATEGIES SHOULD I USE?

On January 23, 2006, President Bush told an audience at Kansas State University that the congressional resolution passed in the wake of the September 11 attacks that authorized the invasion of Afghanistan and other counterterrorism measures gave him the legal authority to initiate a domestic surveillance program. Bush reportedly authorized the National Security Agency to intercept communications between people (including American citizens) within the United States and terrorist suspects overseas without obtaining a court warrant. Critics such as the American Civil Liberties Union call the program illegal, saying that it threatens civil liberties and privacy rights.[5] Now, imagine yourself taking the position of one of the sides of this question. Is the policy necessary for the safety of the country? Does eavesdropping violate your right to privacy? How would you go about establishing your persuasive speech supporting your position?

Effective persuasion is accomplished through the creation and use of several different strategies. Based on your audience, your goals, and the speech purpose, you will establish common ground through credibility; you will appeal to the audience's beliefs, attitudes, and values; and you will create reasoned arguments that allow the audience to think clearly.

Enhancing My Credibility

One of the strategies that you are already familiar with is the concept of *credibility*, the sense that the audience believes in you as a persuasive advocate. At various points in this text, we've referred to the sender's credibility. Your listeners assess your character, intelligence, goodwill, and charisma while you present your message. Their belief in you may come from your looks, your status, your role, your degree, your expertise, your trustworthiness, or any mixture of all of these. That doesn't mean that you should leave such perceptions up to chance. You have the opportunity to use what you know about the perceptional processes of selection, organization, and interpretation to influence the audience to see you as worthy and deserving of attention. Some recommendations include the following.

Demonstrate Personal Involvement in the Subject. You know the role of ego-involvement, according to social judgment theory. Even though your firsthand experience doesn't make you an expert, it can show that you have a stake in it. A speech about problems of people rebuilding houses in hurricane-prone lowlands could be made more personal if you showed before-and-after pictures of your family's vacation home.

Cite Research. If you can use sources that are respected by your audience, not only will you show that you are well read, but also those sources will add objectivity to what you are saying. Make sure you cite those sources accurately, and don't falsify information. Someone who uses elaboration (as described in the elaboration likelihood model) will demand to have evidence so that they can think through the ideas you're presenting. They'll not be satisfied by simple personal involvement, as someone who uses the peripheral route might be.

Create Identification with the Audience. We usually trust speakers who seem to share many similar attitudes and beliefs with us. Show that your background is similar; share beliefs, attitudes, and values. Use *we* language to show that common ground. If your audience sees similarity with you, your ideas may more likely fall into their latitude of acceptance, simply because they feel they share anchor positions with you.

Deliver your Message Confidently and Forcefully. You've already read about delivery techniques. As a reminder, consider some of the findings from a study of nonverbal behaviors, credibility, and persuasion by communication researchers Judee K. Burgoon, Thomas Birk, and Michael Pfau, who wanted to create a more complete and accurate representation of the persuasive impact of nonverbal behaviors.[6] Among their findings:

- Greater vocal pleasantness, kinesic/proxemic immediacy, kinesic dominance, and kinesic relaxation were associated with greater persuasiveness.
- Vocal cues (specifically, fluency and pitch variety) played a larger role in competence and composure judgments than did kinesic/proxemic cues, while the reverse was true for sociability and character judgments (with immediacy most strongly implicated).

- Vocal, kinesic, and proxemic cues that connote pleasantness and immediacy foster favorable credibility judgments on all but the dynamism dimension.[7]
- Greater vocal pleasantness, kinesic/proxemic immediacy, kinesic dominance, and kinesic relaxation were associated with greater persuasiveness.

Credibility is but one of the strategic dimensions of persuasion that you can employ. Although you would like to have your audience perceive you in a positive light, a failure to use reason can cause persuasive breakdown.

Creating Reasoned Argument

As you attempt to persuade someone to accept your ideas, you are trying to influence the way that person thinks. Most of us feel that what we know is superior to what someone else thinks. As you try to get your audience to shift in their beliefs, values, attitudes, or actions, you must lead them through a series of reasons. In ancient terms, this aspect of message creation was called *logos*. With persuasion, you present a claim or position that is supported by reasons for its acceptance; this is known as **argument**. **Reasoning** is a systematic mental process of moving from one idea to another in order to reach a new conclusion.

Types of Reasoning. Two basic types of reasoning might be considered for persuasion. **Inductive reasoning** occurs as we mentally progress from a single impression or example to form a general conclusion. You see someone wearing a certain kind of clothing, and you assume something about that person's values. You see Johnny Depp in a pirate movie and assume that he must be a weird character in real life because of how he looks and acts on screen. You read a story about the famine in a third-world country, and you reason that all people who have emigrated from that country have left there to escape famine. Specific-example-to-general-conclusion reasoning is needed because we can only assimilate so much information. We create categories for generalizations, but sometimes those generalized conclusions are based on limited or incorrect information. **Deductive reasoning,** by contrast, moves your thoughts from a generalized belief to a new specific instance. For example, if you believe that a certain type of ethnic food is too spicy, when offered a sample from that ethnic food group, you might pass it up without tasting it, reasoning that it will be too spicy, too. Television producers may believe that their target audience prefers reality programming; as a result, the newest offering is another reality show. Deduction allows you to take an audience from where they are to where you would like them to be by reasoning from general to specific. Your persuasive speech is a series of reasons, both inductive and deductive, created by the organization and manipulation of your supporting materials into logical structures. As you recall from Chapter 3, you can make use of five essential types of supporting materials, or kinds of evidence, but now you have to think about their successful application.

Based on appearance, what do you assume about her values?
© Ronald Sumners, 2008, Shutterstock.

Let's briefly review three organizing strategies that are effective for persuasive messages and see how they display reasoning; these and other forms have already been explained earlier in Chapter 13.

Cause-effect order is used to show a relationship between a source and its outcomes. You could also reverse the order and show how some effects can be traced back to their origins. Cause-effect order allows you to develop a reasoning chain that uses induction as it demonstrates that a certain end state (effect) is the result of specific causes. If you were giving a persuasive speech of fact that asserts, "Campus parking does not meet the needs of the campus community," you might develop your ideas by describing the locations of the lots, the conditions of the lots, and the number of permits given. By combining these three specific points, you can reason toward the proposition that parking does not meet the needs of the community. If you can get the audience to believe your three specific causes (locations, conditions, and permits), then you can lead them to effect (inadequate parking situation).

Problem-solution order structures ideas by pointing out a dilemma and offering (or supporting) its potential remedies. If you use this structure, you must first demonstrate that a dilemma exists, that it's serious, and that it impacts your audience. Then you are able to move into the potential solutions, perhaps even focusing on one resolution. Problem-solution order may be a more familiar persuasive pattern, and it often mixes inductive and deductive reasoning. It works especially well when you want to create dissonance and then resolve it.[8] Many advertisements begin by envisioning a problem such as "your house smells like a cat." They then suggest that their product will eliminate the problem: New "Cat No Smell" removes all tell-tale signs of Kitty. By getting you to consider that this problem may be occurring in your life, even though you were unaware of it, advertisers can successfully create dissonance and the desire to remove it. When a solution is made available immediately, you are more primed to consider it.

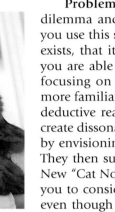

Can an advertisement make you think your house smells like the cat?
© 2008, JupiterImages Corporation.

Finally, there's Monroe's **motivated sequence,** that evolution of the problem-solution format that encourages your audience to take a specific action. As the name implies, the motivated sequence employs psychological principles, especially that of balance, as it moves the audience through five interrelated steps: attention, need, satisfaction, visualization, and action. In the *attention step*, you want to cause the listeners to focus tightly on you and your ideas. This step comes in the introduction of the speech. A speech arguing for the creation of Saturday morning classes could say, "Our college should institute Saturday morning classes." The next three steps constitute the body. *Need* demonstrates to the audience that a serious problem exists that demands change. Remember, in the need step of the body, you try to create in your audience an uncomfortable state of dissonance which they will want to alter. That's the essence of cognitive dissonance theory, which you learned about earlier. When people are made to feel dissonance, they want to resolve it. It is in the need step that you can join evidence with emotion; you can utilize those needs that Maslow described (see Chapter 12).

The second part of the body, *satisfaction*, proposes a plan of action that will solve the need. It's here that you will describe your solution to the problems you just defined. There should be one overall solution to the entire need, not an individual solution to each problem you described. Here's a continuance of the example:

1. Repeat proposition statement: Our college should institute Saturday morning classes.
2. Describe major aspects of the plan: Supports here could be costs, time factors, and people involved.
3. If plan is used elsewhere, tell us about its success.

Example: Using Motivated Sequence to Develop Needs

Linking what motivates us (called *motive appeals*) with reasoned evidence isn't all that difficult. Here's how you might develop the needs, with the motive appeals in parenthesis:

Problem one: There is a severe lack of classroom space (safety, security, timeliness needs)

a. Registrar quote (interview 8/13/07)
b. Statistics on buildings/needs (Muffo report, 9/28/07)
c. Departmental example: lab space (dept. head interview 10/01/07)

Problem two: The university is unable to offer classes (security, esteem)

a. Registrar quote (interview 8/13/07)
b. Advising center statistics (Web site)
c. Personal example
d. Difficulties with labs (peer experience interview 10/03/07)

Problem three (and so on; you determine how many you need to cover to indicate the extent of the problem)

You wouldn't blatantly say, "Now this point brings up the problem of safety," but as you develop your evidence, you could say, for instance, that the lack of lab space has increased safety concerns because of too many people using the lab.

The third part of the body (or fourth step of the motivated sequence) is *visualization,* where you picture for the audience what the world will be like if your plan is adopted. This step projects the audience into the future to intensify their desire for change. It's important to remember that the conditions you picture must seem probable. The visualization step should be a logical counterpart to all of the ideas brought up in the need step. You may choose the positive, negative, or combination method.

The last step is *action,* where you urge the audience to do a specific, explicit act. You want to give them detailed information on how to accomplish this action, so that they will know how to commit themselves. One caution: Asking your audience to "think about this" isn't an action! What behavior do you want them to do? An example for this speech would urge the audience to attend the SGA meeting to be held on Tuesday in Squires at 7 P.M. to voice your support for this controversial change. This is an example of a "passive change" speech, since the audience can't actually make the plan occur.

Take a Closer Look

The positive method of visualization looks like this.

If the college instituted Saturday morning classes, we would enjoy many benefits:

1. Classroom space would be increased by 460 rooms.
   You would support this by doing the math, by quotations, and by illustration.
2. More classes could be offered on Saturdays.
   You would suggest what these new classes could be—in-field labs, for example.

STRATEGIC FACTORS OF REASONING

Beyond order and reasoning come some other strategic considerations for persuasion. Remember, there are many variables that can impact your persuasive situation, so these ideas are simply pieces of experience for you to think about. It's impossible to establish the "perfect" template for any communication event.

Letting the audience know what is about to come, **forewarning,** might work well in informative speaking, but research suggests that for persuaders, the message is more effective when forewarning is minimized. There are some exceptions, however. If your receivers initially agree with you and you are seeking only small changes, it is okay to let them know what is coming. Reconsider that latitude of acceptance: Forewarning stimulates your audience to start thinking about things you want them to think about.

Message sidedness refers to the concept that there are two sides to every issue.[9] A *one-sided message* presents only one perspective; a *two-sided message* presents both sides. However, both types still advocate only one position. Where a one-sided message defends a position and avoids bringing up competing views, a two-sided message also defends a position and attacks the opposite. If a two-sided message simply mentions competing perspectives and there is no attack on the competition, it does no more than a one-sided message. The question is, which approach is better? One-sided messages are more effective when these factors are true:

- Your audience is friendly towards you.
- The audience already favors and/or agrees with your message.
- Listeners do not know much or anything about your topic.
- Counterarguments from the opposition will not be presented.
- You want immediate (not sustained) change, like buying an impulse purchase or signing a petition.

Two-sided messages are more effective when these factors apply:

- The audience is critical, skeptical or unfriendly.
- The audience is well-educated and expects to hear both sides.
- Opposing arguments from your competition are likely to be presented.
- You desire sustained change (you do not want them to agree or do only for the moment; you want them to continue this change).

Two-sided messages appear to be more fair and balanced. For an audience that is not thinking very carefully, two-sided messages make the persuader seem more credible. In addition, for the audience who is thinking carefully, the combination of defense and attack makes them think even more systematically about the issue and may start them questioning the validity of the "other" side. However, by pointing out something about the opposition, you run the risk of having the audience agree with that other side (remember the boomerang effect).

The variables of *primacy* and *recency* refer to a person's tendency to remember what he or she hears at the beginning or at the end of a message. This strategic consideration involves when you should present your *best evidence.* A *primacy effect* means that arguments presented first are more persuasive than later ones. Primacy is especially effective when you need to focus the audience's attention quickly or provide them structure and direction, along with comprehension. This means that primacy works when a topic is controversial or interesting, or when you have an issue that is highly familiar to your audience. The goal is to get to the major point quickly so as to focus them. *Recency*, presenting the most important arguments last for the greatest impact, works under conditions where the subject is uninteresting or the issues are relatively unfamiliar. You can work your way up to the important point you want the audience to act on.

When you use an emotional appeal, you are evoking an emotional response from others.
© Nicholas Sutcliffe, 2008, Shutterstock.

HOW CAN I APPEAL TO THE AUDIENCE'S EMOTIONS?

Consider how often you encounter persuasion based on arousal of feelings of pride or love, sentiment or nostalgia, or those that manipulate our guilt, fear, and shame in an attempt to influence. **Pathos,** or *emotional appeal*, tries to captivate an audience's needs, values, motives, and attitudes. This emotional aspect of persuasion creates immediacy and power, often compelling us to act. When using an emotional appeal, you are trying to evoke a response from the audience based on an emotional response. It is important to remember that emotional appeals should only be used to support your position from its reasoned standpoint, not to distract, mislead, or misrepresent.

Emotion is a state of arousal affected by cognition (beliefs, awareness) and context (it is influenced by external cues). You respond to emotions as a reaction to ward off pain and to seek pleasure. Although emotional appeals do not last long, you may find that this aspect of persuasion has a compelling force, reinforcing the cognitive elements.

So-called *positive* emotional appeals result in warmth. Feelings like love, pride, affection, and comfort, often touched off by some form of association, result in positive attitudes toward issues. Put yourself in the place of a child being promised a McDonald's Happy Meal. The meal itself is "happy"—not only do you get food, but you get a toy. Another example of positive emotional appeal would be Pillsbury telling us that "nothin' says lovin' like somethin' from the oven."

On the opposite end of the spectrum is the most widely studied of all emotional appeals: reflective fear.[10] These are not simple stimulus-response reactions, such as the feelings you might have for a spider; you see it and are scared. In reflective fear, you actually have some cognitive processing behind the fear. You have probably heard the phrase, "Experience is the best teacher." It may be that you never feared living through a natural disaster until you experienced one. Now when a tornado warning comes on or a hurricane nears your coast, you feel fear set in. Maybe when you were younger you never thought that you could get an STD. However, as you learned about statistics for sexually active people and their chances of getting an STD, you began to fear that outcome.

Reflective fear also has varying intensity in an audience; the closer the threat is, the more the fear increases. You are probably not too worried about your final speech for this course today, but the night before it is due, you will feel that concern. Also, the perceived probability of the fear event occurring gets combined with the anticipated magnitude of damage that might happen. If you

After experiencing a natural disaster firsthand, you may feel fear at the thought of facing a similar situation.
© 2008, JupiterImages Corporation.

Remember how the dentist taught you how to brush and floss so you wouldn't get cavities?
© Répási Lajos Attila, 2008, Shutterstock.

think something bad will happen *and* you think that is really bad, then more reflective fear will be felt. As a speaker, you may want to create reflective fear, but only if you are able to ease that fear as you influence. Think back to your earliest dentist visits. The hygienist attempted to get you to brush better; she showed you pictures of cavities forming on teeth and talked about how painful it can be to get rid of "Mr. Cavity." She gave you one of those red pills to chew that show where you miss brushing and where decay could set in. She showed you how to brush and floss; she gave you a free toothbrush and floss packet. In doing this, she was able to create fear by showing you that a real threat exists to you, and then she solved that problem.

So how can a communicator use pathos, or emotional appeals? Remember, their effect is short-lived and they fade over time, so you need to repeat them through rich, vivid examples and meaningful statistics. There are five general findings to consider about your ability to use emotional appeals:

1. Emotional appeals should not be used in lieu of logical persuasion.
2. Higher credible sources are more able to use emotional appeals, because they are already believed. If you do not have much credibility, then emotional appeals might be seen by the audience as a distraction by an unbelievable source.
3. The more important the topic is to the audience, the less effective reflective fear appeals are. People who already believe do not need to be frightened or threatened.
4. The greater reflective fear you can create, the greater the persuasive effect is, up to a point. If you create too great an emotion, that high anxiety might create gridlock, wherein the person simply tunes out.
5. Emotional appeals may be called for and may succeed in specific situations, such as the following:
   - When you want to create interest, such as garnering attention to something the audience knows nothing about
   - When you need to create a difference between generic ideas or products
   - When you want to suggest superiority in a subjective area, like when you attempt to show that your school is the "best" in its student services offerings
   - When it is important to provide continuity across a series of messages in a campaign, such as when an advertiser uses the same slogan for many ads.

WHY DOES PERSUASION FAIL?

There are many ways in which persuasive efforts can fail. You have probably gathered that attempts to influence others can be a combination of credibility, emotion, and reason. It is important to remember that the audience is judging the mix; it is their perceptions that are important. Sometimes people do not listen well or critically. Sometimes they simply accept what they are being given. But more often, your audience will weigh what they are hearing, and so it is important to consider some of the ways that your persuasive choices may be in error. As an ethical communicator, it is your job to present the most well-crafted message possible; being human, you make mistakes. Let us see what some of those possible persuasion flaws are.

Defective Evidence

The first wrong choices you can make are with your supporting materials. The use of **defective evidence,** supports that do not create the belief you are seeking because something is wrong with that data, are pretty typical. The use of *defective data,* supporting materials that are false, is a relatively easy one to correct. For example, the U.S. Census Bureau reported in 2004 in its American Community Survey incorrect data for mean and median earnings for full-time, year-round workers sixteen years and older.[11] You can check your sources, review your statistics, and review your examples.

Hasty generalizations occur when you draw a conclusion from too little data; you supply one example and expect the audience to draw your conclusion from that. For instance, giving an example of one type of computer and then saying that all computers made by this company are the same would be a hasty generalization.

Authority appeals use unidentified or unqualified sources to support an idea. It is easy to identify a source; consider it *verbal footnoting* when you say, "As Barbara Walters said on *The View* on Monday . . ." and your audience will be in a position to judge the veracity of the source. The qualifications of your sources are equally important. Although Coach Krzyzewski of Duke is a wonderful basketball mentor, he should not be considered an expert on global warming. Misuse of statistics occurs when you use incomparable bases of comparisons. For example, if you say that Zander grew one inch last year and Russ grew two, arguing that Russ is catching up, those growth spurts are not necessarily indicative of a catching up. Sometimes, statistical misuse comes from the myth of the mean, the creation of averages where none really exists. Have you ever seen an "average American family," which, according to the Census Bureau, consists of 3.14 people?[12]

Defective Arguments

When you present **defective arguments** or use poor reasoning, your attempts to influence will also be weakened.

False analogies compare two things that are not really comparable. It is an easy step-off of logic to say, "Sue is an outstanding lacrosse player; she'll make a fine coach." Or "Romania, under the dictator Ceausescu, was a model for democratic voting; they held elections just like we do, and they had 100 percent voter turnout." In reality, the elections were staged and citizens voted because if they did not, they would be put in jail. What about a claim from a manufacturer such as, "You eat fruit for breakfast; why not try fruit-flavored gelatin?"

False cause reasoning supplies a linkage between a source and an effect that does not exist. The conclusion does not result from the reasons given, or the claim is unsupported by evidence. Examples would be statements such as, "If this marriage amendment does not pass, American family life is doomed," or "Candidate X did not serve in the military; he could not possibly function as commander-in-chief."

Slippery slopes occur when you mistakenly use the domino effect as your evidence. You supply one piece of evidence and suggest that it will result in a long chain of events, usually leading to doom. McDonald's once ran a television ad that wondered, "What if there was only one McDonald's in the world?" It showed all sorts of people from previous ads entering the sole fast-food restaurant, resulting in tipping the Earth off its axis, ricocheting around the rest of the solar system, and flying off into space. Or consider the argument that if the government restricts the private ownership of guns any more, the next step will be confiscation, and the next will be a total ban on all weapons, and when "they" come to get us, we will have no way to protect our family.

Ad hominem is an irrelevant attack on a source. Let us say, for example, that your opponent on an issue proposes a military draft for all eighteen-year-old males, not just for national defense but for a sense of discipline and responsibility. If you were to come back with the statement, "My opponent only wants this because she is female and forty," that would be an irrelevant attack. You are not arguing that the conclusion is a bad one; you are arguing falsely that the person who made it is not in a position to do so.

You have probably been caught up in *ad populum* errors. They are commonly known as the *bandwagon* approach: Someone argues that a conclusion is true because "most people" believe it. Examples would be, "You should vote for this project because it is going to win anyhow," or "Most people polled believe that fluoride in water may lead to cancer. Fluoride should be banned because of its consequences."

Finally, an *appeal to ignorance* suggests that because something has not been shown to be false or wrong, it must be right. When your friend asserts, "Of course life exists on other planets. No one has shown that it does not," he is using an appeal to ignorance.

Misused Language

The last group of persuasive errors involves **misused language.** *Equivocation* occurs when you use a term that could have multiple meanings, and you fail to clarify which one you mean. Say you are presenting an argument for the legalization of marijuana, and you state that the Bible says that God created the grass and said, "This is good." If you argue that, therefore, marijuana should be legalized because God liked grass, you are exhibiting equivocation.

Amphiboly means that your argument depends on the ambiguity of grammar. When you fail to clearly state something grammatically, it can be taken in multiple ways. One newspaper headline announced, "School needs to be aired." Does that mean that the place smells and needs some freshening, or is it that the school is lacking in something, and that an explanation is going to be talked about or broadcast? It may sound like clever word play to say, "Teacher strikes idle children," but what is it you really mean?

Emotive language appears to be simple description, but in fact it reveals more about values or attitudes. Let us say that you do not spend money frivolously. Are you best described as thrifty, cheap, or a miser? What about that relative of yours who is losing hair? Is he Mr. Clean, a cue-ball head, or just thinning on top?

Errors of evidence, reasoning, and language are very easy to make. We cannot always be correct when we speak, even though we've been schooled in it and usually try to sound appropriate. Most of the time, errors are unintentional and are easily corrected. But there are times when unethical communicators use such errors, or fallacies, in order to confuse or mislead. That is why it is important to be able to spot them and to understand why something is not right.

SUMMARY

Persuasion involves a complex mix of elements: speaker goals, audience demographics and psychographics, and strategies to implement. Although you are exposed to persuasive attempts every day, it may be overwhelming to consider how you can actually engage in successful persuasion, let alone be a competent consumer of persuasive messages. Finally, consider the responsibilities you have when you are a persuasive communicator. You are attempting to influence others—you want them to believe or to act in ways that can benefit or harm society. In 1972, the National Communication Association (then the Speech Communication Association), adopted the Credo for Free and Responsible Communication in a Democratic Society. This credo affirms basic principles essential to living in a free marketplace of ideas. Two paragraphs in particular resound with the concepts of responsibility, especially for the persuasive advocate who has the intent and power to influence others.

> WE ACCEPT the responsibility of cultivating by precepts and example, in our classrooms and in our communities, enlightened uses of communication; of developing in our students a respect for precision and accuracy in communication, and for reasoning based upon evidence and a judicious discrimination among values.
>
> WE ENCOURAGE our students to accept the role of well-informed and articulate citizens, to defend the communication rights of those with whom they may disagree, and to expose abuses of the communication process.
>
> (From "Credo for Free and Responsible Communication in a Democratic Society" by National Communication Association. Copyright © 1972 by National Communication Association. Reprinted by permission.)

This means that we believe that you are accountable for the ideas that you present. You know that you must have sound evidence that serves as the foundation for your message. You cannot exaggerate, stir up emotions in a way that is dangerous, or lie. You must present your position in a way that the audience can interpret and decide for themselves whether to accept it. Essentially, your responsibility is to show respect for the audience. The phrase "a judicious discrimination among values" reminds us that while you might firmly believe your position, the audience has the right to freedom of choice based on their values, which may conflict with yours. This is echoed in the second paragraph, which says that you must defend the rights of others with whom you may disagree. Your listener can disagree with you without penalty. In addition, by being a well-informed and articulate citizen, you have the following responsibility to yourself: You have to know what you are saying, to believe in it, and to present it in a compelling, ethical fashion. Communication professor Richard Johannesen reflected on these responsibilities, noting "To achieve these goals, we must understand their complexity and recognize the difficulty of achieving them."[13]

ENDNOTES

1. Carolyn W. Sherif, Muzafer Sherif, and Roger E. Nebergall, *Attitude and Attitude Change: The Social Judgment-involvement Approach* (Philadelphia: Saunders, 1965).

2. Leon Festinger. *A Theory of Cognitive Dissonance* (Stanford, CA: Stanford University Press, 1957).

3. A recent study of these effects was conducted by Zakary L. Tormala and Joshua J. Clarkson "Assimilation and Contrast in Persuasion," Personality and Social Psychology Bulletin 33 (4) (2007): 559–571, available at http://psp.sagepub.com/cgi/content/abstract/33/4/559.

4. See, for example, Richard E. Petty and John T. Cacioppo, *Attitudes and Persuasion: Classic and Contemporary Approaches* (Dubuque, IA: Wm. C. Brown, 1981). Also Richard E. Petty and John T. Cacioppo, *Communication and Persuasion: Central and Peripheral Routes to Attitude Change* (New York: Springer-Verlag, 1986).

5. Cnn.com, "White House steps up defense of domestic eavesdropping," Cable News Network, *http://www.cnn.com/2006/POLITICS/01/23/nsa.strategy/* (accessed February 24, 2006).

6. Research on delivery and its impact on credibility is vast. For example, Judee K. Burgoon, Thomas Birk, and Michael Pfau, "Nonverbal Behaviors, Persuasion, and Credibility," *Human Communication Research* 17 (Fall 1990): 140–169. Also Sheila Brownlow, "Seeing Is Believing: Facial Appearance, Credibility, and Attitude Change," *Journal of Nonverbal Behavior* 16 (2) (1992): 101–115; Joyce Newman, "Speaker Training: Twenty-Five Experts on Substance and Style," *Public Relations Quarterly* 33 (2) (1988): 15–21; Martha Davis, Keith A. Markus, Stan B. Walters, "Judging the Credibility of Criminal Suspect Statements: Does Mode of Presentation Matter?" *Journal of Nonverbal Behavior* 30 (4) (2006): 181–198; Lanette Pogue, Kimo Ahyun, "The Effect of Teacher Nonverbal Immediacy and Credibility on Student Motivation and Affective Learning," *Communication Education* 55 (3) (2006): 331–344; Katherine G. Hendrix, "Student Perceptions of Verbal and Nonverbal Cues Leading to Images of Black and White Professor Credibility," *Howard Journal of Communications* 8 (3) (1997): 251–273.

7. Burgoon, et al 162.

8. Just like Professor Harold Hill in *The Music Man*, you begin by picturing for your audience the extent of the horrible situation: a pool table will cause young boys to avoid chores, use bad language, stop listening to parents, and wallow in bad morals. (Yes, this is in essence a cause-effect order). Next, you say, "But wait! I have a solution that will resolve this issue! Your town needs a boys' band!" You describe the band's elements: uniforms, musical instruments, determined practice. And then to sell the point, you describe how that band will remove the temptations of avoiding chores, bad language, and so on. What Professor Harold Hill showed was that with a problem-solution order, you can create a need in the audience, and then resolve that need.

9. Mike Allen, "Meta-Analysis Comparing the Persuasiveness of One-Sided and Two-Sided Messages," *Western Journal of Speech Communication* 55 (4) (1991): 390–404.

10. Julia Wood. "A Preliminary Study of Cognitive Impairment as a Function of Reflective Fear-Arousal in Persuasion." http://eric.ed.gov/ERICWebPortal/Home.portal?_nfpb=true&_pageLabel=RecordDetails&ERICExtSearch_SearchValue_0=ED096706&ERICExtSearch_SearchType_0=eric_accno&objectId=0900000b800e6b9e

11. This information was later corrected on the Census Bureau Web site: U.S. Census Bureau, "American Community Survey," United States Census Bureau, *http://www.census.gov/acs/www/UseData/Errata.htm* (accessed July 17, 2007).

12. U.S. Census Bureau, "Average Family Size 2000," United States Census Bureau *http://factfinder.census.gov/servlet/ThematicMapFramesetServlet?_bm=y&-geo_id=01000US&-tm_name=DEC_2000_SF1_U_M00166&-ds_name=DEC_2000_SF1_U&-_MapEvent=displayBy&-_dBy=040,* (accessed July 17, 2007).

13. Richard L. Johannesen, "Perspectives on Ethics in Persuasion," in *Persuasion: Reception and Responsibility*, 7th ed. Charles U. Larson, (Belmont, CA: Wadsworth, 1995), 28.

A

BRAINSTORMING TECHNIQUE

by Don Yoder, University of Dayton

Prescriptive approaches to group decision making assume that groups can make the best possible decision only if they have critically analyzed the problem, considered a variety of information relevant to the problem, and have a choice among a large variety of options. Notice that in the standard agenda model groups must thoroughly analyze a problem *before* they generate ideas about solutions. They also need to generate lots of alternatives, and they need to think about all the positive and negative consequences of each solution before they can choose the specific course of action they want to implement.

A common method groups use to help them accomplish the goal of thoroughly discussing a problem is *brainstorming*. Brainstorming is a group process designed for the simple purpose of generating ideas. To be successful, brainstorming relies on the *synergy* that comes from group interaction and the mutual stimulation of ideas. The interaction allows immediate "stimulus-response" reactions to generate ideas from each other's comments. One person's ideas can spark an idea in other group members that they may have never thought of without the stimulation. Brainstorming groups can generate more and different ideas than a single member working alone because the group members stimulate ideas through their interaction.

Group brainstorming is thus different than merely thinking out loud. Several barriers inhibit the free generation of lots of ideas, however, and groups must use procedures that minimize these barriers.

PROCEDURES FOR EFFECTIVE BRAINSTORMING

Brainstorming requires all members to state any and all ideas that come to mind. The following procedures help to ensure that group members have the time and motivation to generate as many ideas as they can:

1. *Define the problem before beginning the brainstorming session.* Group members should know specifically what they are to brainstorm about. It may be to generate ideas about the problems they are to solve. It may be that they are trying to generate ideas for a solution. Perhaps they are trying to anticipate all the possible consequences of a proposed course of action. Having a clear focus for the brainstorming session helps the members generate pertinent ideas.

2. *All members must participate.* Brainstorming is based on the premise that "many heads are better than one" and that group members stimulate each other to generate ideas they could not think of themselves. Thus, if an individual group member doesn't participate, not only are those ideas lost, but the stimulation those ideas may have for other group members is also lost.

   A strong leader suppresses his or her own ideas. If there is a strong leader in the group, the leader should suppress his or her own ideas so as not to inhibit or unduly influence the other group members. In a work group, the supervisor or manager may have fate control over the other members. Group members may be reluctant to state ideas that are contrary to those of the leader, or they may wish to curry favor with the boss by simply echoing the boss's ideas. In this case, the leader should refrain from contributing ideas so that the members will have free rein to say whatever they think.

3. *No criticism of the ideas is allowed.* This is usually the most difficult criterion for group members to meet. It is natural to react to others' ideas and to make comments or criticisms. If an idea is criticized or laughed at, group members will be unwilling to make any further contributions or will refrain from making suggestions that are similar to the one criticized. Consequently, criticism can undermine the ability of group members to stimulate each others' ideas.

   Even positive reactions can influence the group to generate only similar suggestions that will get a comparable positive response. Reactions can be verbal or nonverbal. Laughing, frowning, shaking the head, nodding the head, grimaces, and looks of shock can be as evaluative and detrimental to the brainstorming process as overt statements. Groups must remember that the goal of brainstorming is to *simply generate ideas.* Evaluation of the ideas will come later, after the brainstorming session is over.

   Self-censorship also occurs in groups and inhibits the brainstorming process. Even if other group members make no overt criticisms of others' ideas, an individual group member could self-censor an idea. The person may decide that the idea is ridiculous, or that it won't work, or that it is trivial, or it will sound stupid and decide not to share it with the group. Remember that brainstorming relies on stimulating ideas in others. Any idea (even ones that initially sound stupid or wrong) may stimulate a great idea in someone else, something they may not have thought of if the member had let self-censorship overrule a contribution. In brainstorming, all ideas are equally valuable and must be expressed.

   A good way to remember that all ideas are necessary and valuable is to adopt the adage of "the wilder, the better." Sometimes the most outrageous idea can be the one that stimulates the best solution. If the group adopts the approach that they should be generating "wild" ideas, the urge to criticize their own or others' ideas will diminish.

   A story of corporate brainstorming that illustrates this principle takes place in an assembly plant. The workers in the packaging department were supposed to wrap porcelain figurines in paper and place them in cartons for shipping. To save money, the company used old newspapers, which they could get for free. However, the workers would sometimes stop and read the newspaper for a few seconds if a cartoon or headline caught their eye. It wasn't blatant or purposefully disruptive, but it happened frequently enough that there was always a holdup in the production line. The supervisors tried to solve the problem through traditional incentive plans, changing to non-English newspapers, and a variety of changes, but nothing worked. During a brainstorming session, one exasperated executive blurted out, "Maybe we should just turn off the lights and let them work in the dark—they couldn't read the newspaper then!" Obviously, this was a wild idea that could never be implemented. But it stimulated another executive to think of the actual solution. The company hired visually impaired workers for the packaging department! They were not distracted by the newspapers; they were very good workers, and the company received accolades for their diversity hiring. Whether this is a true story or an urban legend, it illustrates the process where the "wild" idea, stated without fear of criticism, stimulated the idea that was actually implemented.

4. *Members must stimulate each other's ideas.* The interaction necessary for effective brainstorming requires that group members carefully listen to each other. If members' ideas are going to stimulate ideas in each other, then people must listen closely to what other people are saying. There is a temptation to become absorbed in your own thinking process as you try to come up with additional ideas. You forget to listen to others and build from their ideas.

   To facilitate the interaction and mutual stimulation, group members should keep ideas brief. There is no need for elaborate explanation or justifications of an idea. Since group members are not evaluating ideas during the brainstorming session, it is not necessary to defend the idea or to explain it in any depth. The goal is to generate as many ideas as you can. Quantity of ideas is more important in brainstorming than quality of ideas. The longer a person takes to state, explain, and justify an idea, the less time available for others to contribute their ideas.

   It is often helpful to post ideas where everyone can see them. You can use a variety of media for posting ideas. You can write them on a posterboard, a flipchart, or blackboard, on PowerPoint, or even on a Web site designed for group work. It is important that the ideas are readily available so that they can continue to stimulate new ideas among the group members.

5. *Brainstorming takes time.* The effectiveness of brainstorming requires that groups interact for more than a couple of minutes. In the first few minutes of brainstorming, groups seldom generate more or different ideas than a single person could do alone. It takes time for the obvious ideas to be stated and for the mutual stimulation to take effect to bring out the creative ideas. As a rule of thumb, you should brainstorm for about five minutes per group member. (A four-person group would brainstorm for a minimum of 20 minutes.) Of course, the complexity of the problem being examined may require more or less time. If you are trying to think of a name for a product, you may need less time than if you are trying to solve a complex operational restructuring problem.

SUMMARY

Brainstorming is an effective method for generating ideas that can be used in any stage of the standard agenda model (or other models) of group decision making. The interaction among group members stimulates creativity and produces ideas that a single person cannot generate alone. When done in a climate of openness with no evaluation of ideas, group members can feel free to say whatever comes to mind. When the group members concentrate on the quantity of ideas rather than quality, and when they are willing to risk offering wild ideas to stimulate each others' thinking, brainstorming can help improve the quality of group decisions.

GROUP MEETINGS

by Kimberly Rosenfeld

Too often, meeting participants and leaders take a lackadaisical approach to this critical factor in the decision-making process. If a meeting is not run well, decisions simply do not get made, or if they do, it is twice the work, hurried, and most often not very solid. The acquisition of communication skills can be helpful in setting up a situation conducive to effective decision making. These communication skills are applicable to both leading a meeting and participating in a meeting. Before we examine the types of meetings, let us first clarify what a meeting is and what it is not.

According to the well-known *Robert's Rules of Order* (2004), a meeting is a single official gathering of group members in one room, with a minimum number of people present to make decisions and conduct business for the group. (This number is known as a *quorum*, which is Latin for "of them," a number typically determined by the meeting participants in bylaws.) The members do not leave the meeting except for a short recess, an adjournment by the meeting chair, or when their tasks have been accomplished.

Although meetings are increasingly held in nontraditional environments (Web casts, teleconferences and the like), meetings held as asynchronous discussions are not considered meetings. Rather, they are pre-meeting discussions or forums. E-mailing group members about an upcoming assignment, instant messaging, or posting messages in an e-room do not qualify as meetings.

Meetings fall into one of two major categories. There are formal meetings: meetings that are large in nature, such as conventions, conferences, and other types of mass meetings. There are also informal meetings: meetings that take place on committees, boards, and task forces.[1] The most common of these is the informal meeting. This is the type of meeting that professionals and active community members find themselves participating in, and will be the type that is referred to here.

MEETING TYPES

Virtual

Living in the digital age has afforded us with many methods of connecting groups to discuss an issue. As early as just twenty years ago, meetings had to take place face-to-face; individuals would need to make the time, travel great distances, secure the funds for participation, and go to other lengths to physically be present during the discussion. This is no longer the case. Meetings are still conducted face-to-face; however, in addition to the traditional group meeting, more and more groups are accomplishing their goals through virtual meetings, teleconferencing, or conference calls.

Virtual meetings are those that take place over the Internet as live, synchronous discussions. *Teleconference meetings* are meetings that take place using real-time video projected images of the meeting's participants. *Conference calls* are meetings held over the telephone with multiple parties talking from remote locations on a single line. Many of the same communication skills that ensure a strong face-to-face meeting will also apply to these new venues.

Formal

Formal meetings are meetings in which the entire membership meets to hear reports of officers, boards, and committees and to propose business, discuss it, and then to vote. These meetings are typically scheduled in advance, run on a consistent schedule (e.g., the first Monday of every month), and follow a protocol such as parliamentary procedure. Some examples of formal meetings are annual meetings, regular meetings, executive sessions, and conventions (*Robert's* 2004).

Parliamentary Procedure 101

1. Parliamentary procedure enables group members to take care of business in an efficient manner while still allowing for all group members the right to speak and vote.
2. Adherence to parliamentary procedure is democracy in action.
3. An agenda is used to discuss business items one at a time.
4. Only one member takes the floor (i.e., talk) at a time, with each group member taking turns to speak.
5. Group discussions have a facilitator to keep order.
6. All members of the group have the right to bring up ideas, discuss them, and come to a conclusion.
7. Majority rule is used, but the rights of the minority are protected by assuring them the right to speak and to vote.

Source: *Robert's Rules of Order* 1999

Informal

Informal meetings differ from formal meetings in size and in how they are conducted. Often, these meetings take a more relaxed approach. Although group members may not have time to prepare for these meetings, it is critical that group members follow an agenda and limit discussion to the topic at hand. This will prevent the group from wasting time and helps the group better accomplish its goals. Some examples of informal meetings are board meetings and committee meetings.[2]

Many students may find the groups they work in during class projects to be more informal and unplanned. They are often characterized by meetings that are held with little or no notice (e.g., your instructor gives you the last thirty minutes of class to work in groups). It may also involve sporadic meeting dates, times, and locations. Each meeting may be determined by group member's schedules for that particular week. Informal meetings do not need to be unproductive and chaotic. With a little on-the-spot organization and focus, these meetings can run as efficiently as formal group meetings.

Six Steps to Successfully Managing an Unplanned Meeting

1. Before beginning, take the first few minutes to summarize the group's accomplishments up to this point.
2. Take the next three to five minutes to establish what the group would like to accomplish by the meeting's end.
3. Determine who will take the meeting minutes and who will run the meeting.
4. After the meeting begins, keep the meeting discussion on issues related to the objective.
5. At the end of the meeting, take another five minutes to determine what each group member will do to help the group reach its goal before the next meeting.
6. If the group has not already done so, set the next meeting date, time, and location.

Whether the meeting is formal or informal, assigning a meeting chairperson is critical. A meeting chairperson is responsible for planning and running the meeting. The chairperson is often the leader of the group, but not always. Some groups choose to rotate meeting chairs. Let us take a look at how meeting chairs use their communication skills to help meeting productivity.

CHAIRING THE MEETING

Those who possess effective communication skills often find themselves elected or appointed to lead meetings. This is also known as chairing a meeting. As a meeting chair, there are many steps that can be taken to ensure that effective, open, and efficient communication takes place. The chair is responsible for planning the meeting, running the meeting, and executing the meeting follow-up.

Seven Steps to Successfully Planning a Meeting

1. Call a meeting when no other alternative exists
2. Establish a clear sense of the meeting's purpose. What do you want to accomplish by the meeting's end?
3. Choose an environment conducive to work. Avoid loud, distracting locations such as restaurants or coffee houses.
4. Determine the meeting's start and end times and follow them.
5. Create an agenda; send the agenda to all meeting participants prior to the meeting.
6. Inform the participants in advance (one week is ideal) of the meeting's date, time, location and purpose.
7. Ensure active and productive participation by notifying group members who are scheduled on the agenda to present, report, or speak.

Planning

Before planning a meeting, ask yourself, "Can this task be accomplished any other way?" If the answer is yes, then a meeting does not need to be called. One of the most frequent complaints by those in business and industry is that they "hate meetings" because they are perceived to be a waste of time. If the task can be accomplished through a telephone conversation, or an asynchronous Internet discussion, e-mail, faxing, or letters, then use those methods. If a meeting must be called, minimize attendees and time by limiting those asked to participate to individuals who really need to be there. In short, do not ask people to attend meetings when there is not a clearly articulated reason for doing so.

Once a meeting is called, the meeting's purpose should be clearly established. That purpose should be stated at the time each individual is asked to participate, along with the meeting's date, location, and start and end time.

The Meeting Environment

The meeting environment is critical to the group's decision-making process. There have been numerous nonverbal communication studies linking room environments to mood, ability to concentrate, and one's level of satisfaction or dissatisfaction with a task. For example, the size and shape of the meeting table can impact the decision-making and meeting process. A round table enables more balanced conversation and avoids perceived power hierarchies. A rectangular table requires someone to sit at the head of the table, thereby possessing the most power. Research indicates people seated across from each other communicate more often than people seated next to each other. People who sit at the head of a rectangular table communicate more with the entire group than do people seated in any other position.[3]

Circular or semicircular seating helps foster a sense of equality by focusing the members' attention on the leader and on each other. The semicircle or U-shape should be arranged so the door to the room is at the bottom of the U. This way meeting participants are not distracted by persons coming and going. Finally, it is best to get people to sit close together to promote a feeling of cohesiveness. If someone leaves the meeting and will not return, remove the empty chair and ask the group to move together to fill the empty space.[4]

There are some additional environmental considerations to check. Is the room large enough to seat the group comfortably? Is it quiet enough to conduct your business? Does it have facilities for overhead, video, computers, chalkboards, or whatever else may be needed by the speakers to present their information? Not only is the aesthetic quality important, but a location should be chosen that is free from noise or too many distractions. This is the reason meetings should not be held at restaurants or noisy coffee houses.

In addition to the location, time is critical. Determine the meeting's start and end time, communicate it to the participants, and hold to this firmly. People make special arrangements to attend and participate in meetings. They may have arranged for child care, they may have another meeting scheduled directly before or directly after the meeting, or they may have put other pressing projects and tasks on hold just long enough to attend the meeting.

Whatever their individual situation, when a meeting is called, it is analogous to an appointment. All other commitments stop for that special, carved-out time. To disrespect this is to risk losing your credibility along with the respect, trust, and future commitment of group members.

After the meeting's logistics have been decided and the purpose has been clearly articulated, it is time to construct one of the most powerful meeting tools: an agenda. An agenda is an outline of items to be discussed during the meeting. It helps the meeting participants to stay focused and can be used to help the meeting chair progress through the meeting much more quickly. An agenda is typically organized so the items covered first are those that were left pending at the last meeting, meaning they were not decided upon or voted on before the meeting had to adjourn. Next, unfinished business is listed, which are agenda items carried over from the last meeting not discussed at all. Finally, new business is discussed, which is a list of items scheduled for discussion that day. If you are running a meeting with officers, then officer reports would follow new business. The order of these items will change, depending on the importance of each, with the list being structured to suit the group's needs and the purpose of the meeting.

Once the agenda is completed, it should be mailed or sent to each participant before the meeting. This provides participants with enough information to prepare for meeting participation. For those people who will be asked to report something during the meeting, contact them prior to finalizing the agenda. If they do not have anything to report, then they should be removed from the agenda. Keep in mind the agenda is only an outline and can change from the time it is mailed to the day of the meeting. If you look at the sample agenda, you will find that it need not be too elaborate; it need only contain a brief outline of the meeting contents.

Sample Meeting Agenda

A Group Symposium Speech
[place date, time, and location here]

   I. Call to Order
  II. Approval of agenda
 III. Approval of meeting minutes
  IV. Pending items
      Speaking order (Ana)
   V. Unfinished business
      Symposium topic (Roberto)
      Service learning locations (Claire)
  VI. New business
      Monthly meeting schedule (Mike)
      Topic research (Elizabeth)
 VII. Next meeting
      Location, date, time (Carlos)
VIII. Miscellaneous items
  IX. Adjournment

Running the Meeting

If preparations are completed beforehand, running the meeting should be a fairly easy task. But there are a few guidelines to consider. The chair should have copies of the agenda and minutes of the last meeting to distribute to members, and he or she should review the meeting's purpose. The meeting must begin and end on time. Do not wait for those members who are late. If group members make an effort to arrive on time, it is unfair and unprofessional to ignore this fact by extending the meeting's start time. Many can relate to the frustration of rushing out the door to arrive at a meeting where they are required to wait fifteen minutes before beginning. Not adhering to the scheduled time not only ignores the efforts of those who arrive on time, but it also sets the precedent for others to arrive late to future meetings. If this trend continues to its logical conclusion, then why meet at all? It is better to let those who are late play catch-up than to push the meeting start time. This is also true for ending the meeting on time. There is nothing more frustrating than to be held up in a meeting when you were expecting to leave at a certain time. If there is not enough time to cover all agenda items, set another meeting date; do not try to cram it all in by meeting "overtime."

In addition to time considerations, the meeting chair will open the meeting with an approval of the last meeting's minutes, provide an overview of the agenda, and begin with the agenda's first item. The chair is not expected to present all items on the agenda, as there will probably be some type of division of labor amongst the group that will need to be discussed by those responsible for their portion of the project. Instead, the chair's job is to keep the meeting focused and progressing in a timely fashion. If meeting participants begin to talk about topics unrelated to the agenda or seem to be discussing an agenda item for too long, it is the chair's responsibility to refocus the group. The best way to accomplish this is to refer back to the agenda. This typically helps to remind the participants that additional topics or issues can be discussed under "miscellaneous" if time permits, or pushed (a.k.a. *tabled*) to the next meeting. Before adjourning, be sure to clarify tabled items and to secure the next meeting date, time, and location.

Running the Meeting

1. Copy the agenda and minutes of the last meeting and distribute to meeting participants.
2. Begin and end the meeting on time.
3. Seek approval of the last meeting minutes.
4. Open the discussion by reviewing the meeting's purpose and the agenda.
5. Keep the discussion focused by using the agenda.
6. Clarify the next meeting time, date, and location.
7. Adjourn the meeting.

Source: *Robert's Rules of Order*, 2004

Meeting Follow-Up and Minutes

Although the meeting is adjourned, the chair's job is not quite through. During the meeting, there should be a designated "minute keeper," or group secretary. This person is responsible for recording the decisions made and the meeting's accomplishments. The minutes are a formal record of the group's decision-making and actions. Minutes should be typed up immediately after the meeting and include the meeting date, time, location, and the names of participants. Located at the bottom of the minutes should be the name of the individual who typed them, with that individual's signature. Minutes are not meant to infringe on the privacy rights of the individual group members and should not include intrusive information, such as how an individual group member voted, what his or her opinion may have been on an item, or any other miscellaneous interjections. Once the minutes are completed, they should be sent to all group members for review before the next meeting. If a mistake is detected, it should be communicated to the secretary and changed immediately with the correction noted at the next meeting and a corrected version placed in the minutes log or notebook. Minutes are typically written in bulleted or outline form; people who read the minutes should be able to visualize what was accomplished at the meeting.[5]

After ensuring the meeting minutes have been sent, the chair will then complete any follow-up tasks or follow-through information that needs to be given to the group members before the next meeting.

Sample Meeting Minutes

A Group Symposium Speech
Meeting: Saturday, February 4, 20xx
Time: 12:00 P.M.–1:00 P.M.
Location: College Library Student Conference Room
Meeting Participants: Ana, Roberto, Claire, Mike, Elizabeth, and Carlos

I. *Approval of meeting minutes*
Last week's minutes unanimously approved.

II. *Speaking Order* The speaking order for the symposium presentation will be: opening Mike; first point Ana, second point Carlos, third point Claire, and closing Roberto.

III. *Symposium Topic* homelessness

IV. *Service Learning Locations* Each group member will bring a list of three possible service learning locations to the next meeting.

V. *Monthly Meeting Schedule* Monthly meetings will continue on the first Saturday of the month until two weeks before the presentation. At that time, we begin meeting on a weekly basis: Saturdays 12:00–2:00 P.M. in the college library.

VI. *Topic Research* Tabled to the next meeting

VII. *Next Meeting* 1st Saturday in March 12:00 PM–1:00 PM

VIII. *Miscellaneous* Next Meeting Chair, Claire. Next Meeting Secretary, Mike

Minutes Typed by:
Ana Romero

PARTICIPATING IN THE MEETING

All meetings need active members. The meeting chair is not the only group member who should plan for meeting participation. Meeting participants have an equal obligation to properly prepare to be an active meeting participant.

Planning

Planning begins with questions. It is not necessarily safe to assume that because you are asked to attend a meeting that your participation will be useful to the group. Asking the right questions can help you determine if the meeting is something you should attend. What are the meeting's objectives? Do you have a copy of the agenda? Will you be expected to present anything on the agenda? What will you need to bring to the meeting? What else can you do to prepare to participate? Answers to such questions should provide you with enough information to determine if your presence is needed, and if so, what to do to prepare for participation.

Just because the meeting chair has not informed you of these things does not mean you are not responsible for any type of meeting preparation. As a professional and active meeting participant, your contributions can be more complex and effective if these questions are asked and then preparation is made accordingly.

Participating During the Meeting

In most cases, people in attendance at meetings have been invited for a reason: to participate. Meeting participation is a good time to speak up and show what you have to offer, to be an active member of the group, to help with the group's task, to build trust with fellow group members, and to carry a fair share of the work. Some meeting participants do not speak up due to shyness or increased communication apprehension. The best way to build confidence and voice your contributions is to actively and appropriately prepare and to utilize your listening and speaking skills.

Using Your Listening Skills

As we learned in the listening chapter, listening skills are just as important as speaking skills when it comes to effectively communicating. Your ability to listen actively during meetings and stay focused on the speaker is directly linked to the quality of your contributions. To listen well is challenging, as we have to battle several poor listening habits such as wandering minds, boredom, physiological distractions (e.g., hunger), and our own egos (e.g., thinking of what we will say instead of listening to what others have to say).

The best way to combat some of these poor listening habits during meetings is to follow the following listening guidelines.

1. *Prepare yourself to listen.* This involves clearing your head to remove psychological distractions, removing physical distractions, and working to prevent physiological distractions. When you find during a meeting that you just can't stop thinking about the report that is due tomorrow, or the argument you had with your boss just before the meeting, then you will

want to work to temporarily remove these psychological distractions. One way to accomplish this is to write whatever may be distracting you down on a piece of paper. Then place the paper in your pocket, purse, briefcase, or backpack until the end of the meeting. After the meeting is over, take the paper out and give yourself license to think about it again. This way, the distracting issue isn't going anywhere, it is just placed on psychological "hold" and doesn't get your attention until after the meeting.

In addition to psychological distractions, you should remove physical distractions. This may include shutting down your computer or turning off the pda or cell phone until the meeting is over. Finally, to prevent physiological distractions, take some preemptive measures such as eating before the meeting, getting a good night's sleep the night before, or drinking a cup of coffee just before the meeting. Whatever your physiological needs may be, think through what you will need to do to prevent this serving as a distraction during the meeting.

2. *Work on following what is being said.* There may be a lot of new information shared at a meeting, people talking rapidly and in rapid succession, and decisions made. Part of utilizing your listening skills is to be sure you are comprehending what is said and remembering what has taken place. This can be accomplished by jotting down notes, asking clarifying questions, and actively engaging in the discussion.

3. *Check for accuracy.* When in doubt, utilize your paraphrasing skills (repeating back a person's message in your own words) and perception-checking skills (describe, interpret, and ask) to clarify anything that may be confusing.

Using Your Speaking Skills

When it is your time to say something during the meeting, work to be as organized and succinct as possible. Try to avoid unorganized thought and rambling ideas. It is better to think through the point you want to make and do so as quickly, yet thoroughly, as possible.

This can be accomplished by keeping your public speaking training in mind. Just as you organize a speech, you will want to organize your contribution. For example, open with a statement introducing your point (think thesis statement or topic sentence). If you are making multiple points or have more than one piece of evidence, then briefly preview what you will say (preview statement), and as you state your points, work to support them with plenty of evidence such as examples and statistics (main points and sub points), finally, you should conclude with a brief statement summarizing what you have said. Taking time to organize your thoughts will not only add to your credibility, it will demonstrate your proficient communication skills and set you apart from many of the other participants.

Follow-Up

The end of the meeting is typically the beginning of the participant's work. If possible, complete assigned tasks as soon as possible after the meeting. There are two reasons for this. First, it sends a nonverbal message to fellow members that not only are you efficient but that you take your commitment to the group seriously. Second, it ensures that the task will be completed without the risk of being forgotten or running out of time before the deadline.

ENDNOTES

1. H.M. Robert, W. Evans, D. Honemann and T. Balch. *Robert's Rules of Order Newly Revised* (Cambridge, MA: DaCapo Press, 2004).

2. Ibid.

3. P. Andrews and J. Baird. *Communication for Business and the Professions,* 8th ed. (Long Grove, IL: Waveland Press, 2005).

4. H.M. Robert, W. Evans, D. Honemann and T. Balch. *Robert's Rules of Order Newly Revised* (Cambridge, MA: DaCapo Press, 2004).

5. Ibid.

DEWEY'S REFLECTIVE THINKING MODEL

by Kimberly Rosenfeld

C

The reflective thinking model offers a systematic approach to decision making that allows for more linear approach to the process then some of the other models we will be discussing. The model consists of six steps from problem to solution. Keep in mind many decisions can be viewed as problems to be solved. Thus, the reflective thinking model often refers to the decision itself as the *problem*. To put this into context, we will use, as an example, a problem you may experience while working on a class group project. Many group projects involve research, writing, and some type of oral presentation. Along the path from start to finish, several decisions must be made. Let us look at how you can approach decision-making using the reflective thinking model.

DEFINE THE PROBLEM

The first step in the reflective thinking model is to define the problem. We often think we understand a problem, but upon further reflection, it becomes evident the problem is not what we envisioned, or there is more than one problem to be solved. Using our example, the immediate decision to be made by the group is to determine the topic. In addition, there may be a whole plethora of problems related to the task at hand and group dynamics. Problems related to the task at hand may range from what type of research will be needed to how the final paper and speech will be organized and presented. Problems related to group dynamics are often related to issues such as when and where the group will meet outside of class, how the work will get done, who will be responsible for various tasks, and the timeline for completing each task. It is best to focus on one problem at a time. Some problems may be solved quickly, such as where and when to meet. Other problems, such as topic selection, may take more time to solve.

ESTABLISH CRITERIA FOR SOLUTIONS

After defining the problem, but before discussing possible solutions, it is critical that the group discusses and compiles a list of criteria, or standards, that the decision needs to meet. This helps group members define for themselves all they are looking for in an ideal decision. It also helps keep the decision making on track when the process is at risk for being muddied by emotion or at an impasse as a result of too many viable options.

Going back to our example, think for a moment about choosing a topic. Two of the criteria have been provided by the assignment: (1) It must be a problem facing the community, and (2) It has to be local in nature. The group then thinks of other criteria it would like to see met. This can be accomplished by brainstorming together possible criteria (see explanation of brainstorming in Appendix A). Your criteria might include: (3) the topic should have the greatest impact on children, and (4) it should be in some way related to the health care field. Whatever the criteria, each group member should have a say in what is compiled. A good leader will ensure even participation among the group members at this point and work to draw out shy members and to control bulldozers.

Identify Solutions

In order to come up with the best solution, it is a good idea to allow time for some good old-fashioned brainstorming. Many of us learn about the importance of brainstorming in elementary school. We learn to brainstorm ideas before writing an essay by drawing mind maps or a series of circles and connecting lines. As we move into adult life, we often get out of the habit of allowing ourselves the luxury of idea exploration. If the group's leader creates a supportive and creative climate for brainstorming, the results can truly embody the notion of group synergy. For those of you who may be out of practice, let us take a moment to discuss the brainstorming process.

Brainstorming begins by setting up the ground rules: (1) All group members' ideas are valid no matter how ridiculous they may seem at the time, (2) every idea possible is needed, thus participation is essential, (3) ideas should be expressed as they "pop" into one's head without consideration of their merit, (4) if possible, the brainstorming should take place until the group has exhausted all ideas; if the group does not have this leisure, the time frame for the brainstorming should be set and communicated to the group, (5) the group should have the appropriate materials available to record the ideas for the entire group to see (e.g., computer with LCD projector, flip chart and markers, chalkboard and chalk), and (6) a group member should be appointed (or volunteer) to take notes during the process.

After the ground rules have been established, it is time to let the fun begin. The leader of the group refrains from sharing first, as this may stifle the responsiveness of others; rather, the leader serves as coach, encourager, and facilitator.

Evaluate Solutions

Once a list of possible solutions has been generated, it is time to evaluate them. This is where the list of criteria comes into play. First, the group should read through each item on the list one by one, eliminating anything that is a bit too outlandish or unrealistic. Then, as a group, go through the list a second time to evaluate each item as it relates to the decision-making criteria.

Sample Solution Evaluations

1. Gangs (meets three of the four criteria; three of five group members are interested)
2. Low elementary student performance in math and science (meets three of the four criteria; four of five group members are interested)
3. Childhood obesity (meets all of the criteria, except not sure yet if this a local problem; all five group members are interested)
4. Latchkey children (meets two of the four criteria; one group member is interested)

Select Best Solution

Once you come up with a list of reasonable ideas and use the criteria to see which possible solution best fits, isolate at least two possible solutions and list them according to preference (e.g., first pick, second pick, third pick). The ranking of these possible solutions should be done with much discussion and dialogue. Two of the most popular selection methods are *majority rule* (take a vote) and *consensus* (mutual agreement). Majority rule occurs when group members vote and whichever topic has the most votes wins approval. The problem with majority rule is that it does not allow for discussion and may leave group members who voted in the minority frustrated and dissatisfied with the solution. To arrive at the best possible solution, it is a good idea to strive for group consensus. Group consensus can be more time consuming, but it allows for member input, debate, and a mutually satisfying solution to be chosen. After discussion, if the group cannot reach consensus, the next best step in the decision-making process is to vote. Whatever method the group decides to use, it should be discussed and established before solutions are selected.

Sample Solution Listed from the Topic that Best Meets Criteria

1. Childhood obesity
2. Low elementary student performance in math and science
3. Gangs
4. Latchkey children

Implement and Test Solution

Now it is time to implement and test run the decision. Some decisions seem good on paper and in theory, but in reality, the decisions are not always the best choices for the group. For example, say the group decides they want to work on teen delinquency in their neighborhood. As the group begins to research this problem, they find teen delinquency really is not much of a problem in their local community. Subsequently, there is little literature available and little to report about. At this point, it would be important for the group to reconsider the choice of topic and to implement their next best choice.

Following this six-step process is not always necessary, as some problems are more easily solved than others. When the problem requires more effort or is very important to the group, the reflective thinking model can ensure a higher-quality decision and an easier time arriving at the decision. Although this theory is the most widely used, it is not the only decision-making theory available.

Glossary

A

Acronym—a word abbreviated in such a way that it creates a new word or phrase so that something (a concept or process) is easy to remember

Acrostics—create memory by using the first letter of words to create a sentence

Action—behavior to implement a decision; fifth and final step in Monroe's motivated sequence; you urge the audience to do a specific, definite act

Action model—states that the source of a message is solely responsible for the meaning of a message

Actuate—to move to action; you want the audience to do something

Adaptors—behaviors that can indicate our internal conditions or feelings to other people

Adjourning stage—(dissolution) the group has achieved its goals, solved the problem, or is no longer needed so roles are abandoned

Adoption—taking on a belief or behavior that was not considered before

Affect display—a form of nonverbal behavior that expresses emotions

Age—the first audience demographic to consider; the maturity of the people

Alliteration—the repetition of initial or matching sounds in neighboring words

Analogies—show a similarity between features of two ideas, objects, or people, in order to create a comparison between the familiar and the unfamiliar

Anchor positions—core beliefs and values which serve to center our thoughts

Anecdote—a brief, amusing story that can be used to capture audience attention

Antonyms—words that define your term by presenting another term having an opposite meaning

Apples/oranges method—impromptu strategy that begins by acknowledging that "there are two sides to this argument . . . " and then state the positions

Appropriate interview attire—shows respect for the situation, the company you would like to work for, and the interviewer

Argument—presenting a claim or position that is supported by reasons for its acceptance

Aristotle—philosopher, scientist, and teacher who lived in ancient Greece

Articulation—the physical production of a sound clearly and distinctly

Assimilation effect—occurs when a person perceives the message to advocate a position closer to his or her own position than it actually does; the person minimizes the differences between the message's position and his position

Attention step—first step in Monroe's motivated sequence; you want to cause the listeners to focus tightly on you and your ideas

Attitudes—predispositions to respond to others, ideas, or events in a particular way

Audience analysis—the gathering of demographic and psychographic information about your audience

Audience interest—achieved by giving the audience new, useful information, providing a solution to a concern, or showing a connection

Autocratic leader—leadership method based on direction and control of the leader. There is little discussion among followers

Autonomy/connection—a dialectic that has to do with our need to be connected to significant others at times, and at other times, to exert our independence

B

Belief—your perception of reality; it describes your conception of something

Biased questions—questions phrased in such a way that they would be likely to influence the interviewee's responses

Body—the central part of the interview; where much of the information is exchanged and all or most of the interview goals are accomplished

Boomerang effect—for individuals with high ego-involvement, most messages that are aimed to persuade them that fall within their latitudes of rejection have the opposite effect; by hearing something that is perceived as negating your position, you are made to feel even stronger about your position, rather than the desired persuasive effect of changing your mind

Brainstorming—a free flow of ideas from all participants, and the process can spark initial ideas into new directions and solutions

Briefing—a meeting for giving information or instructions

C

Carrier—a channel of messages

Categorical (topical) order—the "natural" or "relevant" organization pattern

Cause-effect order—organizational pattern used to create a clear connection between the cause of a problem and the potential outcomes

Central route—suggests that people think actively about the message, evaluating information and weighing it against what they already know

Ceremonial speeches—reaffirm common values and strengthen ties among a community

Certainty—behavior that communicates to others a lack of interest in their position on an issue; the person seems to know all the answers

Channel—pathway that carries sound waves created by the voice, or some mediated signal

Character—perceptions of integrity, honor, trust, altruism, and ethics

Charisma—an individual personality set apart from ordinary people; special charm or appeal

Choice—one of at least two viable alternatives

Chronological order—organizational pattern that structures ideas according to a time progression

Claim—represents the desired end result of the speech, the main idea that you want the audience to assume

Cliches—words that have been overused and lose power or impact

Closed question—attempts to limit or restrict the response and focus the interviewee on providing only the desired information

Closing—serves a critical role in the interview process: provides closure; helps to maintain the relationship that was developed during the interview; and can help motivate the interviewee if further cooperation is needed

Code—language

Coercive power—power to punish; members follow coercive leaders to avoid reprimand or punishment

Cognitive dissonance theory—the result of an individual's holding inconsistent attitudes or behaviors is an uncomfortable feeling that motivates the individual to reduce the discomfort by bringing consistency to those attitudes and behaviors

Cognitive restructuring—reduction of speech anxiety by assisting you in how you think about speaking situations

Coherence—the narrative's internal consistency

Collaboration—a win/win approach to conflict with each person in the conflict situation leaving the conflict completely satisfied with the outcome

Collectivistic cultures—cultures in which people practice collaboration with family, friends, and colleagues

Commitment—the willingness and ability to follow through with the plan, even if negative consequences are experienced

Communication—a process by which information is exchanged between individuals through a common system of symbols, signs, and behavior

Communication apprehension—an individual level of fear or anxiety associated with either real or anticipated communication with another person or persons

Communication context—involves time of day, location, setting, and occasion or purpose of the event

Comparison and contrast—structures ideas by showing that there is a similarity and/or difference of your topic with something the audience already knows

Compromise—considered a lose/lose approach to conflict in that each party is required to give up something to solve the situation

Conclusion—in a presentation, re-emphasizes important points and creates psychological closure

Conflict management—strategies used to help resolve group conflict

Conflict model—suggests five ways people make decisions to reduce anxiety

Connective transitions—develop movement from point to point and create a seamless message

Connectives—create the dynamic flow of a speech and help listeners to remember and to recognize where they have been and what to expect next in a speech

Connotative meanings—reflect your personal, subjective definitions

Consequences—the effects of the decision on the decision maker(s), other people, and/or their environment

Constitutive rules—tell us how to "count" different kinds of communication, revealing what we feel is appropriate

Continuance—supplementing, or adding on to, what the audience already knows, without denying previous knowledge

Contrast effect—occurs when a person perceives the message as advocating a position further away from his position than it actually does; the person exaggerates the difference between the message's position and his own

Control strategies—statements that create psychological reactance and lead to defensiveness, which leads to extrinsic conflict

Convince—your goal is to change the way your audience thinks or believes

Coping patterns—how people make decisions to reduce anxiety related to making important decisions

Counseling or helping interview—conducted often by a person in the helping professions (medical, social, psychological) to give advice or help the interviewee solve problems

Cover letter—sent with a resume, it contains information regarding who at the company should receive the resume and specifically what job you are applying for

Credibility—perceptions of believability

Critical thinking—an investigation whose purpose is to explore a situation, phenomenon, question, or problem to arrive at a hypothesis or conclusion that integrates all available information and that can be convincingly justified

Culture—community of meaning; we all belong to multiple cultures and we come into contact with other cultures on a professional and social basis every day; people belong to a variety of nations, traditions, groups and organizations, each of which has its own point of view, values and norms

D

David Berlo—discussed process and the complexity of communication in *The Process of Communication*

Decision-making plan—recognizes that *humans* will be making decisions and not a totally rational and nonemotional machine; provides structure to group members if the group finds itself going nowhere

Decisions of consequence—important life decisions

Decodes—turning the signal again into a message

Deductive reasoning—moves your thoughts from a generalized belief to a new specific instance

Defective arguments—using poor reasoning; weakens your attempts to influence

Defective decision—occurs if you *do not* study the problem, make a thorough search and evaluation of alternatives, deliberate about commitment, and collect feedback during the implementation stage

Defective evidence—supports that do not create the belief you are seeking because something is wrong with that data

Defensive avoidance—psychological coping pattern in which a group tends to avoid a decision when the only available choices are undesirable

Definitions—concise, simple statements that explain what you mean by a word or expression

Democratic leader—adopts the Theory Y assumptions and creates an atmosphere of member integration, self-control, and participatory decision making; the input of subordinates is encouraged and is used to make decisions

Demographics—a broad class of population characteristics such as age, gender, ethnicity/race, and socioeconomic status

Denotative definition—a formal or dictionary definition

Denotative meanings—literal, dictionary definitions that are precise and objective

Derived credibility—the believability you produce in your audience's mind as you present the message

Derogatory language—consists of words that are degrading or tasteless

Descriptive approach—research based and focused on how groups actually *do* make decisions; involves a process that emerges naturally from the interaction of group members

Descriptive speech—attempts to clarify information or to create understanding through vivid language

Destination—the other person; receiver of the message

Deter—influences the audience to stop something before they begin it

Dialectics—polar opposites; Baxter and Montgomery identify three dialectics at work for each individual in a relationship

Dialects—regional or ethnic speech patterns that have variations in grammar, accent, or even vocabulary

Dichotomous questions—restrict responses to one of two possible choices

Discontinue—asking your audience to stop doing something they are currently doing

Disruptive group roles—exhibiting a role that harms the group's productivity, cohesiveness, and harmony

Double-barreled question—asks for a single answer to what might be several questions

Dual perspective—recognize another person's point of view and take that into account as you communicate

E

Effective delivery—involves both verbal and nonverbal message management, tailored for the intended audience and context

Ego-involvement—refers to the importance of an issue to you

Elaboration—involves cognitive processes such as evaluation and recall

Elaboration likelihood model—attempts to explain how people's attitudes are formed and influenced

Emblem—a nonverbal behavior that has a distinct verbal referent or even a denotative definition, and it is often used to send a specific message to others

Emotion—a state of arousal affected by cognition (beliefs, awareness) and context (it is influenced by external cues)

Empathy—approaching a discussion with the intent to understand the other person's position from his or her point of view

Empirical—knowledge claims are based on observations of reality (i.e.; the real world) and are not merely subjective speculation based on the observer's perspective

Employment interview—takes place between an employer and a potential employee

Empty words—overworked exaggerations

Encoded—converted from one system of communication into another

Enumeration—an amplification technique; lets you list all the members of the class to distinguish this one term (the grocery list approach)

Environmental noise—interference with the signal as it moves from the source to the destination

Equality—involves treating others with respect and valuing their thoughts and opinions, regardless of their knowledge about the topic, their status, age, or position

Equivocal words—have more than one correct denotative meaning

Etymology—explains the current meaning of a word based on the historical meaning or origin

Evidence—material that you use to support your ideas, enhance interest, or establish an emotional response

Example—a type of evidence; single instances that illustrate or explain in an attempt to make a concept meaningful

Expectancy violations theory—suggests that we hold expectations about the nonverbal behavior of others, and when communicative norms are violated, the violation may be perceived either favorably or unfavorably, depending on the perception that the receiver has of the violator

Expert power—a person who is able to assist the group in reaching its goals because of his or her expertise on a given topic

Explication—simplify or further define other terms in the denotative definition

Expository message—focuses on teaching a person a process or skill or describing how some process occurs/happens

Expression—(value) sharing or emotional communication; you are seeking an outlet to convey your feelings or values to your audience

Extemporaneous (extemp) speech—one that is carefully planned and practiced, that works from an outline or series of notes yet leaves room for message adjustment, and that maintains a conversational style

Extension—examples of actual instances of the term in use

Extrinsic conflict—conflict related to the personalities and relationships between members

Eye contact—direct visual contact made with another person; helps us to communicate in at least four ways: it can open a channel of communication, demonstrate concern, gather feedback, and moderate anxiety

F

Facial expression—outward emotion shown on your face

Feedback—information that is routed to the source, or fed back, from the receiver

Fidelity—the external standard for judging the truthfulness of a story

Figurative analogies—compare things in two different categories

Final summary—helps the audience recall the main points, improving overall recollection and comprehension

Forewarning—letting the audience know what is about to come

Forming stage—(orientation) characterized by group members: attempting to orient themselves; testing each other and the group boundaries; creating dependence on the group leader or other group members for support during this uncomfortable time

Freedom of expression—the freedoms of speech, of the press, of association, of assembly, and of petition; this set of guarantees, protected by the First Amendment, constitutes this concept

G

Gender—is learned behaviors that constitute masculinity and femininity in a culture

General goal—the primary purpose of your communication

General purpose—guides all choices in your speech; overall goal

Gestures—movement of your head, arms, and hands that you use to emphasize, to reinforce, or to illustrate ideas

Goal—a desired state that decision makers would like to reach; the results you want to achieve

Good reasons—a set of values that let us accept a story as true and worth acceptance

Goodwill—caring for others more than for yourself

Grammar—syntax, a patterned set of rules that aid in meaning

Group contract—a group agreement that outlines group norms and consequences for breaking them

Groupthink—a phenomenon that often results in a flawed decision made by groups whose cohesiveness becomes so strong that they stop challenging each other's ideas

H

Hearing—a passive physiological process where the ear receives sound

High-context culture—uses communication in which most of the information is either in the physical context or internalized in the person

History—events leading up to the current situation

How-to presentations—show how to do aspects of a job in a particular way; often these are training videos or online computer-based training activities

Hypervigilance—involves high anxiety as the current situation is not compatible with the goal, so action is required, and the group thinks it must make a snap decision under pressure

I

Illustrator—a gesture that is used *with* language to emphasize, stress, or repeat what is being said

Imagery—uses words or phrases that appeal to the senses

Impromptu—talking about a topic with little or no preparation

Individual-centered roles—distracts the group or blocks the group from moving forward toward goal or task completion

Individualistic cultures—cultures in which people are taught personal autonomy, privacy, self-realization, individual initiative, independence, individual decision making, and an understanding that their needs and interests are just as important, if not more important, than the needs and interests of others

Inductive reasoning—occurs as we mentally progress from a single impression or example to form a general conclusion

Information giving—communicating data or beliefs in order to develop understanding and awareness

Information-gathering interview—focuses on planning and asking questions, listening to the responses, and recording the information

Informative message—one whose goal is to produce shared understanding, to increase knowledge, to cultivate appreciation, or to develop skills or abilities

Informative speech—the goal is to produce shared understanding, to increase knowledge, to cultivate appreciation, or to develop skills or abilities

Initial credibility—the perception of the source prior to a message (also known as your reputation)

Initial summary—also called the speech preview, forecasts what main points are about to come in the body

Intelligence—a perception of competence, expertise, and knowledge

Intension—a list of attributes/characteristics that something must have to be properly labeled as this term

Interaction model—views the source and receiver as a team in the communication process

Interdependence—members combine their talents and resources, giving them the ability to solve more complex problems than they could as individuals working alone

Internal summary—reviews what has just happened

Interpersonal linkage—power based on who you know and what resources these people control

Interpretation—assigning meaning to your perceptions

Intersubjective—meaning can exist only when people share common interpretations of the symbols they exchange

Interview plan—outlines your strategy for goal achievement and it includes the topics that should be discussed as well as the sequence and wording of specific questions

Interviewing—form of interpersonal conversation that has two parties: interviewer and interviewee, structured around asking and answering questions and having specific goals to accomplish

Intrinsic conflict—conflict that centers on disagreements related to the task facing the group

Introduction—opening remarks that provide the audience with initial message orientation

Intrusion of territory—violation, invasion, or contamination of your space

J

Jargon—specialized professional language

Johari window—created by Joe Luft and Harry Ingham, shows the four aspects of ourselves that are affected by self-disclosure; each is a result of what is known or not known to self and to others

Judgment categories—latitudes or zones that we use to evaluate incoming persuasive messages

K

Kinesics—the study of our use of the body to communicate

Knowledge gathering—identifying the data or evidence that you will need in order to reach your communication goal of information-giving, persuading, or expressing value

Knowledge-gathering skills—include your ability to read and to listen

L

Laissez-faire leader—one who takes a hands-off approach to leadership and provides very little direction to those being led

Language—a shared system of symbols structured in organized patterns to express thoughts and feelings

Leadership—the ability to *influence* the behavior of others to move people to action

Leading question—guides the interviewee in the direction of the response preferred by the interviewer, or otherwise requires the interviewee to give the socially correct or acceptable response

Legitimate power—exists as a function of someone's position in an organization

Level-one (general) goals—the broad, overall goals of the speech

Level-two (specific) goals—provide a definitive, explicit goal for the audience

Listening—the active process of receiving, constructing meaning from, and responding to spoken and/or nonverbal messages

Loaded question—can incite emotional responses, give equally disagreeable response alternatives, or place the interviewee in a paradox where any answer is inappropriate

Loaded words—sound like they're describing, but they're actually revealing your attitude

Low-context culture—the majority of information is stated explicitly

M

Main points—ideas generated by your specific purpose; they divide your message into manageable units for you to present and your audience to consider

Maintenance leaders—focus on relational issues, the development of an open and supportive climate, motivation of members, and conflict management

Maintenance roles—strengthen the group's social and emotional structure and contribute to the group's cohesion

Meaning—symbols must be shared in order to be understood

Meaningfulness—refers to the ways that we project comprehension or understanding onto perceptions

Mental road trips—a place beyond the "here and now" where you go as you listen to others speak; thinking about other things than what the person is saying

Message—the verbal or nonverbal stimulus that is transmitted to an audience

Message sidedness—refers to the concept that there are two sides to every issue

Misused language—a persuasive error that occurs when you use terms incorrectly or ambiguously

Mnemonic device—a method used for enhancing memory

Monroe's motivated sequence—organizational pattern used mostly in persuasion, combines logic and psychology because it models the human thinking process and motivates the audience to action; consists of five major steps: attention, need, satisfaction, visualization, and action

Motives—the drives, urges, or needs you have

Movement—the positioning of your entire body as you speak

Multimedia presentations—involve the combination of sight and sound to create interest and excitement, along with information that is best presented in an audiovisual format

Multiple-choice questions—restrict the interviewee's response options; extremely closed questions

Mystification—the use of special jargon to imply that you have special authority or expertise

N

Narrative rationality—our standard for judging which stories we should believe and which we should ignore

Narrative speech—tells a story that organizes our perceptions of the world, preserves our history, lets us experience other's lives or cultures without being there, entertains and engages us, promotes creativity, and connects each person involved in listening to the story

Narratives—a type of evidence; stories that elaborate an idea

Need—second step in Monroe's motivated sequence; demonstrates to the audience that a serious problem exists that demands change

Negation—defines by saying what your term *is not*

Neutrality—communicates that you simply do not care about the person or what he or she is saying

Noise—anything that can interfere with the signal

Norm of reciprocity—asserts that in order for us to continue to move forward with a relationship, we must feel the person with whom we are communicating is self-disclosing equally, both in depth and breadth

Norming stage—(structure) happens when group cohesion develops, new standards evolve, and new roles are adopted

Norms—shared guidelines for beliefs and behavior

Novelty/predictability—a dialectic that has to do with the excitement and uncertainty level present in a relationship

O

Obstacles—factors, barriers, or constraints preventing movement from the current situation to the desired goal state

Occulesics—use of eye contact

Open question—requests very general or nonspecific information, and there is usually very little direction provided by the interviewer as to the direction of the desired response

Opening—serves at least three functions critical to the success of the interview: sets the foundation of the parties' relationship during the interview; motivates the interviewee to participate fully; and provides an orientation to the interviewee

Openness/closedness—a dialectic that has to do with our need to share information with others versus our need for privacy

Open-to-closed question—the interviewer begins with a question, but then follows up very quickly with a much more narrow, closed question

Organization—structuring perceptions in order to make sense of them

Organized knowledge—often called your intellect; it consists of your informed beliefs; what you think is real

P

Parallel structure—occurs when you use the same pattern of words to show that two or more ideas have the same level of importance

Participant—includes source, receiver, speaker, and listener

Pathos—emotional appeal; tries to captivate an audience's needs, values, motives, and attitudes

Pauses—add emphasis and impact to your speech by stopping your message briefly

People points—draw attention to issues affecting family or team members

Perception—our set of beliefs concerning what is out there

Perceptual skills—engage physical and psychological dimensions, resulting in an interaction between the senses and external environment

Performing stage—(work) most of the productive work is accomplished; group roles become flexible and functional, and group energy is channeled into the task

Peripheral route—used when we do not think about the message very much and are influenced more by the nonargumentative aspects of the message; this is low elaboration

Personal space—a small amount of portable space that you carry with you all the time; you control who is and who is not permitted inside that space

Persuasion—a process of social influence, involving the preparation and presentation of verbal and nonverbal messages to others to influence their beliefs, values, attitudes, or actions

Persuasive claim of fact—attempts to create a belief in an audience

Persuasive claim of policy—argues what should be done by the audience

Persuasive claim of value—goes beyond creation of reality; it attempts to get the audience to accept a judgment based on certain criteria

Persuasive speech—involves the process of social influence in order to influence beliefs, values, attitudes, or actions of others

Phonological rules—regulate how words sound when you pronounce them

Physical context—the space surrounding the communication event, or the place in which the communication event occurs

Physiological dimensions—speech anxiety caused by the body producing hormones and adrenaline that overloads your system, causing your heart to beat faster, blood pressure to rise, etc.

Physiology—physical sensory ability

Pitch—your voice's intonation; how high or low in range your voice sounds to another

Power—the ability to *control* the behavior of others

Power distance—the extent to which the less powerful members of organizations and institutions accept and expect that power is distributed unequally

PPF method—impromptu strategy uses Past, Present, and Future as the main points

Prescriptive approach—logic based and focused on how groups *should* make decisions; involves steps that, if followed correctly, should lead to a quality decision

Presentational aids—any items developed for reinforcing a message; including objects, models, charts, drawings, graphs, videos, and photographs

Previews—give the audience a prompt or advanced warning that movement is about to occur

Primacy—arranges ideas in terms of how convincing they are, moving from most important to least important

Primary question—used to introduce topics on new areas of discussion

Primary territory—space on those items you personally control

Problem orientation—allows others an equal contribution to discussion and decision making

Problem-solution order—structures ideas by pointing out a dilemma and offering (or supporting) its potential remedies

Procedure points—highlight policies that have to be introduced, clarified, changed, or reinforced

Process—implies that communication is continuous and ongoing; dynamic; it never stops

Progress points—describe or clarify steps that have been taken or priorities to be established

Pronunciation—saying a word in an accepted standard of correctness and sound

Provisionalism—behavior that tries to explore issues, look for solutions, and consider the points of view of other group members

Psychographics—involves the audience's cognitive elements—how they think, value, and tend to act

Psychological noise—distraction takes place inside the sender or receiver, such as misunderstanding or failing to remember what was heard

Public territory—available to anyone; so any space you try to claim is only temporary

R

Rate—the speed at which you speak

Reasoning—a systematic mental process of moving from one idea to another in order to reach a new conclusion

Receiver—person who accepts the communication

Recency—moving from the least convincing point to the strongest

Reference(s)—consist of thoughts, experiences, and feelings about the referent

Referent—the thing that we want to communicate about that exists in reality

Referent power—based on the personal liking or respect that one person has for another

Reflective thinking model—based on the premise that a group must adequately understand a problem before it can be solved

Regionalisms—words or phrases that are specific to one part of the country

Regulative rules—tell us when, how, where, and with whom we can talk about certain things

Regulator—a turn-taking signal that helps control the flow, the pace, and turn-taking in conversations

Reliability—the consistency with which other people interpret or give meaning to your questions or statements

Researching skills—consist of your ability to seek and gather information

Resume—a document containing a summary or listing of relevant education and job experience, created for obtaining an employment interview

Reward power—offers access to some desired resource as payment for compliance

S

Satisfaction—third step in Monroe's motivated sequence; proposes a plan of action that will solve the need

Screening interview—used to determine if the interviewee meets the necessary requirements for the available position; typically conducted by a professional in the human resources department

Secondary question—also called a probing question; used to encourage an interviewee to keep talking, to provide additional or more focused info, or to clarify an answer

Secondary territory—not your private property; not owned by you, but typically associated with you

Selection—a method of focusing that narrows your attention to selected stimuli; determining your topic and purpose, meeting the audience's needs and expectations, and recognizing the kinds of supporting materials you will use to build the message

Selection interview—conducted by supervisors or other members of the department that is hiring the position; occurs after the interviewee was successful in the screening interview

Self-disclosure—revealing aspects of ourselves with another person—things the person would not know unless told

Semantic rules—govern the meaning of specific symbols

Semantic triangle—a model that demonstrates how words come to have meaning

Signposts—alert the audience to something important about to come

Simple 6 method—impromptu strategy that uses the common questions of who, what, when, why, where, and how as the main points

Situational anxiety—speech anxiety caused by the result of being placed in a particular context, and the real or imagined aspects of that situation cause anxiety

Situational leadership—assumes that a leader's effectiveness is contingent, or dependent, upon how well the leader's style fits the context

Six degrees of separation—Stanly Milgram's notion that you are likely to cross paths with a stranger more than once

Skill knowledge—consists of your grasp of how to do something

Slang—consists of words that are short-lived, arbitrarily changed, and often vulgar ideas

Small group—a collection of people who work together either voluntarily or involuntarily to achieve a goal or solve a problem

Social context—considers the nature of the event taking place in a physical context

Social exchange theory—relates to perceived relational costs and rewards

Social judgment theory—suggests that attitude change is mediated by a judgment process, and it also supplies a way of thinking about how to persuade others

Socioeconomic status—demographic measure that includes occupation or profession, education, and income level

Solution—supplies the course of action that allows the obstacles to be overcome and the goal realized

Source—person who initiates communication

Spatial order—arranges your main points in terms of their place or position

Specific goal—(specific purpose) answers the question of where you want the audience to be at the end of your message

Specific purpose—states precisely what you hope to accomplish in your speech

Specificity—start with a general illustration and move to a specific one

Speech anxiety—commonly called stage fright; apprehension about communicating in some situations

Speech preview—also called the initial summary, forecasts what main points are about to come in the body

Speech purpose—a statement of a goal and the desired audience response

Spontaneity—communication characterized by honesty, directness, and good faith

SPREE method—impromptu strategy of four points: State your position, provide your Reason(s), Explain by experience or example, End with summary

Stability—refers to the predictability that we need in life

Statistics—a type of evidence; numbers that indicate relationships between phenomena

Stimulate—you assume that the audience already agrees with you, but you want to strengthen that conviction because it is built on a shaky foundation

Storming stage—(conflict) occurs as a result of interpersonal struggles and polarization inherent in responding to the task at hand; different ideas compete for consideration, and group members share and challenge each other's ideas

Strategy—1. a plan; 2. a form of communication often making others defensive because they suspect a hidden agenda

Styles approach—leadership style focused on behaviors of the leader

Subjectivity—perceptions that are unique to your personal experience, views, or mental state

Superiority—creates defensiveness by demonstrating that we perceive ourselves to be better than others, which leads to extrinsic conflict

Symbols—arbitrary labels that we give to some idea or phenomenon

Synergy—suggests that the end product of a group's efforts is superior to the product of the individuals working independently

Synonyms—amplify your term by presenting another term having the same essential meaning

Syntactical rules—present the arrangement of a language; how the symbols are organized

Systematic desensitization—reducing speech anxiety by focusing on reducing tensions that surround a feared event; you learn how to relax

T

Task leaders—group members who help the group with organization and advancement toward making a decision or completing a job

Task roles—contribute to the group's productivity and are concerned with moving the group toward achieving its goals

Terminal credibility—the cumulative result of initial and derived credibility

Testimony—a type of evidence; consists of the comments of others

Thank-you letter—sent as a courtesy to the interview team and company as a way to keep your name and credentials in front of the decision makers

Theory—an attempt to describe, predict, and/or explain an experience or phenomenon

Thesis statement—topic sentence or central idea

Three T method—strategy for effectively using a presentational aid: first touch (or point to) the place you want the audience to focus their attention, second turn your face to the audience and third begin talking

Three-dimensional presentational aids—an item used to reinforce a message that includes people and other animate creatures, objects, and models

Topic—subject of your speech

Traitlike anxiety—speech anxiety that is a result of your temperament and personality; it is a relatively stable and enduring predisposition of an individual towards experiencing fear and/or anxiety across a wide range of communication contexts

Transactional model—incorporates view that all participants are both speakers and listeners with the notion that the creation of the meaning of a message is not the sole responsibility of the source or the receiver, but a responsibility that is shared among all participants in a common situation or event

Transformational leader—someone who possesses the charisma necessary to motivate followers and evoke change

Transitions—phrases or key words used to link ideas

Transmitted—sent the message

Trite words—words that have been overused and lose power or impact

Two-dimensional presentational aids—an item used to reinforce a message that includes images such as drawings, photographs, maps, graphs, charts, overhead transparencies, etc.

Unconflicted adherence—a decisional coping pattern in which there is little or no anxiety related to a decision; results in a decision to do nothing

Unconflicted change—a decisional coping pattern in which there is some anxiety related to a decision; decision maker feels a decision is necessary and generally adopts the first alternative that presents itself

Understanding—combines skill with intellect to create insight

V

Values—enduring judgments or standards about what is good or bad

Vigilance—the best coping strategy; as the current situation is not compatible with the goal, action is required; the group has time to search for and evaluate solutions, promoting a quality decision

Virtual groups—a gathering of people using chat rooms, blogs, social networking sites, bulletin boards, Web sites, listservs, or any form of computer-mediated communication to meet and solve problems, achieve goals, or share experiences

Visualization—fourth step in Monroe's motivated sequence; you picture for the audience what the world will be like if your plan is adopted; reduction of speech anxiety by imagining positive speaking experiences

Volume—projecting your voice loudly enough so that it can be clearly heard by those in your audience

U

Uncertainty—the extent to which risk and ambiguity are acceptable conditions

W

Wilbur Schramm—introduced a model of communication that includes a notion of interaction

Index